D1391339

A Kingdom
in Two Parishes

Tudor stained glass, Smithills Hall, Deane. *Bolton Museums.*

A Kingdom in Two Parishes

Lancashire Religious Writers and the English Monarchy, 1521–1689

MALCOLM HARDMAN

Madison • Teaneck
Fairleigh Dickinson University Press
London: Associated University Presses

Contents

Preface   9

SECTION ONE: REFORMATION

Part One: Henrician Monk

1. Henry Bradshaw: Last of the Old Catholic Order   23
2. "Place Spiritual": The Real Presence of Christ   25
3. "Ghostly Tuition": The Discipline of the Holy Spirit   27
4. "Life Historial": The Transmitted Authority of the Father   30

Part Two: Edwardine Preacher

5. Thomas Lever: Seeking the Place Spiritual   35
6. The Effectual Body of Christ   40
7. Manifesto Contradicted by Revolution   43
8. Negotiation Prevented by the Needs of Power   49
9. The Republic of Christ   55

Part Three: Marian Martyr

10. George Marsh: Following Ghostly Tuition   77
11. Earl and Yeoman   80
12. Royal Lancaster   86
13. Visitors   90
14. From the Monastery to the City   93
15. Mature Tuition   103

Part Four: Elizabethan Bishop

16. James Pilkington: Meditating the Life Historial   117
17. Survival   119
18. Stability   124
19. Restraint   133
20. Measure   137

21. Entourage   144
22. Reinterpretation   148

SECTION TWO: NONCONFORMITY

Part Five: Jacobean Catholic

23. James Anderton: Claiming Equity for the Visible Church   159
24. "The Marks of the True Church"   164
25. "Loyal, and Dutiful"   168
26. "Antiquity and Continuance"   173

Part Six: Parliamentary Stronghold

27. Civil War Bolton: Claiming the Marks of the True Church   181
28. "A Little Ticket of Lead": Presbyterian Divines   184
29. "I Hope I Shall Die in Honour": Royalist Martyrs   194
30. "God's Gifts . . . for Edifying the Body": Roundhead Soldiers   201

Part Seven: Caroline Dissenters

31. Oliver and Nathaniel Heywood: Remaining Loyal, and Dutiful   225
32. Restraint: The Poem of God   230
33. Christ Displayed   236
34. Scope: The Lamentations of Saints   245

Part Eight: Revolution and Thesaurus

35. Revolution as Antiquity and Continuance   255
36. "A Dissuasive from Contention"   260
37. Contention and Continuance   266
38. Antiquity and Continuance: A Reinterpretation   273
39. Thesaurus   278

Notes   294
Bibliography   335
Index   344

Preface

THE geographical focus of this study is provided by the interlocking parishes of Bolton and Deane, Lancashire; to which—as inseparably linked in their economic and religious history—one must add the townships of Aspull, to the west (part of Wigan, but taxed with Blackrod, Bolton); of Ainsworth, to the east, and of Great Lever. The latter, near the heart of both our parishes, but, as a result of medieval inheritance patterns belonging to neither, was technically (like Ainsworth) an "island" of distant Middleton. The whole area thus defined amounts to 90 square miles.

I have added to, and (as I hope) in part corrected, my two chief sources: J. C. Scholes, *Bolton Bibliography* (1886) and Archibald Sparke, *Bibliographia Boltoniensis* (1913). I have not, however, tried to amass evidence so much as to provide a focused, comparative account of local religious writers in their relation to the monarchy. Read together, they form an interesting group, one which amounts to more than the sum of its parts. Chronological as well as geographical boundaries seemed to suggest themselves, though some exclusions had to be decided. Thus Humphrey Walkden, Fellow of Queens' College, Cambridge, and friend of Erasmus, is doubly out of the picture. If (as seems possible) he originated in Walkden, then he falls just outside Henry VIII's new parish of Deane. As a loyal servant of his college and Catholic Christendom (he died in 1525), he could have taken no part in the reevaluation of monarchy impelled on his subjects by Henry's impending attack on its sacred places, including the shrine of the princess Werburgh at Chester, the religious center of the region.

The district defined above was anciently part of the royal appanage, since the days of John O'Gaunt of the royal Duchy of Lancaster. The local grammar school was established, at one remove, by the same educational initiative of Henry VII's mother, Margaret Beaufort, first countess of Derby, that also revived or created Manchester Grammar School and St. John's College, Cambridge, among other institutions. As a separate parish, Deane was the (long overdue) creation of Henry VIII. The monarch was patron. The see of Chester—another Henrician creation—was patron of Bolton. Ancient families who inherited local leadership—"Puritan" Levers and Pilkingtons, "recusant" Andertons—also inherited the opportunity to argue at the national center: to coax the young Elizabeth to be "governor," not "head" of her church, and to goad the dying James I into copy editing a refutation of a treatise aimed against his claim to be "governor." The "old" families were eventually displaced—though their bloodlines did not disappear—to be replaced, as writers of prestige, by commercial "cousins" such as the Heywoods; by "new" gentlemen of the Civil War opportunity bonanza such as Joseph Rigby or (at a lower level of pretension) Ellis Bradshaw; and by official mouthpieces such as the King's Preacher Zachary Taylor (son of the local headmaster and uncle-by-marriage of the eleventh earl of Derby).

One of the chief aims of this book is the recovery, in greater particularity, of significant contributors whose voices are likely to be lost in any attempt to construct what we might please to call a "national" or "European" concourse of impressions and ideas. Those particular terms are in any case more than usually at a loss to accommodate the emergence (from the early seventeenth century) of Protestant cotton traders who looked to the Middle East for their commercial outlets and to Scotland or New England for their higher education. The parochial concourse does permit the voices to be heard a little more clearly and has the advantage of destabilizing assumptions about any larger patterns to which we might wish to concede its right to belong. I have cited all sources in the notes, but, for the sake of accessibility, I have used modern British spelling when quoting, while retaining (as far as possible) the expressive punctuation and capitalizations of the original. Exceptions are indicated.

By way of separate bibliography, I thought the best I could do would be to give an impression of the printed output of the rare authors who form the basis of this essay on "religious writers and the English monarchy." To serve this purpose, Boltonian works from the time of Henry VIII to William and Mary are listed in some detail. For the sake of completeness, Lawrence Anderton, the Jesuit polemicist, is listed with his (for my topic) much more relevant cousin James. I have made no attempt to list the output of the Andertons' secret press, however. George Marsh, as appearing in Foxe and Coverdale, is accounted less rare and is provided with an indicative list only; as is James Pilkington, for similar reasons, in his character as author of the Homily against "Excess of Apparel." William III's Dean of Chester, Lawrence Fogg (whose ancestors virtually "commissioned" Marsh's letters from prison), and Robert Ainsworth, the lexicographer (and kinsman of the nineteenth-century novelist William Harrison Ainsworth), form the conclusion to my account. Since their relationship to the monarchy is radically different from that of their predecessors, they are omitted from the separate bibliography (though fully cited in the notes). Insofar as their "subject" is monarchy at all, it has become the "subject" familiar to us from our own thought-world. That thought-world (though it does not always realize it) is of course itself the child of time. With the flight of James II and (one is tempted to say, "finally") the death of his daughter, Mary II, in 1694, it becomes possible to read back into earlier discourse a project for "depriving the subject (or its substitute) of its role as originator, and of analysing the subject as a variable and complex function of discourse."[1]

The two most costly pieces of discourse in the present collection are also textually the most problematic. Nevertheless, it is fairly clear that when Hewit and Marsh took their "step to the block, to the fire," under Cromwell and Mary Tudor, they had no intellectual project in mind for "depriving the subject . . . of its role as originator." That facility is merely one of their legacies: an only apparently paradoxical outcome of their motivating conviction that the monarch under Providence was the fount of order.

To generalize rather grossly, there is a progression from a Tudor strategy whereby the monarch, as written subject, is semi-magically invoked by the writing subject as the efficacious projection of the writer's own values and sense of worth; through a Stuart palaver that moulds writer and written anew in terms of the self-consciously vulnerable and pitiful, prone to sin and in need of some further intervention; into a post-Revolution discourse in which the double-gendered contrivance of "William-and-Mary" seems no more than a pervasive analogue for precarious new mixtures of thought and feeling, whose note (in Taylor and Ainsworth, particularly) is that of a feminized, gentlemanly "style," no longer nearly so demanding in its expectations for itself or others as the former way of writing. The "settlement" of 1688–89 seems to have induced forms of finessing temporization on the (written) personalities of the highly educated: not a condition built to last. Yet not even at this stage have the old *constitutional* expectations been surrendered: all the writers in the present sample, at least, convince as being in process of exercising a power of influence, howbeit by forms of petition. They are far from parading to the clockwork requirements of some centralized power. Rather are they adventuring themselves on behalf of the serious delights of communality such as, one imagines, originally fostered their capacities and set them in motion. Thus qualified, they measure themselves against national systems obtaining: if not to the point of self-sacrifice, as Marsh and Hewit. Spiritual intentions had constitutional results.

Works to which I am deeply indebted have inevitably pursued other paths. Thus C. H. Garrett's *Marian Exiles* (1938, reprinted 1966) makes no link between Sir John Cheke, Henry's Regius Professor of Greek and chief propagandist of the Marian exile, and the revenge killing of Marsh, of Deane parish, whose leading family, the Heatons, financed Cheke's campaign. H. C. Porter's *Reformation and Reaction in Tudor Cambridge* (1958, reprinted 1972) notes that Thomas Lever, James and Leonard Pilkington, and Richard Longworth were all Boltonians and all Masters of St. John's College; but his mise-en-scène is confined to Cambridge, and there is no link to Marsh or the Heatons. Patrick Collinson's *The Elizabethan Puritan Movement* (1967, new edition, 1990) takes the Presbyterian Conference at Dedham, Essex, as one of his chief exemplars. He is not concerned to discuss John Angier, of Ded-

ham, who was persuaded by Bolton Puritans to take up a local cure instead
of emigrating to Boston, in New England. Angier's son-in-law, Oliver Heywood of Little Lever (the home and manor of the family that included
Thomas and Ralph Lever) is described as a "Yorkshireman" (p.211). Such a
designation is a condonable slip, since Oliver Heywood was accepted minister
at Coley, Halifax, from 1650 and helped to compile its local history, but it
is a blurring of distinctions, nevertheless, one that misses the opportunity to
link Oliver and Nathaniel Heywood to Thomas Lever, whom Collinson defines, along with Latimer and Robert Crowley (first publisher of *Piers Plowman*), as "the social conscience of Edwardine England" (p. 49).

A. F. Allison, in his 1982 article in *Recusant History,* "Who Was John
Brereley?," finally disposed of the disingenuous nonsense enshrined in Joseph
Gillow's *Bibliographical Dictionary of the English Catholics* (1885–1902),
which had "definitely ascertained" that James Anderton, lay impropriator of
Bolton and Deane, had *not* written the famous (and impressive) *Protestants
Apologie for the Roman Church* (1608, translated into Latin by William
Rayner, 1615). In falsely ascribing the work to Anderton's cousin, the Jesuit
Lawrence Anderton, Gillow seems to have hoped that he had tidied away
the English Catholic tradition of refusal of the secular claims of the Papacy
that James Anderton so superbly, and inconveniently, represents. Since Allison's article it is no longer possible to be an expert on the *Apologie* without
having read it. What he necessarily omits, however, is the very large area
of agreement on matters relating to personal conscience about the monarchy
between James Anderton and his neighbor and distant kinsman, James
Pilkington, first Protestant bishop of Durham.

At least as enabling, for my purposes, was the publication by W. E. Brown
in his *History of Bolton School* (1976) of research by M. S. Howe that conclu-
sively established that the school did indeed have a flourishing pre-
Cromwellian existence, leaving for disposal established biographical fancies
based on the conviction (itself the child of old discords and revenges) that it
did not.

I have included no more than a bibliographical notice of Christopher Lever, whose *Historie of the Defendors of the Catholique Faith* is so temptingly
apposite to my main theme. Until more can be discovered about him, he
would seem (perhaps) to be a member of the Bolton *diaspora,* a rather numerous group whose productions lie outside my scope. His churchmanship was
of the high Anglican kind approved by Charles I. He may have been related
to the Reverend John Lever, whose churchmanship was similar, and who
became vicar of Bolton in 1673. As in the case of other local surnames, our
modern confusions reflect the contradictions of those times. John Lever, the
vicar, was apparently fond of strolling the town with another "John Lever"
(no relation), the Presbyterian son of a Papist father. They declared themselves "brothers."

Humor, good sense, and a certain spontaneous theology of laughter are touched on less than they should be in what follows. The most direct approach to these Boltonian qualities is to be met with in one of the least pretentious, most beautiful autobiographies of recent times: *Saintly Billy. A Catholic Boyhood,* by Bill Naughton (Oxford University Press, 1988). In what amounts to a metahistory of the Lancashire Catholic survival, Naughton (himself of Irish descent) records his friendship with one "Sylvanus Anderton," the representative of the Catholic gentry who kept the faith alive by the written word ("Sylvanus," one remembers, was the amanuensis of St. Peter in prison). In the old Catholic church on Pilkington Street, or in St. Patrick's, Great Moor Street, Naughton kneels before the Body of Christ, "waiting for me in the tabernacle." It is only as he goes out, however, and feels on his face the moorland wind blowing into the heart of the town that he recognizes he cannot "go through life without the Holy Spirit" (p. 217). For him, this spirit is the divine laughter (though "divine" is almost too weak a word) of Boltonians of every race and religion. Theirs is a collective memory of townsfolk running through these streets before Prince Rupert's cavalry; of Bolton mothers and children who paid with their lives for Lincoln's victories, when no cotton meant no bread. Diminished and exhausted by the economic depression of the 1930s (their reward for bearing the brunt of the industrial revolution, of the nightmare of the Somme and of Gallipoli), they are about to be hurried into a worldwide civil war. There is nothing to save them (or the world) but their holy spirit.

My account begins and ends with the Bradshaws: Henry Bradshaw, benedictine of Chester, compiled the miraculous *Life of St. Werburgh* that was issued by the king's printer to coincide with the pope's award to Henry VIII of the title, "Defender of the Faith." It provides a final definition of the medieval English theory of monarchy. In 1694, the year Queen Mary II died, another Henry Bradshaw, of Marple, Cheshire, nephew of the regicide President John Bradshaw, purchased Bradshaw Hall, Bolton, and thus made himself, for one final generation, the head of a gentry clan that predated the Norman Conquest.

C. S. Lewis, in his *English Literature in the Sixteenth Century* (pp. 122–3), wrote sympathetically of Bradshaw's *St. Werburgh,* while begging to differ from Carl Horstmann, one of Bradshaw's nineteenth-century editors, who claimed to have found "Homeric qualities" in Bradshaw's work. Very much overstated as a definition of representative quality, the claim is accurate in the largest sense. As in the *Iliad,* in *St. Werburgh* we are given a world conceived as eternal, but whose future is under threat. Homer's fragile eternity depends on Zeus, son of cannibalistic Kronos. Touching divinity by the overthrow of Hector, Achilles (doomed from that moment) becomes more and less than a man. Announcing the ambition to devour his victim "raw",[2] Achilles invokes a return to a world beyond the order of Zeus, a world of inconceivable disorder and indulgence. Such a world is apprehended and prayed against in *St. Werburgh*. Her ancient shrine, the guardian of Christian England against "brutes and Welshmen," is at the mercy of the brutish Henry: Welsh by descent, yet king of England (and, as such, earl of Chester) by his father's right of battle. Henry obliterated England's holy places and put himself in place of the Holy Father, whose long-disputed function was now to be abolished in England. All of Bradshaw's successors discussed in the following pages—"Protestant" and "Catholic" alike—are much more comprehensible as seeking to build a sustainable Christian kingdom amid the aftermath of that overthrow than as vying with each other to produce (what nevertheless they did help to produce) a secular administration in which the personal power and prestige of the monarch are reduced to a bare minimum and religious allegiance becomes purely a matter of personal choice.

I am grateful for early research funding from the Leverhulme Trust and from Warwick University; also for two terms of research leave from Warwick to complete the book.

Among many librarians and archivists who have provided advice and help, I would like especially to thank Dr. Peter McNiven, Special Collections, John Rylands Library; Mrs. K. Lapsley, Local Studies Unit, Central Library; Dr. Michael R. Powell, Chetham's Library, Manchester; colleagues in the Warwick University Library, particularly Janet Gardner, Robin Green, Peter Larkin, and Joan Powell; and Dr. Susan Brock of the Shakespeare Institute, Stratford. I should also like to thank the staffs of the British Library and Students' MSS Room; of the Library of the Society of Friends; of Dr. Williams's Library, London; of University and College libraries, Cambridge; of the Bodleian; of the New York State Library, for copies of the Thomas Cole papers; and of the Education and Arts Department of Metropolitan Bolton, not only for the copy of the annotated *Bibliographia Boltoniensis* but for continual advice and help over a number of years from Mrs. S. L. Harrison, Messrs. F. N. Parker and B. D. Mills; from Mrs. Angela Thomas, Senior Keeper of Human History and all her staff; and also (and especially) from Mr. Kevin Campbell, Archivist. I should also like to thank Mr. George Verwer (whose Operation Mobilisation brought the first bibles into St. Petersburg, the former Leningrad) for writing to me on 16 May 1991 with the information that the idea for the ocean-going book-ship for world evangelism, *The Logos* (which became a reality in 1970), was first mooted in the back room of a Bolton bookshop, formerly the King's Arms public house, during the 1960s. The arrival of his letter—like its contents—was one of those unpredictable developments that in retrospect appear foreshadowed.

——— Parish Boundaries   - - - -   Township Boundaries

Bolton Parish Church is in Great Bolton township. The other Bolton townships are Little Bolton ("L.B."), Anglezarke, Blackrod, Bradshaw, Breightmet, Darcy Lever, Edgeworth, Entwistle, Harwood, Little Lever, Longworth, Lostock, Quarlton, Rivington, Sharples, Tonge with Haulgh, Turton.

Deane Parish Church is in Rumworth township. The other Deane townships are Farnworth, Halliwell, Heaton, Horwich, Kearsley, Little Hulton, Middle Hulton, Over Hulton, Westhoughton.

Great Lever and Ainsworth are "island" townships of Middleton parish. Aspull is in the ecclesiastical parish of Wigan, but for civil purposes taxed with Blackrod.

A Kingdom
in Two Parishes

Section One
Reformation

When Jeffrey Hurst of Shakerley was brought before Justice Leland, he caused a Mass to be sung, and bade Jeffrey go and see his Maker. . . . Jeffrey answered, Sir, my Maker is in Heaven.
—Henry Pendlebury, *A Plain Representation of Transubstantiation* (1687)

PART ONE
Henrician Monk

What were mankind without literature?
Full little worthy, blinded by ignorance.
The way to heaven it declareth right sure
Through perfect living and good perseverance.
—Henry Bradshaw, *The Life of St. Werburgh
of Chester* (1521)

1

Henry Bradshaw: Last of the Old Catholic Order

Bradshaw's *Life of St. Werburgh* is "a legendary epic after the fashion introduced by Lydgate," who died in 1460. "The poem is written in seven-lined stanzas (rhyme royal, introduced by Chaucer)."[1] All this made it distinctly old-fashioned on its first appearance.

Two things make it more than just old-fashioned, however. Bradshaw is a simplifier and also, to some extent, a popularizer. He has absorbed the dreary mass of the relevant medieval chronicles—he made a Latin reduction of them, now lost—and purged them of many of their excesses. Bradshaw has also forsworn the courtly refinements of Lydgate—his northern gentleman's speaking voice can be heard through the springy and moderately alliterative lines. Like the Sunday school pioneers of the eighteenth century, however, or the pioneers of wholesome reading material for the masses of the nineteenth, Bradshaw is dismayed as well as energized by the

> singular condition
> Of the common people, simple and negligent,
> Which without literature and good information
> Be like to brute beasts.[2]

The voice is that of a provincial literary class, audible at any time for the next four hundred years. Like most of his successors, Bradshaw's main target is the commercial class:

> Go forth, little book: Jesu be thy speed
> And save thee alway from misreporting,
> Which art compiled for no clerk indeed,
> But for merchant men.

He prays they "to the monastery be never unkind".[3]

What is mainly interesting about his work is the vanished wholeness it represents. In it can be read what is almost the final statement of a medieval Trinitarian system of real presence, personal assurance, and inherited authority—of sovereignty, assent, and sanction—that would be fragmented and questioned in detail by his Protestant successors. As we shall see, Bradshaw's alienation from part of his own system is an omen of its collapse.

2

"Place Spiritual": The Real Presence of Christ

LIKE the person of the king, or the body of God the Son in the sacrament, Werburgh's bodily presence commanded the immediate reverence due to her spiritual sovereignty.

She had no special connection with Chester (or "West Chester," to give it its old name) during her lifetime. Her body was moved there from Stafford-shire to escape the fury of the Danish invasion of 875, nearly two hundred years after her death. As with other Saxon saints, the church that sheltered her remains underwent a complete rebuilding after the Norman Conquest and was successively reedified and adorned to reach an apogee of magnificence and elaboration, making it ripe for Henry's commissioners of 1539.

Bradshaw is not insensitive to the charms of historical association or of art, but with the austerity of true belief he knows that such things are as nothing besides the immediacy of his saint's physical presence, now and till the end of time, at West Chester,

> In which holy place unto this present day
> She bodily resteth by divine providence
> And so by His grace shall continue alway.[1]

In his "charitable motion" to readers to protect the monastery, Bradshaw twice rhymes "place" with "grace". This is no empty coincidence. In the thought-world that he inhabits, all things exemplify divine providence, and such a rhyme points to the interdependence of the paired terms within the divine scheme. A "place" can be a source of "grace," yet only by "grace" does "place" cohere at all. Bradshaw can describe the little piece of earth where Werburgh "bodily resteth" as "the place spiritual" because her presence there is the assurance that earth is sustained by spirit. Her body, resting in the Lady Chapel at West Chester, is a divine indicator of the sacredness of place and of its importance within a secure plan of revelation and redemption. The quality of her presence depends on her virtues, yet these in turn depend on her election by divine grace as Christ's spouse to exemplify a particular measure of Christ's perfection:

So that no creature more perfect might be
In virtuous gifts (by grace) than she.[2]

Miracle proclaims, with effortless fecundity and simplicity, the divine sovereign power that, if correctly invoked, readily incarnates itself in material
space and time. Thus, the body of the radiantly virtuous Werburgh remains
unblemished two hundred years after her death. Three centuries later still,
a fire threatens to destroy Chester. The monks make procession through the
streets carrying her body on a litter and singing the litany with true devotion:

The fire began to cease—a miracle clear—
Not passing the place where the holy shrine
Was borne by the brethren.[3]

The supreme miracle is also the most frequent. At every mass, the sacred
elements become, by the miracle of transubstantiation, the very substance of
Christ and, as such, contain Christ whole and entire—divinity, humanity,
soul, body, and blood. As each "region" (a favorite word of Bradshaw) has
the assurance of its own particular significance in the bodily presence of its
tutelary saint, so all Christendom is united to its furthest corner by this
renewal of the real presence of Christ Himself. To complete the assurance,
the consecrated host (which lacks nothing that is also in the consecrated
wine) is reserved over the altar, with a light burning perpetually before it.

Anointed mortal sovereignty is a shadowy participator in this divine splen-
dor. The sovereignty of a kingdom rests in the king's person; his bodily
presence is the center and the source of power. He is king, not merely by
analogy with Christ, but by virtue of his election through divine grace to
represent Christ, the only true king.

3

"Ghostly Tuition": The Discipline of the Holy Spirit

L IKE the medieval arrangement whereby Parliament gave support to the king after receiving the sacrament, or like the inspiration of the Holy Ghost functioning within the "tuition" of Catholic discipline, Werburgh was a source of assurance, strengthening personal assent to the promptings of conscience and enabling the perseverance needed to carry them out.

The doctrine of transubstantiation was not officially authorized by the papacy till five hundred years after Werburgh's death. As an Oxford man,[1] Bradshaw must have known that two famous scholars of the University—Ockham and Wycliffe—were among those who made unsuccessful attempts to have the doctrine modified in favor of some compromise formula that would retain the idea of Christ's real presence in the sacrament while stopping short of the notion that the bread and wine were literally "transubstantiated" into his "substance." In common with other papal doctrines, this crucially contentious formula of "transubstantiation" was enshrined in the self-referential dog-Latin jargon of scholasticism. Bradshaw, as a contemporary of Erasmus, was part of the movement of Catholic reformers to free the faith from this barbaric jargon. What Erasmus undertook in neoclassical Latin for the scholars of Europe, Bradshaw attempted, in their native idiom, for the "merchant men" of his own "region."

In his search for consensus, he had ready to hand an "original" whose formulations might command assent. He put his view of the real presence into the mouth of the dying St. Werburgh:

> Thy most blessed body in sacrament
> Thou gave to us for our communion
> To be our defence and ghostly tuition
> Now present here in form of bread.[2]

In this moving attempt to conserve the mystery of the real presence while making it appear accessible, Bradshaw could rely on the affection of his "region" for St. Werburgh and on the desire of his readers to remain part of

27

Catholic Christendom. The ambitions of a nationalistic monarchy were clearly antagonistic to both.

Yet monarchy had fed for centuries on the papal interpretation of the doctrine of the real presence. There is thus a political meaning in Bradshaw's equation of the reception of the sacrament with the acceptance of "ghostly tuition." The doctrine of transubstantiation, in its full scholastic elaboration, and the credal affirmation that the Holy Ghost "proceeds" from the Son as well as the Father, were unique to the Latin church.[3] Insofar as the Spirit seemed a product of the Son, and the Son of the mass, then to receive the wafer was indeed to submit to the version of "ghostly tuition" permitted by authority. A demonstration of this, under the English Catholic monarchy, was made at the opening of each Parliament, since Parliaments were inaugurated by a solemn mass of the Holy Ghost. It was after adoring, and perhaps swallowing, very God that the Parliament of 1485, for instance, asserted the sovereignty of Henry VII. This king of dubious claim went on to revive Edward the Confessor's policy of concentrating sanctity, as well as power, at Westminster.

As one might expect, Bradshaw equates the "ghostly tuition" provided by the sacrament with humble obedience to the discipline of the Roman church. His Saint

> Daily increased more and more in virtue
> In ghostly science and virtuous discipline
> Observing the doctrine of our Lord Jesu.[4]

The cultivation of virtue is a matter of "science," or objective knowledge, founded on disciplined regard for doctrines that are not in question. Individual conscience is simply a matter of reverence for "tuition" or protective authority. If God seems remote, Bradshaw draws close to Werburgh

> Our sure tuition, next to the Trinity.

If personal doubts as to belief and conduct should arise, Werburgh has gone on ahead, triumphant in sanctity:

> In all necessity a sure mediatrice
> From grievous oppression preserving thy place,
> A lantern of light in each woful case,
> To illumine thy people plunged in heaviness
> With great consolation and ghostly solace:
> Now lighten our conscience, sweet patroness.[5]

Clearly, for Bradshaw, the Holy Spirit, which sustains the consciences of true believers, does not tempt his own people into rebelling against "oppression." Yet, also from Bradshaw's viewpoint, Henry VIII's bid to free himself from Rome, while retaining the doctrine of transubstantiation with all its power for solemnizing individual assent, would be a form of perjury and of blasphemy. Contrary to Henry's given word, it pretended to make the king, instead of the vicar of Christ, king of kings, the earthly arbiter of conscience.

4

"Life Historial": The Transmitted Authority of the Father

LIKE the evolutions of the English legal system, or the providential workings of God the Father in history, Bradshaw's Werburgh exerted an authority sanctioned by its success over time. Her authority, however, was in practice vulnerable, since it depended to a great extent on her bodily presence in the Lady Chapel at West Chester. In the same way, the pre-Reformation view of historical process was vulnerable, since it depended on a belief in the eternal here and now of Christ's presence in the sacrament, at the center of history. As it turned out, the desecration of shrines like Werburgh's was the preliminary to the political triumph of a theology that denied transubstantiation, only to find its own political relevance at a discount by virtue of that very denial.

Among the most influential of Tudor propagandists against transubstantiation was John Bale, hagiographer of Anne Askew, who was put to death under Henry VIII for denying the doctrine. Bale, a professional monk-hater, nevertheless had a relatively high opinion of Henry Bradshaw.[1]

If to the mind of a virulent Protestant like Bale Bradshaw is a good man affirming a mistaken creed, where lies his mistake? Perhaps it lies in the exclusion of future possibilities that his sensibility represents. The great strength of Bradshaw's gentle, generous, but unquestioning version of pre-Reformation Trinitarian orthodoxy is his absolute certainty of the bodily presence of the Son in the sacrament. A great weakness is his serene reduction of the Holy Spirit to a function of Roman Catholic discipline. But the fatality which his version of the system carries within itself is his alienation from history. He cannot read the writing on the wall except to wish it away. He cannot embrace for the future what he can record of the past: the providential authority of the Creator-Father, working out the destiny of peoples. This is hardly surprising, and rather to his credit than otherwise. It is symptomatic that, unlike the jealous God of the Old Testament, or the equally aggressive deity to be met with in earlier monastic or later Protestant hagiographies, Werburgh, in Bradshaw's version, works only kindly miracles that help the good and simple or that let off lightly even wickedness itself.

True, a tyrannical bailiff who oppresses a servant has his head twisted round backwards, but he is almost immediately contrite and is rapidly restored to spiritual and bodily health.

Werburgh was a royal princess of the kingdom of Mercia, "Of five mighty kings descended lineally." Due to these connections, she was in life awarded the privilege of acting as spiritual "governor" to all monastic houses in the kingdom. Chester Abbey, as the guardian of her body, claimed the inheritance of this and of more material privileges that had accrued to her as an "enhery-tryce," as Bradshaw spells it.[2]

Wealth and land and inherited spiritual authority were the cold objects of the deliberate pillaging and desecration of Werburgh's shrine, and many others, by Henry's Commissioners of 1539. A calculating brutality extin-guished all traces of the holy bodies of England's saints in order to transfer to the person of Henry Tudor all claims formerly made on their behalf. The king could now command the Church's wealth and its authority. An act of Parliament consigned to the fire all who denied transubstantiation, with lesser penalties for lesser lapses in orthodoxy. Dragged into schism, and then materially and spiritually pillaged, the Church was thus recompensed with fresh powers of persecution. To this arrangement the last abbot of Chester acquiesced, becoming the first dean of Henry's new cathedral. The heraldic carvings that had covered Werburgh's shrine were hastily reassembled to improvise a throne for the king's bishop. The monarchs who had guarded the saint were translated into the basis of an episcopal authority created ex nihilo by royal command. South Lancashire and Cheshire, hitherto a remote and independent-minded region of the huge diocese of Coventry and Lich-field, were now to be spiritually policed from Chester.

To some extent, Bradshaw's system could provide for such things. Ac-cording to the ordinary medieval view, which he accepted, the ultimate sanction for the power of kings rested with divine Providence. Victory in battle, for instance, was a true claim to authority, since victory was sanc-tioned by God. Werburgh herself was not merely "virgin glorious" in her own right but "Descended by ancestry of blood victorial," a figure who inherited effective historical power as the instrument of a greater power. Her "life historial" deserved to be recorded because its historical conse-quences were still operative.

When such consequences threatened to become unbearable, a votary of Werburgh might cease to wish to celebrate them. Desiring a Providence that will conserve his region's spiritual autonomy, Bradshaw becomes narrow and backward looking. He is certainly backward looking in that the Danish inva-sion is still vivid to him and the Norman Conquest still a recent event. Indeed, the Conquest was providential to the pious Saxon Bradshaws. Loyal to Edward and to William and disowning the perjured Harold, they retained their lands on that occasion.[3] Bradshaw is narrow, in that the vanished frontiers of the Kingdom of Mercia still bound his loyalties. In particular, Chester's former function as a border fortress keeping at bay the incursions of "brutes and Welshmen" is something he responds to quite uncritically. His heart is with Edward I, who strengthened and adorned Chester for that purpose, and with the old, original, earls of Chester, who died out in the reign of Edward's father, Henry III.

By a long and tumultuous process which Bradshaw reviews serenely, the Abbey of West Chester and the status of its saintly patroness have been constructed and finalised. It is significant that the rescue of Chester from fire in 1180 is the last miracle of Werburgh that Bradshaw records. Looking back to that providential event, he can only bear to look forward, at the end of Werburgh's story, to the continuance, under the same providence, of the status quo:

> This holy abbess and lady imperial
> Hath been president in Chester monastery,
> Their trust, their treasure, and defence special,
> In much reverence seven hundred year, truly;
> And so shall continue, by grace of God Almighty,
> To the world's end in high magnificence.[4]

One may pity such an intense reliance, forfeit to destiny as it was. Yet by obliterating Werburgh and her like, Henry removed not only his local spirit-ual rivals, but also so many local sanctions against disbelief in himself.

PART TWO
Edwardine Preacher

A man may have just occasion to keep or change any place, but never to yield or agree unto any evil or ungodly thing
—Thomas Lever, *A Treatise of the Right Way*
(Geneva, 1556)

5

Thomas Lever: Seeking the Place Spiritual

Henry Bradshaw died in 1513, shortly after completing his poem. It was issued in London by the king's printer in 1521, to coincide with the award of Henry's new title—"Defender of the Faith"—from a grateful pope. The poem provided a final summary of the medieval mystique of sovereignty, which had power to associate the person of the consecrated king to the absolute supremacy of the King of Kings, bodily present by transubstantiation.

Thomas Lever was a moderate Protestant and natural constitutionalist, with some elements of the Hellenic spirit in him. He was also a man of very individual integrity and was determined to retain the sense of Christ's real presence while denying with equal passion the old Catholic notion of confining that presence to the consecrated wafer. He would spend his life seeking a place from which to begin negotiating a more liberal view of human sovereignty and a new, nonmonastic but still communal setting for the material functioning of the spiritual sovereignty of Christ.

It was the Christianization of the English cultural setting that preoccupied him, even while resident in Europe. That setting was currently dominated by the political needs of the monarchy. No more than the monks of the Pilgrimage of Grace or the Independent ironsides of Cromwell's army could Lever have accepted monarchical authority as the arbiter of conscience. It was his instinct, however, to argue for moderation and compromise, in the search for constitutional workability, seeking to avoid, not foment, rebellion. Circumstances were hopelessly against him. A reductive memorialist view of the sacrament, fostered by upper-class Protestants, was for them a useful means of crushing out the political relevance of Christian theology. Ironically, while this Anglo-Zwinglian view was not shared by Elizabeth, she found it politically more expedient than Lever's type of liberalism, within which lurked a demand for a parliamentary monarchy, if not an absolute republic.

This man, who could charm Elizabeth to a compromise in the matter of her ecclesiastical title—she consented, at his strong suggestion, to be called "Governor" rather than "Head" of the Church, as her father had been[1]— may to some extent be conveniently placed in time between two Bradshaw generations: on the one hand, that of the monk Henry, composer of the last rationale for medieval monarchy; and on the other, that of his kinsman Robert Bradshaw, of the township of Bradshaw, leader of Bolton's military stand against the perjured Charles, and therefore, willingly or otherwise, an ally of his Cheshire cousin, John Bradshaw the Regicide.

Geographical placement is another matter: it was not something Lever ever really found. It turned out that what he was seeking was something outside Europe altogether.

Southwest Lancashire, with its good farmland and rich manors, has been defined as the scene of "medieval prosperity"; whereas southeast Lancashire, with its pastoral landscape of green moorland—a source of wool for the textile trade—has been called the site of "Reformation prosperity."[2] Roughly speaking, the Catholic west confronted at Bolton the Protestant east.

In accordance with this pattern, at the western edge of Bolton parish, in the townships of Lostock and Blackrod, respectively, were the homes of the recusant Andertons and of Laurence Vaux, whose *Catechism for Children* (Antwerp, 1574) was among the outlawed Catholic texts stocked by their secret press in the reigns of Elizabeth and James. Among townships at the parish's eastern edge were Bradshaw, and also—three miles or so to the south—Little Lever, home of Thomas Lever, whose Protestant *Treatise of the Right Way* (Geneva, 1556) was smuggled into England in large numbers during the reign of Mary. Responsible for the smuggling, and for financing the Protestant propaganda campaign, were the five merchant "sustainers" of the Marian exiles. These included George and Thomas Heaton, close relatives of Lever's mother, Elenor Heaton. Elenor was the daughter of the conservative Catholic Richard Heaton, who had helped to bring up Lever's father, John. The continental base of the Protestant Heatons was Emden, Protestant rival of Catholic Antwerp. Their home base, the township of Heaton, formed a section of that central part of Deane that included the parish church of St. Mary, and which intervened between the western and eastern parts of Bolton parish. Richard Heaton's new chantry at Deane was smashed to pieces in 1522, on the eve of the Assumption of the Virgin. No one was ever punished, and whether ultra-Protestants in his own family commissioned the outrage is unknown.

The Tudor conflict between Catholic and Protestant, like the Civil War that followed it, was here what it was in England as a whole: a conflict between different aspects of the same landscape, in which some areas appeared to be on one side, some on the other, and all were traumatically divided. What was true of a parish, or a country, was true of the whole continent of Europe. Lever must have had ample opportunity to observe this in 1551 when, in the role of chaplain and religious adviser, he accompanied Queen Catherine Parr's brother Northampton on his embassy to the Court of Henry II of France and Catherine de' Medici. Lever may also have glimpsed on that occasion the young Mary, Queen of Scots, and her mother and regent, Mary of Guise, who had returned to France to help foil Northampton's embassy.[3]

It is this English and European pattern of conflict and the consequent search for security of place that partly characterises the experience of the Puritan Thomas Lever. Moreover, unlike Counter-Reformation Catholics who led similarly roving lives, Lever can no longer subscribe to Henry Bradshaw's sense that each and every "place" may be made "spiritual" by the mere act of consecration. It sounds like a fine distinction, but it is a radical one. For Lever, each faithful communicating *congregation* is a potential source for the material transmission of the effects of the spirit. It is not a wafer that he worships, but *Emmanuel*: "God with us."

Christ's bodily presence on each and every altar of the old Catholic Europe might seem to have confirmed the absolute value of localities while affirming the material unity of all Christendom. Typically, at Bolton during the early sixteenth century opposing aspects of the local landscape were imaged together in the fabric of the parish church of St. Peter, which reflected the unflinching Pennine character of eastern uplands as well as the softer radiance of westerly meadows. By day, the blunt west tower of dark reddish stone was not merely the sternest and most imposing feature of the busy market place, but a clue to the iron in the gaunt hills beyond it; while the flamboyant east window, with its sanctuary lights, suspended in the night sky like a cluster of butterflies above the heads of those who approached the building from that side (where the ground is still almost sheer, and lonely) provided a transcendent intimation of the softer landscape towards which the wayfarer was climbing. In the morning, at one of the altars—the high altar, perhaps, with its serene picture of the Assumption of the Virgin— James Bolton, vicar and eponymous gentleman of his native place, would say mass in vestments embroidered with golden roses and other colored flowers by the nuns of Amiens.

Conflict between the old manorial and the new pastoral families would be reflected in the architectural history of such local churches. The requirements of national politics were always a factor. Towards the end of her reign, Elizabeth would appoint the Catholic Andertons as lay rectors of Deane and Bolton. As such, they were responsible for the upkeep and adornment of their chancels. During the Puritan reaction, Mrs. Andrews—maintaining the Lever tradition on London money—would set her cohorts of godly women to acts of systematic iconoclasm in both churches. Their towers would be manned by Robert Bradshaw's Parliamentary troops during the Civil War.[4]

Continuity and disruption sustained each other. Father Bolton, who may have helped to educate Pilkington, Lever, and Marsh, graduated from Cambridge in 1504 and kept his living (as did most priests) through the religious upheavals of Henry's reign and Edward's and Mary's, dying in 1556. Catherine Bolton, a young relative of his, married Richard, John Lever's heir. As was usual, Richard did not go to the university, leaving the pursuit of learn-ing and a career to his younger brothers, Thomas, Ralph, and John.[5]

Thus far does Bolton exemplfy the pattern of English and European divi-sion, and of continuity in division. There is also a New World dimension to the significance of Thomas Lever, as there is to the history of Bolton, how-ever. One might in parenthesis exemplify this same Bolton family of Bolton, pioneers of Westchester in the New York colony in North America.[6]

There was a third element in the local landscape besides moor and meadow, one that was more deeply characteristic than either of local poten-tial. It showed itself inside the churches, in the sturdy, tangled screens of carved wood that divided the priests' chancel from the people's nave. These were the product of the wooded, dream-haunted cloughs of Bolton; of a confined and teeming world of swift streams and timber; of coal mines and forges; fully operational by the Tudor period: the birthplace of an industrial empire, and (as we shall see) from the first decade of the seventeenth century the very earliest scene of the British cotton industry. Such was the township of Darcy Lever, an epitome of workshop England, powered by the twisting streams of the forceful little rivers Tonge and Croal. Close-knit and prosper-ous, it began just beyond Blackshaw Brook, five hundred yards north of the back door of Little Lever Hall, where Thomas Lever was born.

Uncoiling from the grimy nest of Darcy Lever, the Tonge and Croal tribu-taries feed into the river Irwell at a point three-quarters of a mile below Little Lever Hall. A few minutes' scramble down steep banks from the front door of their father's house would have brought the Lever brothers to where the waters meet, a place modern children visit to enact their dreams of the Wild West. There is still enough ruggedness in the terrain and flow in the persistent stream to make boys dream of the sea. Yet at no point is the Irwell naturally navigable.

Only through a sequence of eighteenth- and nineteenth-century improve-ments and canal building (including the Bolton-Manchester Canal through Little Lever) were these shallow waters brought to bear traffic. Then by a further effort of engineering, Manchester turned itself—in 1894—into one of the great ports of the world. The Irwell was fed into the newly dug Manchester Ship Canal. Cargoes could at last be floated direct from southeast Lancashire to California, Montreal, and Buenos Aires, the great markets of the New World that first came into human imagination in the 1530s with the discoveries of the naval pioneers.

It is in this altogether broader setting—the insertion into what would otherwise have been an entirely Latin American continent of an English-speaking culture—that one must place the significance of Lever's experimen-tal colony at Aarau, in republican Switzerland, which has been seen as pro-viding the model, after 1630, for the Protestant colonization of New England,

and "westward to the Pacific".[7] Initiative counts here, more than custom. The most striking elements are no longer matters of evolving family tradition, as was the case with the Bradshaws and their relationship with the English monarchy, but matters of education and of individual imagination and will. If we ask where the transitional figure of Thomas Lever could be placed in this context, it would be between Laurence Vaux, from Blackrod, on Bolton's westernmost rim, the civilized yet childlike last Catholic Warden of Manchester under Mary, exiled to Louvain under Elizabeth; and Vaux's Latin pupil Laurence Chaderton, of Oldham,[8] first Master of the "godly house" of Emmanuel College, Cambridge: the greatest source for the Puritan emigration movement to New England. The first president of the "new Emmanuel," Harvard College, would be Henry Dunster,[9] of Bulholt, between Bradshaw and the upper Irwell, just outside the eastern boundary of Bolton.

6

The Effectual Body of Christ

THE matter of personal conversion eludes analysis; its implications cannot be imagined. In 1546 Thomas Lever was a young don at Cambridge. Anne Askew was on trial for her life. Lever was studying a Latin book on navigation, *De Re Navali*. Families were divided, and movement was in the air. Elenor Heaton, Lever's mother, may well have been of Protestant tendency, like her relatives George and Thomas Heaton. Her father Richard Heaton was an old-fashioned Catholic. George's wife Joanna, dying in childbirth in 1552, would dedicate her son to the Reformed Church. Joanna's father was Sir Martin Bowes, who as Lord Mayor of London helped to set in motion the proceedings that led to Askew's martyrdom.

The testimony of Askew was that Christ's presence was not confined to a wafer. As Lever read that testimony in Bale's account, his imagination was fired by the idea of an untethering of the real presence, of an effectual future for the sacrament as a vessel for the material reconciliation and transformation of the human world. This is what would lie behind his choice of the title "Governor" for Elizabeth in 1559. It is the title Bradshaw assigned to Werburgh. It descends from the Latin *gubernator* and the Greek *kubernetes*. It means "pilot."

In November 1548, as Edward VI's new Protestant prayer book was being compiled, Lever took part in a disputation about the mass, in the chapel of his Cambridge college, St. John's. Others had a less academic approach: during this period, someone made Lever's point for him by entering the chapel secretly and cutting the string of the hanging pyx in which the sacred host—or the "god in a box," as the Protestants called it—was reserved.[1] The shocking purity of this act—the untethering of the real presence from its fixed place above the altar, imprisoned and elevated from the congregation—mirrors those positive aspects of Lever's sacramental thinking from which he would never deviate. These positives, however, required to be protected in a world less persuaded of them than he was. He would always be willing to negotiate for their protection; they themselves were nonnegotiable.

An anomaly to observers, Lever possesses a consistent internal logic: one that must have been reached before his Protestant ordination by Ridley in

1550. He is very clear about the special role of the clergy as ministers of the Word and Sacraments: but both Word and Sacraments are for him a leaven whose proper function it is to energize a whole community. Otherwise the power, even the being, of these instruments of grace is somehow diminished. For him, man can indeed resist the grace of God. This view of a function—shared, it might be said, between God and man—which is supremely important and necessary, yet circumstantially or apparently limited, may well reflect the nature of Lever's own busy, efficient, yet thwarted existence. It certainly makes his theology center on the notion of an incarnated, ascended Christ. It sets him equally at odds with systematic Calvinists and Romanists on the one hand and pragmatists on the other.

The gist of his view of sovereignty is to restore traditional Catholic priorities under an evangelical dispensation. Like Henry Bradshaw, he desires the monarchy to defer to the Church's gospel of Christ; but like Askew and Bale he believes that Christ lives in our hearts and in heaven, and cannot be confined to a wafer. Conscience cannot therefore be placed into our mouths by any priest: it is a spiritual indwelling apparent in the daily experience of the Christian community. Here Lever adds a special rider of his own. For him, if Christ is truly present in our hearts, his sovereignty will be manifested in communal efforts of well-doing, apparent in the material sphere. The spiritual sovereignty of this materially effectual Christ cannot be confined to the impulses of any single human embodiment. Like the sacrament, human power becomes effectual only when functioning distributively through the exertions of the communal conscience, either without any bodily monarch at all; or else through a constitutional monarchy acting distributively; or, in the last resort, through pressure brought to bear on a personal ruler.

The apparent oddities of his sacramental practice follow from this. For Lever, it was simply because Christ *was* present, that the eucharist required an evangelical simplicity for its celebration. He would never permit Elizabeth to order him to wear exclusive vestments: not because he denied the priestly power, but because he denied the claim of any secular authority to make liveried flunkeys of those who alone had apostolic power to invoke Christ's sacramental presence, a presence whose essence was unity, however, not exclusion, and whose function was the ordering of the material world in the interests of communal well-being, regardless of the whims of princes. By the same logic, Lever could not abide the use of wafers—a practice common to Romanists, Calvinists, and Lutherans—since the leavened bread of everyday eating did not merely "suffice" for the sacrament (as the Edwardine and Elizabethan prayer books put it) but was the only possible medium for the effective Body of Christ.

Romanist wafer worship; the Zwinglian absentee Christ, whose real presence was confined to heaven; the Calvinist tendency to deny man any cooperation in his own redemption—all these approaches seemed to Lever to refuse efficacy to the sacrament. The Lutherans were more ambiguous and more at the beck of princes. With Luther they emphasised faith (whether or not they shared his personal nostalgia for transubstantiation) yet clung to antic ceremonies as though anxious not to encounter the Christ of the gospels. For Lever, it was bad to rely on "ceremonial religion of man's invention without any word of God," but worse to have "the word of God . . . without any true comfortable knowledge and love of God." That "comfortable knowledge" was of "salvation freely opened and offered unto man through Christ" and that "love" must be functional, if it was to be worth anything. True believers asked of Christ "to have and use a pure love, to minister the gifts of thy good things unto mutual comfort and commodity." Individual conviction of salvation, as predestined, some Calvinists came to regard as the mark of a Christian. For Lever, however, the much-argued contrast between the "security" of the worldling and that of the godly was a distinction without a difference: "security" itself was a sin to be prayed against, along with "blind zeal." He listed both as forms of covetousness, for they greedily pretended to appropriate spiritual gifts that could have no function unless shared, as Christ was shared.[2]

Lever became involved with the "extreme protestant party at court,"[3] but his own outlook is better described as "evangelical" or even "radical Catholic." More implacably than most of his English contemporaries, he raises perennial issues about the incompatibility between secular states (not least monarchical ones) and Christianity itself.

In his *Epistle* to Edward's Council of 1550, Lever summarised his triple manifesto. The "preaching of God's gospel" was not to be separated from "justice and equity" in administration; from a distributive economy of material goods both "cheap and plenty."[4] Only in his busy, cheerful little colony in Switzerland, an experiment lasting only eighteen months or so and involving at most a hundred volunteers, would Lever ever glimpse his ideal republic, based equally on the "free use of the Word of God and the Sacraments and . . . the manufacture of English cloth."[5]

In England, his tactics depended on who was on the throne. Like other well-connected Puritans, he could negotiate with Elizabeth to some extent, yet he remained vulnerable to the needs of monarchical power. The youth and apparent pliability of Edward gave Lever the opportunity to launch a manifesto directed beyond him towards the education of England. When the boy died, however, Lever's impatient idealism (with some prompting, most likely, from his unscrupulous brother Ralph) drove him into the camp of Lady Jane Grey, that pathetic champion of a form of Protestantism scarcely less incompatible with Lever's ideas than Romanism itself.

7

Manifesto Contradicted by Revolution

THE three surviving sermons of Lever were all delivered in London during 1550, and all published by him that year in a number of editions. They were designed to be read as a coherent manifesto and were again reissued in 1572. The February sermon tackles the problem of the individual conscience and political society; in March Lever is concerned with the reformation of the church; in December he spells out the implications of all this for the future of education.

With the arrogance of an idealistic young intellectual (he was not yet thirty), Lever scourges the nepotism of the minority establishment he outwardly supports. "For Papistry," he says, "is not banished out of England by pure religion, but overrun, suppressed and kept under . . . by covetous ambition." Anguished, disdainful and enjoying himself tremendously, he denounces to their faces the spiritual pretensions of his own most likely patrons. The regime has established its favorites in so many deer parks, stolen from former monastic sanctuaries: "the deer thereof, most dearly bought with Christ's blood, have strayed out of their feeding to destroy the corn of all men's livings."[1] Lever has been praised, together with Latimer, for "lending the cause of 'commonweal' the sanction of the Gospel."[2] For Latimer, however, the primary theme remains the medieval one of the sufferings of Christ's poor. Lever's angry pity is honed for the definition of Christ's new rich. These are the "deer," the regime's pets and also its victims—their brashness has provoked popular rebellion. As for the real masters, they are not so much deer as wolves. For, he tells them to their faces in his March sermon, "when the Lord of all Lords shall see the flock scattered . . . if he follow the trace of the blood, it will lead him straight way unto this court".[3]

Lever parodies the cant of the Anglo-Zwinglians, who know not what comes in or goes out of their mouths. Secure in the belief that they at least, by faith, are "saved by Christ's blood," regardless of how they behave, these new landowning Protestants, comfortably annexing salvation along with abbey lands, have conspired to remove all social and political meaning from the sacrament by demoting it to a mere memorial of Christ's death.

Lever will have none of this. Delivered in pouring rain on 2 February in

ganda—he actually uses the word "advertise"—in a spacious style designed from the first for the widest consumption. Edward is idealised, circumvented, manipulated into suggesting a function analogous yet subordinated to that of the sacrament as Lever envisages it: at once high in a serene heaven and yet also present to answer the longings of congregated hearts with materially effectual redress:

> Wherefore according to the example of Christ Jesu, most Christian and Gracious King, for the reverence of God, which hath set you upon the high hill of honour and authority, lift up your gracious eyes of charitable pity, and behold much people throughout all England, coming to seek release, ease and comfort, sent from God unto them, by your excellent Majesty.

Turning to the Lords of the Council—or rather, speaking past them to the listening crowd and yet larger crowd of intended readers—Lever is concussive and without apology. Whereas, in medieval tradition, Latimer still preaches as a priest of the Church, Lever claims the more worldly voice of a Protestant citizen:

> Now my lords, both of the laity and of the clergy, in the name of God, I advertise you to take heed, . . . For you maintain your chaplains to take Pluralities, and your other servants more offices than they can or will discharge. . . . Fie for sin and shame, either give your servants wages, or else let them go and serve those which do give them wages.[7]

Lever's terse style yields subversive information when read at leisure. He is challenging the right of the mighty to tax the productive labor of the poor in order to endow the holders of sinecures. It has been pointed out that Lever, to a far more noticeable degree than Latimer, reproduces in English the effect of the hieratic, antithetical rimed Latin prose of Cyprian and his medieval successors.[8] In fact, Lever varies this style (which had become preeminently the style of royal courts) in order on the one hand to distance, circumvent, and employ the king, as we have seen, and on the other to accommodate the sloganlike directness of phrases such as these, in which the patterns of "homoioteleuton," stripped of courtly glitter, perform their street function of simple outrage:

> And especially landlords take exceeding fines and rents of their tenants, and do no good unto their tenants.

The cumulative effect of these movements back and forth between heraldic proclamation and graffito is to transpose the boy monarch into a functional ideal: the embodiment of a disinterested center through which God's mercy is percolated to nourish the material body of the whole people, not least the "rude lobs of the country, who . . . speak foul and truly as they find it." A courtly style designed to stun listeners into subservience is given one more outing as an instigator of subversion.

If Henry Bradshaw is Bolton's first-ever purveyor in print of pious suste-nance to the commercial classes and their employees, Lever is its first disaf-fected young intellectual of the upper-middle class to claim to be the mouthpiece of the disenfranchised.

His third sermon was preached at Paul's Cross in December 1550 and was immediately published with his open *Epistle to the Council*. The sermon itself is a comprehensive and circumstantial review of the "uncharitable spoil of provision, that was made for the poor" in grammar schools and universities. It completes Lever's manifesto by underlining yet more forcibly the central claim of the whole trilogy: for communicating Christians, "works of mercy" are to be regarded neither as unnecessary to salvation, as was the convenient tendency of Anglo-Zwinglian memorialism, nor as merit-purchasing acts of charity to others, in the old Catholic manner, but are to be understood and performed as simple duties to a part of oneself.

Lever, who was a generation younger—and more comprehensive and radi-cal—than Latimer, had challenged the Council to reform England. All he got by this, however, was a particular favor of the kind that Latimer himself might have requested and obtained. It was in response to Lever's pleas that the despoiled grammar school of the Pennine market town of Sedbergh was graciously refounded with a royal grant. His sermons are said to have helped rescue as many as a dozen such schools:[9] a fine concession, but a different matter in principle from the general nature of Lever's demand. What he had claimed was that education was a basic need of the Christian state, a training for God's people to do on earth the work of Christ, as the Body of Christ. Educational provision was a duty which all Christian people owed each other. The idea of the monarchy as personally monopolizing all sources of beneficence made no sense in such a theory. A human figurehead, a constitu-tional focus for gathering and distribution was more like what was wanted. To an extent, in the case of a Protestant boy king, one could pretend that such an arrangement could become a practicality. Wholesale theories, how-ever, were set aside for particular duties for the rest of Edward's reign, as Lever was now busily administering St. John's College, Cambridge, as its radical new master.

When the boy Edward died, Lever put his faith in the girl Lady Jane Grey and her father-in-law Northumberland. How long she would have remained a lay figure had she survived cannot be guessed. "Tokenism," in modern parlance, would have been the most likely approximation between Lever's theory and her practice, had anything permanent come of the rebellion. Jane was primly sure that good works were not necessary to salvation, but merely "meet for a Christian, in token that he follows his Master," an opinion quite as unsatisfactory from Lever's point of view as it was to the Romish inquisitor to whom she gave it.[10]

Martin Bucer, Regius Professor of Divinity at Cambridge and a personal friend of the Levers, characterized this type of upper-class Zwinglianism as a desire to confine Christ "to a certain limited place in heaven," where, presumably, his inconvenient commands need not affect relations on earth.[11] Just like the Romish doctrine of transubstantiation, this ultra-Protestant view tended to make any kind of intellectual training quite superfluous for the majority who were required merely to accept it.

Lever himself was astute enough to bypass logical puzzles about what the sacrament was, in favour of advertising what he believed it did. He offered the opportunity of agreeing to differ about doctrinal definitions as the sine qua non of initiating discussion about contemporary social and political issues, precisely the development the Tudor state could not afford to tolerate. Less radically threatening and more typical was Thomas's brother Ralph, who was merely unscrupulous and partisan, a player of intellectual games with a taste for plots. Games of mathematical and verbal reasoning were his hobby and stock-in-trade. He discussed with Bucer a new system of "witcraft" or commonsense (Cambridge-style) nomenclature for grammatical and logical terms, and he introduced new varieties of complication into the game of Pythagoras, a "battle of numbers" played on a double chess board, whose aim was to capture the King.[12] Parties of dons would gather for this entertainment, possibly in an ancient little building still known as the "House of Pythagoras," in delightful gardens across the river from St. John's College.

Edward's death on 6 July 1553 brought all these pleasures to an end.

On Sunday 16 July, Edward Sandys, vice-chancellor of Cambridge and a small Lancashire gentleman of similar background to the Levers, preached a sermon to the university in favour of Queen Jane. On the following Wednesday, however, as Thomas Lever and his brother Ralph, "booted and spurred, . . . were about to carry to the London printers the text of Sandys's sermon, the news reached Cambridge that Lady Jane and her husband had been imprisoned and Mary acclaimed as Queen."[13] Northumberland, aristocratic gang boss and chancellor of the University, was arrested in Cambridge that Thursday, and his vice-chancellor gave himself up on Friday.

That September, Thomas Lever led a party of Cambridge academics, including his brothers Ralph and John, into exile. The attempt at quasi-constitutional revolution had failed. The unhappy—if inevitable—alliance between the censorious theorist and his most natural target had served to impress on the former the difference between publishing a manifesto and being in a position to negotiate for real change.

8

Negotiation Prevented by the Needs of Power

ONE may perceive an antagonism between Lever's sacramental theory and the institution of monarchy. He was certainly one of those the "repression" of whose "moderate puritan aspirations" by Elizabeth has been described as encouraging "doctrinaire presbyterianism, and the more extreme and disruptive manifestations of puritanism generally."[1] Yet through all this he was still a Lancashire gentleman, with an inherited sense of responsibility for saving the monarchy from itself. The double nature of his relationship to the Crown is shown clearly enough by his reaction to exaggerated news that reached him in exile about the Wyatt rebellion. As a Protestant, he feared Queen Mary might still be alive, renewing her "grievous persecution of the church"; as a gentleman he dreaded that, with the London mob in control, the English monarchy might be "irrecoverably lost."[2]

A letter of 1560 to the continental Reformer Bullinger gives a clue to Lever's priorities on his return to England. "Authority" is for Lever comprised of "Queen and parliament" (in that order); yet he tilts the balance away from the Privy Council and thus, in effect, from the queen, by defining Parliament as "*summum concilium* [the supreme council]" where others might call it simply "*concilium commune* [the general council]" of the realm. On the delicate matter of the monarch's claim to act without reference to Parliament, Lever makes clear he has no intention of heeding "the injunctions issued by the Queen after parliament was over." These insisted on the wearing of vestments. Many of the clergy—"giving *obedience* as a reason [*obedientiae, ut aiunt, causa*]!"—will do what she asks. For Lever, she asks in vain. The queen's command alone does not constitute sufficient "authority" to block the veto of conscience.[3]

At the Synod of 1562, he was one of a group who lost by one vote a motion in favour of "six new articles of a Protestant cast."[4] These included as part of a package the assertion that in future the "surplice" should be accounted "sufficient" by way of vestments. Yet in 1567 we find his more extremist London admirers approving his continued godly refusal to wear the surplice. Clearly, Lever was prepared to drop his own preference for no vestments whatever in order to achieve a constitutional compromise with fellow Protestants. But ordered to don mass-gear at the queen's bidding, he refuses even the surplice: not out of abstract godliness, but as part of a strategy for advertising that further compromises needed to be made. His idealistic distributive economics is relevant here. In a world where royal chaplains flaunted in jewelled copes, many poor parsons could not afford even a surplice. Lever's upper-middle-class simplicity alluded to that point. He was not a rebel, exactly, but his chosen posture advertised his demands clearly enough. He wanted the right to belong to an establishment from which he claimed also the right of demurral.[5]

The politic refusal on the part of Elizabeth and Secretary Cecil to pursue the reforms desired by the Puritans helped to keep alive anomalies that gave Puritanism an opening. Thus, at Coventry Lever was able to have it both ways. Early in the reign, he accepted a "call" to become town preacher to this rich commercial community with its strong Lollard tradition. He wished to remain as free as possible in relation to the town.[6] This fine antiestablish-ment posture was only made workable by the tact of the establishment—crucially, no doubt, the tact of Lever's old college contemporary William Cecil—in clinging to its bad old habits. It appears that no effort was made to appoint a new vicar to Coventry's largest church till after Lever's death.[7] He was able to enjoy what has been called "an almost episcopal standing" in the town.[8] Personal prestige of this order could be permitted quite safely to such a man in such a place. Under King Edward, such men and such places had wanted a radically reformed episcopacy: more numerous, more modestly financed, distributed not according to hoary precedent but in line with the current needs of the population: local pastors rather than instru-ments of the national monarchy. Allowing Lever to minister to Coventry while a complaisant bishop—far enough off in Lichfield—looked the other way, exemplified Elizabeth's need to economise on reform.

She went a little further. Lever's reformist desire to institute some "disci-pline" for ministers and preachers was legitimised—and put under monitor-ing—through Bishop Bentham of Coventry and Lichfield, who appointed him archdeacon, an ancient office with (in practice often nominal) responsi-bilities for the education and management of the lower clergy which Lever intended to make fully real. Not tied on a day-to-day basis to any local parish ministry, yet welcome everywhere by civic arrangement and bringing everywhere as archdeacon of Coventry a reminder of the national establish-ment's right of veto on local aspirations, it seems that Lever was allowed an apparently personal power base in the redundant royal chantry of St. John, Bablake, a building of moderate but handsome proportions with a tower over the crossing. The Coventry city fathers repaired the roof in 1570. The monarchy was content to retain the endowments. In the same spirit of make and mend compromise, the old Catholic mystery plays continued throughout

Lever's time at Coventry. He was in no hurry to foreclose such a popular showcase of local talents and trades.

Such amiable arrangments, suited to the peaceable administration of regions, left too much choice to localities and individuals to be conceded on a more than temporary basis by the national authority. Places and people whose subversive tendencies put them at risk might be indulged only for a time with what looked like extraordinary privilege, but which was really only the liberty of enough rope.

Education was the inevitable source of conflict between monarchy and those Lever spoke for. During his time in Coventry, Bablake School was founded in the college buildings attached to the former royal chantry. Its first endowment came from a crate of silver ingots consigned by mistake to a Coventry servant sent to Spain to collect the steel gad-nails his master had ordered: a providential "plundering of the Egyptians," as it must have seemed to men who had seen Protestants burned at Coventry at the bidding of Philip and Mary. In keeping with Lever's theory of the effectuality of the sacramental life in promoting economic welfare, Bablake School was specially concerned in raising trade apprentices.

A more advanced literary training was required for the learned professions, including the ministry. The general inspiration of Lever's third London sermon, if not his direct prompting, lay behind a royal furor on this topic.

When Elizabeth visited Coventry in the summer of 1565, she stayed in the despoiled Whitefriars, recently reedified to receive her. Since its connection with the Black Prince, Coventry had been granted the title of *Camera Principis*. The city was not for its citizens, but was a "prince's chamber." The function of its professionals was to sweeten it for the royal presence.

When Elizabeth emerged on 17 August, expecting to receive a loyal address from the city recorder, Throgmorton, she was confronted by a tirade against the spoliation of local charitable funds. When Henry VIII destroyed the English arm of the Knights Hospitallers, the traditional defenders of the faith, he granted that rich cluster of their properties that appertained to their house in Coventry to John Hales, his official and favorite, who had certainly driven the poor from the hospital, but had never founded the grand institution of learning he had undertaken to endow. Throgmorton demanded redress, in a lengthy speech. "What fools ye be!" interjected Elizabeth audibly and famously. No doubt she was not in the mood for a local instance.[9] At that very moment, the survival of Christendom itself was imperilled by the Turkish onslaught on the Knights Hospitallers' headquarters at Malta, key to the Mediterranean. She had not sent Christendom any assistance.[10]

The Tudor Reformation was half-baked and provincial, whatever else it was. Even John Knox, who despised Lever's moderation, praised his essential insight. The spoiling of monasteries, hospitals and chantries, as Lever summarised it, was nothing more than "worldly covetousness taking and abusing [what was] pertaining unto the Church of Christ," an attack on Christ, not the Pope of Rome, a secular hypocrisy that veiled itself behind the muddled and eclectic theology it commissioned. So far, Knox and Lever were in agreement.[11] The English church was only half reformed. Like Bishop Jewel of Salisbury, whose prose style has been compared with his, and whom he befriended in exile (to Knox's disgust), Lever was "in a class of his own."[12] However, whereas Jewel in his officially sponsored *Apology of the Church of England* erected defences only against a tendency in himself and others towards Romanism, Lever's more shadowy career was spent in defending himself and those for whom he felt responsible against those pressures arising from royal intransigence that tended to encourage Protestant dissent. It was this arm of her own defence that Elizabeth now proceeded to attack.

At the start of her reign, she had had great need of her Puritan intellectuals. They were shunted through a series of preferments with almost embarrassing speed. Thus, for three years between 1559 and 1562, the honorable and moderate Grindal, a Cumberland man and no natural pluralist, was wanted in two places at once: as master of Pembroke, Cambridge, and as bishop of London. Those Bolton alumni who were trusty fellow Johnians of Secretary Cecil were shifted round the board with the cynicism of necessity. Twenty months of 1559–60 saw James Pilkington as Prayer Book Commissioner, as master of St. John's and Regius Professor of Divinity at Cambridge. He also had time to decline the see of Winchester before being renominated, this time for Durham. His brother Leonard replaced him in both Cambridge jobs. The peak year for Bolton Puritans was 1564. James Pilkington, melancholy scholar of delicate constitution, was policing Elizabeth's turbulent northern borders as prince-bishop. His brother John (formerly Grindal's deputy at Pembroke) was beside him as archdeacon of Durham; Thomas Lever, archdeacon of Coventry, was also now a canon and prebend at Durham and master of Sherburn Hospital there; his brother Ralph had attached himself to the rising Protestant family of Devereux as logic tutor;[13] and Leonard Pilkington had been replaced at John's by yet another Boltonian, Richard Longworth. The hour had found its fall guy.

The Longworth township was a narrow strip of high moor, trailing up to the northern boundary of Bolton parish. The Longworth family were its hillbilly squires.

Richard graduated from John's, but spent Mary's reign as a fellow of Queens', returning to John's as fellow under James Pilkington. Cecil may have regarded him as pliable. As master, he proved merely a broken reed, but one whose removal could be used to damage radicals of more serious growth.

Once elected, Longworth launched an antisurplice campaign, a moral purity crusade (a poor relation, or perhaps nephew, of his, Thomas Longworth, was given a watch on the brothels), and some ultra-Protestant ceremonies at communion. These involved the celebrant scurrying from stall to stall in an irreverent manner with the "holy bread," and reminded onlookers of the worst decadencies of popery, except that black gowns were worn and people made an effort never to kneel. In all this, Longworth was aided and abetted by William Fulke, a fellow with scabrous rhetorical powers and a taste for plotting honed by games of Pythagoras with Ralph Lever.

In 1565 Elizabeth commanded Cecil to put his old college in order or earn her displeasure.

A game of Pythagoras, with living pieces, now ensued. Various pressures were brought to bear on Longworth. He retreated to the high moral ground, denouncing in pamphlet and sermon the hypocrisy of an establishment that made a "rebel" of any man who might "offend in external matters, which is nothing," while lavishing stipends on absentees.

In 1567 Cecil called his bluff. He told Pilkington to deprive Lever of his canonry and prebend's stall at Durham for not conforming on vestments. These—with their stipends—were offered to Longworth, who accepted them, in absentia, retaining his mastership and reflating, with ever less credibility, what was left of his dialectic.[14]

It had been necessary to prune back these Boltonian Protestants, but only in order to conserve their growth. People like them had their uses in the country at large, even if they were a little too noticeable at Cambridge and in London.

Protestant dissenters, brought to book in 1567 by Bishop Grindal for holding a conventicle in the Plumbers' Hall in the City, recorded their admiration for Thomas Lever. Less accurately than they realized, they lauded what they deemed his absolute and godly refusal of the surplice. With very fair accuracy, they summarised beliefs whose gist no one could fail to infer from Lever's writings. "You preach Christ to be priest and prophet," they told the bishop, "but you preach him not to be king. . . . [T]he pope's canon law and the will of the prince must have first place."[15] That was the crux. No more than Herod could the Governor of the Church of England permit Christ to be preached as king. And Lever was publishing in London again—an edition of Bradford's *Meditations*, completed and prefaced by himself.

In 1569 Longworth was expelled from St. John's. But in the same year, the Catholic gentry of northeast England staged an armed uprising in favor of Mary, Queen of Scots. Walter Devereux was among the Protestant warriors Elizabeth turned to in this emergency.

Pilkington—under medical attention in London—was ordered north to preside over the mopping-up operations. Meanwhile, Mary herself was hurried south to a city with a long tradition of hostility to the Catholic monarchy: Coventry, safely stewing in Puritan resentment with Lever's ambiguous aid.

Mary was of course already queen of England in the pope's eyes, and Elizabeth's heir in any case. As long as it looked as though Mary might succeed, she was to that extent Elizabeth's safeguard against invasion by a Catholic power—in particular, Spain, which had no wish to see a French queen dowager made queen of England. It was about as important to comfort Mary's enemies, at home and abroad, as it was to placate her friends, but no more. The days of open flirtation with Puritanism were long gone. To come to details, a Puritan like Longworth could not expect a bishopric, but in 1572 he settled for the Chester deanery. Coventry, meanwhile, did not get the grand college for which its hospital had been pillaged. In 1572 Elizabeth merely released some of its land towards a grammar school, to be named "of Henry VIII," after the pillager. Tentative and piecemeal was the order of the day. Reformist intellectuals like Lever and Grindal were never to be allowed to restructure the national establishment, but they had some local victories. In 1574, for instance, the finances of Sherburn Hospital (where Lever was still master) were restructured on lines fairer to its tenants:[16] a small gesture towards meeting the discontent on Elizabeth's northern borders. Grindal acted in this as archbishop of York. He was nominated for Canterbury the following year.

The pattern that had looked farcical in the case of Longworth was now replayed as tragedy. If not by design, yet almost inevitably, the incompatibility between what Grindal believed in and what Elizabeth needed meant that, under prevailing conditions, he had to be prevented: since negotiation was not an option. Was he promoted in order to be prevented? He was not deprived: but he was put under house arrest in very short order by the Privy Council, in June 1577. The whole world now knew that Elizabeth had turned against the kind of moderate Protestant reformism he represented.

9

The Republic of Christ

THE spirit of compromise in which Grindal, Pilkington, and the other Prayer Book Commissioners of 1558-9 had operated was now to be reversed. True, the doctrines of the Church of England were as muddled as ever: nevertheless, conformity to whatever they were was to be demanded. This sorry tale has often been told, and there is no need to repeat here the story of Elizabeth's attempt to strengthen the force of the royal prerogative by setting up the High Commission, in 1583, a body which gave what has been called a "spiritual tyranny" to the archbishops;[1] or to recall that—for better or worse—the workings of the Ecclesiastical Commission, supposed to reduce the realm to conformity, ran into insuperable difficulties through its own inner contradictions. The archbishops were simply not consistent either with themselves, with each other, or with the monarch whose instruments they were.

Having expended moderates like Grindal and Pilkington—men of character who had some knowledge of the world—the regime reached for brittler and more pedantic instruments, tools that broke in the hand even as they were used. A replacement archbishop of Canterbury—Whitgift—with the aid of yet another Lancashire Master of St. John's —Whitaker—compiled a set of Lambeth Articles of 1595 so ultra-Calvinist in tone that the queen and her secretary quite agreed they must never be published, as any attempt to enforce them would render the realm ungovernable.[2] What suited Elizabeth in Whitgift was not his theology but his manner, which was courtly towards her and schoolmasterish towards her subjects. And he was very rich.

Most of the theologians appeared to think that what was at issue was the question of which beliefs were the right ones; and therefore what ceremonies, and pattern of living, were the correct ones to be prescribed to the nation. This self-referential mode of thinking suited the regime's pattern of behavior: coercive and rigid modes of control were justified by the phantom of doctrinal authority: the Lambeth ghost that failed to walk in 1595.

It is to Lever's very considerable credit that he did not think in this way at all. It followed that the hierarchical determinism into which the Tudor regime tended to degenerate had no use for his preferred modes of procedure. The papacy was in the same boat.

Thomas Lever's *Treatise of the Right Way,* first issued during his exile in 1556, appeared in a London edition in 1571 with a new preface, and was again reprinted in 1575. In its Elizabethan context, it contrasts quite as sharply with the officially sponsored catechism by Nowell of 1570 as with the recusant catechism of Laurence Vaux, which began to appear from 1567. Obviously, Lever has no time for the mass, though he is also very little at home with Nowell's Anglo-Zwinglian tendency to debase the consecrated elements to "tokens" and to confine their effectiveness to the individual and the next world. Far more important than any particulars is the fact that the *Treatise* on the one hand invites its readers to enter into their own spiritual sovereignty, whereas the catechisms, on the other, demand submission to the sovereignty of others.

Vaux, the Boltonian sub-prior of Louvain, represents the English recusant aspiration for the past. What Lancashire people—Protestants included—called with tender nostalgia "the old religion" is what Vaux wants break-aways to return to, not forward to the Counter-Reformation, but backwards to a childhood in which bells were hallowed and "every one of the Apostles made an article of the creed." In all its editions—up to 1605—his catechism retains the pre-Tridentine form of the Hail Mary. His is a code "necessary for children and the ignorant people," pleading with its readers to turn back through the gate into paradise and the mental submission of the wise child. When Vaux himself was a little child at Blackrod, fanatics came at dead of night and smashed to pieces gilded statuary and screens in Deane Church, five miles to the southeast, which was at that time served by Whalley monks. In middle age he writes, "God gave every man grace, not to be wise more than he ought, but to be humble and rather to seek what an unknown ceremony meaneth, than to laugh when he knoweth not."[3] His is the trau-matised heart of Catholic England, subject to a feeling not foreign even to the Nowells' clever protégé, Edmund Spenser.

If Vaux's form of submission involves a return to ignorant bliss, what Nowell demands is the sort of brainy servitude well-disciplined schoolboys grow up to resent. He was educated at Middleton, the main stronghold of the Ashton clan, and became master of Westminster under Henry and Edward and dean of St. Paul's under Elizabeth. His own family home was hard by Whalley Abbey, whose flamboyant last abbot, Paslew, fed the cold loath-ing of the ambitious local gentry for all things monastic with his displays of wealth and power.[4] When his abbey fell, it was the Levers' neighbours, the Ashtons of Great Lever, who got their hands on the land. Nowell's catechism (which he wrote in Latin) is a lengthy dialogue between "Master" and "Scholar." The scholar's first answer is enough:

I for my part, right worshipful Master, shall willingly answer your demands, so far as I have been able with wit to conceive or keep in memory, and can at this present call to mind and remember, what I have heard you teach me out of the holy scriptures.[5]

Lever's *Treatise* had no designs on the mind of any child. Some of those who read it in the shadow of death under Mary may well have turned to it again as Elizabeth's reign settled into repression. It revealed Lever's inimitable blend of subjective piety and intellectually alert refusal to be trapped by definitions. It was not the product of a woolly mind, but of a mind which could probably outfox Ralph Lever, D.D., at logical games, but infinitely preferred to keep open a dialogue with the "English man and woman, who or where so ever thou art" who chose to engage with it. A beautiful feature of Henry Bynneman's edition of 1575 is that in the main body of the work, the eye is drawn from the density of the black letter in which Lever's own comments are printed into the serene clarity of the Renaissance script in which the English versions of the ancient prayers and creeds of the Church are set out. This arrangement seems to fix Lever himself in time, while releasing his subject matter into a more civilised future.

An absolutely key moment comes when Lever introduces the text of the Apostles' Creed. His tone is one of the most fastidious liberalism. One is convinced he means what he says:

> I do not meane that they be taught, only to say, I beleeve as the Church doth . . . but that . . . as every one of them . . . may say with the holie Catholike Church: "I beleeve in God, the father almightie, maker of heaven and earth."[6]

Coercive and fixed in essence, the mutually exclusive sovereignties of Crown and papacy prescribed for children an education in conformity of belief. Lever—still retaining the spirit of the New Learning—desires for men and women education for the possibility of individual belief. His syntax here dismisses the idea of conformity as a virtue and suggests that each decision to say the creed proclaims the distinctiveness of the individual. It is a momentary, if frequently renewed, act of voluntary alignment—not an assertion or an abdication, but the joining in a prayer: "I believe; help thou mine unbelief."[7] For Lever, the quality of belief has reference to its object: an infinitely mysterious godhead requires one kind of attention; a set of verbal propositions quite another.

The refusal to pay lip service to either transubstantiation or memorialism (his inquistors sought to rescue him by pretending the ideas were interchangeable), and the claim to believe the Catholic creeds for oneself, and not because the pope says to do so, were the beginning and end of Marsh's heresy. More flippantly, Ralph Lever's *Witcraft*—most likely penned with one eye on the precocious Robert Devereux—would be a child-centered learning experience for clever boys, an introduction from within to grammar and logic, a rejection of the rote learning encouraged by Ralph's dim rival at John's, the old-fashioned dialectical logician Peter Carter. Pilkington's favored method of initiating the rebuttal of a rash arguer, who might seek to wrench a text to serve narrow ends, would take such form as this: "Cyprian's words are not altogether so plain as he sets them."[8]

Marsh, James Pilkington, and Thomas Lever clearly know not merely that there are limits to their own intelligence but that, in developing, the human mind experiences limit, in particular the limitations of language. This is rare enough to suggest a common origin, perhaps in a common teacher at Bolton Grammar School. While John Lever and Leonard Pilkington are merely of ordinary distinction—a headmaster, and a Regius professor—Ralph Lever, too, knows the human mind has limits, but he recoils from them to romp infinitely within himself. In this he typifies the secular Renaissance spirit familiar from Elizabethan poetry. The spirit is joined in origin, perhaps, to the Reformation spirit that is so clear in Marsh, yet is forced by circumstance to sever itself from it. While Elizabeth could tolerate games in a box in the Ralph Lever manner, she was compelled to deny for a little longer what Marsh exemplified: the impossibility of living in a box constructed to fit others.

It is one sign of the times—and given the school's early distinction rather a sad one—that in 1572, at the urging of the trustees, the pedantic and reactionary Peter Carter—driven from John's by the antics of Longworth—accepted the headmastership of the Bolton Grammar School.[9] Another sign—this time of the futility of Elizabeth's own reaction—is the fact that no sooner had Richard Longworth been sent packing from St. John's than another of the same species—Adam Longworth—sprang up nearby as a fellow of Corpus Christi, a protégé—inevitably—of one of the intransigent academic supporters of Thomas Cartwright,[10] the main mover of Presbyterian dissent in England and, moreover, at one time a Johnian, though not one who owed any preferment to Thomas Lever.

During the 1570s, Lever must often have been reminded of his days of exile. At Frankfurt he had been able to achieve a compromise with Knox and was also able to work with Jewel, who had signed Romanist articles in England. But Jewel and Knox were unhappy with each other, and any chance of concord was ruined by the arrival of establishment-minded bullies of an Anglo-Lutheran variety, as self-righteous as Knox and with fewer scruples. Knox was ousted; Lever withdrew to find his own peace elsewhere.[11] This pattern now entered its final phase.

The story of the uneven battle between Elizabeth's new hard-line bishops of the 1570s and those young men—notably Cartwright—who wanted a Knoxian system in England has often been told. It suffices here to say that Lever was on neither side.

With his liking for discussion and for constitutional forms, it was natural that, in the spring of 1572, Lever should join in talks with other Puritans about the possibility of presenting an admonition to Parliament. He had been one of those who had urged Cartwright to return from Switzerland the previous January. As it turned out, in the absence of their natural leader, two of Cartwright's hotter disciples rushed out their own findings from the talks in two somewhat conflicting statements under the same cover.[12] They were put in prison, where, of course, Lever visited them, as he would have visited Cecil or Elizabeth, in appropriate circumstances. "I scorn to fear or falter"[13] was not his family motto for nothing.

Pilkington's family motto—"Now thus, Now thus"—reflected their capacity for adaptation.[14] The good bishop had spent a lifetime protecting the slightly younger Lever from himself. He now seems to have experienced a sense of personal betrayal. Without mentioning Lever's name, he made a direct connection between the old antisurplice movement and this new attack on "our whole ecclesiastical polity," muttering darkly about "dissimulation." Grindal, however, perhaps from better knowledge, spoke of the new developments as the work of "young men," and held that many of the old antivestiarians were opposed to the formation of a dissenting "party."[15]

Without freedom of discussion, there was of course no chance of resolving any of these issues. Once her brief honeymoon with the Marian exiles and their intellectual sympathisers was over, Elizabeth was driven to force the lid down on the whole boiling with a ban against the preaching of the gospel as Grindal, Lever, and other Puritans of their type and generation understood it, that is, as information that was relevant to the governing of a Christian society and that therefore required airing. For Elizabeth, during the 1570s it became a matter of urgency to prevent Christ being preached as king, since there were clearly many Christs, and only one Queen Elizabeth.

At its most conservative, the argument for the "prophesyings"—or Puritan preaching conferences—has been summarized thus: "There would be no security without subjection to the gospel, and no understanding of the gospel without preaching."[16] What Elizabeth feared—and Lever most likely welcomed—was that even in the most carefully regulated circumstances, differing views of biblical and other texts, and of their contemporary relevance, were bound to emerge. For Lever, conscious and intelligent wrestling with the Word of God was a necessary part of the work of cooperation with the living Christ, effective in the real world. Elizabeth herself refused to see any difference between the most conservative arrangements, whereby only the clergy were present, and the wildest scenes of schismatic ranting, in which disaffected laity were not only present, but held the floor. Lever's exercises naturally fell between the two: he fostered preachers of high quality and drew respectable lay auditories.

Unfortunately for the "prophesyings" in general, and for Lever in particular, the queen got wind of the most notorious "prophesyings" in the realm, those that took place at Southam, a vigorous little market town just 15 miles from Coventry. People traveled far and wide to such affairs, and Southam's anarchic extremism was in a measure a rival to, and possibly exacerbated by, the more diginified arrangements in the local metropolis. Thus best and worst coexisted in their usual polarity.

Warwickshire was the patronage area of the queen's favorite and ticket-of-leave man, the earl of Leicester and his brother Ambrose, earl of Warwick, sons of the traitor Northumberland. She may well have been "informed" about Southam as part of a court plot against Leicester. She was only too ready to conflate Lever and other questionable intellectuals with the likes of Oxenbridge, Southam's wild rector.[17] The confusion was prophetic: places like Coventry, as well as places like Southam, would be on Parliament's side in the Civl War.

From 1576 the queen issued peremptory orders to put down the prophesy-ings. Her commands were delayed, but not deflected, by the resistance of Grindal. "Remember, Madam," he advised her, "that you are a mortal crea-ture. . . . Bear with me, I beseech you, Madam, if I choose rather to offend your earthly majesty than to offend against the heavenly majesty of God."[18]

For Lever, the final blow came late in June 1577. Bishop Bentham of Coventry and Lichfield was sympathetic—his successor Overton would con-tinue to believe that Lever's type of approach tended to "win . . . to conform-ity"[19]—but bishops were Elizabeth's creatures de facto, and when she communicated a personal veto to them, that must be that. As James I would put it, "No bishops, no king." Without bishops, how was a monarch to control the mind of the people? So much the worse for bishops, thought the young men of the Cartwright school.

The queen, wrote Bentham to Lever on 18 June 1577, had "been informed of some matters handled and abused in the exercise at Coventry." Apologeti-cally, his lordship suggested the prophesyings be abandoned until "we may . . . obtain the full use thereof with her good pleasure and full authority."[20] In Ralph Lever's game of Pythagoras, several small pieces together can take an equivalent large piece, always provided that "the King can not be taken with equality." Thomas Lever died suddenly at Ware as he was leaving London for the north, shortly after receiving his sovereign's veto on his life work. *Virtutum in omni mansuetudine inseminator,* Bale had called him: "A planter of virtues in all gentleness."[21]

He had believed in a Christ both vulnerable and dynamic. Whereas a Roman priest offered Christ to the Father for the intentions of a particular mass; and whereas for an Anglo-Zwinglian like Sandys the Eucharist was a memorial, confined to the elect, of the death of a celestial absentee whose "body is there, therefore not here," for Lever the Lord's Supper "offereth in spirit and truth to be seen and received by faith, the body and blood of Christ glorified in heaven." Christ offers himself to his people, and through them to the world, so that there is no longer any division between heaven and earth, no separation (such as Nowell insisted on) between Christ and the consecrated bread and wine, and no discussion necessary as to which places may qualify as spiritual, since all places imaginable or unimaginable, are potentially so.[22] The discussion that is required is of how, in practice, they may become so. It is this reliance on the material effectiveness of Christianity in the world that gives Lever's Christ his vulnerability. Here it was that Elizabeth struck, piercing some of her own most loyal allies.

In his new preface to the Elizabethan editions of his *Treatise,* Lever had not advised subjecting the individual conscience to royal authority. Instead, he had urged a grown-up citizenry to share the responsibility of a Christian monarchy come of age: let there be no more "suspecting, envying, misliking, and misreporting of others, especially of such as be in authority." For him, all, including the monarch, were members of the same body. The preacher's task consisted of "advertising and desiring . . . so to search the heavenly scriptures, and their own consciences, that they may see and take occasion to pity and pray for themselves, for all men, and especially for the Queen's most excellent Majesty."

Pity for Elizabeth? He must have felt that, at least, as he opened her desperately opportunistic veto on her friends.

For Henry Bradshaw, the sovereignty of the earthly monarch depended on that of Christ himself, bodily present as the consecrated elements which the Roman Church alone could guarantee. For Lever, Bradshaw's central notion of a "place" made "spiritual" through the bodily presence of a Holy One must be abandoned for a dynamic of moral energy effective within and beyond, yet also vulnerable within, the whole universe. The saints are with us, "albeit not their persons in bodily presence, yet their examples of living." Where another theologian might claim to "believe" such and such an inert doctrine about the presence or otherwise of Christ, in or out of any heaven or any church, Lever is more evasive in expression and more dynamic in implication:

> I know and think assuredly, that I and all Christians, be one Church, one congregation, in such unity of lively Faith which worketh by charity, as doth ever keep us together as members of one body in Christ . . . made one mystical body in Christ of many men in all places.

His *Sermons* of 1550—reprinted in 1572—offered Protestants the opportunity of agreeing to differ about doctrinal definitions in order to initiate an awareness of the needs on earth and in England of the Body of Christ. His *Treatise,* from which the above is quoted, releases a pioneering dynamic which draws directly on the evangelical example of Christ's people going "into all the world, . . . the Lord working with them."[23]

Such a vision did not exclude the possibility of a liberalized constitutional monarchy, but it turned out to be something the Tudor system was not calculated to survive. Even so, the queen's edict against her moderate Puritans left a propaganda vacuum that she has occupied ever since, as well as dividing her subjects against each other to her own short-term advantage. For the record, it was not under Lever's persuasion, but after good Queen Bess had destroyed him that the Coventry city fathers started their notorious campaign against maypoles, plays, processions, and other remnants of Merrie England.[24]

Lever's spirit was driven from England as surely as he had been driven from Frankfurt by his squabbling fellow countrymen and from Wesel by the Lutheran establishment. "Then it was," early in 1556, "that Lever, shepherding his flock to a new asylum, . . . became the prototype of those New England ministers . . . of the future who were the organisers of a new type of colonisation upon Lever's model." The canton of Berne offered shelter. Discouraged, however, at Basle, Lever and his companions finally settled at Aarau, around the disused church of St. Ursula, the English virgin martyr to the Teutons. Miles Coverdale, the Bible translator, whose version of the psalms in particular has been a major influence on all subsequent literature in the language, came to preach there. John Lever, too, was with his brother. Ralph had gone off by himself. There were a number of English weavers, and the little colony was self-supporting. One may imagine some elements of democracy as well as some elements of the provincial gentleman's perennial dream of a locality free from government control.[25]

Here, amid breathtaking scenery,[26] Lever was able to enjoy a purified Little Lever in exile: a distributive sacramental life and an experiment in distributive sovereignty, with himself in the gratifying role of constitutional governor.

Acknowledging the receipt of some sermons from Bullinger, he can repress neither his sincerity nor its cleansing element of irony. "While others are wont to dedicate their writings to princes," he writes, "you alone have made choice of us poor exiles to whom to address your midnight studies." If the colony is a distributive prince, it is also a consecrated body: a tiny, voluntary republic whose constitution is "glorious if we regard him to whom we have consecrated ourselves, namely Christ."[27]

Frontispiece of Christopher Lever's *Defendors Of The Catholique Faith* (1627) woos dedicatee Charles I. *By permission of The British Library.* 859.h.7.

Breeches: Adam and Eve. Post-Conquest fragment from old St. Peter's. *Bolton Museums.*

Gowns: Early Tudor Angels. Bench-end detail, old St Peter's. *Bolton Museums.*

Bolton c. 1750. Old print. The "chapel," to the left of church, is Robert Lever's school of 1656. *Bolton Libraries.*

Deane Church, c. 1834. Old drawing. A fence rims sheer Deane Clough. J. Boardman, *Records and Traditions of Deane* (1904). Author's copy.

Spiritual and secular power—St. Werburgh and an idealized King—are set back-to-back on her Abbey's seal. *By permission of* The British Library. Circ. 47.b.

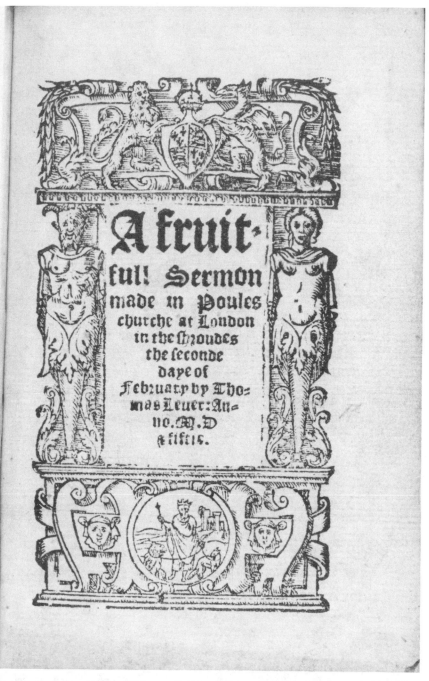

A fruit-
full Sermon
made in Poules
churche at London
in the shroudes
the seconde
daye of
February by Tho-
mas Leuer: An-
no.M.D
& fiftie.

Frontispiece to a 1550 edition of Thomas Lever's *Fruitfull Sermon* combines pastoral nymph and satyr, royal arms, and a king taming beastly disorders with the cross. *By permission of The British Library.* c.122.c.16.

The cruell burning of George Marſh, Martyr.

Wherein this in him is to be noted, then when as he had bin a long time tormented in the fire without mouing, hauing his fleſh ſo broiled and puſte vp, that they which ſtode before him vnneth could ſée the chaine wherewith hee was faſtened, and therefore ſuppoſed no leſſe but he had binne dead, notwithſtanding ſodainly hee ſpreade abroad his armes, ſaying: father of heauen haue mercy vpon me, and ſo yéelded his ſpirit into the hands of the Lord.

Chiasmic patterning and pierced side link Marsh to Christ. J. Foxe, *Actes and Monuments* (1610). *By permission of The British Library.* Fol.478.i.3.

Rivington School seal of 1585. The Master (an image of Pilkington?) holds birches and *Galatians* 3.1: "O Folyshe Galatians," infidel despite Christ "crucified among" them. M. D. Smith, *Rivington*, by permission.

Jacobean Darcy Lever Hall: yeoman-capitalist house in traditional half-timbering. *Bolton Museums.*

Jacobean Bradshaw Hall. Stone-built gentry house in new, many-windowed style. *Bolton Museums.*

PART THREE
Marian Martyr

They advised me . . . to . . . fly the country as I had intended. . . .
my weak flesh would gladly have consented, but my spirit did not
fully agree.
　　　　　—George Marsh, "His Own Examination" (1555)

10

George Marsh: Following Ghostly Tuition

ELIZABETH'S ban on preaching in 1576–77 came as a reminder that the Tudor monarchy could have no competent policy on the reception of ideas. At the beginning of her reign, she had felt compelled to pretend that all the moral education her realm required was the regular public reading of "the ten commandments in the vulgar tongue, without exposition."[1] Her sister had shown a similar blend of political disingenuousness and human bewilderment. In August 1553, at the beginning of her reign, Mary had briskly offered to resolve an epoch of religious upheaval by "leaving those new found devilish terms of papist or heretic, and such like."[2]

In the case of both monarchs, early personal intentions were complicated and confused by the deliberations of Parliament. Mary, for instance, had no more success than Thomas Lever in persuading the beneficiaries of the sack of the monasteries to part with their plunder, though most of them rediscovered their papal allegiance. As had been usual, her first Parliament was inaugurated with "the solemn mass of the Holy Ghost." The two Protestant bishops who attended—Harley of Hereford and Taylor of Lincoln (he had ordained Marsh)—walked out, "not abiding the sight."[3]

Death—rather than mere detention—for indiscreet and unrepentant Protestants became likely with Mary's marriage to Philip in July 1554. It became certain after Cardinal Pole's "absolution to the whole Parliament of England" that November and was ordained by the Act of 26 January, 1555, which revived fourteenth- and fifteenth-century statutes against "heretics," on whom there was now open season.

Till about the end of 1553, Marsh may have functioned in semisecrecy as pastor and schoolmaster to the Protestants of the Langton district of Leicestershire, continuing unofficially the role he had performed in Edward's reign, nominally as curate to Lawrence Saunders, who had also held the living of All Hallows, Bread Street, in the City of London. Both were close to John Bradford, and it seems that, in effect, by serving the two parishes between them, they formed a cell in that network of provincial Protestant growth points having links with London congregations that the preaching tours of Bradford had been designed to draw together. All three were Cambridge men and products of the educational initiatives of the house of Lancaster. Saunders—courtesy of Henry VI—was educated at Eton and King's College. Bradford's essentially mathematical intelligence was trained at Manchester Grammar School, while Marsh was a product of Bolton Grammar School and of Christ's College. These last three institutions, in their different ways, were all indebted to the revival of learning fostered by Lady Margaret Beaufort.

But while Saunders thought in grooves, like an intransigent young partisan, and Bradford strove to hammer English Protestantism into a self-contained system, Marsh showed the obstinate depth and restraint of the mature student he was. Not till 1551, when he was already in his thirties, did he matriculate at Cambridge. A widower, he had left his children in Lancashire in the care of their grandmothers.

Saunders was burnt at Coventry in February 1555, having been taken there from London. Marsh suffered two months later at Chester, after incarceration and baiting at Smithills, Lathom, and Lancaster. Not only their martyrdoms, but the economic nexus they exemplified—Marsh as a Lancashire farmer and woolstapler, Saunders as a member of a London mercantile family—provided an irreversible challenge to the mind-controls of the Tudor state. Saunders probably had roots in Coventry Lollardy. His example was followed by two local martyrs that September: Robert Glover, a Coventry merchant from nearby Mancetter, and Cornelius Bungey, of the Coventry Cappers' Guild, whose pageant of the "Harrowing of Hell" had been performed with the usual panache the previous Corpus Christi.

While the personalities of Marsh and Saunders were complementary, the strategy of their martyrdoms—their modes of following the leading of the Spirit—were discrepant. Marsh, for instance, seems to have been much more discreet in avoiding anything that could have been interpreted as public preaching. He certainly addressed secret congregations in his home vicinity, however, and thus helped to initiate the house service that has been described as the normal form of worship among Bolton Puritans for the next century or so.[4]

Just to the north of Church Langton can still be traced the straight line of the Roman Via Devana, or "Chester Way." One may imagine Marsh, perhaps at around Christmas 1553, traveling the three miles or so of country lane that would bring him to this ancient road. His vicar Saunders was in prison in London. Should he turn right, southeastwards, towards Huntingdon and Cambridge, perhaps to flee from some East Anglian sea port, perhaps to pass boldly south to London? Or should he turn northwestwards, towards Leicester, Derby, Manchester, and his home region?

It has been said of Mary's repressive measures that they "tested not only the sincerity and courage but also the political strength and tactical wisdom of the opposition group."[5] Whatever his actual route, Marsh's tactical decision was to turn north westwards towards home, Chester, and death. He would continue in secret Bradford's preaching mission to Lancashire and Cheshire, while at the same time putting a clear distance between his own modest but unshakeable revisions of the Catholic faith and the full-blown Protestant sectarianisms of Bradford or Saunders. In effect, he had decided neither to flee the country along with Lever and Pilkington, nor to become one of the three hundred Marian martyrs of the southern province of the English Church. He would be the martyr to the north.

It is useful to distinguish Marsh from the four men nearest to him.

His most interesting quality is an almost Socratic sense of the "spirit," a quiet, internal voice that prevents him saying or doing things about whose rightness he is uncertain. This prompts him in turn to give an account of his faith in scrupulously moderate terms. His following of what Henry Bradshaw called "ghostly tuition" shows a mature and pastoral discrimination: mature, in its avoidance of any attempt to construct a rival theology, or to designate the parameters of a rival communion (characteristics, respectively, of Brad-ford and Saunders), and pastoral in its wariness of offending simplicity. His advice about children is a sample of the whole tenor of his communication: "Love" them, he says, "but [be]rate them not, lest they be of a desperate mind." For Marsh, as for his great inspiration, Philip Melanchthon, truth is a gradual assimilation that sophistry and tyranny are alike powerless to evade or capture. One might die for it, but never in it.

His most obvious claim to be remembered, however, is that while like Lever and Pilkington he decided to oppose the theology of the Marian regime, his "spirit" did not quite permit him to do so from the security of exile. To leave the country without permission was to break the law. This scruple, which had availed also for Socrates, came to Marsh's aid. There was no need to seek any other field of battle than the one that offered. He could stay and not fear the outcome. "In this our spiritual warfare," he reflected, "is no man overcome, unless he traitrously leave and forsake his Captain."[6]

11
Earl and Yeoman

W<small>HEN</small> we enquire what kind of martyr Marsh was, we are compelled to notice the influence on him of the humanistic New Learning. But this does not explain why he was a martyr at all—indeed, it may be said to suggest tendencies in the opposite direction. Humanist training had been fostered by the Lady Margaret Beaufort, mother of Henry VII and first countess of Derby, as a means of providing cultivated and loyal administrators for the Tudor regime. She began, modestly enough, with an experimental school on the Stanley estates in Lancashire, and then, once her husband had won the crown for his stepson at Bosworth, came the endowment of colleges and schools by her and on her behalf by her Lancashire protégés and other northerners. Their intention was to enlighten and deploy a barbaric region in which Lollard discontents simmered side by side with the most old-fashioned Catholicism, not to mention superstitions that antedated Christianity by many centuries.

Without her intervention, there would have been no Bolton Grammar School and no Christ's College, Cambridge, to supply Marsh—the son of a modest farmer—with the enlightenment that enabled him (among other things) to function as a Latin master in Leicestershire.[1]

But of course, he was on the edge of this cultivated world—touched and transformed by it though he was. He was not a gentleman and a scholar, like Pilkington, a close associate of Sir John Cheke, the first Regius Professor of Greek; nor did he—as Lever did—correspond intimately and at length with that other great Cambridge Hellenist, Roger Ascham.[2] Scholarship has always had its enemies. "What does not the itch of seeking out Truth compel men to do?" Mary's chancellor and inquisitor, Bishop Gardiner asked, suspiciously.[3] Yet it is not at all certain Lady Margaret was not right: there is little to suggest any corollary between a high degree of literary sophistication and the final intransigence of martyrdom.

Pilkington, Ascham, and Cheke were academic experts when it came to the text of the *Phaedo*—Plato's account of the martyrdom of Socrates and a favorite teaching text of the Renaissance—but Pilkington returned from exile to become prince-bishop of Durham, and Ascham survived discreetly in England, to glean emoluments from Queen Elizabeth, his Greek pupil. Cheke did not follow the Socratic method of almost choosing martyrdom, but had to be kidnapped in Brussels and dragged on a sedition charge to London, where he died in prison, in 1557, aged 43. It was a brutal loss to scholarship, but hardly a gain for the Reformation.[4]

It is when we ask why Mary's officials went to such lengths to punish Cheke that we come nearer to realising Marsh's usefulness as a scapegoat for better-connected men.

Though he acted in a Socratic manner, it is very unlikely Marsh could read the *Phaedo* in Greek—though it is quite probable that he knew the story of Socrates. His presence on the edge of Cambridge humanism helps to define the quality of his martyrdom. But it is his presence on the edge of the parish of Deane that has more to do with the determination of the authorities to kill him.

Mary's government feared and hated Cheke because they suspected him of masterminding what has been called the "ministry of information" of the Protestant exiles. This was at Emden, in Germany, and it was the center of a ceaseless propaganda campaign against Mary's regime. It was funded by Thomas and George Heaton, merchant bankers and representatives of the leading family of Marsh's home parish of Deane. George Heaton, a correspondent and secret supporter of John Bradford,[5] may have spent at least part of Mary's reign in London, the center of heresy and persecution. He should have been easy to arrest. His father-in-law, however, happened to be the egregious Martin Bowes, former Lord Mayor and persecutor of Anne Askew and now the equally respectable M.P. for the City of London. George Heaton's kinswoman Elenor Heaton was mother to Thomas Lever.

Marsh's old family home was most probably at Marsh Fold. Marsh Fold Lane survives. Local tradition connects him also with a farm called Broadgate, west of Deane Church. Since his family seems to have been moderately prosperous, Broadgate was perhaps George's own separate home as a young family man. The farmhouse at Broadgate survived into the Victorian age: a rough stone building with a thatched roof. Marsh Fold may have been similar. The account books of nearby Smithills Hall give one idea of the family's status under Elizabeth. One Humphrey Marsh, we read, was paid an undisclosed sum in 1587 "for putting in the shoulder of a cow that was out of joint." A slightly different, though not incompatible, idea is suggested by the fact that from 1590 the Marsh family contributed money to the founding of a small parish school at Deane.[6] Its lineal descendant is still in existence, as a Church of England junior school, just as the lineal descendant of Pilkington's grammar school, founded in 1566 with the flourish of a royal charter, survives as a state secondary school.

A "fold" was a farm where sheep or cattle were "folded," or penned for feeding, in the old days of moorland farming when beasts survived the barren months of winter only through the most strenuous and careful management. It is possible that "Marsh" is more properly "March" or "Marche." "March Fold" would mean "the fold on the boundary, or on disputed land on a boundary line." Certainly, Marsh Fold was right on the boundary between the parishes of Bolton and Deane. But like everywhere else, it had to be somewhere, and in Deane it was.

The pattern provides a rough analogy of Marsh's martyrdom. It has been said of England in general and of remote areas like Lancashire in particular that the "Reformation . . . collided . . . with a revitalised spirit of medieval Catholicism."[7] Marsh shows the influence of both, yet he stands on one side of the divide. In defending himself against his persecutors, he shows himself to be a cautious example of a Cambridge student who has studied Protestant apologetics. In comforting his friends, his prose reflects the inwardness and melody and depth of pietism of a provincial farmer touched by the *Imitation of Christ*. Nevertheless, that finer courage of refusing retreat into antithetical enclosure that distinguishes him from Bradford and Saunders is also the more ordinary courage of opposition that distinguishes him from Lever and Pilkington. At Lathom House before Lord Derby, at the county headquarters in Lancaster Castle, and at the heart of the region's ecclesiastical center—the Lady Chapel which had once housed the body of St. Werburgh—all Marsh had to do was to press on where he was while the world, as it must have seemed to him, was spun backwards into the dark night of the past.

Marsh continued preaching in secret in his local region till March 1554. Evasion became increasingly difficult, both for Derby and his local deputy Barton of Smithills, no less than for Marsh himself. Barton's delay is quite understandable. Elderly and lame, he had barely completed the reedification, on Protestant lines, of his family chapel. Of Saxon origin, this had been only too recently adorned with the arms of Edward VI and Archbishop Cranmer, in jewel-like stained glass. With Edward's death, such loyalty became suspect.

It was now the end of winter—the "chiefest time of feeding," (and also of ploughing), for the year to come. Every hand was needed. As so often before and since, the grand people resigned invidious initiatives to others. Winstone, Barton's servant, took the decision to put relatives of Marsh under a charge to deliver him to Smithills. To flee now would ensure their immediate arrest; with the loss of their beasts and of the year's crop. He went before them to Smithills Hall.

Parish legend—which Nathaniel Hawthorne would refashion more than once[8]—tells how the steadfastness he showed alone in that moment at Smithills seared itself into the sandstone pavement where he stood. A red depression in its surface shaped like a deep footprint (actually of ancient geological origin) has ever since been associated with him.

Marsh's relatives were now charged to deliver him to the earl at Lathom

House, some fifteen miles west of Bolton. The confrontation between them there can be seen as a stage in the history of that negotiated loyalty in terms of which—from medieval times to the first World War—south Lancashire conducted its affairs. Historians have pointed out that while the region, because part of the royal demesne, never actually experienced "feudalism" in its strict historical sense,[9] it retained much later than might have been expected a sort of sentimental "feudalism," or habit of looking for leadership to its local aristocrats. Chief of these were the earls of Derby.

Their title—reinvented by Henry VII for his Stanley stepfather—was an example of the Tudor regime's redeployment of antique loyalties for modern ends: a political gothic revival that anticipated that of the nineteenth century. It had been in 1351 that Henry, earl of Derby, became also first duke of Lancaster. John O'Gaunt married this man's daughter and inherited both titles. Henry VII, Gaunt's descendant, was in a position to dispose of them once Stanley had secured the crown for him at Bosworth in 1485. Retaining the major title for himself, Henry made Stanley "Earl of Derby," thus confirming him and his heirs as second to the crown in the "Duchy of Lancaster." The Stanley lieutenancy was at various times also extended to Cheshire, a plausible arrangement insofar as the Earldom of Chester, like the Dukedom of Lancaster, was joined to the crown. Claiming also by inheritance the title of Prince of Wales, Henry Tudor, as a native Welshman of formidable intellect, brought a new mystique and a new wizardry to the red dragon of Wales.

Such blurred and dazzling heraldic arrangements remained a focus of loyalty, but were never its source. It was not real feudalism, but a collusion between ruler and ruled that depended on cooperation for its maintenance.

At Bosworth, Lord Stanley had relied on four culturally constructed characteristics, working together: Henry Tudor's physical certainty of his own sovereignty; the near suicidal opportunism of an expendable aristocrat (that of Stanley's own younger brother Sir William, chamberlain of north Wales); the efficient animal ferocity of the "low-born Welshmen" who were Richard's most likely killers; and, cohering and lending effectiveness to the whole enterprise, the presence of a middling class—the Lancashire and Cheshire yeomen who were the pith of that "military muscle of the Stanleys"[10] on which the Tudors relied, not merely at Bosworth but again at Flodden in 1513, when Stanley forces seized the opportunity to kill James IV, crippling Scottish national sovereignty beyond repair and making England safe for Henry VIII.

This sort of pattern made the English hegemony and laid the foundations for its empire. Divided against itself, it made for debacle. The Essex Rebellion of 1601 would have on one side a suicidally opportunistic aristocrat and his Celtic warriors,[11] but the respectable Lancashire element—in the person of Richard Bancroft, bishop of London—soon organised pikemen and propaganda against them. And of course, there was Elizabeth.

It was the key to a whole system that the third earl of Derby confronted in the capable yeoman George Marsh. Both of them knew very well how matters stood. Just as the well-being of his ancestral farm was a factor in Marsh's decision to give himself up, so the continued management of his region under his own dynasty was a factor in Derby's conduct. To kill a monarch in battle—your own or anyone else's—was not quite the sort of decision any gentleman could take. Neither was martyrdom a gentleman's death. To wait and see, and still be master in the outcome, was the path of honor. The whole region, in the person of its earl, may be described as waiting to see how this man of the middling sort would move, now that—like others of his sort at Bosworth and Flodden—so many lines of initiative and communication centered on him.

Battles are not won by wasting men or by putting commanders in impossible positions. Perhaps the outcome was tacitly understood between them. As long as Marsh proved firm but modest, loyal to the Crown, though a Protestant, and, above all, named no names, Derby could protect the region from any further unnecessary embarrassment. In Marsh's account, there is a sort of professional equality about their modes of address to each other. Marsh felt free to remind Derby to his face how much the earl's current policy contrasted with his lordship's procedure under Edward, and Derby felt obliged to make some brief account of himself on that score. Even though they appear to be on opposite sides in this engagement, Marsh and Derby rely on a certain common discipline and, at the secular level, have some common aims.

The prestige of the Stanleys rested on their capacity to mediate between central government and their own region. They rarely allowed their own loyalty to any particular regime to undermine local loyalties to themselves. With its sharp divisions, south Lancashire was always a problem. Even the Stanleys had to tread softly and in both directions. After Henry's break with Rome, they scrupulously avoided any challenge to the Catholic prejudices of southwest Lancashire. When Mary returned England to the Roman fold, they did what they could to avoid making permanent enemies of the Protestants of the southeast.[12]

On Marsh's side, there were deeper things at issue than the maintenance of a stability favorable to the Stanleys. His very modesty would make a rock of conviction for those local Puritans of the Civil War period who reduced Lathom House to a ruin and ended its dominance of their landscape forever. In the balance of things, Marsh's burning at conservative Chester would find an answer (and for some an expiation) in the beheading in Bolton market place of an earl of Derby, under the Commonwealth. While neither George nor his lordship could have planned to arrange or to prevent such things, it is significant that Marsh refused the trap of consistency into which Bradford charged with all his superior intelligence. Marsh refused to give the earl the "definite answer" he needed to quieten his own political nerves. He was determined to provide his own answer and—just as Lever had done with his London sermons—to get it published as widely as possible as soon as possible after delivery. His account of his examinations—sent off to and virtually commissioned by his four wealthy supporters in Darcy Lever—was circulated throughout the Manchester district on the writer's advice. Exactly like Henry Bradshaw, he had identified the "merchant men" as the audience that must be reached. The four families involved would all be fined for refusing knighthoods under James and would all show Parliamentary sympathies under Charles.[13]

Just as Lever's sermons used the monarch to reach another public, so Marsh deployed the monarch's lieutenant in his own campaign. His initiative is significant and it anticipates relations between Bolton and Lathom House in the next two reigns. It became an understood thing that while most local preachers were subject to Stanley scrutiny, an exception was always to be made for preachers from Bolton. The Stanleys might own land there, but not souls, apparently.[14]

Marsh the martyr is poised between history and drama—between the Stanley pikemen and bowmen who made and maintained the early Tudors and the Stanley acrobats and stage players who entertained Elizabeth. Unlike both these groups (and Shakespeare had connections with the second) Marsh could not be induced to wear the Stanley livery. At Lathom, he slept in an outhouse among the tent canvases of old campaigns. He was treated to joshing by the earl and his recruiting officers: "the favourers of the religion now used had wondrous good luck," he was reminded and "it was a great pity" that he, "being a well-favoured young man, and one that might have good living . . . would so foolishly cast [himself] away." George said he would be as loath to lose the world as another would, if he might retain it with a good conscience. As if in apology, "I could not do that," he said. Might his friends be permitted to relieve him? He trusted God would strengthen him with his Holy Spirit. He was no doubt composing the next instalment of his account in his head even as he spoke.[15]

An unfettered prisoner, he left Lathom under light guard for the castle at Lancaster.

12

Royal Lancaster

I⊤ is difficult to assess how much support Marsh won during the eight months or so he spent in the "highest prison" in Lancaster Castle, or the four months at Chester, much of it in an almost lightless dungeon in the city wall. There are no letters from Chester.

His most significant letters—preserved in Foxe—provide fascinating detail on his examinations at Lathom. They constitute the witness he wished to leave behind him of his particular views. After writing them, he put aside apologetics in order to continue by letter from Lancaster his ministry to his friends in Lancashire and Leicestershire. A letter to Manchester and another to Langton are in Foxe and Coverdale, and Foxe has also a moving letter to Darcy Lever.

Imprisonment in Lancaster was itself an opportunity to begin a new ministry. This possibility he had won by turning homeward instead of to London. By doing so, he had evaded not only confusion with his associates such as Bradford and Saunders, but also interminable bouts of sophistry with the medley of papist disputants, English and foreign, who were fielded against them, not to mention the even more enervating daily collisions with Protestant sectarians, including anabaptists, who were shrewdly herded by the London authorities into the same prisons with the late king's preachers.

Marsh, who had walked unfettered for two days from Lathom to Lancaster and spent a night in their Lancaster lodging with his two guards from Lathom, who "out of good nature" gave him those last hours of trust and liberty, was now dragged in chains four times from one end of the strong castle to the other to appear before the sessions of the judges, who chose thus to treat him as a malefactor rather than a heretic. Since leading citizens were known to favor Marsh, this was perhaps their way of ignoring, and thus protecting, the tendency he represented.

Always eschewing "captious arguments" Marsh relied on demeanor to make his case beyond argument. The Lancaster authorities appear to have been uninterested or incapable of teasing out the details of the "heresy" of such a man. Their reticence is not surprising, since at its most extreme this consisted of acknowledging the authority of the prayer book of 1552 to which they had all conformed. Had they probed more closely, they would have been embarrassed to encounter an outlook actually more conformable with the more conservative prayer book of 1549, which had not been found intolerable by Gardiner, now Mary's chancellor and inquisitor.[1]

The strategy of Marsh's performance during these encounters—as would be the case in his show trial before the bishop of Chester—was to rely on the perceived contrast between his own fair-mindedness and the unfairness of his ghastly position. The actorly quality—which in a different form runs through the whimsical force of Lever's rhetorical style—shows itself in Marsh in a more transcendent, yet also more personal and somatic form. "I thought it good to certify you by my own handwriting," he writes, "that God would assist us with his Holy Spirit, and that we may with boldness confess his holy name; and that Christ may be magnified in our bodies, that we may stand full and perfect in all the will of God."[2]

At Lancaster, his policy was to provide the town with services in English twice daily. He was lodged with a companion called Warburton in the "highest prison," and they performed the English liturgy twice a day, with extra Bible passages in the evenings, all enunciated "with so high and loud a voice, that the people without in the street, might hear us." Some supporters regularly "sat down in our sights under the windows." A twentieth-century Boltonian of Irish Catholic background gives an idea (and it is not exaggerated) of the impact of voices such as these:

> A born Boltonian uses words like others might use hammer and chisel, and it seemed to me as though I were not listening so much as having them engraved on the cerebrum, so forceful each vowel, so inflexible each consonant, and so penetrating the delivery.[3]

Not surprisingly, some citizens objected to such muezzin-like proclamations. The authorities dallied, estimating the pros and cons.

Propaganda must be paid for. There is a suspicion that Marsh's death—among many others—was the price of the propaganda drive of the Marian exiles. This should not detract from the exiles' part in making possible the transition to a Protestant regime, yet neither should Marsh's own propaganda, which was so much more heroic in performance, yet so much milder in content than most of theirs, be forgotten. The pain of death and the (equally real) pain of survival were broadly to the same end, in worldly terms, yet there was a difference. In a society that was still very hierarchical, humbler folk who could never aspire to a yeoman's independence might count themselves lucky to get within reach of a gentleman's protection. The name of Marsh's companion—Warburton—calls to mind a Thomas Warburton, a poor weaver from Lancashire, who joined Lever at Aarau, and was married in the colony's church of St. Ursula.[4]

Only once does Marsh hint at the contrast between his choice and Lever's. Speaking generally of "faithful ministers of Jesus Christ," he describes how they "are willing and ready . . . to forsake not only the chief and principal delights of this life—I mean their native countries, friends, livings—but also to fulfil their ministry to the uttermost, that is, to wit, with their painful imprisonments and blood-shedding, if need shall require." The stumbling after the phrase, "fulfil their ministry to the uttermost" serves to show the intensity with which he equated its meaning with his own choice.[5] Part of that ministry—in Marsh's case—was to encourage discretion and survival insofar as was compatible with faithfulness. Lever, in the peroration to that *Treatise* of 1556, which he sent out anonymously from exile, would warn of the long fire of remorse that, for the rest of their days, lay ready to plague those who denied their faith when challenged to declare it. Surely, he wrote, "speedy passage" to the great hereafter "by a fiery faggot" would be preferable? He could rarely resist an alliteration or a nautical metaphor.

Lever's Heaton relatives had connections in the Furness district, beyond Lancaster.[6] It is permissible to imagine Lever's *Treatise* being smuggled in to local ports—maybe Piel Island, where Lambert Simnel had once landed to claim his kingdom—in barrels of salt pork, perhaps.

Whereas Lever gathered to himself a select flock, folded for the winter into their purified little Lancashire in Switzerland, Marsh addressed in his letters his own Church, as he defined it: "dispersed and scattered abroad in the midst of wolves" at Langton, Deane, Bread Street, or Darcy Lever. Whereas Lever aimed to invade his native county in print with secret incitements, Marsh claimed it in his own voice for Christ from its chief citadel.

For Lever, heaven is like Aarau: an alluring retreat that beckons. For Marsh, it is a city one must climb to see from the "highest prison" of Lancaster Castle. The "entrance is narrow and sudden," and the way up so steep one might easily "stagger or turn back." Looking out at a city that is already his, he recognises what he must still do to gain it: "If this city were now given to an heir, and he never went through this perilous way, how could he receive his inheritance?" To receive heaven meant claiming Lancaster: "our Captain . . . must lead us to our journey's end, and open to us the door of everlasting life." As for Socrates in his prison, so for Marsh in his, the only true door of escape leads homewards, not into the suicide of exiles. Elizabeth was of their mind: she never quite trusted runaways.

In July 1554, amid the splendors of the Latin Mass, Gardiner officiated at Mary's wedding to Philip, who shared her descent from the dukes of Lancaster. Derby, their lieutenant, gave the queen of England away to her Spanish husband and bore the sword before them to signify his family's continued protection.

From the tower of Lancaster Castle, Marsh, too, on every day he could throughout that summer and early autumn, broke into Te Deums and psalms of thanksgiving, but in English. Every day, he prayed aloud for the queen, in English, and declaimed the English Bible in so vivid a manner that his auditors thought he was preaching in his own words. He was claiming another protection, another husband, and another future, for the soul of England: "Let us take to us the sword of the spirit, which is the word of God, and learn to use the same according to the example of our Grand Captain Christ."[7]

13

Visitors

UNDER Mary, one-sixth of the English clergy were deprived for having wives. Among these was Bishop Bird of Chester, replaced in May 1554 by Dr. Cotes. With the arrival of the papal legate and the submission of the English Parliament to Rome that November, it was high time for George Cotes to be dealing with irregularities in his diocese. Among other scenes of liturgical inadequacy was the former priory of St. Mary, which lay in the shadow of Lancaster Castle, being divided from it by the long, irregularly shaped yard that was the scene of public executions.

George Marsh was apparently amused: "The bishop being at Lancaster, there set up . . . holy water casting, procession gadding, mattins mumbling, mass hearing, idols-upsetting. . . . [H]e was informed of me, and was desired to send for me and examine me; which thing he refused to do, saying he would have nothing to do with heretics so hastily."[1]

Before his departure, however, the bishop saw to it that Marsh was "more straightly kept and dieted." His visitors, and their gifts of food, were sharply reduced. "If his lordship were tabled but one week with me, I think he would judge our fare but slender enough," Marsh wrote. He added, in perhaps the last sentence he ever wrote: "God lay it not to their charges but forgive them and turn their hard hearts, if it be His will."

That the arrival of his final antagonist should lead to a lightening of tone in Marsh's writing is not surprising. The dreadful games of the powerful and their impact on the lives they diminish have always been a source of dark comedy, as they have been the genesis of the clown. To judge from Foxe's account, Gardiner and his fellow inquisitors were in the grip of nervous exhilaration as they baited the first of their victims, the pedantic, bewildered John Rogers. In some cases—and this is very noticeable in Lawrence Saunders—it is the doomed who exhibit a flow of high spirits. In Marsh's case, one might imagine an uprush of adrenalin at the approach of his life's last challenge and also a sense of relief that he had been able to achieve a little.

During his months at Lancaster, he had had a number of visitors. Some brought money or food, and having journeyed from a distance, called in every day during the time of their stay in Lancaster. That favorite point of reference for so many Lancashire traditionalists—John O'Gaunt—had for a time be-friended Wycliffe and, partly in alliance with Lollardism, partly to forestall the discontents it drew on, had liberated his remaining bondsmen in a grand popular gesture. The blend of "gospel" Christianity and populism to which Marsh appealed was an old-established English emotion. In Lancashire to some extent it was even a way of life,[2] rather than a newly imported conti-nental theology. Thus, the mood of *Piers Plowman* (first printed under Ed-ward VI, though written much earlier) is an almost constant background to the historical perspective of Pilkington. His was a not uncommon country-man's distaste for the mumbo jumbo, celibacy, and tinsel of a religious estab-lishment that seemed only to mock the hardships of the workaday world.

While "some" people may thus have seen Marsh as a champion in an old cause, "many"—as he puts it—came to tell him to do himself a favor and submit. He "made them plain answer."

With the not very scholarly local priests who were sent to cross swords with him—"by 2, 3, 4, 5 or 6 at once"—he was gentler. "At their departing they either agreed with me, or else had nothing to say against me." His "communication with them was about the sacrament." It is perhaps not super-fluous to note again the contrast with Bradford and Saunders: communica-tion, not disputation, the effort to agree instead of disagree. "Empty and bestow those five loaves and two fishes that ye have," he wrote encouragingly and typically to his friends in Bolton. Knowledge shared was knowledge increased, he thought. If he was able to communicate some of that supportive tuition to these equally simple Romish interlocutors, he was a very dangerous heretic indeed.

His more distinguished supporters fell into three groups: members of the ancien régime, new men seeking entry to the establishment through com-merce, and individuals who had achieved some claim on public opinion be-cause of their careers.

This last group included the master of the grammar school—whom Bishop Cotes was especially cross with—and the mayor of the town. This latter lived to celebrate fifty years as a Protestant and was Marsh's victualler in jail. His attitude to popish idolatry was an aggressively humorous contempt, which (according to Foxe) he took opportunity to display from the bench during Mary's reign.[3]

The group of Darcy Lever supporters Marsh relied on to circulate his letters in southeast Lancashire included the Fogg and Crompton families of that township—yeomen seeking entrance to the landed establishment through commerce—and also the Bradshaws and Levers, representatives (it may be) of dispossessed or junior branches of the gentry families of Bradshaw and Great Lever, respectively, who might be described as seeking to reenter the establishment by the same route. For this group, Puritanism and Parlia-

mentarianism would go hand in hand, without necessarily excluding affection for the monarchy or the Church of England.

Marsh also had the privilege of supportive or speculative visits from the
"real" old gentry, including two representatives of the multifarious Lancashire clan of Ashton, which had long been, and would long remain, prominent in church and state within and beyond the county. In the reign of
Henry VIII, an Ashton cleric had worked to found St. John's College, Cambridge, under Bishop Fisher, Lady Margaret's nominee. Thirty years after
George's martyrdom, one of a number of Ashton high sheriffs would refortify
the keep of Lancaster Castle against the Spanish menace, finishing it off with
a look-out turret patriotically dubbed "John O'Gaunt's chair."

Perhaps the most significant visitor was Robert Langley. Unknown to
Marsh before his arrest, Langley arrived to offer himself as Marsh's publicist
within Protestant circles "about Manchester or elsewhere." He was able to
offer the Darcy Lever group a wider range of contacts than they could supply
unaided. He was a link man in another important sense. The Langleys were
a distinguished local family, whose fifteenth-century representatives had included a bishop of Durham, and—perhaps even more tellingly—Ralph Langley, third warden of Manchester, who had built the nave of the Manchester
Collegiate Church. Robert Langley, in promoting Marsh, may well have
considered that he was not abrogating, but continuing, the religious responsibilities of his family. This, more than anything, is the clue to Marsh's intentions. By a different method from Lever, he was anxious to confront his
generation with some version of Christianity credible for the times. He had
tasted enough of academic theology to know its worthlessness for that
purpose.

A few weeks after the bishop's visit, George was brought to Chester.

14

From the Monastery to the City

Before becoming bishop of Chester, Dr. Cotes had been master of Balliol College, Oxford. This had been refounded in 1507, on the particular orders of Pope Julius II, who had laid the cornerstone of the present St. Peter's the year before. His indulgences, sold for the building fund of his new basilica, would provide the occasion for Luther's Ninety-Five Theses, and his use of military force in support of the temporal power of the papacy would be attacked in Erasmus's *Praise of Folly*. Thanks to the protection of the Emperor Maximilian, he was able to avoid calling a General Council of the Church. The new Balliol was thus intended to be a cell in the structure being devised for the regaining of Western Christendom by an indurated Papacy, holding out against consultation on doctrinal matters and confronting the world with an absolutism that offered itself as an administrative instrument to the secular power on which it relied.

Balliol's new statutes reflected the mentality behind them. Formerly, members had elected their own principal, but the college had also been monitored by two independent "masters," appointed from outside. For a few years during the fourteenth century, Wycliffe had been one of these. This policy was now reversed. External controls were reduced to a single visitor, elected—paradoxically—by the college itself: a unique arrangement. He was allowed only one visit a year, unless specially invited. Meanwhile, each of the ten fellows nominated his own scholar, who became his personal servant. Scholars were elected to vacant fellowships. Further privileges bolstered the master's position at the top of the heap. It was a format unique—even by Oxford standards—for its servility, petty jealousy, and collateral irresponsibility—a matrix for the implements of higher control.

The pope's deputy in making these arrangements was Bishop Fox of Winchester. Ten years later his scheme for the founding of Corpus Christi College came into collision with Bishop Oldham of Exeter, a protégé of the Lady Margaret Beaufort and an apostle of the new humanism.

Fox had wanted to found a college for monks. Oldham offered a large contribution to the endowment, on condition that it became instead a college for the training of secular clergy, with special provision for Greek as well as

Latin and theology. He got his way, and the college was given the oversight of Oldham's new grammar school in his native Manchester.[1] This school's Horatian motto—*Sapere Aude* (literally, "Dare to be Wise")—summarised its policy. The antithesis of the new Balliol, it offered, like Colet's contemporary and similar school at St. Paul's in London, to forge an alliance between classical humanism and the modern commercial city, in a context of Christian piety replenished from its source in the Greek New Testament.

Marsh's school at Bolton was refounded from an old chantry school in rapid—and successful—emulation of Manchester Grammar School. John Lever, Oldham's ward, and father of Thomas Lever, was a prime mover. Cambridge, to which its brightest pupils were inevitably drawn, was buzzing with the ideas of Erasmus and soon with those of Melanchthon, Erasmus's most civilised Protestant successor. St. John's College, and Christ's College—where Marsh became a self-financing "pensioner"—were both Lady Margaret endowments. Both had become hot-beds of Reformation ideas.

Under the bludgeoning of questions from Cotes's chancellor at his final trial, Marsh is reported to have used a phrase eloquent of the preciousness of that time to him: "his continuance was at Cambridge," he said. It is quite possible that, like other scholars of modest means, he worked in the town and studied on the fringe of the university for a while before officially enrolling.

The polarity between Cotes and Marsh could hardly have been more complete. Counter-Reformation Oxford had collided with the Cambridge Reformation. The pensioner of Christ's, with its mission to supply "new blood" initiatives to the Tudor monarchy, had met the master of Balliol, which existed to justify the papacy in its alliance with the empire.

That alliance was thriving just at present. Quizzed by Derby on his deferred plans for escape, Marsh had answered that, had he not decided to surrender himself, lest disloyalty to the Tudors should stain his conscience, he would have fled to Germany. The emperor had destroyed the heretics of Germany, Derby replied.[2] In a few months, he would give his sovereign in marriage to the emperor's son.

The brief, largely ineffectual joint reign of Philip and Mary was more like the "reign" of Lady Jane Grey than might at first appear. What chiefly distinguishes them from her is not the duration of their political credibility—about thirteen months, compared with less than nine days—but the effective source of their claim to legitimacy. Both initiatives were experiments in cultural hijacking: the earlier one was certainly premature, but its replacement was rather more forlorn. The Janeites were a Protestant élite who required a weak sovereign whose legitimacy depended on their own power over her predecessor. A pious young woman was a suitable figurehead for the imposition by a packed Parliament of a "moderate" Protestantism empowered to persecute in both directions. Something not very different in essential pattern would eventually be realised in the "constitutional" Revolution of 1688–89.

Had Northumberland got his way, his son, Jane's husband, would have reigned jointly with her.

Mary's legitimacy, on the other hand, was the product of the military power of the Emperor Charles V. This had prevented the papal annulment of his aunt's uncanonical marriage to Henry. Their pious daughter duly became the first effective female sovereign of England. After his marriage to her in July 1554, Charles's son Philip was officially regarded as ruling with her, but Parliament would never consent to his hallowing at Westminster. In one fatal respect, this double-headed Catholic monarchy was less viable than the Protestant alternative it had displaced. By contemporary standards, the bride was all but too old for childbearing.

When, at the end of the following summer, Philip returned to the continent to assume the responsibilities that fell on him with his father's abdication, their English experiment was over as surely as Northumberland's experiment had collapsed with the arrest of Jane. The following year, Philip renewed his father's policy of going to war against a pope who crossed him.[3] His Catholic soldiers were soon in Italy, battling for supremacy with the pope's Lutheran mercenaries. Mary was dying—her support was still worth invoking against some of Philip's other European enemies—but the English experiment was running out of time. Perhaps, in the eyes of Charles V, it had never been more than an unavoidable reassertion of family honor. Others saw it differently. For some Protestant readers of Lever's sermons—including Knox—it was God's vengeance on Protestant misconduct. For Gardiner, perhaps, it was the answer to all his prayers.

What the experiment had looked like—and in England the burning went on as though there were still juice in it—was an attempt to align England by wedlock and heredity with the Holy Roman Empire and its desired tool of thought control, the new absolutist papacy. What it was not—and this is even suggested by the revulsion its methods aroused in many conservative English Catholics—was a return to the good old days. Like Northumberland's conspiracy, it had a theory of the future, but unlike the vague notions of constitutional monarchy that animated Lever and other Janeite academics, the ideas that filled the heads of Gardiner and his northern lieutenant George Cotes had been found wanting rather too often before.

Much of the moral resource of Western Christianity in its battle with the secular world had been derived from monasticism. This force was shattered with virtual impunity in England because it was almost everywhere seen to be dying. A new kind of religious revival—associated with, but by no means confined to the free cities of the empire—was mingling spiritual and material discontents in forms that made it again urgent to consider the central question of the relation between Christianity and the world. Ever since the emergence of the Church as an institution to be reckoned with, secular authority had repeatedly answered this question in its own terms: Christianity must be as uniform as was necessary, not for the truth's sake, but for the sake of obedi-ence. The Church was grasped as an implement of repression. To reformers of many kinds for many centuries, the papacy itself—insofar as it claimed secular as well as spiritual absolutism—was the chief enemy of rational orthodoxy.

In the late fourth century, two great Catholic saints had opposed in vain a hideous development in the Christian commonwealth: the introduction of capital punishment for heresy. The Emperor Maximus, for political reasons, resorted to this method of repressing the Manichean sect that had arisen in Spain. Inevitably, it increased their numbers. Of his chief opponents, one was Martin of Tours, formerly a Roman soldier, who became a founder of Gallic monasticism. The other was Ambrose, bishop of Milan. He, too, encouraged monasticism. His most famous convert—Augustine—would de-velop the rather different ideal of the *Civitas Dei,* the utopian city of the elusive future, which lies directly behind Lever's colony at Aarau. Monastic retirement or utopian colony: there might be a third way, and it is suggested by Marsh's call to Lancaster. The respect in which Ambrose was held by certain sixteenth-century Reformers was due to his heroic perseverance in this third way: the patient Christianization of the great city of Milan itself.

He stood above all for the idea of the Catholic Church triumphantly defending itself with the sword of the spirit against schism and superstition on the one hand (Ambrose was an enemy of Arianism) and against the arrogance and cruelty of the world on the other (he resisted other imperial atrocities besides the introduction of capital punishment for heresy). In this latter capacity, he was frequently, and courageously, quoted by Archbishop Grindal when arguing against Elizabeth's resolution to put down "prophesying."

Moreover, the writings of Ambrose seemed to Protestants to be in favor of the practice of extending communion in both kinds to the laity and to be hostile to the doctrine of transubstantiation. Marsh certainly knew these arguments and seems to have alluded to Ambrose in that context during his own examination for heresy at Lathom.[4] Though he called on theological "experts," the earl was of course chiefly interested in limiting the political damage of one more experiment in the school of Maximus.

The atmosphere of Chester was very different. The city had once been of great strategic importance. It was garrisoned by Roman and Plantagenet armies as a fortress from which to control north Wales. Royal connections gave its merchants privileges that failed to prevent its relegation to merely local importance during the seventeenth century, in face of competition from the brash Lancashire port of Liverpool. During the Civil War, a "minority of racketeers" held the city for Charles.[5] The last episode of its military history was almost decisive. The king narrowly escaped rebel fire while viewing the siege of Chester from its cathedral tower.

When Marsh entered it, it was a recently despoiled center of monasticism. Physically dominated by its various monastic buildings, it was spiritually dominated by the trauma of their despoliation sixteen years before. The feelings and pockets of many had been adversely affected, and Marsh was going to pay for it. It was in the precincts of St. Werburgh—now Dr. Cotes's residence—that the two Georges held their rehearsal for the inevitable show trial in the cathedral, which both must have been anxious to conduct as decorously as possible.

Between an inquisitor too well trained for curiosity and a heretic whose whole strategy was to minimise irrelevant differences, the central irreconcilability was soon made clear. What all such exchanges came down to sooner or later—in this case, sooner—had been established by Lord Chancellor Gardiner in his examination of Rogers before the Council, a kind of training seminar for inquisitors. The heretic usually professed his belief in the Catholic Church. By this, the heretic proceeded to explain, he meant the faith of Ambrose and Augustine, as set out in the Athanasian Creed. But the inquisitor was not to be deflected by such a trick as that: "Make a direct answer whether thou wilt be one of *this* catholic church or not, with us in that state in which we are *now?*"[6]

At this moment, in England, what was required was submission to the notion of the pope and the power of the monarchy, which de facto controlled that notion as far as England was concerned. The tone was set by Gardiner, who was very keen on royal authority, and could at first hardly bear the idea of Mary's renouncing her father's title as Head of the Church. But, with her marriage to Philip, Philip and Mary, as joint monarchs, perfectly submissive to papal authority, could achieve directly what Gardiner's poor master Henry had only aimed for by his break with Rome. Philip, as the representative of the most powerful family in Christendom—the great-grandson of Maximilian and moral heir of Maximus—could deploy Rome, or so it seemed. Ambrose, that outstanding champion of the Church's right to independence from the civil power, had been aware that a Church that relied on persecution was a Church at the mercy of the empire. Doubtless in a later age he would have concurred with John Henry Newman's strictures on the "fallacy of persecution." That fallacy was peculiarly attractive to Gardiner. Like John Stuart Mill, he knew that the minority were likely to be right and had a duty, in the end, to inform the people.[7]

It was not that he was a monster. Routinely refuting one more heretic's objections against images of the Holy Ghost in June 1555, Gardiner was momentarily discomposed by a view that, from so polluted a source, touched his own vulnerability. We must not make to ourselves images of doves to worship, the heretic reports himself as saying, "for though the Holy Ghost appeared like a dove, yet he was not like in shape, but in certain qualities, and therefore when I saw the dove which is God's creature, indeed I might

remember the Spirit to be simple and loving." For a moment, the Lord Chancellor appeared "somewhat moved." But his reply showed the invincibility
of the official habit. That thought and feeling might be connected; that form,
in the end, might matter much less than impalpable "qualities"; or that the
individual imagination might function as a voluntary agent in recalling these,
were none of them items on that day's agenda. The heretic, one of a batch
of four burnt in Canterbury the following month, reports that Gardiner "said
I had learned my lesson, and asked who taught me."[8]

The stronger and more united the masters, the more easily doubts are
quieted in the servile heart. Gardiner—like the staff of Kafka's castle—was
an instrument of the Hapsburg world ideal. The sovereigns he had united in
holy matrimony could exact more than protestations of secular allegiance.
They could control and thus redeem countless wayward souls. God had given
them the duty of demanding of their subjects unprovisional submission to
anything they or their heirs for ever might permit the pope to teach. Their
partnership would bind England into a trading community with former
rivals, most particularly the Low Countries. Throughout Europe, and beyond, the greatest happiness of the greatest number—happy because they
were obedient, prosperous, and sanctified—might thus be ensured. The blood
of heretics—a misguided few—would be the life blood of the *Civitas Dei*.

The system Marsh confronted had very little to do with Ambrose and
everything to do with Maximus—very little—one might say by analogy—to
do with Marx, and everything to do with Lenin. Cotes, like his variants,
was merely the apparatchik of utopia, a poor thing that was there to be
denied. This does not mean that Marsh had right on his side.

Both men had been christened in honor of St. George, patron of chivalry
and England. Any attempt to outline the implications of their confrontation
for the future energies of England might identify three areas where distinctions might be made.

First, the area of spiritual conflict is perhaps the least obvious and most
intractable. No doubt both men felt the absolute claim of the otherworldly
over the worldly. It was just that George Marsh desired the Christianization
of the everyday by the direct witness of the faithful, working at all the
ordinary tasks of the city in which they found themselves: an All Hallows
in Bread Street, a Church in Church Langton. In this respect he is much
nearer to the Lever of Coventry than to the Lever of St. John's College,
Cambridge, or of St. Ursula's Aarau, and is somewhat distinct from George
Cotes, with his reliance on those residues of monasticism, the college, or the
cathedral precinct.

Second, a difference of intellectual strategy may be detected alongside the
difference of spiritual focus. Gardiner's academic and episcopal assumption,
that enlightenment is simply a "lesson" to be "taught" by higher authority,
was clearly shared by Cotes. This was clearly at variance with the ghostly

tuition Marsh shared with some of his fellow Protestants, a scattered and persecuted fellowship whose leading intellectual propagandists were in jail or in exile and who reached out towards agreement with each other in a voluntary process rooted in personal experience and observation.

Third, the most obvious things about Marsh are his insistence on the use of English and his refusal to defer to Rome. Given the race for the Americas as the background to this cultural intransigence, Marsh at Chester, like Lever at Aarau, may be seen as making one of innumerable individual decisions whose broad result may be seen as the distinction that still exists between Latin America and the North that, as Bismarck noted in a memorable phrase, "speaks English." It is not, perhaps, necessary to be an Anglo-Saxon or a Protestant to feel that there has been some connection between Marsh's kind of intellectuality and the political aspirations of English-speaking communities all over the world or that the break with Rome and its cult of authoritarianism has been beneficial as well as inevitable.

It is when collating the first and third areas that doubts arise and distinctions become blurred. How far has the Christianization of the city of men in the here and now been affected by the rise of a cultural empire refusing deference to Rome? The absolutely transcendental nature of that "simple and loving" spirit that Marsh and martyrs of many kinds have been unable to stifle in their hearts may be suggested by a single example: the distinction without a difference that marked in Ireland the end of a Latin Empire and the beginning of an English-speaking one.

The only English pope—Adrian IV—had in the twelfth century claimed Ireland as the appanage of Peter and transferred that claim forever to the English sovereign. Gardiner must have appreciated the logic of such a claim and would have rejoiced that Philip as king of England had papal right as well as imperial power on his side in making it good. Shipwrecked officers from Philip's armada of 1588 would look on the Irish as they looked on their converted Indian slaves of the Americas—as barbarians with access to the mass.[9] The king's own view of subject races was equally predictable. His policy for Ireland—borrowed from his continental experience—was *divide et impera*: he planned for its permanent destabilization by importing plantations of English and Welsh immigrants into Leix and Offaly, henceforth to be renamed Queen's County and King's County. Derby was ordered to dispatch recruits from his region via Chester "to inhabit the realm of Ireland." By May 1558 "Many hundreds of men, women and children are dead of famine" came the report on the progress of this policy.[10]

Once the Elizabethan regime had settled down, there began an almost invisible but irreversible process of transition, whereby the Latin empire that had obsessed men's minds for centuries was to be overtaken by a new Protestant and Anglo-Saxon imperialism. The wicked old port of Chester, for instance—founded by Agricola, father-in-law of the Roman historian Tacitus—

was made to yield its status to Liverpool, which as yet had very little historical baggage. Papal superstition went the way of Roman militarism. Never
again would there be an abbot of St. Werburgh, the Saxon princess the zeal
of whose house for Rome had assured her canonisation. The Protestant future
was safe with Richard Longworth, Elizabeth's new dean of 1572, loyal to
her as to her predecessor. This part of the English coast was the key to
Ireland as well as north Wales. St. Patrick himself had launched his mission
from a Lancashire beach. English Protestants vowed to free their Celtic
neighbors from the yoke of Rome.

With a large force of armed invaders, Walter Devereux left Liverpool for
Ireland in 1573, Ralph Lever's new logic (it may be) in his pocket. Before
long, the earl of Derby knew what to do with his Bolton hard men. A
number of them would join Walter Devereux—and later his son Robert—
in pacifying Ireland. A leading light among these Boltonians was Dr. Richard
Rothwell, whose surname suggests a relationship with the vicar of Deane,
who conformed from Henry to Elizabeth. A Greek and Hebrew scholar, the
good doctor was also an accomplished exorcist and a mighty warrior, a "rough
hewer" of both flesh and spirit. All in all, he was a worthy successor to the
armored ecclesiastics of the middle ages.[11]

Other, more peaceable, Boltonians were planted in a new colony at Liverpool. The earl of Derby's deer park at Toxteth was turned into a victualing
station for the Irish enterprise, staffed and inspired by Bolton Puritans. They
were efficient agents in the smooth continuation of King Philip's policy of
achieving the permanent destabilization of Ireland by importing alien elements, though henceforth Ulster was the more favored target and (as under
Edward) Protestant Scots, rather than Catholic Welsh, the favored allies.
Such was the price the Stanleys exacted of Puritan Bolton for leaving its
preachers alone.[12]

To most later observers, Marsh's colloquy with Cotes was simply an exchange between Protestantism and Romanism, to be judged according to
affiliation. If one were to try to summarize it through the eyes of the protago-
nists, one might call it a collision between anarchy and irreligion on the one
hand (looking through Cotes's eyes at Marsh), and the worldly manipulation
of superstition in the interests of creating servile fear on the other (looking
through Marsh's eyes at Cotes). It was a conversation without communication between the smooth administration of "ghostly tuition" by wafer and a
disputed Pentecost.

The Theses of Melanchthon had persuaded Marsh that God does not
demand lip service to propositions to which the intelligence cannot assent.[13]
For both men, as for the Elizabethan high churchman Richard Hooker, it
was important to try to overcome error. What was of supreme importance,
however, was to retain the belief that "God may be merciful to save men
even when they err."[14] Otherwise, we are driven to prefer our own proposi-

tions about God to God himself. Now, transubstantiation was a doctrine particularly offensive to the reason of many. What Marsh found in Melanchthon was the reassurance that a loving and wise God could not demand that out of servile fear he should pretend to believe it. Not to believe it could not make him truly vulnerable to a charge of heresy.

Of course, for Cotes, transubstantiation was the fulcrum by which all things in heaven and earth were turned. Marsh could not quite believe that and was (which was the main point) absolutely certain that this did not make him a heretic. Of course, it did, since the Pope had forever concluded the argument by proclaiming the dogma of transubstantiation early in the thirteenth century. This proposed in effect that the consecrated wafer was materially informed by Christ, not merely a proposition about Christ. To deny this proposition was therefore to be materially sundered from Christ.

Next on the checklist of condemnation came errors about what Protestants thought of as the abuses of the mass (all mainly amounting to an investment in the extra-biblical notion of Purgatory). George refused to be drawn very far here, again following Melanchthon's advice. But he claimed to be certain of one thing, at least: the laity as well as the clergy had the right to communion in both kinds. This was a matter of canon law, not of dogma. Was Marsh content to have this point of canon law referred to His Holiness? No. The papacy might one day concede the point (and in fact would do so, during the twentieth century, on its own terms)[15] but Marsh was sure it was a right now, for Christ had so intended. He could cite scripture—as well as St. Ambrose—on this.

Ambrose was irrelevant. The legacy of Maximus saw to that. To claim the "right" to differ from the pope on canon law was effectively to claim for oneself the emperor's right to force the pope to change that law. Of course this gave the emperor (or his nominees) the right and duty to put an end to the subject's "liberty," by which was meant the concessionary terms on which the subject's existence was tolerated. To be "mistaken" about canon law was one thing, but an apparatchik like Cotes saw with perfect clarity that to *claim the right* to differ from it was to cease to be fit to live. Indeed, Chancellor Gardiner had indicated as much.[16]

There was no need to take the case further at rehearsal. Cotes returned Marsh to his keeping-room over the abbey gateway, and supplied him with a sequence of carefully monitored visitors, notably "one Wrench, the schoolmaster."[17] A much worse prison was available if he held to his obstinacy.

Late-twentieth-century visitors may still savor much of the beauty of the St. Werburgh's Abbey known and loved by Henry Bradshaw. Most beautiful—and a rare English survival—are the lofty and elaborate canopies of the choir stalls, which, dating from the very end of the reign of Richard II, have the appearance of a forest on fire. The dean's stall, formerly the abbot's, is on the right of the entrance to the choir. Marsh would hardly have been permitted any sight of this, being most probably admitted by an outer door directly to the Lady Chapel, a virtually distinct, though connected, building in the austere thirteenth-century style, with lancets in groups of three. On this spot, for over seven hundred years, had been the shrine of St. Werburgh, just beyond the high altar of the main church. Bishop Cotes had doubtless made efforts to soften the visual devastation of its removal, but these fell short of taking to pieces in its favor the temporary episcopal throne that had been made of it. Standing somewhere between the broken shrine of the kind Saxon princess and the patched-up altar of the Mother of Jesus, Marsh was teased into condemning himself to death.

He was then taken from the former monastery to a deep prison, like a well, set in the city wall at the Northgate. He was there in the same place for four months. There were very few who called to him or dropped coins or food down to him through a small hole in the wall.

15

Mature Tuition

For Mary—as for Elizabeth and Henry—there was no very clear distinction, in monarch or subject, between acting on personal conviction and acting as one pleased. The distinction that mattered lay between monarch and subject. It was the royal pleasure that had the exclusive permission of Providence. The whole "liberty" of the subject consisted in awaiting that pleasure. In the little local matter of George Marsh, the deputy chamberlain of Chester went through the routine of showing the heretic, as he waited by the stake, the official expression, under her seal, of Her Majesty's pleasure, which was that he should be pardoned at the expense of his personal conviction. His refusal to forgo that figment sent him to hell, leaving her guiltless of his death.

In such a context, there could in theory be no distinction between dialogue and treason. Nevertheless, dialogue of a kind divided the official mind of Chester at that moment. One of the sheriffs, whose name was Amry, vetoed the routine address from the condemned. His anxiety to get things going was motivated by the fear that his colleague, Sheriff Cowper, might use the delay to attempt a rescue. There was apparently a scuffle. Cowper fled over the bridge into Wales and outlawry.[1] As for the common people, some of them were quite as oblivious of the Protestant fact that Purgatory did not exist as of the papal fact that Marsh did not deserve to enter it, for, as was usual at public executions, they offered him purses to buy masses for the safe conduct of his soul through Purgatory to Paradise. Bewilderingly, he refused them.

For Mary, such temporary ripples of disturbance, physical or mental, had danger in them, but did not qualify for significance. Such things had vexed England since Richard II's day—the days of Wycliffe and the Peasants' Revolt—and indeed, like all evidence of evil, were coterminous with a fallen world. But the eternal reality was otherwise. The ghostly tuition that lived in conscience was guaranteed throughout Christendom by papal administration of Christ's body by wafer, and the conditions and continuity of that administration were locally guaranteed by the favor extended to her own regime—now mercifully allied to the empire—by a paternal Providence. God the Spirit, Son, and Father, worked in unity on her behalf, a fact she had the comfort of celebrating by initiating the building of a chapel for her father's Cambridge foundation, Trinity College. This building—a very poor relation of the nearby King's College Chapel of Henry VI, VII, and VIII—has been well described by a twentieth-century architectural historian as "a typical Marian product,"[2] and it is precisely the stereotype *routine,* or pseudo-routine, of "back to normal" that represents the most woeful aspect of the experiment that was Bloody Mary's reign.

The experiment lay in tightening up a routine that had ceased to work and in proclaiming with unprecedented conviction a consistency that had never really obtained. What passed for state popery reached Cambridge in January 1557. It proved a rather bizarre interlude. It was also, from several points of view, no more than a figment. Mary's consort was now at war with the pope and Cardinal Pole's legation—in the name of which these things were done—had been canceled by the Holy Father, and his doctrine declared unsound. He nevertheless appointed a commission for the reclamation of Cambridge headed by Cuthbert Scot. Perhaps coincidentally, this man shared his surname with Derby's resident jailer at Lathom. He was Mary's master of Christ's—Marsh's old college—and had recently been consecrated as the new bishop of Chester. Under his supervision, two foreign Protestant professors—Martin Bucer and Paul Phagius—were tried and condemned. Their corpses were dug up from the Cambridge churches where they had lain since the previous reign. Placed in a box which was then chained to a stake in the market place, these were then burned, together with a pile of heretical books. The Body of Christ could now be returned for perpetual reservation to those churches temporarily polluted by the material residue of the professors. The new bishop of Chester carried the host from the new Trinity Chapel, and after a solemn and extensive detour, housed it over the high altar of the university church.[3] The Cambridge Reformation was scotched. Insofar as Bucer's unpleasant schemes for a theocratic police state were also scotched, the English people were entirely the gainer.

Routines are also causes. Any attempt to reconstruct that mature tuition of the spirit that forbade Marsh to settle for the closed systems of either Bucer or Mary's two bishops of Chester must be fraught with imponderables. More manageable—and it might be said more typically Lancastrian—is his doggedness in maintaining as publicly as possible the routine of a previous administration, in expectation of its re-adoption by the next. This liturgical intransigence he shares with a martyr of the next century, Dr. Hewit, who invented and used, in London under the Protectorate, an Anglican litany for the restoration of Charles II. In Marsh's case, the most intransigent petition— "From . . . the tyranny of the bishop of Rome, . . . Good Lord, deliver us"— would be omitted from the prayer book on the restoration of his coreligionists. The new English litany, while it softened the claims of the monarch—adopting Lever's compromise title of "Governor"—consigned His Holiness to irrelevance.[4] This suited the view of those of Elizabeth's commissioners—including Pilkington—for whom the occasional heresies of the bishops of Rome were merely incidents in the long history of the worldwide Church. Such a view was perhaps arrogant enough to need an alternative empire to contain it.

With less arrogance or learning, Marsh's mature tuition nevertheless prompted him also to deny death or the pontiff much relevance to the continuing life of the spirit. At his final trial, were not Popes "Linus, Anacletus and Clement," the Bishop urged, looking at him over his spectacles, "all good men?" "Others also," Marsh is said to have answered "but claimed no authority in England."

About 20 April 1555 Mary withdrew to Hampton Court and commissioned the litanies that were to turn the fatal disease within her into a child. On 23 April Cotes celebrated for the last time his own name day and England's patronal festival, no doubt with appropriate magnificence. Dying in the fire the following morning, Marsh began the English litany again. His flesh boiled, Foxe writes, so that the chain that held him to the stake was hidden.

"At his death was a new invention of cruelty," it was later recorded. "A firkin of pitch was hung over his head, that the fire melting it, it might scald his head as it dropped on it."[5] Bored, or indifferent to mere burning, and desiring to degrade both its victim and those who, watching, might be made accessories of their own degradation, some inventive spirit had decided to add a little visual comedy to George's transformation into "a firebrand in hell."[6] The general motivation was as old as Chester itself: *pereuntibus addita ludibria,* as Tacitus put it—"dying was enhanced with comedy"—*unde . . . miseratio oriebatur:* "which only provoked compassion."[7]

History repeated itself on this occasion, though with less éclat. One may imagine the obscene glee of Sheriff Amry. "No sermoning, now!" he shouted, doubtless anticipating the effect of boiling tar on that once well-favored and voluble head. But the Chester of Philip and Mary lacked the panache of Nero's Rome. The fire did not burn brightly enough to ignite the firkin, and the full "human torch" effect was spoiled.[8]

Worse was to follow. Popish enemies may have failed to make a clown of Marsh, but his Puritan sympathisers were more successful. At Foxe's hands he is reduced to intransigent anonymity in the—undocumented—account of the final Chester trial, and in a passage of Pilkington that shocks the reader as a sentimental lapse in the writings of one so scholarly, humorous, and sad, there occurs this maudlin degradation of the martyr:

Consider whether they ["the bloody bishops"], or the simple souls which they tormented, have gotten the victory. The simple soul offered himself to die, rather than offend God by superstition or idolatry . . . so God ever confounds the wisdom of the world, and is glorified in the fools and abjects.[9]

Dissent, under the Protestant Tudors, was sometimes punished by promotion. In 1560, immediately after publishing the above attack on authoritarian episcopacy, Pilkington was nominated as Elizabeth's bishop of Durham. Lever had been trapped by the same method under Edward VI. Immediately after delivering his first two London sermons, with their refined incitement to disobey the magistrate at the bidding of conscience, he was commanded to join the heresy commissioners engaged in questioning the anabaptist Joan of Kent, whose utterances might well have sounded like an untutored exaggeration of his own. She burned, and doubtless Lever, who piqued himself as an impresario of compromise, suffered. Persecution, as an instrument of persuasion in matters of belief, was not his intellectual style. Revenge might be different. Such a simple emotion might be safely imputed to simpler beings, and in his Geneva *Treatise* he does so: "The priests of Baal shall not escape the rage of the people,"[10] he prophesies, once Protestantism is reestablished.

Neither Lever nor Pilkington mentions Marsh in this context. It would be strange if so very local an instance was entirely absent from their minds, but exorcism rather than homage may have been a motive. There is no evidence, either, that Marsh's outraged relatives—not even his brother-in-law, Jeffrey Hurst of Shakerley, who was released from Lancaster Castle only by Mary's death—had any plans for the priests of Baal in the shape of conforming clergy like old vicar Rothwell of Deane, even though they waited till he died, well into the reign of Elizabeth, before founding their parish school. It was not blood they were after, apparently.[11]

Without assuming that there was a particular conspiracy, it is hard to avoid feeling that Marsh—and others like him—were scapegoats for provincial gentry like the Levers and Pilkingtons and for City merchants like the Heatons. Few members of the influential classes chose to be martyrs. Among heroic exceptions to this pattern were the two men nearest to Marsh: John Bradford, the Levers' county neighbour; and Lawrence Saunders, whose City family were a generation or two ahead of the Heatons in the eternal quest to "get on." Their class, as well as their character, contributed to Marsh's respect for them. Inevitably, however, he had a different consciousness, and a different conscience, from theirs. Their social position imposed on its possessors a habit of behaving as though, broadly speaking, they were in the right. Both men were rather free with the word "infallible." A man of middling status like Marsh, on the other hand, was always likely to be blamed by both ends of the social spectrum. He had to prove his integrity every day.

"Written up" by Foxe as are all these martyrdoms, a difference in character emerges between Saunders and Bradford as well as a more radical difference between them and Marsh.

Bradford cannot be charged with denying the possibility of cooperation between man and God, or the importance of the moral conscience, or the presence of Christ in the sacrament. But he is anxious to construct an alter native establishment to the Roman one and to defend it with a block of doctrine—scripturally based, of course—to serve as an excluder. As foreshad owed in his writings, that establishment looks meanly contractual, exclusive, and pedantic. Providing a groundwork for a type of mercantile Protestantism which (had he lived to see it) his own heroic purity would certainly have put to shame, he insists above all on dividing mere human experience from the imputed faith that is to redeem a minority of human beings. For him, the consecrated elements remain to human experience nothing but bread and wine: Christ's presence depends only on faith, which is either "infallible" or nothing. It is important to have in general a "good intention towards God," but the particularities of right and wrong in daily life are solved *ambulando* once one is seized by "infallible faith." As for auricular confession to a priest, for instance, he defines this as an "indifferent" matter in itself, but lists eight reasons why under any conceivable practical arrangement it is "unlawful and wicked."

Bradford's last words were apparently an exclusion: "Strait is the way, and narrow is the gate that leadeth to eternal salvation, and few there be that find it." Even this was magnificent in him, a gentleman's call to battle addressed to the trembling apprentice Leaf, dying beside him in the fire. But in less desperate straits, there might be a short step from Bradford's separation in principle, to the "Manchester man's" separation in practice, between faith and life. It is a short step from Bradford's moral grandeur to the overweening alienation of the self-made man that would characterize Manchester in the world's eyes in later years. Improving Christ's prayer to his Father to forgive his persecutors, Bradford asked all the world forgiveness and forgave all the world.[12]

Saunders, on the other hand, claims for himself and his associates the Holy Spirit as a remunerative commodity and does so with enough confidence for an Exchange full of merchants and a sprightly enough flow of words to talk up a sure thing. He speaks of his "conscience" as "grounded . . . upon the infallible truth of God's word." He will not change his "uncorrupt religion . . . though an angel out of heaven should preach another gospel." Unsurpris ingly, he is able to assure Cranmer, Ridley, and Latimer that "we, believing, are sealed with the Holy Spirit of promise . . . (which spirit certifies our spirit, that we are the children of God)." Like them, he is confident of belonging to an authentic, exclusive, and persecuting Church. "Joan of Kent," whispers a "wily" Romanist to Saunders, "was of your church." "No," Saunders can thankfully reply, "we did condemn her as an heretic."[13] There speaks the sangfroid of a City of London élite (one is tempted to add, "also of a Boston élite") that will one day know what is best for the world and insure it. It is as though the sense of its own rightness inherent in a certain élite is claiming to replace the sovereign inviolability of princes.

Among other differences, Marsh is of course a Deanite. Bolton and Deane, taken together, would be doubly provincial—to London and Manchester—and would prosper through inventive resistance to and exploitation of that position. Deane parish in itself would be Bolton's inextricable "other half," epitomising an England (and a New England) of deeper tilth, modester, more traditional and surprising than the busy commercial centers. "Bolton," that strenuous epitome of England as a world center, would commandeer the platforms of Manchester on behalf of the Anti-Corn-Law League (very little corn could be grown on the Pennine uplands of Bolton parish) and would lobby imperial statesmen to secure Egypt and the Sudan so that Bolton might import entire the cotton crops of those exotic regions (thus undercutting rival industries in Asia, America, and the rest of Europe). But "Deane," Bolton's meditative hinterland, would remain in the lee of all that bustle and achievement. In Mary's reign, the best of Deane was at its post while the Bolton Levers and Pilkingtons were bustling and achieving—something else—in the safety of exile.

Marsh was a mature student whose official period of study at Cambridge was very brief and whose second career as a schoolmaster and parson was ended almost before it began. Copied over and over again, his letters circulated in secret in his home region before being published by Foxe and Coverdale. It was in his home region that they remained influential. Private piety, but also forms of civil and ecclesiastical resistance and dispute, were nurtured by them over the next three and a half centuries.

In particular, there are three modes of inner being that Marsh has inherited or developed and that he transmits: a sensitive kind of attention, an unshakeable grasp on what constitutes a distinction, and an acutely cautious approach to formulating a definition.

In writing to friends, he alludes to a habit of attending on God through an almost continuous registering of the little events of daily life. The priestly eternity of the daily mass is replaced for him by the no less traditional idea of each life as a brief, eventful progress into an altogether transcendent eternity. He tells his own story through Bible allusions: the old Deane life is "that pleasant Euphrates"; London is "that glorious Babylon"; Langton his "vineyard." Celibate security is not for him: nothing has been the same since "the Lord . . . took my dear and beloved wife from me." Melanchthon's stress on the priesthood of all believers sheds light here.[14] When Marsh urges his former parishioners to continue ministering to each other, while he supplies them with his own careful account of his life's chief crisis, he is adding his weight to the Protestant cult of journal making. Praise and confession combine in a record of God's achievement in transcending the failures of one sinful life. Degrees of grace, or degrees of spiritual authority, cease to be relevant in describing the inner life of the world. Marsh, in addressing his enemies, defends auricular confession as useful to bring comfort to those not well advanced in faith. But he recommends to his friends a form of private confession that has no reference to priestly function. Each sinner in private is invited to open to the divine tree surgeon "the evil tree of our heart, with all the roots, boughs, leaves and fruits, and with all the crooks, knots and knowres, all which thou knowest."[15]

Most moving is his account of his decision to give himself up at Smithills. We are as far as possible here from the administration of "ghostly tuition" by wafer. It is a faint, Socratic negative within him which is the determinant: "my spirit did not fully agree" he writes, with those who advised flight. He visits friends in their houses—including his mother—and prays on Deane Moor at sunset with another friend. Lest he upset his mother further, he spends his last night at Deane with yet another friend, at Hulme Barn farm, "taking ill rest, and consulting with myself of my trouble." The occasion of his final decision is a letter he does not need to open. This is delivered, "at my first waking," by one who brings it, sealed, "from a faithful friend of mine." Marsh's "mind and conscience" are now "cheerful and in a quiet state." He rises, and "after I had said the English Litany (as my custom was) with other prayers kneeling by my friend's bed-side, I prepared myself to go towards Smithills." On the way there, he calls at other houses, to beg the comfort of more prayers and to make arrangements for his family. Perhaps not truly in error, Marsh's male relatives, under orders from Smithills, had gone to seek him with his sister in Atherton, a few miles away, and had thus left him to present himself at Smithills alone, where they afterwards joined him. It is as though the "spirit" Marsh refers to is nurtured in him out of a whole inhabited landscape. "My friends," he writes, "thought I would not [recant] and, . . . God strengthening and assisting me with His Holy Spirit, I never will." The divine imperative that sets his conscience at ease is mediated to him through a series of almost wordless communications with those who share his form of consciousness. Their tact leaves him, in the last analysis, free to make the decision that their support almost expects of him.[16]

Mutually exclusive polarities are drearily similar since they exist to polarize and exclude, feeding the appetites of the powerful from the bewildered alienation of the many. Marsh and his associates at Deane and Langton represent a "middling" class that has borne the main brunt of such arrangements for hundreds of years, negotiating the rival claims of sacred and secular authority to receive the unthinking obedience of the people. They are not charmed by the appearance of a rival pair of absolutes, in the shape of ultra-Protestant land-grabbers and their scripture-fetishist pastors. In Deane parish, in particular, one can detect the distinction without a difference between its leading clan of Heatons in their former role as monastic tithe farmers and the same clan converted into bankers to the Reformation. Moreover, a

Protestant establishment driven to control or expel its own inner contradictions might become as oppressive as the Catholic version has always been
during its own periods of reasserting coherence. Mary's regime claims almost
unprecedented coherence. The fact that it does so in the name of Catholicism
is almost secondary.

It is in this context that Marsh's notion of what constitutes a true distinction becomes vitally important. At one level, it represents the intellectual
heroism of a mature student holding out for the rights of individual thought.
At another, it is a blow aimed—consciously or otherwise—against the trans-
parent devices of coherence.

Power and the construction of coherence are what motivate Marsh's
priestly inquisitors at Lathom. This makes them extremely obliging. He reports even-handedly the "gentle and far-sought interpretations" with which
they seek to "mitigate" the real-life abuses of the mass.

The tenor of his inquisitors' argument may be indicated as follows. The
Roman Mass describes itself at one point as *sacrificium laudis*—a "sacrifice
of praise" and thanksgiving—which is *all* you ultra-Protestants think the
communion to be. Why, therefore, cannot you rest content with that definition, and save your life by outward conformity? They go even further and
insist that when they refer to the mass as a "sacrifice" they mean nothing
other than "a memorial of a sacrifice." Clearly, in their endeavor to save him,
these good fathers will take on themselves the very heresy of which they
seek to relieve him. They are the priests of Marsh's tribe as surely as Derby
is its warlord, and they are just as bewildered.

Marsh is neither a Romanist nor an Anglo-Zwinglian memorialist: he can't
quite accept transubstantiation; still less can he deny Christ's bodily presence
in the eucharist altogether. He sees that two such mutually exclusive absolutes may be sophistically defined as equivalents—they are both "resolu-
tions," and as such tend to deny to individuals any contact with what they
are able to experience and believe of themselves—but for him there remains
the unalterable distinction between what one can and cannot freely believe.
He almost recognizes as a failure his own incapacity to take orders any more,
but he has assented to Melanchthon's conviction that human nature would
rather *bene esse*—enjoy "well-being"—than *esse*—merely "survive." He cannot turn back. Like Hooker, he "would neither wish to speak nor to live"
under the assumption that God is a "captious sophister." In the same anti-
Calvinist spirit he exclaims, "What need we to dispute and reason of our
own merits?" He is not tempted to resolve either way the puzzle of determinism and free will. The question of irrresistible "election" is also suspended:
every failure to help a neighbor is a hint against it in every man's case, he
is sure.[17]

He is equally unbiddable—as appears from his letters—on the subject of
Bible authority. Of course he does not accept Rome as the arbiter of all texts.

But neither can he bear the idea—popular with Protestants like Rogers and Saunders—of applying the Holy Spirit like a secret formula so as to produce a supposedly "uncorrupt" and consistent set of biblical rules. The Bible is simply seen as a daily companion to be meditated anew through every day of practical Christian endeavor. This humility is the one intellectual conviction he refuses to abdicate. He is intransigently tentative.[18]

Theological definitions, for such a mind, must be formulated with caution and held provisionally as mere verbal forms deserve to be. They are subject to improvement by mutual agreement in an atmosphere guided by the "simple and loving" spirit of inquiry. They cannot be abdicated to order. Threats are no argument. Marsh dare not play "Caesar"—the ancient yard game of Bolton Grammar School,[19] in which boys contended for supremacy of the school dunghill—with his immortal soul. For him, as for Thomas à Kempis, it is Christ within each who teaches truth and promotes good actions, and it is better to forsake all things than to confound both truth and action with sophistical subtleties.[20]

The flaw—if that is what it is—in Marsh's position is that, in the real world, it is not tenable except either as part of an act of submission to an absolute Church (something he rejects) or as initiating a liberalisation of sacred influences so far-reaching as to make them no longer usable—and therefore no longer worth tolerating or supporting—as a tool of coercion by their polarity, the secular power.

Once her Puritan intellectuals have been expended in helping to establish her regime, Elizabeth will commence the struggle—sometimes grisly, sometimes farcical—to emulate the spiritual police system of her sister. In his enthusiasm for compelling logic, Ralph Lever will provide her with a series of "assertions . . . touching the canon law," which now read like an Elizabethan form of Newspeak. "English laws," he claims, have throughout all ages been solidly grounded (insofar as they have been "English laws") on the "written word of God." Therefore all the "Pope's laws" that are not so founded have represented treasonable innovations, repugnant to "the positive laws of this realm." Not to "punish all Papists and Transgressors" is in itself therefore a perilous "change in the commonwealth," and one that merits "God's Curse" and its material manifestations.[21] Elizabeth welcomes arguments of this kind, applying them judiciously in the maintenance of the necessary fantasy that despite all her pragmatic shifts of policy she remains, in the words of her chosen motto, *Semper Eadem*—"forever the same."

For Marsh, God and God only can offer such security. Like Henry Bradshaw, he looks away from this world to God's transcendent future:

He will set before us His own holy Body, which is given to us to be our meat, and his precious Blood, which was shed for us and for many for the remission of sins, to be our drink. He biddeth, willeth, and calleth for guests, which hunger and thirst. *Come* (saith he) *all ye that labour and are laden, and I will refresh you, cool and ease you, and you shall find rest unto your souls.*[22]

This was for him the experience of the eucharist: an invitation to eternity, not a capturing of the divine for the purposes of men. Violence cannot redress violence. To refuse violence is for Marsh to refuse "exhortation, . . . to do and believe as the Catholic Church did."[23] Like Thomas Lever, he will not now say, "I believe as the Church doth." He desires every credal affirmation to be a fresh, unforced, decision to say the prayerful words of assent "*with* the . . . Church." Otherwise, belief is impossible.

Beyond that, Marsh and Thomas Lever become less similar. Both reject the practice of imposing "ghostly tuition" by wafer for the purposes of state popery. The yeoman Marsh also reflects, in a gentler, more scrupulous way, some of the values of the sort of bustling, public-spirited, education-minded commonwealth Lever desires to see. What can have no place in Marsh, however, is Lever's tendency to reduce the presence of Christ in the eucharist to a sort of divine lubricant for the machinery of such enlightened social arrangements. Liberalized, middle-class, and intellectually alert, this "reformation" is as worldly, from the point of view suggested by Marsh, as the Renaissance papacy itself. Both have forgotten the absolute, transcendent demands of that free spirit for which no regime, however canonical or innovative, can legislate. In a simple style more frequent and admirable than his occasional bursts of sentimentality, Pilkington provides a theological rationale for that scrupulous discrimination and reticence in the use of language that is also of the essence of Marsh's mature sense of ghostly tuition. Truly to cooperate with the Word Incarnate is to postpone final judgment to where he has placed it, at the end of history. Pilkington cannot now claim for his own party a god sealed in scripture, or a wafer, and reduced thus to an implement of government, but he believes "we shall understand," more and more, "His Holy Spirit, the schoolmaster of all truth" who 'worketh all in all', yet not without us."[24]

Asked to give his "belief of the sacrament of the altar," Marsh weighed his words:

> I answered, I believed that whosoever according to Christ's institution did receive the holy sacrament of Christ's Body and Blood, did eat and drink Christ's Body and Blood, with all the benefits of His death and resurrection, to their eternal salvation; for Christ, said I, is ever present with His sacrament.[25]

Marsh's tone is almost blithe as he records his fatal final clause. "In" would have been orthodox, but "with" was damnable. Syntactical orthodoxy was important to churchmen, but it was the secular authorities who incurred the opprobrium of killing the solecist. Derby was anxious, and he knew his own.

Thomas Holcroft, a die-hard Catholic, and Mary's knight marshal, intrigued for the release and connived at the exile of Edwin Sandys rather than be responsible for the disgrace and death of a fellow Lancashire gentleman who happened to be a die-hard Protestant.[26] Marsh was a useful scapegoat for such arrangements and ought to die, but an earl does not burn even a yeoman for misusing a preposition. There is something unbearable in being bully to a set of clerks.

Marsh's mature view of the sacrament—the question of questions in his examiners' eyes—may be classified under the heading of the philosophy of "consubstantiation," a compromise view that predated the dogma of transubstantiation that was designed to silence it. In English theology, it had for many generations coexisted with the philosophic determinism of Ockham as well as with the free-will ethics of Wycliffe. The words Marsh found were similar to those formulated by Melanchthon in the Wittenberg Concord of 1540,[27] except that Marsh, lacking the intellectual's incapacity for leaving well alone, refused to elaborate.

Such reticence was unusual. What was astonishing, however, was Marsh's obstinacy in refusing to deny that his inquisitors, too, might have right on their side, as far as definitions went. One might take this as supportive evidence for the local tradition that he remained close to the conforming vicar of Deane, Father Rothwell.[28] It is certainly an important point in reconstructing the kind of affection in which his memory would be held in his native place. Unlike his more contentious associates, he would not deny the heart of his village's "old religion" in reaching out for a definition more satisfactory to his own intelligence. If his body must burn—and he says his reticence was partly aimed at avoiding that outcome—he must take the goodwill of a whole people with him and not merely a chosen few.

Pestered by the theological experts actually to deny or positively to affirm transubstantiation (Were the bread and wine *changed into* the flesh and blood of Christ? Was the sacrament, received or reserved, the *very body* of Christ?), Marsh "made answer, I knew no further than I had showed already. 'For my knowledge is unperfect,' said I." Pestered by Derby to write a more "direct answer"—or shame his family as a "traitor" by failing to provide the state with clear, and therefore loyal, justification for his own destruction—he "took the pen and wrote that I knew not."

Nothing that was done to him over the next thirteen months would induce him to pretend to know.

PART FOUR
Elizabethan Bishop

Eternal God and loving Father, who lovedst us when we hated
Thee, ... make us often worthily to consider this Thy fatherly
dealing with us, that from henceforth we may become new men.
—James Pilkington, *Statutes of
Rivington School* (1566)

16

James Pilkington: Meditating the Life Historial

IN surviving as a dynasty, the Tudors imposed discontinuity on their subjects. Henry VIII burned Protestants, but raised his son as one. Mary fought the heresy in her body politic as fiercely as the disease in her own dying body, yet shrank from actually eliminating Elizabeth from the succession.

In adapting to such events, our three Boltonian Protestants also confronted them, and together they provide a relatively coherent chain of thought which amounts to their commentary on their age. The most obvious implications of this are also the most significant. People were thinking. There was a market for the products of thought. The Tudors—who were to a great extent its subject matter—were thus made subject to forces they had no means of comprehending or preventing. The monarchy became almost a product of the discontinuity it had produced. Beneath the Elizabethan slogan—*Semper Eadem*—lay a pragmatism that was not mindless, for it was beset with so many admonitions to adapt.

Thomas Lever, preacher to Edward VI, claimed for the conscience of a Protestant community, nurtured by the effective sacramental presence of Christ, a sovereignty to which law itself was subject. He made himself a mouthpiece for the educational and economic aspirations of the whole people of Christ. Alas, the most powerful among his hearers were busy privatizing common land and extinguishing the Church's charitable assets. George Marsh, as he awaited death under Mary, provided evidence for a view of the Holy Spirit as preventitive guardian of communal well-being, testing the individual conscience in matters of intellectual assent so as to curtail the formulation of required doctrine well short of the point where, ceasing to be useful, it could become a source of fetishism, polarization, and moral nihilism. But the authority that condemned him was nihilist: the state, claiming a perfect collusion with the church, could require without the need to justify.

And so also under Elizabeth. Pilkington was not capable of pretending that the whimsical cruelties and piratical economics of her reign were likely to produce permanence or harmony in church or state. It has been said that his career "illustrates the trials of a divided allegiance."[1] Yet by itself this

117

judgment misses his individuality and also his broader significance. From his vulnerable position as an agent and maintainer of the Elizabethan settlement, he meditated the various exemplars of what for him was the unchangeable fact of history, that "God and the world are enemies."[2] As a corollary of this preoccupation, he emerged—albeit posthumously—into something like political controversy. Published in 1585 by his protégé John Foxe, Pilkington's commentary on Nehemiah deals with the providential role of God the Father working through human history and raises a central but forbidden topic of the Tudor age, the question as to what are the true sanctions of authority, and how far it might be possible or desirable to seek to resolve clashes between the Christian conscience and the laws of society.

The writings that emerged during his lifetime treat of the same theme, but prepared as they were for publication by their author, they show a more controlled amalgam of those contradictory qualities indispensable in any age for a Christian bishop, the qualities of the serpent and the dove.

17

Survival

THE Marian exiles have been described as executing "one of the most astute manoeuvres that has ever carried a defeated political party to ultimate power." Five English merchants who had connections with Protestants on the continent paid for the exiles' propaganda campaign and for the education abroad of a number of students of divinity "who it was intended, should one day become the clergy of a reformed Anglican Communion."[1]

Yet the key to political—if not "ultimate"—power remained with those of the legitimized descendants of Henry VII who survived to inherit it. In Lancashire, the lieutenancy remained with the Stanley family, who negotiated this crisis as one among so many others in their long history. Their behavior as Mary's reign drew to a close exemplifies the wisdom of maximizing one's own options while foreclosing those of others. Thus, the ecclesiastical center of southeast Lancashire—the most vulnerable part of the region under Mary—was the Manchester College of vicars choral, which had been dissolved in 1547. Ten years later, it was being used as a prison for suspected Protestant heretics and was even in danger of being revived. Lord Derby bought it. The innocent and delightful Laurence Vaux was installed as Warden and as Lord Derby's inquisitor of choice. No George Cotes or Stephen Gardiner, he was "well beloved and highly honoured" by his notional victims in the memory of one of these, the future Presbyterian Hollingworth.[2] As soon as Mary died, prisoners and priests (the latter with all the sacred vessels of the college) were let go, and the Stanleys were left with a handsome town house and barrack for their retainers. Ever up-to-date, members of this survivalist clan would not only plot for the release of Mary Queen of Scots but in due course be numbered among the commissioners at her trial.[3]

The Lancashire divines who went into exile under Mary, and the Lancashire merchants who financed them, had a far narrower set of options.

Martin Heaton, no doubt named after his maternal grandfather, Sir Martin Bowes, lord mayor of London, was born at Heaton Hall, Deane, in 1552. His mother Joanna, who did not long survive his birth, dedicated him to the service of God and the Reformed Church. His father George was one of

119

the five merchant "sustainers" of the Marian exiles. Under the Elizabethan settlement, which his father's money and his yeoman neighbour's blood had helped to pay for, Martin rose to become dean of Winchester, and in due course was persuaded by Elizabeth to accept the see of Ely (long kept vacant and bled of funds by her) on condition that he signed away its remaining rich manors. As in the case of Whitgift, Elizabeth favored a prelate who had his own money to spend.

Plump and hospitable, Heaton drew praise for his sermons from King James, and his marble effigy (complete with cope) was spared by the Cromwellian soldiery who spared very little of the figure work of his cathedral. One may wonder, however, whether his family's investment in Protestant education got value for outlay in his case. He is recorded as a benefactor of the Bodleian Library, to the tune of £40, not a very great sum, even then.[4]

On the debit side, the Heatons seem to have spread their financial resources, and their energies, rather too thinly. As early as the 1570s, their Deane properties were being claimed—and violently invaded—by their financial rivals and neighbors, the Andertons. From 1592 the Andertons were devoting themselves to Catholic education and propaganda.[5] By the time Heaton was enthroned at Ely (1599)—or not long after—mass was being celebrated again at Heaton Hall.[6]

Thomas Heaton, another relative and another sustainer of the Marian exiles, died in poverty after expending his fortune endeavoring to promote the German port of Emden as a secure base for Protestant traders. Margaret of Parma's policy of granting a measure of tolerance to Protestant merchants within her own Catholic sphere of influence may be said to have helped to ruin him, among others.[7] Like his relative Thomas Lever and other Janeites, he dimly foreshadows a Protestant revolution that would not come home to England till 1688–9. He had been a friend of Grindal, who had at one time shown an interest in the Emden scheme, and who in his will of 1583 forgave him a debt of £50.[8] Grindal himself, of course, like all other minor pieces in the European game of Pythagoras, or "battle of numbers," was not put on the board to modify the absolute supremacy (on the board) of his own monarch. The whole point of the rules was to achieve overwhelming superiority against the rival side, so that the winning prince might celebrate "a triumph" over the rival monarch and the board be cleared as by some providential hand for another variant of the same game.

In 1568, having abdicated in Scotland, Mary Stuart fled south into the prison of the neighboring kingdom of which she was heiress and, in Catholic eyes, queen. Till her execution in 1587, England was now occupied by a pair of rival monarchs, each claiming to be "exempt from human jurisdiction and subject only to the judgment of God."[9] Bolton's Marian exiles were useful in such a context, but they were not to be permitted to interfere very much with the rules of the game. James Pilkington would serve as bishop of Durham, on the Scottish border, aided by his two archdeacons: his brother John in County Durham and Ralph Lever in Northumberland. Ecclesiastical pre-ferment within the diocese was also found for Laurence Pilkington and for John and Thomas Lever, among other family connections. This pool of talent made Durham's first Protestant episcopacy possible, if not credible.[10]

James would be allowed to help found a grammar school at Darlington in his diocese and to found another one at Rivington whose governor would be his brother George, the head of the family. Erasmus and Petrarch were studied there as models of Latin prose (the international language) and there was Greek for older boys, and singing was available as an option. There was a scrupulous avoidance, in the prayers drawn up for the school, of anything suggestive of predestinationist pedantry. By the time of its founder's death, the school had 114 pupils, many of them (in agreeable contrast, it may be, to Bolton Grammar School) drawn from the local gentry.[11]

The center of this propaganda system was to have been St. John's College, Cambridge, which was accorded the supervision of Rivington Grammar School. Preparations were thus being made to provide a network of educated Protestants loyal to the new regime.

But Elizabeth wanted loyalty only on her own terms. Cambridge was the center of the Protestant web being spun to protect and hamper her, and there she accordingly struck. On the eve of her visit of 1564, Leonard Pilkington was still master of John's and Regius Professor of Divinity, in substitution for his brother. On Elizabeth's orders, he was relieved of both these duties. James Pilkington was manipulated into suggesting the next best thing for John's, and—with disastrous consequences for the Protestant cause—Cecil snapped up his suggestion of Longworth for master, a blatant and nervous rebel who proved almost too easy to eliminate, in due course. Leonard Pilkington withdrew to the family diocese, eventually finding a niche as treasurer of Durham Cathedral. Unlike Longworth, he was a firm and suc-cessful administrator, feasted by his old college whenever he returned. But meanwhile Elizabeth's visit to Cambridge was a success. She promised to found a new college (words are cheap). She excused herself from having to sit through a tragedy by Sophocles.

Pilkington's diocese was reduced to order by similar royal methods. In 1569 the Catholic majority in that part of the world, under their traditional leaders the earls of Westmorland and Northumberland, were beginning to turn towards Mary. The Privy Council got wind of possible Spanish landings on the Durham coast. Elizabeth's lieutenants in the north—the earls of Sus-sex and Bedford—urged gentle measures. Time, winter weather, readiness and absence of panic would soon restore this volatile region to loyalty.[12]

But Elizabeth wanted loyalty only on her own terms. She arranged—against advice—for the potentially rebellious earls to be summoned to York to submit themselves to whatever she chose to do with them. Their honor forbade this, and blatant and nervous rebels they became, to be eliminated in due course.

Pilkington, in "constant ill health," as Grindal describes him, was in London during the insurrection. He was, however, allowed to petition Cecil on behalf of his defeated diocese now under martial law. "The country is in great misery. . . . [F]ew innocent are left to try the guilty," he pleads. Without the queen's pardon the country will be "desert": "if I go down in displeasure, my presence shall do more harm than good," and "if the forfeited lands be bestowed among . . . strangers," the people will have no leaders, and there will be no freeholders able or willing to do service in peace or war.[13] The bishop is here directing towards his sovereign much the same sentiments as those addressed by the priest to Oedipus, at the beginning of Sophocles's play:

> Let us not have to remember your reign
> As beginning in prosperity only to stumble later:
> Establish the state in safety!
> With happy augury you blessed
> Us once: be equal to yourself!
> For if you will be prince, as now you are,
> It will be better not to reign
> Over a desert kingdom: a tower, a ship, is nothing
> Emptied of the men who shared a life within it![14]

A hint was enough. Northumberland was executed, and Westmorland died in exile. Their heirs were deprived, the passionate loyalty of the region to its old families was discarded, and the queen took the land, which was farmed out to absentees. Freeholders—those rich enough to purchase the queen's mercy—were let go. Her northern advisers begged especially for mercy for "men of the meaner sort," but these were not worth anything except as examples of terror. She ordered hundreds of them to be hanged. And yet, as Grindal understood it, the rebels themselves "put no one to death."

Pilkington summed up the dilemma to Henry Bullinger: "The world cannot bear two suns, much less can the kingdom endure two queens or two religions."[15] Yet, leafing through his Sophocles, he might have asked himself whether the survival of two princes, or even of one, was worth so many other lives. In the Athenian play, the prince is the source of the evil he pretends to heal, and so perhaps with Elizabeth. It is not difficult to collect from Pilkington's *Nehemiah* any number of quasi-Sophoclean aphorisms against arbitrary power: "Common things would be done with common consent"; against princely irresponsibility: "The people are worthy no less praise than the rulers: for they are as ready to obey as the other to command"; and in favor of respect for humanity as being something quite other than pieces in a game: "Man is God's good creature, and to be beloved of all sorts."

If the arbitrary sacrifice of the people was the lifeblood of monarchs, what right had monarchy to claim the special protection of Providence? As a matter of common observation, did monarchy have such protection? Was it not strange that "Poor cities in Germany, compassed about with their ene- mies, dare reform religion thoroughly, . . . yet this noble realm, which all princes have feared, dare not"?[16]

18

Stability

"F<small>ATHER</small> of Heaven have mercy"—a fragment from the opening of the English litany—are the words recorded as Marsh's last utterance in the fire. It was the sixteenth day of the pontificate of Marcellus II, which had yet six more days to run. This pope is more often remembered for the epochal *Missa Papae Marcelli* of Palestrina,[1] who was indebted for his musical education to Claude Goudimel, founder of Rome's first school of music and one of the many thousands of French Protestants massacred by opportunist Roman Catholics in 1572.

Thus celebrated above a pattern of human agony with which he seems to have nothing to do, Marcellus provides one model of God the Father, and Palestrina's mass one model of the *bene esse,* or "blessedness," an eternal music rising above the contradictions of a dying world. Not to question, but to celebrate an unquestioned, eternal pattern: that was the capacity the English surrendered in favour of the Reformation.

Marsh's own *bene esse,* on the other hand, may not improperly be called "Socratic," in that it begins with the refusal to pretend to know. At the same time, it would rather doubt the evidence of the senses than certain moral convictions of its own nature. It does not despise the attempt to make common sense of everyday objects or pretend that the material world is other than it is, but it refuses to regard material common sense as an answer to its own desire for meaning.

There are of course great differences. Marsh endeavors to obey what he calls the Holy Spirit because for him it comes with the promises of Christ, whereas for the Socrates of the *Phaedo* loyalty to the λόγος is much more abstract. What matters, however, is that for both of them mere tradition must often yield to the fresh insights of honest intelligence and that there is no authority that can prevent this divine process. Marsh believes biblical texts dealing with the afterlife contain news of actualities, whereas for Socrates the myth of Er's otherworldly experiences may be only a story. Both, however, are aware that in such matters all language is figurative and that there is no human group who have knowledge that is exclusive, exploitable, yet incommunicable. Both rely on the ordinary decencies of their culture in avoiding the fanciful priorities of cultists, of whatever kind.

Most particularly, for the Socrates of the *Phaedo* it is important, but not very important, to notice that when a straight stick is partly dipped in water so that it looks bent, it does not as a matter of fact "turn into" a bent stick. Such commonsense touchstones are no more than checks that we are not devoting ourselves to trivial delusions before passing on to the ethical and spiritual questions that await the exploration of the eternal soul. Similarly, Marsh is aware of something most English Protestants insisted on: that the wafer does not "turn into" the body of Christ, for all the words and postures of the priest. For Marsh, the Eucharist is a corporate celebration of all the mysteries of being, physical and spiritual, commanded by Christ to the world's end and guaranteed to bring health to body and soul. It is important, but not very important, to notice that it is not a conjuring trick.

In all these respects, Pilkington is similar to Marsh. His viewpoint may be further clarified by contrast with Luther, who in his *De Servo Arbitrio* asserted God to be unknowable, yet to have provided man with a perfectly clear set of rules in the Bible.[2] For Pilkington, the opposite of these assertions is true: God is present with us as a familiar friend at all places and times, while the Bible is a collection of Hebrew and Greek writings the very text of which is not absolute, for as with all other texts there are conflicting readings. The *bene esse* is therefore neither "knowing" nor "not knowing," but "finding out" in the presence of One who is no captious sophister. Nurture, development, gradual increase of knowledge, and mutual trust—such is Pilkington's view of God's relationship with the universe, insofar as he feels able to subject that relationship to rational scrutiny. Such therefore is his rationale of stability in the human commonwealth. When Lever persuaded Elizabeth to take the title of "Governor" of the Church, he was probably aware of the word's descent from the *kubernetes* or "governor" of the human soul in Plato's *Phaedrus*. In the same spirit he speaks of Christ's soul-governance in terms of "allure." Pilkington, even more familiar with Plato's work, assigns Elizabeth a role comparable with that of Diotima, the kindly instructress of Socrates in the *Symposium*. This is the pattern he wishes to see substituted for that of the Renaissance papacy. In the second century A.D., he says, Pope Eleutherius reminded King Lucius of Britain that a king was "God's vicar" on earth. Elizabeth, too, it seems, must be God's vicar, the representative of a nurturing, sympathetic, and intelligent god. Without naming her, it is clear that in her he hopes to see realised some of those divine qualities which in human terms are seen as maternal. Rather clumsy if offered merely as flattery, the passage connects with others in his writings to suggest a desire to escape from any false equation between masculinity and the divine:

God made kings and queens to be nurses to his church. The nurse's duty is to feed, guide, and cherish the child; yea, to correct, instruct and reform him when he does a fault. She must not be a dry nurse, but with the two paps of the new testament and old feed her children; she must teach him to go; when he is fallen, take him up again; and give him such wholesome meat, that she may and dare taste and try it herself. God grant princes thus to be nurses, and not stepmothers.[3]

Pilkington believes in predestination, in the sense that he is sure God is in charge of history, despite human error and crime. He is also anxious to stress that man cannot save himself or do anything good of his own will without God. At the same time, he is adamant that God can never be regarded as responsible for sin. He is in agreement with and, perhaps, influenced by Plato's warning against any tendency to anthropomorphize divine powers that are, if worth our respect at all, infinitely better than we are. In the Christian context, this means that Pilkington refuses to see Christ and the Father as different gods: the latter, also, may be defined as showing reasonableness and restraint, as never offering a threat without time for repentance and mercy. His laws are the laws of nature and require all our intelligence for their observance. "Give place to nature, fear God," he says, as though these were equivalents. As for superstitions about such things as burial rites and their power to affect divine decisions, "Socrates bade bury him so as were most easy for his friends" is a typical touchstone of his. Thus, to set land aside for a graveyard and to keep it decent is rational: to pretend to "hallow" it with mumbo jumbo is absurd.[4]

He holds the doctrine of human degeneracy—a corollary of predestination—in a peculiarly humanist form. Far from thinking that human degeneracy requires repressive antihumane measures for its control, it is precisely the futile resort to antihumane measures throughout history that is itself one of the major evidences for human degeneracy. That the poor will not amend for the fury of the powerful is not surprising: what is wonderful is that the powerful have not yet learned this. Whereas for some devotees of Original Sin—Roman Catholic as well as Protestant—human degeneracy implies the continual necessity of the rod in teaching, for Pilkington what is predestined (for it is a matter of common observation) is the uselessness of the rod for promoting learning. Spare the rod, if you would not spoil the child.[5]

It is permissible to call him a "Calvinist," but only with the proviso that this tells us very little about him. He is equally a Hellenist and humanist in the Erasmus tradition. He was certainly much more at home at Cambridge than at Geneva. Perhaps his greatest moment came in the early 1540s with the delivery of a well-received series of lectures on Acts in the same university schools where Erasmus had lectured a generation before. He would always be alert to the subtleties of language and impatient with the dogmatic mentality. He more than once refers to "those whom" God "hath chosen in Christ before the world was made," yet he differs from later intellectual Calvinists, such as Perkins, by denying the possibility of individual certainty, either of damnation or redemption. He also shows none of Perkins's tendency to reduce God merely to the Father of power, devaluing the surprises of the Spirit and the compassion of the Son. Clearly, for Pilkington there can be no such thing as philosophic free will—otherwise different results might follow from identical causes, something that could happen only in a nonsensical universe whose laws existed only to be suspended—but a practical sense of free will is enforced on almost every page. Tellingly, he never refers to Calvin in such discussions, but to Bernard of Clairvaux, who was content to set grace and free will together as an unresolved paradox.[6]

An essay, giving the main arguments for predestination in stiff student Latin, is regarded as an early work of James Pilkington (though it might possibly be by one of his brothers). Everything he chose to publish in English must be regarded as offering a considerable revision to this early piece, which, in any case, contrasts almost to the point of contradiction with the verbal and intellectual suppleness of his later Latin pieces. In one of these—a letter of advice to Andrew Kingsmill, his young brother-in-law, written in 1564— the bishop chooses to argue that theology can provide as great an intellectual challenge and risk as the study of law (which Andrew seems to prefer). Pilkington "tempts" him with the dangerous challenge of the two *clarissima lumina*—"brightest luminaries"—of the recent past. Peter Martyr has sufficient subtlety to investigate the due weight of serious things, though he is a trifle inclined to get carried away with himself (*facilitate sua fluit*), whereas Calvin needs to be read attentively, especially since *exlex est et devius*. This can be read as a gentle reproof of his style—"He is a law to himself and so discursive!"—or else as a grave warning against his content: "He is beyond the pale, quite astray." The reader must choose, after contending with Calvin for himself. Genuflection does not come into it.

Here we have the essence of Pilkington's notion of stability in church and state as well as the terms on which he supported Elizabeth. Conformity of the heart depends on the freedom to "find out." This in turn cannot happen with safety and for sufficient numbers of people unless there is an adequately endowed establishment able to advise with integrity and without undue pressure from philistines in or out of office. It is a gentlemanly ideal of enlightened usefulness, and it is perhaps more than a coincidence that by far the most likely classical source for the amusedly dissentive adjective—*exlex*— is that epitome of good style and good sense, Horace's *De Arte Poetica*.[7]

At his death, his fellow exile and fellow prelate, Bishop Horne of Winchester, described Pilkington as *episcopus Dunelmiae vigilantissimus*. At the same time he reaffirmed his own allegiance to Elizabeth as one hating popery from her infancy, yet also never likely to provide an opening for "Lutheranism," by which he meant the arrangement whereby the personal views of the prince prevailed absolutely in doctrine and ceremonies. Horne himself seems covertly to have fostered Presbyterianism as the best bulwark against such a development.[8] As it had shown under Henry and would show again under James and Charles, the Church of England was liable to degenerate into the condition Horne feared. Pilkington, intellectually if not administra- tively "most vigilant," raises the question of what he calls a discipline of "seniors" in a passage of his *Nehemiah*. Typically, and briefly, he combines great sympathy for some of the disaffections of Presbyterians with sharp doubts about practicalities and principle: doubts which turn on the, for him not negotiable, matter of loyalty to the "prince." For him, such loyalty was not an abstraction but a personal decision to cooperate with the regime of Elizabeth.

Pilkington's fierce belief in the necessity for mildness emerges from his writings. Much more than a zealot of ambiguous loyalty like Horne, he may be seen as a victim, as well as an implement, of the Elizabethan regime. It was Horne who, as Dean of Durham from 1551 to 1553 and again from 1559 to 1561, did much to stir up the resentment against Protestantism that Pilkington then inherited as bishop. It was Horne who pruned or dismantled a number of Durham's monuments and who shocked local feeling by permit- ting women to advance beyond the very westernmost part of the cathedral to which their presence had hitherto been confined.[9] While Pilkington would have concurred in essence with these changes, his character was much more suited to the role of pacifier that he was now called upon to play. Unfortu- nately, of course, this role was now virtually unplayable.

Like the rest of his family, the Pilkingtons of Rivington, pastoral gentry and poor relations of the flamboyantly ambitious Pilkingtons of Pilkington, the bishop would prefer not to have to take sides. Apart from a couple of "divorces" (of persons betrothed in childhood, by medieval custom), the Pilkingtons of Rivington offer little to historical sensation seekers, from the thirteenth century onwards. A Pilkington of Pilkington might murder a royal favorite, marry a fabulously wealthy heiress, die charging at Agincourt, or glitter in close proximity to John O'Gaunt or Richard III. No doubt the Rivington Pilkingtons got to hear of such things.

Bosworth was truly a battle between rival monarchs, for numerous local rivalries were settled there: of which not the least significant was the contest between Stanleys and Pilkingtons (of Pilkington) for the control of northwest England. Pilkingtons lost, and the Stanleys took their land. Not Rivington: those smaller Pilkingtons were left to sink or swim. The not very satisfactory arrangements by which they held their land could no longer be guaranteed by the power of the Pilkingtons of Pilkington. True, these latter, even after attainder, still held rich estates in five counties, by virtue of an inheritance acquired by a marriage of 1383. They were politically defunct, however, and in the reign of Henry VIII their male line died out.[10] The Rivington Pilking- tons, partly simply to survive, partly because now on them devolved the opportunity and responsibility of maintaining a name some centuries older than the Norman Conquest, emerged for the first time into national life for one final generation.

When Elizabeth succeeded, Thomas Lever, from his fastness at Aarau, joined with Englishmen at Geneva in demurring in advance from any ungodly ceremonies Elizabeth might choose to favor. Pilkington, at Frankfurt, headed the party who felt it prudent to affirm their support for the Tudors at this delicate stage of their providential destiny. He organized and, perhaps, composed the crucial offer to "submit to such orders as should be established by authority, being not of themselves wicked."[11] This maneuver suggests a desire to be placatory, but not to the point of taking sides. With the "masterly ambiguity"[12] for which the Elizabethan settlement has been praised, it left open to negotiation the question of exactly what constituted "authority" and retained a conscience clause to cover in advance any withdrawal of support. It was not an intellectual and moral submission to Elizabeth, as of divine right, whatever she did, it was an offer to cooperate with such lawful arrangements as might be made, for as long as they appeared to be divinely approved. It was an altogether more serious and delicate measuring of royal pretensions than the almost irrelevant fleabite of the Geneva "protest."

Most important of all, it was the opening shot of a holding campaign against contemporary polarities and their nemesis of moral and political nihilism. In 1570 Pius V absolved Elizabeth's subjects of their loyalty with a bull so generalised in expression as to be meaningless except as a gesture of nihilism: "They shall not dare to obey her or any of her laws." Decent Catholics ignored it and also failed to claim, in any significant numbers, the celestial "merit" promised them by papal secretaries of state for the Christian enterprise of murdering Elizabeth. Her own archbishop of Canterbury, the brittle Calvinist Whitgift, had no better ethics to offer: he was the only one of her Counsellors to support a scheme for the privy assassination of Mary Queen of Scots.[13] Quasi-constitutional means had to be found for her removal: a bad omen, as Elizabeth well knew, for the future of personal monarchy itself.

High above the shrine of St. Werburgh in Chester Lady Chapel is still to be seen a roof boss depicting Thomas à Becket, the pope's "stinking martyr and traitor to his prince,"[14] as Pilkington calls him, for whose murder Henry II was forced to do penance. Henry Bradshaw's medieval system of stability ultimately depended on the state's willingness to defer to the Church, a pattern exemplified virtually for the last time (for even Mary spent part of her reign as an official enemy of the pope) when Henry VIII accepted the title "Defender of the Faith" from the Holy Father in 1521. It is not surprising to see Pilkington rejecting this old order, yet in desiring to see the secular arm strengthened at the expense of ecclesiastical arrogance, he was not necessarily anxious to strengthen the monarchy as such, nor was he necessarily subtracting from the true dignity of the episcopate. Secular power, he recognized, cannot be compelled to obey spiritual authority without having its own

reasons for doing so. Retelling the improving story of Theodosius's submission to St. Ambrose, Pilkington tartly comments that he wonders whom to
praise more, the good bishop who "durst rebuke" his lord or the good emperor
who "willingly submitted." For Pilkington, the overworked story is not an
argument about the relative potency of institutions, but a (rather unusual)
example of human integrities finding their match.[15]

God shows his omnipotence through gentle leading and through spiritual
impulses that provide arguments for the heart. This is the only invincible
power in the universe, and it is the duty of a bishop to be the "scout watch"
of this divine strategy. Its victories are not won by force, however. Issuing
a "Confutation" of an anti-Protestant pamphlet posted about Chester by
Bishop Bonner's Welsh chaplain, John Morwen, in 1561, Pilkington tells of
his own encounter with Bonner. Henry's bishop of London, who would later
be a driving force of the Marian persecutions, was at that time in prison
under Edward VI. "*Ad regendam ecclesiam,*" he affirmed, from Acts 20 in
the Vulgate translation—"to rule the church as a king"—is the duty enjoined
on ecclesiastical authorities. "No," countered Pilkington, remembering his
own Cambridge lectures on the Greek text,

> if ye will be judged by the word, the Greek word is ποιμαίνειν, which signifies
> *to feed,* as the shepherd feeds his sheep, . . . a simple kind of rule and authority,
> as shepherds have. . . . Also, 'I am the good Shepherd,' says Christ; where likewise
> is the same Greek word placed. . . . His kingdom was not of this world; but he
> came to teach his Father's will. Likewise he taught his apostles not to challenge
> this superiority, saying 'The princes of the people have rule over them, but it shall
> not be so among you; but he that would be greatest, shall be the least.'"[16]

This dovelike gentleness in Pilkington could be deployed with serpentine
adroitness. He was one of the Commissioners for Cambridge of 1559. In
1560 he undertook the duty of preaching a sermon of restitution for Professors Bucer and Phagius. He was careful to say the least he could about them,
in order to achieve the greatest possible contrast with the extravagancies of
1557. Poor Phagius published nothing but translations from Hebrew and
Chaldee, it seems, and died soon after reaching England. As for Bucer, it
was true that he was married, but it seems that Pope Paul III, a dozen years
before, was of opinion that, while there are weighty arguments in favor of
married priests' setting aside their wives, the balance of Catholic authority
is in favor of their keeping their marriage vows, once contracted. Dare one
add anything to this?

The master of understatement provides an epigram—naturally, a modest
one—that puts the political gloss on his method of "least said, soonest
mended." This takes the form of a calculated throwaway on "Charles the
fifth (than whom all Christendom had not a more prudent prince, nor the
church of Christ almost a sorer enemy)."[17] Note the past tense. Clearly—

and the message was being put out in various ways for the benefit of papists at home and abroad as part of the calculated policy of Elizabeth's early years—England's new prince, the more than adequate successor to Charles's cousin and daughter-in-law, is now in a position to demonstrate fully Christian prudence, healing the sores of Christ's church with astutely applied balms and a ready fund of soft, but quite adequately deadly answers for turning away wrath. In Cambridge terms, the Elizabethan settlement has taken its place—and that a noble one—among the states of Christendom.

Cecil, Parker, Pilkington, and the other commissioners made sure that changes in the university went through with as little drama as possible; when Pilkington replaced his Marian predecessor as master of St. John's, the "proceedings were conducted with a courtesy that was more than nominal."

On the other hand, Pilkington erased much of the Romish figure-work from the college chapel and elsewhere. Yet even here (it was Secretary Cecil's college, too, and a model to follow) selection rather than vandalism was the method. The chapel has been swept away by the far greater desecration of a Victorian rebuilding, but the tomb effigy of Archdeacon Ashton remains intact, a rare survival, as does the lovely carving of flowers and fanciful heraldic animals over the main gate. The principal figure of St. John, apparently removed but not destroyed either in Lever's time or Pilkington's, was replaced in 1662.[18]

More damage to the Anglican establishment was done by a different kind of rescue: among the bright young men admitted as fellows of John's under Pilkington's brief mastership was Thomas Cartwright, the future Presbyterian.[19]

On 10 April 1561, under the earliest rib vault in the western world, anticipator of all the glories of Gothic that came after, James Pilkington was placed on the "highest throne of Christendom," as the cathedra of the bishop of Durham is known, a vertiginous stone structure completed in 1381, the year that reverberated to Wycliffe's lecture against transubstantiation at Oxford, the death knell in England of the Gothic universe. The first Protestant to sit there, he was its first occupant to be overpowered by an incompatible décor which the Anglican Church has never lived up to, never escaped, and never had the finances to maintain.

Durham, with its cathedral, castle, and monastery, has been described by a twentieth-century expert as comparable only to the papal palace at Avignon or the imperial castle at Prague.[20] Its prince-bishop enjoyed by tradition enormous power. He was count palatine and earl, chief judge and temporal ruler of northeast England, as well as its supreme ecclesiastical authority, with powers of patronage and excommunication. But the Tudors knew how to cut prelates down to size. In 1536 the question of final authority in the administration of justice was settled in the Crown's favor, and in 1537 the diocese was placed under the authority of the Council of the North. Durham

House, the London palace adorned by Wolsey in his time of favor, was annexed; Durham College, the Oxford endowment reserved for Durham monks, was extinguished and its premises appropriated for another foundation. Under Edward, Pilkington's predecessor Tunstall had been robbed wholesale, as well as imprisoned.[21] Elizabeth would make sure her new appointee incurred any obloquy that was going for the failure of her policies (which were not his), while depriving him of the income to make them work. The ghost of a feudal anomaly must be kept in place, at economy rate.

Pilkington refused the use of miter and crozier and demonstrated his aspiration towards secularization and modernization by granting the tiny boroughs, clustered abjectly round his own massive but now much less significant domain, the hopeful status of an incorporated city in 1566. Several trade companies of the city were incorporated at the same time. He was forward-looking in other ways, having a generous view of the potential role of women as teachers of Christianity, for instance, that was in glaring contrast with the cult of misogyny fostered for centuries at Durham along with the sacred bones of that prince of woman-haters, St. Cuthbert.

Such things cut no ice with Elizabeth. She knew the motto, *Divide and Rule*. Pilkington was provided with a dean in the shape of William Whittingham, an opponent of female authority in church and state so fanatical as to be an embarrassment to her in any other place. And Pilkington's dreamy vision of a modern church of the prosperous city, with the laity, including women, holding positions of dignity and responsibility, received an icy check from Elizabeth's personal order of 9 August 1561, banning the very presence of "families of young women and children" from the sacred precincts of all colleges, cathedrals, and other "societies of learned men professing study and prayer."[22] Exclusion, not mission, was to be the function of her establishment.

While her Puritan intellectuals well knew that Elizabeth was their best guarantor of stability, they might also have suspected that one of the prices of monarchy itself was a reliance on antiquated modes of thought and behavior that, in the longer term, were the enemies of stability.

19

Restraint

Thanks to the pioneering generosity of Lord Leverhulme, whose father was raised at Pilkington's grammar school, the "grand, but not forbidding"[1] little world of Rivington is still a place of beauty and refreshment, public ownership having succeeeded to that of its squires. The middlemen, or grubcapitalists, those "merchants of mischief that go betwixt the bark and the tree,"[2] as Thomas Lever called them, may ruin other woods and hills.

Pilkington, too, led a charmed existence by comparison with most of his contemporaries and coreligionists. We are told that the Rivington branch of his ancient family "had early embraced the doctrines of the reformed religion." Born to a godly inheritance, there are wistful questionings in him that never venture to displace a devolved faith. At other times, he shows the nervous determination of the sensitive. One suspects that he held the legacy of his parents' convictions all the more dear because of a greater sense of his own weakness, as compared with some of his brothers. (There were twelve surviving children; James could not bear cold, and spent some of the crises of his life being ill.)

He may have found in Virgil a kind of stoicism natural also to the interplay between his own nature and upbringing. Observing history's triumphs, he feels much more deeply the universality of its defeat, and yet he refuses the indulgence of despair. It might be argued that for him, as for Lever, the English Church was never more than half-reformed. But there is a deep conviction in him, deeper than Protestantism or Christianity itself, against hoping, believing, or attempting too much.

His home background and his classical education made it inevitable that "Nothing in excess"—the motto placed over the Delphic shrine of the shepherd-god Apollo—should be his watchword. Its corollary is also deeply true for him: we must often be content with oracular ambiguities of expression in our quest for the truth. These qualities, and his scholarly interest in the history of liturgies, made him a natural choice as one of Elizabeth's Prayer Book Commissioners. Like Marsh, he recognized many valid "orders of ministering the communion," provided priest and people prayed together in their own tongue, and all received for the comfort of their souls. He would have been amused, and perhaps reassured, to note that when the Parker Society began to research the history of Elizabeth's Prayer Book, they were unable to locate a single surviving copy actually "answering in all points to the Book" authorized by Parliament. But what pleases scholars is rarely good enough for political enforcers.

Pilkington seems to have gone along with and perhaps influenced the Thirty-Nine Articles as a tolerable compromise. His signature comes fourth after Archbishops Parker and Young and Grindal of London on a Christmas Eve petition of 1566, urging the queen not to veto the Commons' decision in favor of their implementation. But, beyond a certain point, he would become almost uncontrollably enraged by any attempt to enforce detailed ordinances governing faith and practice. A humorous but urgent letter of 1565 from Parker to Cecil—both of whom knew Pilkington from Cambridge days—makes this clear. Cecil has been trailing a new policy of considerably tightening up on uniformity of ceremonies. Parker objects to being made the scapegoat for a "seek and destroy" fishing operation he would rather had never been started. Lightly veiled in deferential language, the gist of the archbishop's anxiety reveals itself to the modern reader, as it must have done to Cecil. The gossip is, he warns, that the queen is indifferent; that men blame me, not you, only because they need your honor's patronage; that honest Grindal is of course unwilling; and that dear Pilkington—you know what he is like—has vowed to give up his diocese rather than issue any new demands.[3]

This insight is important. Pilkington—now charged with policing his charming, tiresome, new prebend Thomas Lever as well as the ghastly Whittingham—has almost had as much as he can bear. Sensitivity, scholarship, and those powers of intellect and persuasion the new regime has taken and used, must now be unlearned and the energies of a lifetime must be deflected into hectoring advocacy of the shallow pedantic ordinances of worldly fools. It was at this point that the drive that got Pilkington to the "highest throne in Christendom" turned inward. He confined himself more and more to working with small groups at his residence at Bishop Auckland. The monarchy that killed Marsh, and deprived Lever of his raison d'être, made it unwise from about 1566 for James Pilkington to publish anymore. He founded Rivington Grammar School in that year, however.

He had refused, or been refused, Winchester:[4] perhaps because he objected to signing away much of the see's income to Elizabeth; perhaps because she had no intention of seeing Pilkington's wife, a Hampshire gentlewoman with connections in the neighborhood, playing the great lady where Mary and Philip had spent their nuptials. And so they were sent to Durham, and Elizabeth bled his finances anyway. The local gentry, almost to a man, hated everything to do with Protestantism. Great numbers of the common people in remote areas were virtually in a pre-Christian state.[5] To a native of the western Pennines, Hampshire might appear almost excessively sweet—the diocese included the Channel Islands, which geographically speaking are part of France—but by the same token northeastern England might seem like a desolate parody of home. Like Nehemiah, the new prince-bishop felt abandoned where "out of sight is out of mind and soon forgotten, in an old, torn, and decayed city, a rude people and poor country, where he should not live quietly for his enemies, but take pains to build himself a house, and the city where he would dwell." Mary's reign had been terrible: "But alas! the fiery faggots of those days were not so grievous then, as the slanderous tongues be now."[6]

Weakness of the flesh and the more tender passages of the Old Testament fed Pilkington's sentimentality in his exile at Durham and Coldharbour, his London residence. The same weakness had been braced, in his continental exile, by Swiss doctors and the example of Sophoclean tragedy. Writing from Geneva to Rodolph Gualter at Zurich, he surely had the Oedipus plays in mind: "You have formerly acted a part in this tragedy. . . . [W]e are now brought upon the stage, that, being humbled by adversity, we may discover him, whom in our prosperity we did not acknowledge as we ought, to be a kind and merciful father." Just as Oedipus, amid the scenery of Sophocles's native Colonus, is finally reconciled to Apollo, so in some heavenly Rivington the pattern of the universe will again be as clear to Pilkington as it was in childhood. He supplies his own chorus: "We commonly say of ourselves that the English will never let well alone."[7]

But if he disliked the excesses of Protestantism, the same doctrine of restraint was simply fatal to the papal supremacy: "There hath been no man so holy (except Christ Jesus) but he has been deceived." Any claim beyond that was just nonsense, and hubris, too. Yet—by the same line of reasoning— what is good in the Roman tradition is to be embraced. Pope Gregory the Great is a handy authority against the irrationalities of lesser popes. Aquinas is a principal authority against Romanist excess: "St. Thomas . . . writes that 'it is superstition when a man is too holy.'" Aquinas of course writes in Latin, a language which is not very friendly to ideas, in Pilkington's eyes. He reminds his readers that the English borrowing of the Latin word "superstition" is apt to be confusing. Pilkington has almost a genius for conveying subtle ideas with clarity and charm. The explanation of the "two Greek words signifying this superstition" that he then gives (in his Confutation) is of a sort to make one wish that his publications had been much more numerous.[8] The Bible, of course, is the Christians' chief source of belief: but perhaps especially in its regard, we must show restraint, warns Pilkington. Whereas Lawrence Saunders used a remark of St. Paul in arguing that Rome had the wrong gospel and his own coreligionists the right one, Pilkington draws on the same remark in arguing that Rome's gospel does not go wrong, exactly, but simply goes too far. Its excesses defy belief.[9] Again, the same passage of

Nehemiah that drew from Pilkington the tearful effusion quoted above has also a puzzling omission in the logic of its narrative that draws this touch of Ockham's razor from him: "we may content ourselves to be ignorant of it, as of all . . . unnecessary truths." In the same spirit, he declines to join Bradford and other codifiers of an alternative theological system in their great project of "disproving" transubstantiation, preferring to stay with the negative observation that it cannot be proved from any text a thousand years old.[10]

Pilkington is at his most delightful when—in conversational mood—he develops the theme of restraint as an antidote to partisanship. Thus, in another passage of the *Confutation*, having acknowledged Cranmer as a "holy martyr" and shown up his predecessors at Canterbury—Augustine, and Anselm—as arrogant stalking horses of papal supremacy, he nevertheless concludes that it is those great theological pioneers who are "of our religion in some opinion of the greatest matters, more than Cranmer."[11] At moments like this, Pilkington seems the soul of the English Church and the enemy of its manipulators.

Man can learn from the humbler creation. Pilkington quotes with delight the remark of the illiterate Antony, the popular saint whose shrines provided a refuge in lonely places in Lancashire and elsewhere: "all the creatures of God are my books." Clever people should perhaps be forbidden the Bible: simple people hardly need it, he adds. To find a way to read it is to learn also how to live.

And so with prayer. Public worship should be comely and dignified, never excessive. God is "our heavenly father." Dare we address him in anything less appropriate than "familiar and reverent talk"? Anticipating the Quaker tradition, he notes that the most intense prayer is silent. Moses was so earnest "in his sorrowful meditation, that the Lord said to him, 'Why criest thou to me?' yet we read not that he spake any word at all." Learn from the reticence of the animals. Sin has natural consequences that represent God's punishment: but "it is against all humanity that . . . man should also lay on more sorrow besides. No beast, if another stick fast in the mire, or fall under his load, will stand mocking or hurting him." Like Virgil, Pilkington fears and despises the human perversion that is love of violence. He likens it to the violence of papal superstition. In the old days, St. Paul's Cathedral had a giant censer that flew about the inside of the building like a deus ex machina. Meanwhile, outside, to please men's eyes and to earn a few coppers, poor human beings flung themselves from the spire tied to ropes, sometimes losing their lives.

Methodically simplifying the gorgeously ornamented silver and gold plate of Durham Cathedral, Pilkington and his dean (whose actual responsibility it was) drew Elizabeth's caustic comment that it was no wonder the people now preferred bloodsports to religion. For Pilkington, of course, the old cruelties and the old religious excesses were two sides of the same coin.[12]

20

Measure

THERE is another side to Pilkington's mildness.

Badly mutilated internally during the Civil War, savaged by a "thoroughly insensitive" restoration during the next century,[1] his cathedral was also subjected to the ignorant good will of the early Victorians. It was at this time, for instance, that the fifteenth-century reredos of Bishop Langley's altar, at the west end, was scrapped. Nevertheless—though with a peculiar massiveness of its own—it retains the essential elements of the Anglican esthetic: an uncluttered exposure of structure; a sense of coolness; a feeling of security and freedom within a fabric so large and so well founded; and—if one has ever experienced the weltering saturation of a Spanish cathedral, for instance—a sense of elation not unconnected with a sense of relief. This latter point is important, lest we forget the depth of ferocity with which intellectual Protestants like Pilkington experienced their longing for moderation as well as for release.

One of the cathedral's treasures remains the Neville Screen, behind the high altar. It was consecrated in 1380. It consists of a number of airy canopies, each of which once housed an appropriately accoutred saint. It was the gift of the Neville family, a great power in the north. Dean Horne was most likely responsible for removing the images or "puppets," as Puritans called them. Pilkington and Whittingham demurred from pulverizing the canopies. A Counter-Reformation prelate would certainly have disposed of the screen altogether.

It is important not to confuse Horne's action with vandalism or Pilkington's inaction with pusillanimity. One may recognise the sense of spiritual enablement that the compromise implied, yet it is also necessary to acknowledge how enraging to both extremes must have been such acts of iconic and credal pruning. Removing the statues did not mean there were no saints. As Lever put it, the saints are still with us, "albeit not their person in bodily presence, yet their examples of living." The puppets had to vanish; yet their vacated staging might subsist:

> these our actors,
> As I foretold you, were all spirits, and
> Are melted into air, into thin air.[2]

137

Determined to nurture the sense of Christ's living presence "in the midst," Pilkington always celebrated the Eucharist at a table kept in "the midst of the quire" (the Elizabethan prayer book was typically ambiguous on this point). The motivating idea of communality which lay behind this practice is one that in the late twentieth century has come to govern the liturgies of most Western Christians, Roman Catholic as well as Protestant. It was accompanied, in Pilkington's case, by a conviction about the nature of the Eucharist whose best expression he preferred to identify with his own trans' lation of the fifth-century Greek of Gelasius, historian of the Nicene Council of 325.[3]

When an infuriated Catholic mob, with Charles Neville and other nobles at their head, irrupted into the Cathedral on 16 November 1569, they tore and trampled under foot the Protestant Bible and prayer book before passing rapidly south to celebrate mass in Ripon Minster. After 1643, Scots Presbyte' rians, victorious at Marston Moor, not only destroyed most of the medieval woodwork but systematically beheaded all the figures on the Neville tombs and wrecked other pieces hitherto untouched. They also broke the cherubs' heads on the little gimcrack pseudoaltar of pink and black marble that an Arminian cleric, following his own taste, had substituted for Pilkington's boldly simple wooden table.[4]

The contrast betwen these last two objects may serve to introduce what might be called Pilkington's idea of *measure,* an idea that enforces connections between the meaning of the Eucharist and political morality. It may be seen as partly a corollary, partly a reversion, of the Apolline doctrine of restraint. Like that, it springs from a fusion of the three major influences on him: the pastoral lore of Rivington, the Bible, and Greek mythology. From these he draws together a view of man's relationship to the rest of creation—a sacred harmony whose disturbance provokes terrible retribution—compounded of the observable laws of nature, the miracle of divine providence, and the tragic and sublime mysteries of the human organism.

As is appropriate in matters of great importance, he suggests these things very simply:

> to feed our bodies . . . is as great a miracle, if it be well considered, as any other such thing that God works. [For in this miracle is God to be found] changing the good nature of his other creatures, which never sinned. . . . All the works of God are miracles. . . . [W]e should eat and drink with more reverence than we do.

And so, in describing the celebration of the eternal miracle in the Eucharist, he enforces—with typical humanist understatement—the sublime and joyful meaning of what a "table" is. Giving his translation of the canon of the Nicene Council on the Eucharist, he adds, "I note that they call it a table, and not an altar."[5]

This point is of central importance. Without the miracle of transubstantia'
tion, which only a celibate priesthood could perform, there was no altar. No
Anglican, however elegant and festive his sanctuary, believed in transubstan'
tiation. Arminian efforts to provide communion tables positioned and con'
structed "like an altar"[6]—down to pink marble and gilt cherubs—could not
disguise that fact. Unable—and unwilling—to revive the "sacrifice of the
mass," Arminian prelates were equally unwilling to develop the organic doc'
trine of the "table." They were left with a hierarchy shorn of mystical power,
yet at the same time a social consciousness that, while it might borrow (as
Laud[7] sometimes did) the phraseology of Latimer, could not draw the people
together, since its own deadly ambition for deference had placed most of
them outside the railings of its sanctuary. Such prelates were mostly the sons
of merchants.

Nevertheless, in their respect for the sacrament, their claim to act on
behalf of the whole nation, and their refusal of doctrinaire Calvinism, they
have as good a claim to be heirs of the English Reformation as their adversar'
ies. In some lights, Pilkington is more like his Arminian successor Richard
Neile (another Johnian) than he is like Neile's predecessor at Durham, the
stiff Calvinist William James.

Born in 1520—nine years after Erasmus's arrival at Cambridge—and made
a fellow of St. John's in 1539—five years after Henry's break with Rome—
Pilkington exemplifies a generation of English intellectuals set free from Rome
by the spirit of Greece, in poetry, philosophy, and the gospels. By definition,
such an experience could not be duplicated. Any attempt to describe it must
avoid trying to parcel it up among its feuding heirs, for it was truly whole
and indivisible. Yet it also had contradiction built into it. It responded not
merely to the idea of Apollo, whose anger is manifested in natural plagues,
but also to a feeling for his antagonist and antitype, the suave, long-suffering
Dionysus, who may with little warning unleash apocalyptic cruelties. Apollo
continually reaffirms the division between the human and the divine, but
Dionysus, or Bacchus, is god, not only of wine, but of everything that is
dangerous, vulnerable and awesome in the mysteries of life and death. He
beguiles the imagination with transcendental hints, surprising humanity with
the dream of entering another world. At its most palpable, this area of con'
sciousness, like the Apolline, may have its origins in *metron,* or "measure,"
the homely nemesis of farming communities attuned to the laws of a vital
power that is abundant, gentle, and remorseless. Where, as in the gospels,
this idea is set in a transcendental context, we are firmly in the realm of
Dionysus. This passage from Luke, in the King James version, is well known:

Be ye therefore merciful, as your Father is merciful. Judge not, and ye shall not
be judged. . . . Give, and it shall be given unto you; good measure, pressed down,

and shaken together, and running over. For with the same measure that ye mete withal it shall be measured to you.[8]

In terms of the *Phaedo,* a pagan text very familiar to Reformation human-ists, the philosopher is required not merely to "make harmony" in homage to Apollo, but as a true follower of Bacchus to take up in reverent spirit the *narthex* of initiation into the mysteries of the afterlife. Insinuating, danger-ous, and teasing, this transcendental frisson connotes with the ancient story of Ariadne, rescued for heaven by Bacchus-Dionysus in his chariot drawn by leopards. For Dante, the leopard that impedes him at the outset of his mystical way is many things, but ultimately a messenger of that divine love that moves all things. Despite occasional lapses into sentimentality, Pilking-ton retains, as pedantic Calvinists and evasive Arminians among his succes-sors would not, some of this Dantean sense (what, looking ahead, we might now call a "Blakean" sense) of the ferocity and reality of God: "These cruel beasts are set before us for examples of greater things [and, ultimately, of] the Almighty and living God, whose anger is a thousand times more grievous than the cruelness of any beast."[9]

And so Pilkington can provide, not merely an Apolline distinction such as "thou mayst choose whether thou wilt be remembered to thy praise or thy shame," but also a sly and mysterious Dionysian intimation: "God is here so good to his people, that he makes them judge themselves." He can not merely warn us to beware of wine, beauty, and the enchantment of words, but, as a paradoxical corollary, invite us to acknowledge "thy God to work thy salvation . . . by such his creatures." Where Lever preaches, in resound-ing rhythms, against leaving the poor in cold and nakedness, Pilkington inti-mates, in much subtler rhythms, the Dionysian recognition that "We are in the number of those rich men to whom St. James saith, 'Woe,' because they had so great plenty of apparel, that the moths did eat them, and their poor neighbours went cold and naked, wanting them."[10]

Apolline reason, to which all humanity is subject, functions most appropri-ately by ministering to that Dionysian suffering that it contains and that unites humanity with the divine; and also with the animal creation. In a homely image drawn from contemporary medical practice, Pilkington com-pares the reasonable word of God to a clean glass, within which the urine of ill humanity may be held up to the light. Our inmost disease cannot pollute the vessel, which was graciously created for its benefit, since the act of recognising our pollution, in such a context, is simultaneous with the begin-nings of recovery. The exercise of our brains, which are subject to the laws of God's universe, will be necessary yet we dare not hope for success except as we are one with him who incurred the taunt, "Physician, heal thyself."[11]

The incompatibility between such "biblical humanism"[12] and the arro-gations of Elizabethan monarchy, with its ceremonial acts of whimsical cru-

elty, is clear enough. To quote one typical example: "Once at Kenilworth
the hart she was chasing took to a pool in the park where it was caught
alive. 'Her Majesty granted him his life on condition that he lost his ears as
a ransom.'"[13] Arrogating to oneself in such a way the cold judgment of
Apollo, as though one were not subject to the same misery one inflicts, is a
suicidal act of hubris, even in a pagan tragedy. What does it look like as the
modus operandi of a Christian government? Writing the Evening Prayer for
the school he founded in his native chapelry—Wordsworth's school—the
Calvinistic Edmund Sandys made the boys acknowledge their "election, creation, redemption, justification, and sanctification." Pilkington, in identical
circumstances, reminds them of something quite other, and much more, than
a string of abstract nouns: "O Lord, our God and only Saviour, which hast
ordained all creatures to serve and obey us, . . . grant . . . that we may never
abuse them."[14]

Subversion, and a fairer redistribution of necessities, are inseparable from
the cult of Dionysus. In Luke's gospel—and only there—was the great hymn
of Dionysian Christianity, the *Magnificat,* recorded;[15] there also, and nowhere else, was Christ identified with the newborn Dionysus, the divine
βρέφος as Euripides (in a play later adapted for Christian purposes) had
called him.[16] Lying in the crib of the ox, he was clearly seen, not as something
to be subjected to rational scrutiny or intellectual definition but as a new life
which those who—in Luke's words—"found" him, "seeing, made known," so
that "all who heard wondered."[17] Here was also humanity, not merely as
capable of being disciplined by the skills required to cultivate food and chastened by Pilkington's Apolline reminder ("The Lord hath promised nothing
to idle bellies"), but as capable of being driven beyond all reason by the sheer
hunger within it, the hunger that is itself, the hunger that, as Pilkington puts
it, "will break stony walls," the terrible famine whose literal meaning lies
behind the quaint and dreadful legend of the Dionysian βρέφος.

Pilkington presents the poorer classes of humanity as torn between two
desires: for liberty, which their hearts long for above all things, and for simple
food, of which their bellies are kept in continual need, a need that allows
"the richer sort" to enslave them and thus to make the bad world. "Nay,
hunger is so pinching a pain, that a woman will eat her own child."[18] It is
in this context that Pilkington's God the Father is in permanent opposition
to the world. The vulnerability of the divine child is the source of the nemesis
of God.

Deep within the traditions of his native county lay fear of anarchy, yet
also hatred of pretentiousness and wrong. In 1533, when Pilkington was a
boy at Rivington, "the Heralds . . . made their way gingerly into the county
to investigate claims to gentility" and coats of arms.[19] One may imagine his
youthful scorn of such pretensions, and his eagerness to hear family stories
of the days of Wycliffe and the Peasants' Revolt. He might have heard how

even the proud Pilkingtons of Pilkington had not been too proud to dance attendance on the noble attendants of such as John Holland, earl of Huntingdon and duke of Exeter, King Richard's half-brother. That Holland was an acknowledged murderer was bad enough. His absolutely unforgivable offence, however, in local eyes, was his status as the grandson of a minor landowner of Breightmet, in Bolton parish.[20]

As though all this were yesterday, Bishop Pilkington asks "If the poor and rich man's blood were both in one basin, how should the one be known to be better?" He cites the propaganda of 1381,

> When Adam dalve, and Eve span,
> Who was then a gentleman?
> Up start the carle, and gathered good,
> And thereof came the gentle blood.[21]

In the interests of stability, not disruption, Pilkington sees the future Church as a meeting place of minds, where "we shall . . . not disdain to be admonished of our duty at mean men's hands." In any case, "a gentle kind of preaching is better to win weak minds, than terrible thundering of vengeance." He shares Marsh's recognition that a firm and gentle manage, and no berating, hardens a boy for good: "bring him to love it earnestly, and nothing shall make him afraid to stand to it manfully."[22]

Women have an honorable part to play, in Pilkington's eyes, a view that requires him to deploy a little Socratic irony to get round St. Paul: "St. Paul saith, 'Christ died for our sins, and rose for our righteousness'." His words contain "most and only sufficient doctrine to save our souls," but "mark who were the first preachers" of that supreme sermon. Pilkington is far too sly to mention that Paul notoriously forbade women even to raise their voice sufficiently to ask questions in church. Let their husbands explain things to them at home, commands the bachelor Apostle. Pilkington and the angels have something to say about that:

> Mary Magdalene and the other women, which went early in the morning with ointments to the sepulchre, they see Christ first of all other after his resurrection, and were sent to teach it to the apostles and [i.e., "even"] Peter.

It is worth noting Pilkington's humanist method here. With the grammatical finesse not unworthy of one who has lectured where Erasmus lectured, he places the women's vision in an eternal present—they "see" Christ first. Their preaching of that vision, however, may appear to be set discreetly in the past: "they were sent to teach." But if we read the phrases more carefully, we might well decide that what belongs in the past is not the preaching exactly, but the divine command to women to begin preaching. In any case, in Erasmus's manner, Pilkington transcends the argument with a sentence of sufficient literary quality to move our sensibilities into a new mode of response: "Should we not believe this resurrection, because that women taught it first?"

While of course never actually mentioning the question of women preach-ers within the church building, Pilkington insists that they—among Chris-tians of every order—will increasingly teach Christ outside it. He completes his Dionysian reading of the Christian message by trumping the apostle with his (and Pilkington's) favorite evangelist. Luke's symbolic story from Acts is cited: "Apollo, a mighty learned man ... submitted himself to be further taught in true religion of Priscilla and Aquila, a simple man and his wife."

In such passages as these—this is from *Haggai* (1560, second edition 1562)—Pilkington seems to offer to prolong into the theologically dreary reign of Elizabeth some of the dangerous possibilities of 1539, when, not yet twenty but already a fellow of his college, he was preparing himself to deliver those admired lectures of his on Acts which he never afterwards rallied heart to publish.

His heart was in Rivington. He placed Euripides on the syllabus of the school, and granted to local inhabitants a unique influence over its affairs. In 1828, they were able to compel the Charity Commission to condone their practice of allowing girls to attend on equal terms with boys.[23]

21

Entourage

WHETHER as a schoolboy scrambling these hills with his brothers, or as a bishop traveling in some state between Durham and London and back again, Pilkington found in his native landscape his intellectual entourage.

Since the industrial revolution of the late eighteenth century, major routes no longer pass through Rivington. But in Pilkington's day and for centuries before that, Rivington was not merely a little world of its own—a remote chapelry of a large moorland parish—but also a place for which the clichéd description "crossroads of history" might have been coined. It was crossed by an old causeway, which ran south from the port of Preston—on the River Ribble—and passed over the moors via Rivington before going on to Bolton (via Smithills) and so to Manchester. Bonnie Prince Charlie and his doomed highlanders passed this way in 1745, taking good care to skirt Bolton itself.[1]

The monk Henry Bradshaw and the bishop James Pilkington both represent intensely conservative families from the same region of south Lancashire who predated the Norman Conquest by some centuries. It will be the Bradshaws—or some of them—whose most memorable act will be to revolt against the Stuart monarchy. In the pages of Bishop Pilkington can be traced an unwilling development—culminating in the posthumously published *Nehemiah*—from the celebration of timeless paradoxes towards preparing for the moment where one might have to take sides. Turning from Bradshaw's chronicles of effortless miracles towards what Marsh recognised as man's "perpetual warfare upon earth," Pilkington, with extreme discomfort, submits himself to envisage the next stage of that history of perpetual change and conflict that can be read all about one at Rivington. Here in miniature there opens a map of the borderland territory of south Lancashire—stretching from the Mersey in the south to the Ribble in the north—itself an epitome of the borderland that is the human terrain.

Blackrod, Rivington's neighbor township to the southwest, was a Roman station "high above the dense forest of Roman Lancashire" where the "British resistance" skulked and plotted.[2] Near Edgeworth over the moor just to the northeast is believed to have been the Roman fort of Coccium, its native name deriving from the red color of the local streams, which are rich in iron (from the Welsh *coch,* meaning red).[3] An irresistible local legend claims that the river Douglas (the word is British) flowed red all the way to Wigan with the blood of men slain in the last battle fought by King Arthur, a memory, maybe, of Saxon invaders of the fifth or sixth century, and a vivid parable, most certainly, of battles in all places and at all times.[4]

Anglezarke Moor, which shelters Rivington from the north, is the "ark of the Angles," offering protection, perhaps, from Viking raiders moving inland from the Ribble. In the days of King Alfred, when Winchester was the capital and London a border town, the walls of Chester formed the apex of the narrow triangle that was the Saxon kingdom, and the sacred body of Werburgh seemed all that intervened between the Britons of Wales and the Norsemen who had overrun Lancashire, across the Mersey.[5]

The extinction of Werburgh by the Tudors was part of an immense process of centralization and consolidation, yet it was inevitably the beginning of more division. By the 1570 edition of Foxe's *Actes and Monuments,* some pious forger seems to have manufactured a letter, purportedly from Marsh, which gives him a place in the system of salvation analogous to (and evidently rivaling) that once taken by such saints as Werburgh.[6] This rivalry, and even older ones, would still be fighting matters into the eighteenth century, but only just.

While British influence retreated across the Mersey and into Wales, the Ribble was long understood to be the true boundary between the spheres of influence of Scottish and English kings. It was only when the Old Pretender's forces crossed that boundary on their way south (in 1715) that Bolton Catholics marched north to join them and Bolton Presbyterians to repel them.[7]

By 1745 religious polarities and ancient borders mattered much less. Deane and Bolton parishes stayed quiet as the highlanders marched through, though there was later a fuss—and a sermon—about the theft of Squire Hulton's horse.[8] The Hultons—Norman-Welsh arrivistes into Deane parish—survived as gentry in the district till the end of the nineteenth century, having in 1819 achieved anonymous notoriety in the person of the magistrate who presided over the Massacre of Peterloo.[9]

Those ancient Bolton families so useful to Elizabeth's religious settlement in its early stages did not long survive the Tudor dynasty. The executors of the will of Robert Pilkington, the bishop's nephew, in 1605, had no option but to transfer his Rivington estate to the mortgagees in settlement of outstanding debts. George, the bishop's brother, had spent his tenure of Rivington in a losing battle against aggressive litigation.[10]

Money problems would also dictate that neither the Levers of Little Lever nor the Longworths of Longworth would retain their estates into the reign of Charles I. Money made in, or through, the City of London bought them out. Then in 1629 the Great Lever branch of the ubiquitous Ashton clan, handsomely enriched by the acquisition of monastic lands in the previous century, moved right away to Downham, near Whalley. John Bridgeman, bishop of Chester—one of the hard-nosed new mercantile breed of prelate—purchased the Great Lever lands on which Ashtons had replaced Levers of Great Lever in the fifteenth century.

As though history were an endless cycle, it might be said that the Levers of Great Lever came back from dispossession with a vengeance in this century in the form of the great international firm of Lever Brothers, whose founder claimed that descent, while the Pilkingtons (whose products still carry the floriated cross from the bishop's family arms) came to preside over the great firm of glass manufacturers of that name.

Yet, until the late nineteenth century, any such recrudescence—however fancifully or seriously it might be regarded—remained unimaginable. As though what the old monk of Chester called the "life historial" had in that place completed its circle and come to a stop, two Bronze Age burial cairns on the Rivington Moors were known with affectionate melancholy as "Bishop Pilkington's sons," in memory of Isaac and Joshua, his two sons who died in childhood, ending his own hopes for a dynasty.[11]

James Marsh, the martyr's descendant, was still helping to work the family farm at Broadgate during the 1850s. Humor, diffidence, a certain whimsical invincibility characterize his face: he has a dark cutaway coat, pale baggy trousers, and holds a silk hat. A young man in his early twenties, he is moderately tall. He looks at the camera as though waiting to say something.[12]

Rex Olim et Futurus—the legend of Arthur, the "once and future king" of a united Britain—remains to this day a potent (and unfulfilled) dream. It was an important aspect of the propaganda system of Henry VII, whose Prince of Wales was christened Arthur. Spenser, the poet of the Leicester faction, provided an Elizabethan version in Prince Arthur, the imaginary consort of Elizabeth-Gloriana. The vision was somewhat tarnished by 1585, when Foxe published Pilkington's *Nehemiah*. Nevertheless the figure of Nehemiah, cupbearer and courtier, who achieves the great and godly work of rebuilding the walls of Jerusalem with the approval of his royal protector, suggests obvious parallels with those once and future Elizabethan favorites to whom Puritans looked for comfort, such as Leicester, Sidney, and the second earl of Essex, Robert Devereux.[13]

What is much more striking, however, is how antiaristocratic and even antimonarchical Pilkington's text is. The idea of a once and future Britain—particularly a once and future British Church—may be called a central obsession of all his writing,[14] but from the opening pages of his *Nehemiah* there is very little respect left for princes or courtiers. When we first meet the Persian kings and their people, we read that the "people were temperate in their living, but their kings passed in excess." Nehemiah is introduced to us as one whose "pedigree is unknown, and his father's too." And Pilkington's alienation proceeds through to the last pages that survive, till he returns to the complaint of Lever and Latimer and other moralists of King Edward's reign. A great contradiction was built into England with the restoration of true religion: "if we look into ourselves, we shall find there was never greater cruelty, oppression of the poor, hypocrisy and dissembling . . . than hath been since the beginning of the reforming of religion amongst us; yea . . . of such as would pretend to be favourers of religion."[15]

22

Reinterpretation

THE most significant aspect of Pilkington's modest but troubling legacy is connected with his reading of ancient texts. He positively welcomes the opportunity of alerting even "unlearned" readers to the fact that Greek or Hebrew texts are disputed bodies of material subject to a variety of readings and open to continual reinterpretation. He never pursues this to the point where it becomes bewildering or disabling, but emphatically delights in the range of possibilities and the opening for choice that it presents. A sense of natural justice goes along with his method of reading. A telling example of alternative interpretation from Pilkington's *Nehemiah* is his gloss on "a word in the Hebrew, as signifieth those uproars and outcries which are made in rebellious or seditious riots, or else of such as cry out for great grief and anguish of heart."[1] Like Marsh and Lever, his notion of education is of one centered, not merely on the Bible, but on the continual, civilized reinterpretation of the Bible, the continual battle against mystification, nit-picking, and bibliolatry.

Whatever the precise details of their schooling, this fine feeling of theirs became articulate through the educational initiative of the Lady Margaret Beaufort. One might note with some dismay that it was another Lancashire beneficiary of the same initiative—Archbishop Bancroft, raised at Farnworth Grammar School[2]—who instituted the production of an authorized version of the Bible, which (because it was authorized) offered itself like a lamb as an instrument of tigerish rapacity. It removed the possibility, while pretending to remove the necessity, of what Marsh, Lever, and Pilkington, among so many others, lived and died for: the free flow of ideas from the most advanced textual scholars to the least advantaged of the poor, and back again—a state of affairs to be envisaged only under certain conditions of social and political generosity. The authority of Augustine of Canterbury, transmitted from Reginald Pole towards Bancroft, devolved from ghostly tuition by reception of wafer towards ghostly tuition by reception of texts. Only for a while, from Elizabeth's accession to Grindal's internment in 1577, might it have seemed as though enablement, rather than repression, was the risk that was emerging. In the English context, one may speak of the year 1577 as an end of "Reformation" and a beginning of a new section of ecclesiastical history: "Nonconformity."

Early in the reign, it might have seemed as though Elizabeth's regime might gather the will to make a positive investment in Protestant education as an alternative to pursuing in a negative spirit the "fallacy of persecution." At St. Paul's Cross in 1560 Pilkington renewed the challenge Lever had made at the same spot a decade before: let there be positive investment in university scholarships for bright and needy boys. With that as a corollary, his *Haggai* and *Obadiah* are able to present a theme of reconciliation. In the former, the story of the effort to rebuild the temple is turned into a challenge to England to become, not a chosen few, but a chosen people. The latter deals with the feud between Israel and the Edomites. Pilkington transposes Old Testament vendetta into New Testament expectation: the ungodly are smitten as Saul only to be raised up as so many Pauls. The brevity of the chosen texts permits Pilkington's scholarly effort at a serious completeness of reading to offer itself to a broad range of readers as an accessible introduction to a mode of serious reading. Humorous, ironic, and warm, Pilkington presents an idea of England's providential destiny that, however comparable in broad outline to the theoretical machine of John Foxe, for instance, retains its humanity because it retains a compassionate awareness of the distance between the necessary ideal and the inevitable reality, between man's pretensions and his need for forgiveness. Great theoretical issues like the doctrine of predestination are subject to continual reinterpretation, and divisive items of canon law—like the question of auricular confession—are seen to have more than one side to them.

Enablement such as this was of no use to the mind-controllers. William James and Richard Neile, who succeeded each other as bishops of Durham under King James, have been described as "typical representatives of the two clerical groups"—Calvinist and Arminian—"who thenceforward came increasingly to vie for control."[3] Of course Calvinists aimed to stamp out individual auricular confession; of course Arminians set out to restore and codify its use. And of course Pilkington hates the very idea of imposing it and scorns with venom the mind-slaves who would seek to deny it to any who, being at "liberty," seek it for their comfort. Christ after his resurrection, Pilkington reminds us, sent not only a general "comfort of forgiveness" to all his disciples, but also a particular comfort by name to Peter who "had need to be comforted more than all." From this humanist and evangelical standpoint, Pilkington will not budge an inch, identifying thereby his sensibility as something that by all means must be excluded from significance and prevented from reproducing itself. Like Lever, he is not afraid of reminding readers that the "King is God's under officer, and not to be obeyed before him."[4]

Almost equally inconvenient—to such a mind as Whitgift's—is Pilkington's determination to use the theory of predestination against worldly arrogance while refusing to deploy it to frighten and control the bewildered. A pedant like Whitgift (Bradford's pupil) worried about logical contradiction as though he had discovered it. For Pilkington, it is part of our fallen condi tion, one that is not improved by resolving the contradiction at the expense of the mercy of God. He cites the words of the woman accused and found guilty before Alexander the Great:

> "I know thee to be above thy laws . . . and therefore I appeal from justice to mercy, and for my faults desire pardon." So we . . . must appeal from justice and our deservings unto his pardon and forgiveness, and both call and trust to be partakers of that salvation, which he hath purchased and offered to the whole world. His mercies do pass all our miseries, as far as God is greater than man; and his pardon can forgive all that call on him.[5]

After a decade, the possibilities of the early 1560s closed in. Pilkington's intellectual tone owed much to the volatile period when new ideas were abroad among the "younker," as he calls his younger contemporaries, the junior fellows of Edwardine Cambridge.[6] These "young men in a hurry"[7] had had a constitutional part to play in running the university, which was very perceptibly strengthened by the new statutes of 1559, in which Pilking ton had a hand. In 1570 Whitgift reversed the process, effectively disenfran chising those he identified as "the younger sort"—and his opponents identified as "the body of the University"—in favor of the old men, in par ticular the masters of colleges, who have ever since remained the usual means of external political control over the University. Having doused Cambridge, the regime turned its attention to the pulpits.

Some strong and humorous phrases from Pilkington's *Haggai* were repub lished as part of the homily against "Excess of Apparel," one of the sequence which, failing a preacher of approved adequacy, was ordered to be read by rote in churches. This piece by Pilkington is the only one in the tome with the good manners to be entertaining, the only one to cite his favorite Greek authorities Sophocles and Socrates, the only one (with the possible exception of Grindal's piece against "Gluttony and Drunkenness") that hints that the literary genius of England is about to enter its greatest phase. Nor is it misogynist. Pilkington has little mercy on the male dandy, but he ends the piece with the acknowledgement that, in the war between good and evil, a woman may use "sumptuous apparel" as a defense against the enemy.[8] This doubtless reflects his own good sense, and may also be an example of the compassion and personal loyalty Elizabeth—whose armor it was—could in spire in her so-called "Puritans", as we have seen in the case of Lever.

Yet the queen's policy brought the new *Book of Homilies* (most of which were printed by 1563) to final form only as part of a campaign of mind control in the wake of the Northern Rebellion of 1569–70. This disaster—

the gravest internal crisis of Elizabeth's reign—was contained at the expense of minds as well as lives. The final, new Homily 21, of 1571, is a dreary piece of berating that chooses to know nothing of northern conditions. Pilkington, well aware of regional difficulties, urged the godly to have their children baptised by Romish priests if (as would often be the case) there was no other minister available.[9] The author of the new "Homily against Disobedience and Wilful Rebellion," on the other hand, offers diabolical consistency with Cranmer's earlier but still authorized Homily on the "Salva- tion of Mankind," in the pugnaciously Lutheran second part of which the term "Christian" is expressly confined to those who believe in salvation by faith alone. Since the 700 poor northerners hanged in the wake of the rebel- lion at Elizabeth's personal insistence could with fair safety be presumed not to be solifidians, there is theological justification for claiming that "God of his mercy miraculously calmed the raging tempest, not only without any shipwreck of the commonwealth, but almost without any shedding of Chris- tian and English blood at all."[10]

What harlot could do more? In explanation of the word "English" it must be presumed that any solifidians regrettably slain were almost all nonpersons because they were Scottish.

It is hard not to feel sympathy with Pilkington's doubts about Cranmer and about the English tendency for not leaving well alone, which led all too easily to a crude mutuality between self-referential theological pedantry, polishing its exclusions, and the bloody will of the prince. Yet that will would have been seen as England's best defense against foreign threat. Elizabethan coercion of the regions, and of the theologians, was the inner side of an ambition for their safety which required a world and a historical providence transformed to meet the needs of Elizabeth, who was England. What the regions felt, or the theologians thought, was naturally subordinated to that precarious ambition.

The style of the new homily—all six parts of it—is inevitably deplorable. Sophistry, not Socrates, is in charge of its "logic." A death-count more than double that of the Marian martyrs is simultaneously disowned and attributed to Providence. Any spiritual influence Pilkington might seek to gain over his diocese is irreversibly frustrated.

The following year—1572—Elizabeth's more than worthy ethical equiva- lent, Catherine de' Medici, presided over the mass murder of French Protes- tants now usually referred to as the "Massacre of St. Bartholemew's," an event alluded to as recent in Pilkington's commentary on Nehemiah.[11] This unfinished work was edited by John Foxe and published in 1585, ten years after the bishop's death. Robert Some, who had matriculated at St. John's during Pilkington's mastership and was to become master of Peterhouse in 1589, added a godly "Treatise against Oppression" to bring Pilkington's argu- ments up to date. It has been said that Some's predestinationist "pessimism" was countered by a personally held "evangelical optimism,"[12] an aspect of his thought that reminds one of Pilkington. Nevertheless, Some was certainly a most rigid predestinationist and one who believed that God's elect were chosen without regard to "any kind of sin." It was a common claim of Counter-Reformation propaganda—amply exemplified by works issued from the Andertons' secret press[13]—that any tendency to deny practical free will was a tendency to encourage moral nihilism. Pilkington agreed with his recusant neighbors to that extent and would certainly have regarded Some's position as deserving the worst they could have said against it. The fact that Some and other young dons were turning to Cartwright's Presbyterian theories had been a factor in Whitgift's decision to revise the University Statutes in 1570. In due course, however, Some became one of those Calvinist heads of colleges who could claim—thanks to Whitgift's statutes—that they alone were the fit interpreters of the Thirty-Nine Articles. Here was a double nemesis, for Whitgift and for Pilkington. Whitgift's empowering of college heads had produced rivals in intransigence who made his own Calvinism seem almost libertarian and humane.[14] More ambiguously, Pilkington's enabling of the "young men in a hurry" of 1559 had helped to enkindle, not only a little enlightenment, but also a good deal of *odium theologicum,* blazing up in more eccentric and unmanageable forms than ever before.

Theoretical intransigence is far from being incompatible with political subservience. It is not surprising that resort to the magistrate is the best Some can offer by way of safeguard against oppression.[15] Placing his "Treatise" with the rest of his career, one might deduce that he requires a magistrate of his own imagining before whom he can then safely abase himself. Pilkington, on the other hand, claims the right to continue arguing with the magistrate we have got. These are the final words of *Nehemiah:*

> We must be judged by God's word, and not it by us: we must be ruled by it, and not overrule it according to our fantasies: we must hang on God's true saying, and not on man's evil living.

He is describing, and fulfilling, the continual, physical effort of "prophesying"; a process that requires a lively secular consciousness as well as a living spiritual conscience, both strengthened through an intellectual, but not intellectualist, wrestling with the text of the Bible. Whereas the Some of 1585 is mainly anxious to defend his party from the charge of theoretically justifying oppression through theological error, the Pilkington of the 1570s can still invoke the tradition of "Master Latimer's sermons." He details such matters as the pillaging of charitable endowments by the queen's deputies, "enhancing of rents to the highest" on royal estates, the despoliation of woods and other natural resources by monopolists for purposes of industrial exploitation; and the symbiotic plagues of "engrossers, forestallers, regraters, leasemongers, . . . [and] lawyers."[16]

The Northern Rebellion, in particular, seems to have made Pilkington think about the duties of patriarchy in monitoring and directing aggressive youthful males, those perennial "lusty younkers" who "think themselves not brave enough, except they can . . . pick a quarrel."[17] Sharing Marsh's sense that conflict is always part of man's spiritual existence on earth, Pilkington sharpens the perception to insist that conflict is coeval with human intelligence. He takes Plato's point that "our battle is immortal," and that the peace—the "solution"—we seek is always beyond us. In intellectual as in military history, every victory is but the prelude of a defeat.[18] Thus, there can never be—what Bancroft would demand—an "end of translating,"[19] or an end of adjusting the whole balance of society to take account of disruptive innovations. The potential soldier—or rebel—is for Pilkington "God's good creature." No attempt to extinguish or to ignore his better qualities will ever, in the end, make him capable of defending, or submitting to, the indefensible.

In arguing for a more disciplined army to defend the realm, Pilkington argues also for regional loyalties and a more credible ethic. Contrary to Elizabethan military habit, a foreign campaign, he thinks, cannot be worth much if it is sustained by the mixed dregs of various regions, brought together for the private profit of a strange captain, "but when neighbours, friends and cousins are together under a captain whom they love and know, . . . they cleave together like burrs." Similarly, lack of preachers accompanying armies leads to licentiousness "and the enemy to prevail." For a preacher to have credit, he must be credible, however. Warning against devilish indulgence, he must share what the soldier knows, that "mirth is not ill." Again, soldiers might be content with their wages if they got them on time. Altogether, an army cannot but be the reflection of the society it defends.[20]

More dangerously, Pilkington argues for a distinction to be made between the will of princes and the credible behavior of subjects. True, "to rebel and draw thy sword against the lawful prince for religion, I have not yet learned," but let the prince beware: "God requireth not such piquishness in a man, that he allow himself to be wounded."[21]

In these and other ways, Pilkington steers a course between the deterministic nihilism of Luther, who never questions that it is useful to insist, and go on insisting, that man is a "captive, subject and slave, either to God's will or Satan's," and the free-will nihilism of Erasmus, with its symmetrical paradoxes reflexive of both sides of every argument, a timeless looking-glass kingdom that excludes the necessity of choice in its own more agreeable style.[22]

It is not necessary to assume that Pilkington's text was much altered by his editor, but it is worth noting that Foxe has hustled the dead bishop into a setting the living scholar chose not to enter.

Dying at his residence at Bishop Auckland on 23 January 1576, and by his own will buried obscurely there in the oratory where he had prepared and ordained the small number of men who felt called to enter the Protestant ministry in his conservative diocese,[23] Pilkington was subsequently disin-terred and buried again before the high altar (as it once had been) of Durham Cathedral. A monument was erected, to which plates of brass were affixed bearing fulsome inscriptions—none of Horatian quality—including an epice-dium by Foxe.[24] The rage and indifference of time have removed all trace of this, and his dust lies somewhere within the sanctuary, as anonymous as the dust of Bishop Cotes, somewhere near the foot of the bishop's throne, at Chester.[25]

With the gift of hindsight, one can see that two of his most striking prophecies concern the twin threats to the English monarchy of an ignorant, intransigent local Presbyterianism, offering to control the weak while itself at the mercy of the powerful, and a reckless, half-barbaric Scots army poised for the invasion of England[26]—the combination that would ruin Charles I. There are other matters, but Elizabeth's refusal to support her moderate Puritans and the failure of her regime to finance Protestant education or to make it possible for the pastors of her Church to initiate intelligent debate about God and the world within a context of loyalty to the crown would seem to lie behind the prayer Pilkington made from the fourth chapter of Nehemiah:

> Most merciful Father, for thine own mercy's sake look pitifully at thy ragged and torn church, the contemned spouse of thy dearly beloved Son, Christ Jesus. . . . Turn away all open violence, that shall be devised against us outwardly: keep us from civil war and sedition inwardly. . . . [T]each us as a schoolmaster, feed us as a shepherd.

Providence would prove harsher than the Bolton schoolmaster, slower to intervene than the Rivington shepherd. Only through civil war would En-gland be granted an ambiguous lesson. Lever's old chapel of St. John, Bablake, would become a prison for Warwickshire cavaliers "sent to Coventry": evi-dence that in the current struggle, commerce and Protestantism would pre-vail over country matters and the "old religion." But the immortal battle was not so easily won. In 1647, after gaining a military victory, Chester's Roundhead authorities would be thrust "like beasts" into Marsh's old Northgate prison by their unpaid and hungry soldiers, no doubt rebellious or seditious, no doubt also suffering great grief and anguish of heart.[27]

Section Two
Nonconformity

David knowing Saul the king to be a wicked man and his deadly
enemy . . . had a good conscience not to touch the Lord's anointed.
—Thomas Lever, *A Fruitfull Sermon* (1550)

PART FIVE
Jacobean Catholic

Under pretence of Reformation, I find the ancient Catholic much
wronged by the modern Protestant; the Protestant condemned by
the later Puritan: every latter still impugning and forsaking the
former.
　　　　　—James Anderton, *The Reformed Protestant* (1621)

23

James Anderton: Claiming Equity for the Visible Church

JAMES Anderton's father, Christopher Anderton of Lostock Hall in Bolton parish, was protonotary of the Court of Common Pleas at Lancaster, the equity court for the royal duchy, which included extensive properties in addition to the county itself. The holder of such an office might well regard himself as having a special duty in regard to the monarch. In 1573 Christopher took out a fresh patent assigning the office jointly to himself and to James. When Christopher died in 1592, James inherited his large estate and also continued to hold the office of protonotary. Christopher had conformed in religion, but James's mother (and his bride of 1583, Margaret Tyldesley) were Catholics. Resigning office in 1608 to travel for his health on the continent, James also issued at this time the second (much enlarged) edition of *The Protestants' Apology for the Roman Church,* his most famous controversial work and the only one he chose to publish in his lifetime. It was against his will that a first edition had been rushed out in 1604.[1]

James's brother Roger was most likely responsible.[2] He seems to have exemplified the traditions of pugnacious generations of Lancashire gentry, never doubting that one must always take sides and must always fight to win. No doubt it was in something of this spirit that Roger's son, also called James, and other Catholic gentry, would arm themselves for Charles. At the conscious level, their motive was the same as that of James Anderton's *Apology*: to wring some religious compromise from the king.[3] But there was a deeper instinct that they shared with such as Roger Anderton. Simply, not to fight was to lose all claim to honor and with it all things in heaven and earth. One is reminded of the robust gatehouse to Lostock Hall, raised by Christopher in 1563. Its ridge of semicircular castellation had the appearance (and the meaning) of the row of shields on some ancestral Viking longboat, poised for a raid on the neighborhood.[4] Vigorous intervention was certainly Roger's style. Whoever issued the unfinished *Apology* in 1604 wanted to be seen to be taking part in the battery of propaganda aimed at the new king during this year, when he was showing himself disposed to consult with his subjects on religious matters and, in particular, seemed to want to mitigate in practice the penal laws against Catholics.[5]

Lawrence Anderton, cousin to Roger and the elder James, was an altogether more modern phenomenon. Known at Christ's College, Cambridge, as "Golden-mouth Anderton," he was ordained in Spain in 1603 and returned to England on mission, becoming Jesuit superior of the Lancashire district in 1621. By 1627 he was at Jesuit headquarters in London and traveled on official business to Rome the following year. His own books were published in France. One presumes that he was an extremely busy man of affairs. His writing appears hurried—or "brilliant," in a slightly pejorative sense—and carries a somewhat disdainful tone. He is efficient, even entertaining, rather than persuasive.[6] Books now regarded as posthumous works of James Anderton were issued during the early 1620s. It seemed at this time that Prince Charles might marry a Spanish princess, and Catholics dared to hope that England's system of alliances would thereby shift permanently in a Catholic direction.

But James Anderton himself was neither an atavistic provincial warrior nor a well-honed international bureaucrat. Arousing in Roger a slightly bullying protectiveness, he drew from Lawrence the entirely deserved tribute that the three treatises of his *Apology* constituted a "sincere and solid proceeding."[7]

A member of the establishment, yet a devout Catholic, James refuses to regard himself as an anomaly. His central concern is with the question of equity as it applies to those who remain loyal to Lancashire's, and England's, "old religion." Secular authority has no power to abolish the Catholic Church, he thinks, which remains the only true and visible Church in England. Parliament has, however, given itself the power to abolish the privileges of what remains the one visible Church. Now, where there is a clash between traditional practice and legislative innovation, the balance of fairness between the two, in English law, is a matter of equity. For James Anderton, it is in the name of "equity" that the Catholic Church, which has "Priority of Possession," claims tolerance for herself from the Protestant heresiarchs who have deprived her.[8]

By such reasoning, he affirms the integrity of England's native Catholicism and proclaims its long-term survival. War of any kind for religion does not interest him. Nor is he energized by the prospect of England as a passive receptacle for Rome's international mission. In proclaiming the survival of the "old religion," he claims also its right to adapt.

For the monk Bradshaw, the sovereignty of Christ, really present in the Sacrament, was also the guarantor of the sovereignty of Catholic kings. The Catholic sanctuary was the "place spiritual," which guaranteed the sacredness of the earthly king's presence and with it the security of the kingdom. In approaching his own "lawful sovereign," James I, Anderton merely begs "private freedom" for Catholics to celebrate the mass. In the words of his second treatise, only the Catholic religion has "the Marks of the true Church" and only the Catholic Sacrament is capable of sustaining the sovereignty even of a Protestant kingdom.[9] The guarantor of sovereignty is no longer literally within the king: rather it shields his presence with a faith the king does not share. The king is to be sanctified by negotiation and revered on terms that include tolerance for views personally alien to the king. Like Thomas Lever, Anderton pushes the king beyond dispute the better to review the terms on which he may remain in place. Paradoxically, he invades the king's presence in order to do so.

That King James himself "deigned to peruse" passages of Anderton's *Apology* we learn from the epistle dedicatory to the posthumous *Liturgy of the Mass* (1620). As in the case of Thomas Lever's sermon for King Edward, there is also another sense in which Anderton's apologetics actually break in, as it were, upon the mystery of the royal presence. Civil War Boltonians would claim to determine the sacramental "Marks of the true Church" and their implications for the status-order of rival localities within the kingdom. Triumph and tragedy alike become tokens of assurance. For John Tilsley, Deane's Edinburgh-educated Presbyterian vicar, the sack of Bolton by Royalist troops can ultimately be read as a divine mark of the high *political* destiny within the realm of the local godly. By the same logic, for John Hewit, Charles's high Anglican preacher at Oxford, the king's noble martyrdom at Whitehall is God's proof of the inviolability of hereditary monarchy as a *constitutional* principle at the heart of the realm. For both of them, as for many Englishmen on both sides of the Civil War, secular power is perceived as royal power under certain constitutional safeguards. Neither of them ventures to explore the limits of secular power itself. For Anderton, however, the early years of King James offer what Edward's reign offered Lever: the chance actually to renegotiate the current terms of the Crown's authority in its relationship to the worldwide sovereignty of Christ. For them, it is not enough, as it seems to be for Tilsley and Hewit, to obtain a secular government worthy of one's *mere* obedience. Conscience, nurtured on Christ's sacrament, remains absolutely superior to any secular power, and is moreover the source for the continual constitutional readjustment of the terms upon which, in practice, secular power may be worthy of being obeyed.

Anderton touches sublimity in the area of personal conscience and assent that is associated with the Holy Spirit. Notions of a "ghostly tuition" passively ingested with the consecrated wafer, which so enraged Henrician Protestants, are displaced by a vigorous Christian humanism, urgent in its plea to all men to continue to revere and practice the doctrine of free will, without which human responsibility is impossible, and which for Anderton is conserved only in the security of the Roman communion. Any stable pattern of mutual responsibility between the monarch and all the people must be negotiated—on both sides—from the premise of Anderton's third treatise, "That the Catholics are no less loyal, and dutiful to the Sovereign, than Protestants."[10] As with George Marsh, one senses in James Anderton a double motive for publication: to defend oneself against ideological opponents and to distinguish oneself from narrower friends. The same double allegiance—to the lawful sovereign on the one hand and to the inner convictions of religion on the other—makes for Anderton as for Marsh the working practicality of conscience. Renouncing, like Marsh, the luxury of exile, Anderton came home to die, having made "choice to die in the Lord."[11] Circumstances were different from Marsh's day. Anderton was the chief landowner of Bolton and Deane, and impropriator of both parishes, not a poor yeoman curate hunted for his life. But—as would also be the case with Oliver and Nathaniel Heywood, royalist dissenters under Charles II—there is in Marsh and Anderton the same integrity between outer and inner, between the perceived spirit of law and the individual's own spirit, without which neither can be said to develop or exist. The posthumous *The Reformed Protestant* (1621) provides Anderton's most powerful defence of free will as a life-availing doctrine.

The weakest part of Henry Bradshaw's threefold system, in its own terms, had been its alienation from the "life historial," its incapacity to embrace the providential authority of the Creator-Father, shaping the destinies of successive mortal authorities. The first of the three treatises of Anderton's *Apology* reaffirms the "Antiquity and Continuance" of the Roman Church, and the theme is elaborated further in the posthumous *Saint Austin's Religion* (1620). Unlike Pilkington, Anderton is no Greek scholar. His attitudes are those of medieval scholasticism, and his arguments are essentially circular. The consistency of the Roman tradition is for him proved because the inconsistencies it produces are disowned. The gist of his thesis is that the whole of Protestant theology is a disordered corruption of Catholic truth. This may be demonstrated by using the partial and contradictory Protestant texts themselves in support of the unified orthodoxy they despoil. The serene body of Catholicism rises again from the *disjecta membra* of its nullified rivals. In this process can be discerned "the very Finger of God."[12] His use of texts is by definition partisan, but it is also vigorous and of honest intent. Like Pilkington, he rejoices that "one text of Scripture may have divers understandings and all of them true." Like Pilkington, he dreads and loathes the one-sided inhumanity of the predestinationist system, which must wrench every text into the same half-truth, and he notes with grim humor the ploys of English Calvinists to disown the Epistle of St. James, the apostle of free will.[13]

The residue of toughness and resilience in his thinking allows him to grasp the nettle of the "life historial," which had understandably caused the Henrician monk to falter. God's providence truly secures the "Roman

Church and Religion," Anderton affirms, yet this is compatible with God's benign surveillance of Protestant princes. No sensible Englishman need be alarmed about the pope's temporal pretensions. He "pronounced sentence of deprivation" against Elizabeth, and her reign was untroubled by major rebellion. Every year he claims Naples from the king of Spain, and the "King of Spain detains Naples, . . . notwithstanding the Pope's yearly claiming of it."[14]

Anderton hails the "successful and blessed event" of King James's accession, which brings with it "the most happy union of our long divided continent." This is surely God's purpose working through the "grave and prudent foresight" of the Lancastrian hero and marriage broker Henry VII. In the name of King James's mother, and "by the most humble intercession of Allegiance, and ever resolved Loyalty," Anderton only begs "that we might adore the God of our Fathers."[15] Here is a mentality of long-term negotiation, which (as in the case of James Pilkington and Queen Elizabeth), confronts a new monarch from a background of eight centuries or so of small-gentry survivalism. In their own version of the national trend, the attempt to capture history and rewrite the future would remain a major concern of Bolton's religious writers, reaching a stylised, assured, yet somehow insubstantial balance after 1689 in Zachary Taylor, the first Boltonian writer (since Bradshaw's death in 1513) whose output may be defined as convenient to the uses of current national orthodoxy. But James Anderton's *Apology* is the only successor to James Pilkington's address to Elizabeth from Frankfurt, as an honorable approach, as of right, from an independent-minded gentleman to his sovereign.

24

"The Marks of the True Church"

In 1591 Christopher Anderton adorned his gatehouse at Lostock with the royal arms. The following year, his widow heard mass and a Catholic sermon in the house. Such was James Anderton's parentage. That same year, he was named on a secret list of Lancashire Catholics sent to Lord Burghley. Yet he remained undisturbed, a counterweight to the alternative nonconformity exemplified by Bolton's antivestiarian vicar and yet wilder curate, James Gosnell. The polarization of the kingdom is suggested by the language of these two Jameses. For Gosnell, Bolton swarms with "Jesuits, seminaries, masses and plenty of whoredom." He may be accounted a middle-class radical in the Thomas Lever tradition, but with distinctly less finesse. He used his private income to endow the grammar school and to found a parish lecture-ship. Relatives of Marsh's Darcy Lever friends were the trustees.[1] For Anderton, Puritans like Gosnell "do so tediously and tragically riot in their pulpits, with so much want of matter, and wasteful prodigality of time" that their true motive is all too clear: "to exasperate the State against us."[2]

As a rich and learned servant of the Crown connected through the network of Lancashire gentry to Sir Gilbert Gerard,[3] Elizabeth's attorney-general, and other notables, Anderton was as useful (and perhaps as conscious) a cat's-paw in his place and time as the maverick Puritan Thomas Lever had been in his. Both employed the "liberty of sincere and plain speaking"[4] proper to the loyalist Lancashire gentry. Both knew such outspoken loyalty carried a risk, but they recognized no other kind.

Receiver for the county of certain former monastic properties, James Anderton consolidated his father's acquisitions of land and power. In 1593, for instance, he finally acquired the manor of Heaton which his father had been attempting to wrest, by fair means and foul, from the Heaton family for the previous thirty years. The manor of Horwich was obtained at the same time. It became the home of James's uncle Thomas, father to Lawrence Anderton. Among other colonies of the Lostock imperium was Birchley, which made a home for Roger and his family.[5] James Anderton naturally added his signature to the loyal address presented to the king by the Lancashire gentry in 1603. He had already demonstrated his patriotism not merely by contributing in 1598 to the funds for Elizabeth's Irish campaign, but by standing surety for another Catholic who was "lunatic and penniless." Anderton's devotion to Rome was an act of will, sincerely made and kept, but his loyalty to the Crown was, if possible, more fundamental and stemmed from a pre-Christian sense of honor and tribal identity. Fully reconciled to the Roman Church on his deathbed by cousin Lawrence, he bequeathed money for the support of priests. This decision went against the king's law. It was a hard one for him to make. Policy and faith determined that one who saw himself as a defender of the true visible Church must prosper sufficiently in the world to be of service therein. These were testing economic times that would redraw the map of land-tenure, locally and nationally. Variety was being replaced by confrontation. Locally, Protestant Ashtons moved away to become county magnates, while Protestant Longworths, Levers, Pilkingtons, and Heatons were dispossessed. Bolton's second Catholic family—the Orrells of Turton—suffered the same fate. Rich Catholic Andertons confronted the rising Puritan clan of Andrews, London merchants who bought and married their way into the Lever inheritance and would eventually acquire the Pilkington inheritance, also.[6]

There had been a tension between Lever's inherited loyalty to the monarch and the new directions in which his radical ideas about the Sacrament were taking him. Whatever his personal feelings, the atrophy if not abolition of earthly monarchy is a corollary of those ideas. Anderton thought and felt differently. His devotion to the doctrine of transubstantiation required—or was required by—convictions in favor of materially apparent schemes of order whose indicators could be seen and handled. His writings exemplify precise citation of printed authority as strikingly as Lever's exemplify the calculated evasion of formal definition. Just as Anderton desires to have the substantial and palpable presence of Christ in the Sacrament, so he desires to compel belief therein by a system of citations secure even to "the very number of the line, that so the Reader may . . . point thereto with his finger." To such a mind, the idea of earthly sovereignty must be embodied in an earthly sovereign, and the idea of the Church militant cannot exist apart from a visible and identifiable Church militant. In faithless England, the very "Churches and Colleges . . . impropriated to our Adversaries . . . make . . . mournful intercession." In the African Congo, the Catholic faith is kindled by indisputable and "confessed miracles." Calvin's wickedness is to be seen and handled in the "loathsome ulcer . . . about his private parts." The Sacraments "not only signify, but truly confer grace."[7]

Lever's tendency toward a kind of charismatic whimsicality in doctrinal matters was part of his enchantment with the newly discovered effectiveness of Christ's presence in the hearts and minds of the Christian commonwealth. But for Anderton the only sustainable system in the real world is the Catholic sacrifice of the mass, in which "is offered . . . the sacred humanity of

Christ our Saviour." Nothing less (in the very "mouth" and "stomach" of the recipient) can "testify and work" those "admirable effects of love and grace" without which there is no safety in or beyond the world. Not dispersed in the "confused Chaos" wherein Protestantism is "diversely uttered," but "digested . . . into one contracted volume," the consistency and coherence of Catholicism is "convincing testimony" of its divine origin. Comparing Lever's Christ with Anderton's, one might say that the former, like some will o' the wisp, can only "allure" his votaries towards a vaguely apprehended truth. But the latter can "offer to the view" of his ingesters "a distinct, full and clear notion" as befits those who belong with him at "a pyramidal point."[8]

Receiving the Sacrament, Lever expands—or dissipates—into intimations of a republican commonwealth. Receiving a rather different Sacrament, Anderton consolidates convictions about monarchy as a solid and reliable system. Nevertheless, they are not as incompatible as may at first appear. The one fanciful and radical, the other conservative and pedantic, and both of them partisan, they agree in the notion of distributive totality which the Eucharist itself enjoins. Constitutionalism and negotiation are their bottom line. Lever affirms the supremacy of Parliament. Anderton confessedly takes his tone and his main ground of argument from the great champion of Common Law, Sir Edward Coke, currently (1608) chief-justice of the common pleas, and thus England's leading equity judge. Anderton affirms it as the duty of the "honourable court of Parliament" to represent fully and without exception all the "members" of the "politic body," which is the "Nation."[9] It has no power, under Common Law, to make a nonperson of any citizen for sectarian reasons.

On the title page of the 1608 Apology appears the generic pseudonym Anderton chose to adopt—"John Brereley Priest." One of the meanings of this is that the "Priest" is a kind of Aristotelian final cause in relation to the work. Modestly and sincerely (for such is his style), Anderton acknowledges that, under God, it is from the faithful witness of priests, general and particular, that he derives such qualities as his work possesses. At the same time, vigorously and tenaciously (for such also is his style) he reminds us of the main *purpose* of the work: not to score abstract points but to secure the physical survival in England of the Catholic priesthood, for the good of souls. The "Christian Reader, Catholic or Protestant" is thus compelled to consider the right relationship between a Catholic priesthood, centered on the mass, and a Protestant monarchy. That the mass itself is seditious is something, says Anderton, "I eternally deny." In apportioning equity, however, something must be granted on the other side. Catholics need to accept that with the great consistency of Catholic truth the secular claims of the papacy have nothing to do. What is essential for the good of Catholic souls and (if it but knew it) for the security of the Protestant state itself, is the continued exercise of the "priestly offices." Let us agree, then, that the "power . . . communicated" by God to kings "is in them absolute and independent, as also is the sacred authority of priestly function likewise from God." We must return to a sense of "these two estates, as being several, absolute, and independent." Disloyal Protestants threaten the king with rebellion if the mass is so much as tolerated. Loyal Catholics must make it clear that the mass is the very ground and sustenance of all order. It is of its very nature incompatible with the notion that the royal "Lieutenancy . . . next under God" is a "Tenancy-at-will to any earthly power, either Papal or Consistorial."[10] As a matter of fact, such notions are not Catholic at all, says Anderton, being typical of the heresy of Wycliffe and the pseudotheocratic Protestant sects that follow him.[11]

The central and most characteristic argument of "John Brereley Priest" is based on precedent. "Church government and priestly offices," he writes, "have heretofore been (and therefore may again be) subsisting, though there were no Christian temporal magistrate." "Brereley" or "Brierlie" (modern spelling, "Brierley") is a northern word for "a raised piece of untilled ground where briars take root." Tradition has always been most resistant in such places. The "John" subsisting in such an obstinate wilderness keeps faith till Christ come. Any threat to his saving offices must be avoided, not provoked by open sedition or (equally disgraceful) the "immoderate" theory of those Catholics who would "overcharge the supreme Pastor with incompetent attributes of Authority in Temporalities."[12]

25

"Loyal, and Dutiful"

ANDERTON refrains from any direct discussion of the Oath of Allegiance of 1606. But his views as set out in the *Apology* of 1608 may be said to be the expression of a Catholic case for conformity with that oath, which he had doubtless been required to affirm. It had been designed "for the better dis-covering and repressing of Popish Recusants" insofar as they might feel tempted to any disloyalty to the Crown.

In 1610 Parliament was engaged in tightening up the administration of the oath, with the intention of barring from every area and degree of public life all who retained any sympathy with papal claims to absolve subjects of their allegiance. Clearly, any Catholic sympathisers who refused to take it would put themselves beyond the pale of influence, and most likely at risk.[1]

English Catholics who shared Anderton's views had something in common with the French Jesuits. These enjoyed the special favor of the former Huguenot Henry IV, whose Edict of Nantes had extended a degree of toler-ance to his former coreligionists. French Jesuits were currently arguing that English Catholics might take the Oath of Allegiance to King James. No doubt they shared Anderton's view that secular conformity and the lessening of tension that might follow were "the only sure approved means to restore" the Catholic faith.[2] Like him, they found no dogma that warranted papal interference in the affairs of stable kingdoms, French, English, or other. More than that, however, they were eager to come to terms with the emerging absolute monarchy as the shortest route to influence for themselves.

In this they were opposed by Jesuits in Spain and elsewhere who main-tained the more traditional Catholic view that any heretical monarch was by definition a tyrant and liable to be deposed, if not killed, for the good of the people. The assassination of Henry IV in 1610 made the whole subject too dangerous. In 1613 a decree of the Jesuit general, Aquaviva, put an end to all such discussions by members of his order.

In the light of this chronology, it is interesting to note that James Ander-ton's *Liturgy of the Mass,* written in 1612, contains an "Epistle Dedicatory" to Prince Charles as "heir apparent to the crown" that employs language that echoes to some extent the elegant monarchist codes of French Jesuits of

1610, notably Père Coton's propositions on government. There are national differences, however.[3]

In 1608 Anderton had already affirmed (as would Coton in 1610) that disloyalty to government incurs "damnation," but the Englishman did not share the French Jesuit's abjection. "Qui résiste aus rois acquiert damnation" is rather more nakedly absolutist in implication than Anderton's more measured statement that "obedience ... to [the] temporal sovereign" is a "duty to be observed, for Conscience, and to avoid damnation." Most particularly, Anderton defines the monarch, not as untrammeled autocrat, but as "the Royal head" of the "politic body" of the realm. Ultimately, it is to England herself, "our dearest country," that Anderton feels is owing "the dearest regards of all love" by "the law of nature." With his frequent appeals to English Common Law and to Parliamentary procedures, it is clear that Anderton revered the king as constitutional head. Insofar as the monarchy acted according to precedent, he would feel bound in conscience to support it. But equally clearly, he would not support any un-English development designed to strengthen the monarchy further, such as King James's campaign for the selective importation of aspects of the European (and Scottish) tradition of Roman Law. As for the sort of homage Coton found it convenient to offer to French absolutism, Anderton has an inbred moral instinct against it, just like his Protestant neighbors.

In the matter of the metaphysical status of the sovereign, there is a profound distinction between the two writers. The Coton of 1610 deploys elegant semiblasphemy, with fashionable neo-Greek allusions. The Anderton of 1612 seems alert to the new Grecian fashion (which is quite a different matter from the old humanism of the Tudor age), but he is at pains not to commit, but to expose, a blasphemy that prefers worldly idolatry to Christian reverence. In taking this approach, he seems to be addressing Charles's own anxious piety as though from private information. The passage throws an interesting light on the English tradition of addressing the monarch seriously as another human being, capable of heeding appeals to conscience.

This is Coton's "proposition":

Que les rois sont, comme les appellait Homère, les enfants et nourissons de Dieu, ou plutot, comme dit Menandre, son image animée.

Strictly speaking, the graceful blasphemy is against man and through him, against God. The God of Genesis created man (and not merely kings) in his own "image," and the Apostle John, among others, named all Christian people (and not merely His Christian Majesty of France) "children of God." St. Augustine advised using pagan authors to support Christian values. Coton deploys them to displace the biblical God, to suppress humanity, and to deify the monarch of the world.

To his credit, the English Catholic cannot manage this style of "proposition" very convincingly; or rather, he applies some of its fashionable pretensions to quite a different purpose:

> What can be proposed more proper for so generous and heroical a spirit, or so
> pleasant and delightsome for so perfect an image of our great God, as the lively
> portraiture and true description of that highest honour and religion, which solely
> and peculiarly is by Christians to be exhibited to the first Prototypon of divine
> majesty?

By the Greek word *prototypon,* Anderton appears to suggest what Aquinas
implies by referring to each mass as *exemplum* or *imago* of the sacrifice and
passion of Christ. It is not the mass that is adored, but through and in each
mass it is the Divine Original—the "only Begotten of the Father"—that is
adored. At the same time, there is a mystical identity between Christ as
Prototype and these "examples" or "images." Charles is given a peculiar status
in relation to this Original, insofar as he is called "so perfect an image of our
great God," but by definition this does not exclude other images or the great-
ness of God. In a touching reversion of the story of the Epiphany, when great
kings made presents to Christ, Anderton offers Christ, Prince of all creation,
to one who will be a great king, and whom he already addresses as "sovereign": "Now this is that most puissant Prince, whereof I presume to make
my present by this treatise following."[4]

It is the tone of reverent conviction, and the sense of priorities, that make
all the difference. Behind the fashionable Greek jargon is a deeper biblical
humanism, by no means exclusive to Protestants.

The mass is Anderton's center. There are two topics in respect of which
he displays indignation in its defense. These are loyalty to the monarch, and
the principle of free will, which for him makes loyalty and all virtue possible.
If he can somehow maintain these, despite all the odds, then England will
be safe for the mass. Presbyterian disloyalty, in Scotland and England, is so
threatening that surely the king will need, and reward with toleration, a
loyalty such as his.

He repels any suggestion that loyalty to king and country can ever be a
matter of personal or sectarian convenience. Pilkington had been so deeply
moved by the account of Christ's individual reassurance of forgiveness to
Peter that he would have nothing to do with those of his own party who
would have denied individual confession and absolution to any who sought
them. In the same way, Anderton will not believe the "commandment of
obedience [to Caesar] prescribed by our Saviour and his Apostles to have
been only for fear or in regard to outward policy, and not in respect of
religion or conscience." To accuse Christ of such sophistry is literally to
number Him among the malefactors.[5] Mistaken persons among Anderton's

own party attribute deposing power over monarchs to "the sentence of the supreme Pastor." This is admittedly "less passionate and able to hurt" than the "promiscuous multitude" regarded as sovereign by certain Protestants. But Anderton identifies himself as "undertaking ... the patronage of nei-ther."[6] Unmoved by arguments of fear or convenience, Anderton stands alone and is in that sense linked with Marsh, or any other believer at the moment when their belief is real to them. Anderton writes in a library, not a prison. His references are so profuse that footnotes often cover more page than text: nevertheless, what he is building with all these words is a space that his own conscience may inherit, worldly consequences notwithstanding.

Deploying partisan arguments with some relish, Anderton nevertheless has something more to offer than a double negative. His posthumous *The Reformed Protestant, Tending Directly to Atheism and All Impiety* (1621) fulfils the brief of its title, but it also affirms the author's own moral core. Anderton echoed the usual Romanist claim that, amid the doctrinal and moral disintegration exemplified by Protestantism, the Roman communion remained the only safeguard of virtue. He regarded the Marian persecution as entirely just and necessary "to affright the common people ... by course of exemplary punishment, against Novelism and Innovation of Religion." It was carried out "according to the most ancient laws of all Christian King-doms."[7] No doubt for him even the most reticent demurrer such as Marsh was an inducer of sin. There could be no defense in the claim that many individual Protestants (some of whom he quotes) stressed (as Marsh did) the importance of individual moral responsibility. Anderton's point was that the break from the Roman *system* could at best produce only an alternative (and therefore vicious) *system*: Lutheranism, for example, which Catholics equated with the Turkish tyranny, since it joined secular and sacred authority in one person and in that order, to the ruin of morals; or predestinationist Calvinism, which was simply an organized wickedness, founded on the belief that God was "the Author of sin." As for the Anabaptists, even Calvin recognised they were fit only to be burned. Consistent only with inconsistency, and believing in nothing but themselves, they actively advocated an anarchy that was merely the practical result to be looked for from the pseudosystem of their rivals the Presbyterians.

The Arminians might be considered more congenial to Anderton. It is perhaps not surprising that having returned to England by 1611, he does not mention in this context the Five Points that the Arminians tendered to the States-General in that year. Considerably modifying Calvinism in a free-will direction (very much as James Pilkington had done, for example), they represented a position that many Anglicans had already reached, and would advance from. There can be no doubt, however, that Anderton would have found "Arminianism," as he found "Anti-Trinitarianism," to be only one shade among many in the great night of "Novelism," where skulked all eva-

sion of Catholic truth. Protestantism "began . . . with . . . denial," and remained trapped in a disintegrating pattern of self-indulgence, which made
free will impossible.

But Anderton has more to do than to condemn what he sees as the nega-
tions of Protestantism. The "Epistle Dedicatory" to *The Reformed Protestant*
proposes a broader and deeper basis for the future of Catholicism than does
the "Epistle Dedicatory" to Prince Charles that graces *The Liturgy of the
Mass.* There is considerable poignancy in its appeal, offered as it were from
the grave to the world, in the eccentric typeface of a secret press:

THE EPISTLE DEDICATORIE
TO MAN.

CURTEOUS READER,
   Whether Christian Catholike, Protestant, Jew, Turke, or Pagan, I Dedicate this
small Treatise to thee, because I offer it to MAN, the only reasonable creature
upon earth, whom I finde by late Novelisme so greatly injured, as that I therefore
appeale, and make my complaint to all men, of what profession or sect soever.

Anderton's "appeal to Caesar" of 1608 was for an "open and equal Disputation" on religious matters. In *The Reformed Protestant* the appeal goes beyond
Caesar to "the light of reason and experimental knowledge." The Calvinistic
preachers and lecturers to whom the Scottish king has mortgaged the moral
future of his "united kingdoms" may rant away loyalty and all other virtues
with their "brutish denial of Free-will," but the heavenly kingdom remains.
For the attaining of that kingdom, there remains "that most certain, infallible
and experimental Lecture, written with great legible letters in the book of
every man's conscience."[8]

26

"Antiquity and Continuance"

JAMES Anderton's *St. Austin's Religion* appeared posthumously, in 1620. It was prefaced by a dedicatory epistle to King James. Making reference to the learned Protestant divines who were regularly summoned to stand arguing theology behind the king's chair as he dined, the author proffers St. Augustine's works as "sovereign Antidotes" against any heretical "contagion" from that quarter. Restored to their proper unity from the writings of learned Protestants, the "particulars of St. Austin's professed religion" are "now placed on the table before your highness."[1]

That such a scene was enacted literally may be doubted, but the king certainly took an interest in *St. Austin's Religion,* personally supervising a treatise designed to refute it, which issued from the pen of William Crompton, a Puritan controversialist and lecturer (of a rather flowery type) who might be called a mirror image of Anderton himself. Crompton hied from Bedford Grange, in the nearby parish of Leigh, in the West Derby Hundred of Lancashire. Bedford Leigh was a place of mine shafts and Catholicism in Crompton's day and could still be so described when Gerard Manley Hopkins served as Catholic curate there in the 1870s. Over the same period, Bolton would typify Salford Hundred as a center of Protestantism and textiles.[2] Mavericks in their adjacent, rival, and mutually sustaining native parishes, Anderton and Crompton provide a model of the contest in loyalty waged by religionists excluded from the establishment in opposite directions. William Crompton's son and namesake would be one of the Nonconformist divines evicted from their livings in 1662.[3] James's nephew and eventual heir Christopher Anderton would dither through the Civil War, now thrown into prison in the king's name, now dispossessed of his lands in the name of Parliament.[4] There is a poignant congruity between such (not uncommon) bewilderment and his uncle's sense that secular loyalty was owed, neither to king nor to Parliament alone, but only to both acting in unison.

For James Anderton, the king inherited by birth his constitutional position as secular head of the body politic, whatever any pope might say. But spiritual authority was quite another matter. The whole Christian world owed spiritual allegiance, in conscience, to the pope as spiritual legatee of Peter. It is the dialectic between these two positions that gives Anderton's *Apology* the force of a genuine intellectual document. *St. Austin's Religion,* on the other hand, a more routine compilation, may be said to fall foul of the circumstances of its publication and reception.

Alongside renewed protestations of secular loyalty, *St. Austin's Religion* rebuts the claim of any earthly monarch to "make himself prince of Bishops, and to be president in Ecclesiastical judgements." Crompton's counterrebuttal might be called King James's testament as Governor of his Church. St. Augustine, we are assured, "gives to the supreme Magistrate, active and coactive power in matters of Religion, leaving to the clergy passive and directive power." It is relevant to note that Anderton (or an editor on his behalf) makes reference in this context to "the poison of Arminianism." To judge from the tone of this phrase, English Catholics now saw themselves as confronting, not a Calvinist system as uncompromising as their own in its recension of the Augustinian tradition, but an insidious group of revisionists, eager to serve what Anderton calls "the abomination of desolation," by which he means the suborning of the spiritual heritage to the temporary requirements of a political system.[5] This was all too relevant to his own case. *St. Austin's Religion* was caught in the impasse of all intellectualist nonconformity. It was compelled to offer itself to be judged by a regime whose right of judgment in spiritual matters it could not but refuse. Yet, like other thoughtful nonconformists, Anderton does not want a monarchy powerful enough to relieve him of his disabilities by unconstitutional means.

Contrasting with such high-mindedness, yet in curious complicity with its otherwise baffled aims, there are voices more strident and more routine. As with Bishop Pilkington's *Nehemiah,* partisans hustle a posthumous work into print for their own purposes. Pugnacity and formalism, the wisdom of the foolish and the wisdom of the world in the shape of Roger and Lawrence Anderton, collaborate to issue what James Anderton the intellectual ruminator had chosen not to issue.

For the time being, Crompton had merely to rearrange the same legacy of Augustinian and pseudo-Augustinian texts so as to reaffirm his royal master's right of judgment. When controversy is as predictable as this, the chances of evidence being subjected to scrutiny are slight.

Crompton's status as a cog in the establishment sector of a mutually depressing machine is particularly apparent. His own patron, tutor, and father-in-law—an Archdeacon Pilkington of the second generation—was himself a protégé of Abbot, the primate charged with producing that Anglican oxymoron, an "Authorized Version" of the Bible. King James placed himself at the head of the editorial staff of Crompton's text, whose subject and nullifier was himself. The matter was one of his last concerns, an "authorized version" being achieved only a few weeks before the king's death.

Early in his own reign, King Charles was busy commissioning a fresh edition, revised and extended under the interested supervision of William Laud, soon to be promised the succession to Canterbury.[6] Anderton's usefulness as an antagonist for ambitious clerics had already been demonstrated in the case of Thomas Morton, successively Bishop of Chester, of Coventry-and-Lichfield, and (from 1632) of Durham.[7] He lived like the ideal Catholic Bishop—celibate, and noted for heroic acts of charity. Yet in doctrine he was of Calvinist tendency, though more moderate than some. Born at York, where he received his early education, he knew how dubious was the routine Romanist claim (repeated by Anderton) that the authenticity of English Christianity originated[8] with Pope Gregory's mission to Canterbury in the sixth century. York's bishopric was known to date from the time of Constantine, proclaimed emperor at York in 306. Morton is also important in the succession of the Church of England because he continued to hold secret ordinations during the Commonwealth. He was a living alternative, in other words, to the history of Christianity as constructed by the papacy. Given his conscientious objection to papal claims of secular authority, so was Anderton. Yet neither had any option but to engage on terms set by Rome: the only evidence that could enter their enclosed debate was the textual legacy of the Latin fathers as monitored and transmitted over time by the needs of the Roman see.

The first appearance of Anderton's *Apology,* in 1604, alarmed Archbishop Bancroft into commissioning a reply. Morton was found to write it (in Latin), perhaps with the aid of his friend the poet John Donne. Morton was promoted soon after to the deanery of Gloucester, his career assured. In October 1609 (the year he was promoted dean of Winchester), Morton sent the king an elaborate English work on the same theme, *A Catholic Appeal for Protestants.* The very next day he was for the first time made aware, by an aggressive letter from one signing himself "Roger Brereley" (almost certainly Roger Anderton) of the existence of the new 1608 edition of the *Apology.* Hastily inserting Roger's letter and his own "Answer" into the introductory material of his (now even longer) *Catholic Appeal,* Morton felt moved to define the incident as proof of conspiratorial collusion by "two brothers (as I am informed) both by priesthood and blood." Much more likely, the bad timing was the result of a clash of personality and aim between Roger and James Anderton, a clash, essentially, between opportunistic confrontationalism and the laying down of a case for the long-term future. Morton was certainly aware of this latter aspect of James Anderton's own formidable method. Morton himself could really do no more than invoke those "Protestant" views emerging from the Catholic tradition that were simply disavowed by Counter-Reformation Catholics (notably Bellarmine, with whom Morton also crossed swords).

In such a context, the transmission of Christianity becomes an elaborate masculist game, and not even as such a fair game, since those with access to

New Testament Greek are kept so few in number as to render their marginalia of no practical or political relevance. Doubt is the bogey and subtext of discourse. For Anderton, as for his antagonists, to have "varied from himself" is sufficient condemnation of any man. Without naming his old county neighbor and distant relative James Pilkington, Anderton cites in horrified stupefaction the rehabilitation sermon for Martin Bucer that Pilkington delivered. How can a man like Bucer, who so often changed his mind, be accounted "most learned and holy," Anderton asks?[9] The Pilkingtons of the bishop's generation would have answered with reference to the Platonic tradition. John Pilkington, the Bishop's brother and associate of Ascham, was much interested in Robert Grosseteste, the thirteenth-century reformer and Neo-Platonist, for whom God was revealed to humanity in terms of light and motion.[10] Beyond all knowledge, God is nevertheless immediately with us in all that is dynamic, all that illumines. The possibilities of variety tend godwards.

All this is nonsense to the Andertons and to their contemporary Protestant opponents. For Lawrence Anderton, Protestantism is defined as a "Platonical Idea." This means that, in the only terms in which he condescends to discuss such matters—the sub-Aristotelian "School-Divinity" left over from the Middle Ages—it is simply "a bare Notion of the mind," lacking the guarantee of "Personal Succession" proper to all stable systems. It contains discrepancy and cannot therefore be transmitted. A nonentity (non-ens) such as this must inevitably lack that quasi-Aristotelian entity, the transubstantiated wafer. And behold, it does so lack.[11]

The Protestant Morton has the same scholastic mindset. Since the doctrine of transubstantiation *differs* from the transmitted texts of Gregory the Great, transubstantiation (and every pope who ever taught it) is for Morton *non-ens*, somehow not really there. Maintaining the opposite position, the Jesuit is driven to perform an equivalent, and of course opponent, circuit. He writes *The Progeny of Catholics* and ironically dedicates it to Morton, "the principal motor for me to compose this treatise."[12]

In such a context, it is impossible to talk of a "history of ideas." As an episode in the history of printing, however, it is only appropriate that funds under Morton's control helped to pay for the transmission of Anderton texts. "I. B. P."—as Roger prints his brother's chosen pseudonym—stands not merely for "John Brereley Priest," but also for "Impropriator of Bolton Parish." The jest is as good as a punch in the ribs, for the Andertons hold their right to farm local tithes from successive bishops of Chester, including in his turn Thomas Morton himself.

A disturbing example of this mindless pattern of oppositional symmetry and deductive intransigence enters even James Anderton's *Apology*, albeit in a footnote. Among other documentary certifiers of the real presence of Christ in the sacrament, he cites (down to the subdivision of a page) three gossiping chronicles that "report the . . . miraculous appearance of blood" as a result of "violent sacrilege done by Jews to the Blessed Sacrament" in Poland during 1556. The date of their public burning—the Friday after Ascension Day— is piously noted. The dynamic illumination of their tortured bodies in the fire is of course passed over as *non-ens,* but the brute fact of their annihilation is left to prove, by a sort of deductive symmetry, that Christ is exclusively present in the Roman mass.[13]

That alertness of the human imagination that is common to all vital lan- guage—whether we are thinking of Plato or of Chaucer—has no place in such polemics, which draw such intellectual sustenance as they possess from the international jargon known as "academic Latin," a thing long since cut off from its once living root. In 1615, Anderton's own *Apology* entered this galère, being translated into Latin by the exile priest William Rayner for the benefit of continental scholars.

For James Pilkington, the bloom of eternity had to be gathered daily from the life we know, whereas the mechanics of controversy in which Anderton was trapped exhausted themselves to preempt an unknowable world out of time. When James Pilkington's God asserts his fatherly authority, it is a scene from contemporary Rivington. He is to be discovered, we might now say, in the Hopkinsian *instress* that lives dynamically in the human landscape. Touched by nothing less than a divine idea, men "buskle and bowne them- selves to this work; they spit on their hands, and take better hold than afore; they buckle themselves to labour with courage, not to be driven from it any more."[14] But the dynamic and the intuitive were no longer relevant for Crompton's patron, Archdeacon Richard Pilkington, named after his pater- nal grandfather and raised at his uncle's Rivington School. Providence is now to be guessed at through a maze of printed evidence. From these arid sources the archdeacon assembles *Parallela,* a book put together from the opponent arguments of others, stretching on and on like parallel lines towards a theoretical infinity where God waits, to punish or reward.

Equity, based on the separation of political and spiritual authority, was truly the only way into a dialogue of ideas and out of this deadly interdepen- dence in negation. The implication of James Anderton's *Apology* is that the survival of the "old religion" in a Protestant country necessitated a liberal reading of the tradition of Common Law. At root, tolerance for Catholics must mean tolerance as such. Behind his partisan claim (and in spite of his Aristotelianism) Anderton had glimpsed a universal idea. This makes him unusual in wider contexts than seventeenth-century Bolton.

PART SIX
Parliamentary Stronghold

It is said of Thales the Philosopher, that being asked of one, *What was the greatest?* He answered (*place*) wherein all things stand, or have subsistence.
— Ellis Bradshaw, *A Week-day's Lecture* (1649)

27

Civil War Bolton: Claiming the Marks of the True Church

I⊤ is often said that the Civil War derived from the "Problem of Multiple Kingdoms."[1] That problem necessarily included the frustrations of the regions. In the case of southeast Lancashire, these included the frustrations of economic expansion. The wealth of Boltonian merchants, for instance, increased greatly during the early Stuart period. A fair portion of it was spent on educational charities, who are still reaping the benefits.

In 1628 the Puritan merchant Humphrey Chetham purchased Turton Tower, the former home of the recusant Orrells. His endowed library in Manchester (destined to be a favorite haunt of Friedrich Engels, among others) is still in existence, as is the lineal descendant of his hospital, founded as an orphanage and now a school for music and the arts. In 1646 the trustees of the old Bolton Grammar School—never adequately financed—handed over their charge to the executors of the will of Robert Lever, a London merchant with origins and connections in Darcy Lever. A new stone building—which continued to comprise the school's premises until 1880—and a more adequate financial basis, were arranged by 1658. The "Lever" connection would provide the legal basis for a later Bolton Puritan, W. H. Lever, to transform the school's fortunes in the early twentieth century. William Hulme (1631–91), antiquarian and merchant of Kearsley, in Deane parish and a schoolfellow of Oliver Heywood at Bolton, left grants for study at Oxford, and money to Manchester Grammar School, which remains its chief source of endowment. Increasing enormously over time till 1881, the funds were in that year additionally applied to the founding of two further schools and a residence hall for students at an institution, which, at a still later date, was at last graced by Parliament with the independent status and title of "Manchester University."[2]

In his classic account of the Civil War in Lancashire, Broxap mentions a petition of March 1640–41, brought forward by James Stanley, of Lathom House, the region's leading aristocrat and royalist, whose wife was a daughter of the royal and princely houses of France and Orange. The petition—which had wide local support—was for the founding of an independent Manchester university.[3]

Knowledge is power, and local Puritans in particular were interested in knowledge that had economically beneficial effects. Richard Heywood of Little Lever (Oliver's father), for instance, was an intelligent merchant well aware of the trade depressions of the late 1630s and of the need to learn from them. He was something of a spiritual client of Mrs. Andrews, a Lever of Darcy Lever by birth, whose husband was kin to Thomas Lever. She divided with Lathom House the vetting of local preachers. (The Stanleys had enough tact not to interfere with her arrangements for Bolton.) She and Heywood would seem to have inherited Lever's view that education, trade, and spiritual well-being were natural concomitants of the Christian commonwealth viewed as the Body of Christ. In this context must be placed the arrival, in 1641, under Heywood's patronage, of Richard Goodwin, a graduate of Emmanuel College, Cambridge. This promising young curate—he would become Bolton's Presbyterian vicar in due course—was not merely godly, but an adept at chemical experiments, a key to the future prosperity of the region.[4] Elizabeth's eccentric and arrogant warden of the Manchester College, the mathematician and alchemist Dr. John Dee, had not been popular, but the technological possibilities of what he represented were taken to heart. A "Manchester University" would surely have been rather different from Oxford and Cambridge, which opened their gates to science scholars— a very high proportion of them from Manchester Grammar School—only after the reforms of the 1870s.[5] In 1641, it was intended to use the old College buildings of Manchester as the basis of a university designed to meet local needs.

Broxap mentions Stanley's petition as an interesting question, not very relevant to the Civil War. One might equally fairly describe the war as the gratuitously irrelevant answer. There was, of course, Stanley was assured, no possibility of the petition's even being considered.

Richard Heyrick, current warden of the Manchester College, and a supporter of the "university," was a constitutional royalist like most middle-class Puritans. His background was a cultivated one (his cousin was the poet Robert Herrick). In May 1642 he brought another petition to the king, then resident at York. Signed by eight thousand respectable Lancashire subjects, it begged His Majesty to find an accommodation with Parliament. It was graciously acknowledged and ignored. The signatories would form the core of the king's loyal Presbyterian opponents in the county.[6]

In July 1642 James Stanley attempted to secure his property, the old college buildings in Manchester. They were currently in use as the county arsenal. The Manchester "rebels" acted quickly. With the assistance of troops commanded by Robert Bradshaw of Bradshaw, they drove Stanley out and fortified the town with the aid of German engineers. This action—the speed and

efficiency with which it was completed suggest a degree of preparation—
went far to determine that Parliament would prevail in Lancashire and the
north of England.

James Stanley, now seventh earl of Derby, begged the king to raise his
standard at Warrington, to rally the overwhelming regional loyalty of Lancashire, Cheshire, and Wales that had created the Tudor dynasty. Charles
preferred to raise it at Nottingham, 22 August 1642. He surrendered himself
to the Scots at Southwell, a dozen leafy miles away just three years, nine
months, and several thousand lives later. In January 1649, on the scaffold at
Whitehall, he became the only kind of monarch the English would ever
again care for: a perfect, powerless actor performing motions determined
by others.

If a "University of Manchester" was only a dream and an absurdity, the
Four Horsemen of the Apocalypse were tutors more readily commissioned.
War against civilians in its most ghastly shape—Trevelyan would liken the
scene to the "furies of Alva," but he might have said "the obscenities of
Guernica"—was "unloosed in the streets of Bolton" by Prince Rupert's cavalry on 28 May 1644. Richard Heywood's valuable library was also destroyed
on that occasion. Famine and Pestilence, in the wake of invading armies,
collapsing trade, and the ruinous expenses of the war, became common neighbors. Death, finally, came to the bewildered James Stanley in Bolton market
place on 15 October 1651. His scaffold was made of timber from the ruins
of Lathom House, so long defended, but in vain, by his heroic countess ("It
was the glory of the county," mourned an opponent). Parliament had selected
the earl as an obvious scapegoat, but even some of those defined by the new
regime as his victims now openly lamented him. About to die, he made a
gesture of reverence towards the tower of the parish church, as though it
still guarded the Body of Christ.[7]

Such is the setting for the literary efforts of Boltonians in this traumatic
period, which may be said to have branded a peculiar consciousness of itself
as a town, and as a uniquely Parliamentary town, upon the place. Its Civil
War defenses of chains and mud and rubble gave it a particular place in the
contest to determine the sacramental "marks of the true church" as evidence
for the particular presence of Christ, and with it the true status of rival
localities and modes of sovereignty.

28

"A Little Ticket of Lead": Presbyterian Divines

JOHN Tilsley was a relative of Humphrey Chetham by marriage. His father had refused communion at Deane because the vicar (a drunkard and fornicator, according to charges of 1601) had worn a surplice. Typifying the Puritan disaffection with Oxford and Cambridge, he graduated with an M.A. from Edinburgh University in 1637. Since in due course he delivered Robert Bradshaw's funeral eulogy, he doubtless approved of his preemptive strike against James Stanley in Manchester in July 1642. After the capture of Preston by Parliamentary forces in 1643 (an event he described in a vivid firsthand account to Parliament), he was appointed vicar of Deane, his native parish. Rectory tithes, hitherto payable to Christopher Anderton, were sequestered, the vicar's stipend raised from ten pounds to sixty pounds per annum, and the old vicarage house restored to its intended use.

Tilsley became an energetic (and censorious) trustee of Chetham's Hospital and Library, housed in the old college buildings in Manchester. The churches of the region housed book collections that were in effect branches of this library, subject to Tilsley's campaign against "infection." Whatever compromises might have been achieved in a "Manchester University" presided over by the earl of Derby, only one view of the universe was now permitted. This was defined in the "Harmonious Consent" drawn up for the signature of the ministers of Lancashire by a now bullish Richard Heyrick in 1648. There was to be an end of the "universal toleration . . . of heretical doctrines, broached in these times." Tilsley was a signatory to this, and one of three attestors to the "petition of twelve thousand four hundred and upwards" of the well-to-do Protestants of Lancashire, calling for the institution of a Presbyterian discipline in 1646. Anxious to strengthen support in the House of Lords and to foil the ambitions of left-wing sectaries, Tilsley published a rebuttal of a Leveller attack that dismissed the petitioners as "a rabble of Cavaliers."

Behind such intransigence lay the bewilderment of a self-canceling experience. The greatest battle of the Civil War, for instance, was fought and won at Marston Moor, near York, in July 1644 by Scottish Covenanter forces in alliance with Oliver Cromwell. But—denying the dreams of such as Tilsley in the moment of realizing them—the result was a propaganda victory not for "our dear brethren of Scotland" and their sober Presbyterian institutions but for the Cromwellian army, in which far wilder forms of religious and political radicalism were known to harbor. Yet at least the defeat of Arminianism and recusancy provided an opening for Presbyterianism as their only coherent rival. Ceremonies were arranged for the "setting aside" of godly new ministers, such as those ordained by Tilsley and his colleagues at Turton, in 1650. But in the same year, ministers were required to sign the "Engagement" of loyalty to the republican Parliament. Deane was a living in the gift of the Crown. Sharing to the full that self-identifying loyalty to his king and duke and patron typical of Lancashire Presbyterians, Tilsley could not sign, and was deprived of his living. He may have sympathized with Christopher Love's royalist plot of 1651, in which Heyrick was implicated. Meanwhile Francis Anderton, Christopher's heir, took the opportunity to profess conformity to the new regime. He reacquired the Deane tithes and other family impropriations, which it had been the privilege of his great-uncle James, the Catholic controversialist, to consolidate and deplore.

Tilsley was made a small official grant in 1655, the year after the "Engagement" was rescinded, but he was still negotiating for the funding of his enormous parish (which included the large chapelries of Horwich and West-houghton) in December 1659, on the eve of the Restoration. The last meeting of the local classis was held on 14 August 1660.

Like all other ministers of Deane and Bolton, Tilsley was deprived in 1662. Circumstances mitigated the experience in his case. It was ironic that a minister who had literally fortified his church to defend the aspiration typified by Lever's sermons of 1550—a figurehead king presiding over an honest and efficient commonwealth—should have had his prestige salvaged by a collusion that had everything to do with personalities and their failings and very little to do with the law. Crypto-Catholic Andertons, basking in the return of a monarch like themselves (they would achieve a baronetcy in 1677) saw no reason to demand the eviction of a fellow nonconformist from his vicarage house. With perhaps a touch of fellow feeling, the merry monarch appointed as Tilsley's official replacement John Angier junior, scapegrace son and namesake of a famous Presbyterian divine, who had been given another chance at Harvard after wasting his portion at England's Cambridge. The choice was a shrewd one, insofar as it gave every excuse to easygoing Bishop Wilkins of Chester (who happened to be Oliver Cromwell's brother-in-law) to permit Tilsley to continue preaching, Angier's deficiencies being obvious to everybody. And so a kind of compromise obtained for a time, in good King Charles's golden days. Like others, Tilsley perhaps mellowed. But clearly what he and his Presbyterian colleagues had wanted in 1646—a

United Kingdom made morally invincible by unity in religion—was never to be.[1]

The token of that moral invincibility was a pathetically strange one. The local lay elders nominated by Parliament to arrange for the setting up of the Presbyterian classis were so inappropriate, in the case of Bolton, that only one of the four "ever appeared at any of the subsequent . . . meetings," once the classis was formed. One of those nominated for Deane had harbored Cavalier troops, and showed no interest in Presbyterianism. Not surprisingly, there was an aggressive reaction once the local discipline was up and running. Oliver Heywood, commencing study at Trinity College, Cambridge, felt disillusioned with his home town. He describes the moral police system designed to determine which parishioners were fit to receive communion:

> In the year 1647, or thereabouts the Presbyterian government being settled in Bolton the ministers Mr John Harpur and Mr Richard Goodwin, together with the Eldership made an order (after examination and approbation of the communicants) that every time they were to come to the Lord's supper, every particular communicant should upon the Friday before fetch a little ticket (as they called it) of lead of the Elders, and shew it to the Elders again in Church before they were to receive the Sacrament, that they might know that none but such as were admitted did intrude themselves.

During this period, tradesmen commonly made up for the failure of the Royal Mint to provide an adequate supply of small coins by issuing their own leaden tokens, whose currency depended on their own good name, and on which the king's image was replaced by some private emblem. An American Indian, for instance, was the chosen symbol of William Boardman of Halliwell, who clearly found nothing anomalous about appropriating a continent to further a concern whose own location had to be spelt out rather precisely, on the same token, as "nere Smithilles." The imitation of this practice by the petty inquisition now monitoring access to the Sacrament in Bolton had the result Bishop Pilkington anticipated: the poor and timid complied and the rich and forceful rebelled. At Bolton, the dissidents were led by Richard Heywood. Among his supporters was Ellis Bradshaw, husbandman and soldier, distinguished from others of his class as a thoughtful, vigorous (and eccentric) pamphleteer.[2]

The purchasing of the means of redemption by a token of lead, the privileged currency of a local system of moral management, was far removed from the dynamic "allure" of Thomas Lever's vision, with its legacy in the "whole Puritan movement westward to the Pacific from Massachusetts Bay." Between their international trading requirements and their cult of private worship, the Heywoods had no time for such parochial contrivances. Known as the "Chapel"—since heart-of-oak timbers from the Levers' former chapel were thriftily redeployed in its construction—the house of John Heywood,

Richard's brother, represented a more robust and adaptable ethic than Harpur's little stereotype. The Heywoods thought "getting a ticket" would become a substitute for active righteousness, not its emblem. To one nostalgic for the "old religion," the leaden "ticket" would appear to be sordid as well as inadequate, set against the monk Bradshaw's rich and static images of Werburgh's jewelled sanctuary, itself but a shadow of the *volupte* (a favorite word of his) of heaven's own region.

Appearances can be deceiving, however. Only persons of good family were acceptable as choir monks. Henry Bradshaw's poverty, his monkish encomiast stresses, was "*wilful*" that is, virtuous only because voluntary. The impression of Werburgh's shrine, as of every other throughout Europe, most current in the life of the poor was a little pilgrimage badge of lead not very different from Mr. Harpur's "ticket." Surviving examples of late-medieval stained glass exhibit dandified saints or angels, golden as on the king's coin, chillingly indifferent to the labor that made them possible.[3] England in particular was obsessed with royal saints (and was about to make itself another). The royalist Oliver Heywood praises the frugality of John Angier senior precisely because it was the *chosen* lifestyle of one having a "good Portion" in the world. For a complete antithesis to this Bolton ticket we may turn to the scented rhetoric of John Hewit, Lancashire weaver's son turned royal preacher. He spent just long enough in the old Bolton Grammar School—a little thatched, half-timbered building,[4] crowded with the youth of trading families—to learn to shun (but never escape) everything the place represented. Truly neither dynamic nor static, his sermons are richly *vibrative,* a consolation prize for reality: part of the baroque-derived taste of Van Dyck's portraits of Charles Stuart or James Stanley, Hewit's fellow martyrs at the block. His sermons are synesthetic: sound-pictures of a pious clique of English high society savoring its own taste, vibrating in the taste of itself.

In such a context, the leaden ticket appears less repellent. It is truly the emblem of a pilgrimage. Contrary to any supralapsarian doctrine one may suppose to be current among them, it is the offering by Presbyterian communicants to God of something *earned.* As James Anderton offered the host to Charles Stuart as an Epiphany gift, so these offer to Christ in the small currency of work and bread their week of moral effort and in return take "stars for money; stars not to be told . . . yet to be purchased."[5] The quotation is from George Herbert, but is not out of place. The idea of a coherent spiritual culture had not yet been quite abandoned. At least one of Bolton's Presbyterian divines—Henry Pendlebury—was fond of quoting Herbert. What truly joins and differences the sacraments of court and classis is the shared contradiction between class role and belief theory. The aristocrats who cluster round Hewit believe in free will, yet they refresh themselves with the bouquet of heaven's presence as a compliment to their mere sensibility. The Bolton communicants believe in divine election; yet they steel themselves to earn the memento of a heaven perceived as the wages of a lifetime's effort. The king, to whom the nobility look for approval, has been replaced in their line of vision by middle-class elders. Aristocratic self-regard is transposed into the self-respect of a new class, the ascetic and aspiring upper echelons of the workforce.

The processes that evolved this Presbyterian moment were not exhausted at its demise. Aspiration, supervision, and the acquired instinct for corporate betterment, all with a moral cast and in biblical terms of reference, would long remain the literate culture of the place, and would include most Christian denominations and a number of secular groups by the end of the nineteenth century. In all its many forms, respectability would continue to monitor all the many forms of backsliding. And always, in south Lancashire, there would be the appropriation of stereotypes of America. Here was a great potential; but it was not a transformative one. It went towards the construction of the still hierarchical anthill of Victorian England.

It was from the trap of this all-too-slowly evolving polarity of management and labor that so many sought the dynamic spiritual adventure of a New World. Yet as we have seen in the case of John Angier junior, the New World was only another chance, not another mode of existence. The real "new world" was of the nature of a mental event. In Ellis Bradshaw's case, and that of innumerable others, it began at home in the middle of the seventeenth century. His writing already anticipates the radical "new" democratic spirit, sweeping *back* from America, that intelligent Boltonians of just his sort of class would seize upon in the writings of their hero and friend, Walt Whitman. It was no accident that the two leading Whitmanites were Bolton Scots, raised as strict Presbyterians.[6]

As for the Presbyterian system, its totalitarian pretensions proved even less appropriate to England than to Scotland (which itself evolved a number of rival kirks). In Scotland, the clergy and systems of education and theology were paramount, but English Presbyterianism was rather an experiment in tightening the control of the *cosa nostra* of wealthy Protestants, a further chapter of that Babylonian captivity of the Church that Thomas Lever, to Knox's approval, had deplored. Its eternal verities decayed, but the divisions that had produced them survived. Sole minister by 1657, vicar in 1660, Richard Goodwin was evicted in 1662 and then resumed his chemical experiments in Manchester. But the bulk of Bolton's commercial elite, to many of whom he was related by marriage, persuaded him to return as their preacher by 1669, a situation that was legalized by the Declaration of Indulgence of 1672. In 1696 they built a chapel on what became Bank Street, the northern continuation of Bradshawgate whence their ancestors had sallied to repel the earl of Derby's forces. It was some 250 yards northwest of the parish church. This small-scale but absolute marginalization may fairly be described as the price of eliminating Lathom House and shifting the Stanley headquarters permanently south to Knowsley, ending Stanley dominance (though not in-fluence) in the region. As in other towns with strong Roundhead traditions, the Church of the national establishment would never be the Bolton estab-lishment. The parish church could not help but remain, literally, "Bolton," the "settlement on the boll" or sudden knop of land, St. Peter's rock above the twisting river Croal—the numinous and defensive touchstone (the *place*) it had always been. As elsewhere, nonconformists would continue to claim theoretical rights in it and in its adjacent grammar school, which in Bolton's case they had reedified and endowed. But, as elsewhere, the eye of the land-scape had been put out.

Compelled to justify their beliefs to a powerful and industrious laity, the intellectualist Bank Street clergy had turned their inherited doctrines inside out by the middle of the eighteenth century. Unitarianism, with its denial of the godhead of Christ, its message of human perfectibility, and its practice of opening communion to all without test became the creed of a Brahmin elite, as elsewhere in England and New England. A remnant of true Presbyte-rians withdrew to join Congregationalists in their makeshift conventicle in a dismal alley nearby, the site of a great preaching by the Calvinistic George Whitfield (and were shunned for that reason by Bolton's free-will Method-ists). These Congregationalists prospered in their turn. Within a generation an adjacent orchard was occupied by a new chapel due to expand in elegance and diminish in severity. In 1803 a godly handful fled thence to Moor Lane, and it was there that native Presbyterianism "virtually died in 1817," almost unnoticed amid the inrush of Scots, who had their own chapels and ideas.[7]

It was into this context of controversy and collapse that the works of Henry Pendlebury (1626–95), the most interesting of the Turton ordinands of 1650, emerged. He remained in print from 1687, which saw the publication of his *Plain Representation of Transubstantiation* till 1816, which saw the last issues of his *Invisible Realities* and *The Books Opened*. It was John Tillot-son, another of Cromwell's relatives by marriage and a friend of Bishop Wilkins, who arranged the first publication as part of that undeviating cam-paign against popery that would make him William III's natural choice to be archbishop of Canterbury, in 1691.

Pendlebury's *Plain Representation* was sped on its way by a flamboyant preface from J. Johnson, the London publisher.[8] Pendlebury himself prefers quieter evidence. Yet he is not interested in fine shades of thought, so much as in precise arguments for sustaining an ethical conviction, which he shares with the Boltonian writers of every party we have hitherto met. Also percep-tible is the usual double motive: predictable attacks on the "other" side frame a particular quarrel with one's own side. One might almost define the convic-tion and the quarrel in the same terms. We have seen how at Frankfurt Thomas Lever felt superior to the purely political logic of his fellow exiles, Knox and Jewel, mutually bent as they were on the achievement of irreconcilable difference. We have noted Marsh's incapacity, at Lathom, to concede to his persecutors the clear *denial* they demanded of their own principles. What is common to both events is the same aggressive hunger for more and more enlightenment, the same contempt typical of those "Raw towns that we believe and die in"[9] for nationalistic, imperial, or party "solutions." Here is the provincial "rage to know" first tapped by Margaret Beaufort's school at Knowsley. How Anderton *despises* fellow Romanists who burden the Holy Father with temporal claims. How Pilkington *loathes* fellow Puritans who deny private confession to those who seek it. Pendlebury's eighteenth-century editor put the same idea in a rather trite way, when he defined his author as combining all the "Freedom ... of a Chillingworth" with all the "Dignity of a Hooker."[10]

Anticipating a Catholic backlash, Pendlebury recalls anti-transubstantiationists of the sixteenth century. Like Marsh, he studied at Christ's College, Cambridge, but he makes no mention of Marsh's refined demurrals, finding the straightforward denials of Marsh's brother-in-law Hurst more appropriate to his purpose. Still wrestling with Bellarmine, he reduces the eucharistic bread to a "figurative ... Sign." Very much like Anderton, he places the weight of his argument on moral responsibility, but turns it against the mass. Transubstantiation would indeed be a shift within the power of the deity, but the character of the biblical Jesus is such that we cannot believe he wishes us to be passive ingesters of such an extraordinary miracle, endlessly duplicated in our favor. An American Indian would "determine against" such an impotence of the spirit. In this way, Pendlebury turns his distaste for the supralapsarian tendencies of his own party into denunciation of the mass, which he regards as an equivalent superstition, an abdication of the moral effort of the will. For him, the Sacrament both celebrates and feeds the hunger for enlightenment. Like his own appetite for the printed word, however, his appetite for the Sacrament has become an exercise in the sovereignty of the *inner* life, only. Place is no longer even the background to action. It has somehow ceased to exist, and much of the value of action has gone with it. It is not surprising to learn that Pendlebury seems to have left to his wife responsibility for everything but the preparation of his weekly "ministerial performances":

> such as our Hunger is, that makes us desire this Meat; such as this Meat is, that we desire; and such as the Life is, that is maintained by it, such also is our eating of it.[11]

Elsewhere, he attacks the habit of regarding the mass as "a present Remedy" for "Immoralities and Impurities," but he has himself clearly imbibed the Neoplatonic thirst for intellectual and moral "purity," in its negative aspects. A Turton ordinand, he is in part a product of the power vacuum created by the demise of the Orrells. When the Andertons are forced to vacate Lostock, there will be an opening in that place for James Anderton's worst nightmare. A "high supralapsarian" sect of Johnsonian Baptists—named for its founder John Johnson, a Lostock autodidact—will emerge to promote the message that there is absolutely no connection between the preaching of the gospel and the fostering of good morals.[12] Pendlebury represents a theoretical median point between such desperation and the Unitarian recovery, both of which owed something to him.

The aversion from the world he represents is sufficiently indicated by his *Invisible Realities the Real Christian's Greatest Concernment*. "Seen things," he says, "are the World's Portion, the Crust that God casts out to Dogs, as *Luther* said of the Turkish Empire." Using emphasis, repetition, homely humor, and the magic of Greek and Latin (half-revealing and half-hiding a meaning beyond the laity, like the movements of a mass priest behind a screen), he strives to pull the Sunday minds of his auditors away from loom and byre and counting house to contemplate the shopping list of eternity, which is all that concerns him and all that should chiefly concern them: the Great White Throne, the sounding of the Trumpet, the opening of the Graves, the rising of the Dead. Driven from Holcombe Chapel in 1662, he will be dependent on a share in the Hilton Lectureship at Bolton, a mercantile bequest, and on the voluntary contributions of working auditors in the parishes around. Yet he loves to repeat "the Saying of Sir Thomas More: 'There is a Devil that is termed Business, that carrieth away more Souls . . . than all the Devils in Hell beside.'" Thomas Lever's impetus to explore the world is replaced by a reliance on unvisited regions as providing criteria for Bolton. The American Indian on William Boardman's token (a schoolboy's collectable once such things were banned as currency in 1672) now has the casting vote on the mass. Holy Land dendrology ("the Barren Fig-Tree") must be memorized in all its peculiarities to yield a "Practical Exposition of the Parable," as though any tree visible in northern England has shed all meaning.[13]

Pendlebury writes with a discreet power and deploys much learning with some panache. It is otherwise with James Livesey, relative, client, and theological barker to the Chethams. Down-market from Sir Thomas Browne, his stall is crammed with second-hand ware from many sources. The contradictions stalking Pendlebury have invaded his text. Provincial rawness has yielded to pedantic crassness. There is no longer any reason to believe or any capacity to die.

Death, when it snatches Humphrey Chetham's nephew and namesake (Livesey's brother-in-law) from one state of unearned blessedness to another, remains entirely enigmatic under a spate of words. Wafted from earthly perfection to heavenly bliss (calling aloud in impeccable Latin on uncle Humphrey, all but visible beyond the veil), the young man takes with him the remainder of Livesey's worldly hopes.[14] Three years earlier, he had to lament the passing of John Atherton of Atherton, another patron, under the heading of *catastrophe magnatum* ("a dreadful downfall of great ones"), one of a list of calamities visiting the elders of Zion and Lancashire. In Livesey's opening sentence of compliment to the afflicted widow, Augustine, Tirinus, the Book of Psalms, Juvenal, Chrysostom, Ezekiel, Seneca, and (a favorite) Epictetus whirl past the eye, and Greek, Latin, Hebrew spot the page like currants in an English pudding.[15] Yet he will stoop to explain the most elementary metaphors.

His page is a veil between the life of the Lancashire gentry, all too tellingly anticipated by Epictetus, in which men are "long in exercising, in eating, in drinking" and that future "Kingdom of grace and glory" where "every subject is a Sovereign." To reach it, one must pray for no small miracle in one's favor: "to know His mind, and do His will exactly, universally, and continually." Nothing so specious as common sense will meet the case. Plead not old age and incapacity as an excuse to lay down duty, Lancaster's judges are sternly warned. True, the old Levites were released at fifty, but *Augustine* preached into his last sickness, at seventy-six. Dare to echo Paul's justification in the sight of God: "I *laboured* more than they." Remit no duty to younger men, this first and last generation of Presbyterian grandees is urged, but discharge it to the very edge of the grave—"sincerely, though slenderly."[16] For an elite with no future, it seems, there can be no responsibility to the community, or to the idea of justice, only to one's personal eternity.

In half-realizing this, and in the unction and crassness such a prospect exacerbates, Livesey anticipates those nonconformist divines chained to the denominational zones of influence of Victorian employers and congregations. Dickens himself might have written Livesey's egregious dedication to "George Chetham Esq., late Alderman of London . . . And his virtuous consort Mrs Katharine Chetham with their hopeful Progeny . . . And the Rest of that Worthy Family."[17] Only very rarely, and in a more private context, does he remit his crippling anxiety sufficiently to make a pedantic little joke.[18]

Yet he is capable of producing passages of sinister power. In tracing damnation to its source, he attributes it to final impenitence, itself the issue of infidelity. Infidelity in its turn is at root an indefinable "depraved disposition," which Livesey knows well how to describe. Here—in the hissingly titled ΨΥΧΗΣΗΜΙΑ (pp. 113–14)—is revealed a conscience that remains proud, as the support of external authority crumbles away, to be corroded from within by the atmosphere of inquisition that still leaches from it. He is caught between the allurements of persecution and independence, between the old incense and fresh air. Here in anticipation is that "spiritual luxury" of transatlantic high Victorianism, which sought its moral vacations in ether or Emerson. Here commences that maimed esthetic that made Nathaniel Hawthorne so curious about Bolton and so obsessive of its traditions:

Depraved Nature, there is ἔνδον τι κακὸν connatural corruption which (were there no Devil on earth) would bring you to a Devil in hell. . . . [T]here is a thief in thy house, a spark in the chest, a snake in the bosom, an enemy in thy heart, man, would undo thee for ever: This corrupt nature meets us at board and bed, is ever hunting and haunting us; 'tis a potent enemy; a politic enemy, ever lusting against the Spirit, ever warring against the soul; Christ alone was free from this . . . and Adam in innocency; thou hast need to pray, Good God, deliver me from my self, my sinful self: This was that thorn in the flesh (I humbly conceive) which Paul was so molested with; 'tis called the *Messenger of Satan,* because Satan set on his sinful nature to work. . . . I know Heinsius and Hammond and others think it was some sore and sharp affliction inflicted on Paul by the followers of *Simon Magus;* but let them say who can what it was!

29

"I Hope I Shall Die in Honour":
Royalist Martyrs

"Honor" was an abstract quality, implying a certain dignity and courage of conduct and demeanor. It was also a concrete legal term for "a number of manors held in plurality." The possession of the latter was anciently a very necessary foundation for attaining to the former. Lancashire's most spectacular royalist martyr, James Stanley, earl of Derby, executed on the site of the market cross of his manor of Bolton in 1651, retained his dignity and courage to the last moment. Like his royal master and fellow martyr Charles I, he was incapable of apologizing for his political and military errors, not because he did not recognize them as such but because he could never recognize the right of a lesser being to replace him in his inherited responsibility.

To sustain itself, the attribute of honor required deference from below. What makes Lancashire's second royalist martyr—John Hewit—more interesting than Derby is that he expressed a new direction for the use of honor as a verb. Despite his status as a court preacher to Charles I, he employed honor to imply respect, not offered vertically to wealth and power, but extended laterally to others whose conscience differs from one's own. He was, in other words, a martyr catalyst, dying in the expression of a viewpoint not yet generally acknowledged. Derby (like Charles) on the other hand, was only a martyr lord, buying in blood the continuity of his species in the absence of what Hewit asked of his fellow Cavaliers: repentance.

While the meaning of honor in the context of social values and ethical relationships was undergoing traumatic adaptation, its hard legal implications were more resistant. If the Civil War had immediate winners in Bolton or elsewhere, they were most easily found among those who stuck to the money and accumulated the manors, regardless of dignity or conduct, relationships or respect. A "cash-nexus" elite continued to gain ground at the expense of Derby's past and Hewit's future. Relatively minor local survivalists were the Cromptons, merchant gentry of Darcy Lever, who took no part in the fighting, and the Hultons of Over Hulton, who changed sides at the right moment.[1] But the palm belongs to the Bridgeman family.

Turton Tower, which Henry Chetham annexed for Puritanism in 1628, was the most southerly of the old northern peel towers erected to defend the realm against Scottish invasion. Turton was Bolton's filter for all influences from that quarter. Indeed, with its stern little church "among precipices" (as Camden described it), the place retains to this day a Scottish look, particularly when the heather is in bloom. Very different is Great Lever, immediately south of the center of Bolton. Here there are still some grazing meadows, and the greenest grass out of Ireland. As the gateway to everything south—Manchester, Oxford, London—the site of its picturesque old hall is now buried under an urban freeway. It was this hall and its lands that John Bridgeman, bishop of Chester, bought in 1629.

The bishop's quarters in the dilapidated precincts of St. Werburgh's were not very suitable for a married prelate. Holding in plurality the rich rectory of Wigan (Bolton's royalist rival, nine miles west), Bridgeman varied his residence between there and Great Lever while learning commercial skills from the nonconformist entrepreneurs he was ostensibly policing. Coal mining, in Deane parish and elsewhere, made a shrewd investment and promoted the growth of a section of the working class that would long continue to look to conservative landowners rather than to nonconformist merchants for bread and guidance.[2] An "ardent defender" of Bridgeman "rights and finances," the bishop "showed a complete disregard for the financial policies of Charles I's government."[3] Such behavior was not going to win any wars for the king. Once the Restoration was inevitable, it was going to win the peace for its own kind. His conduct anticipates the Whig state after 1689 as Disraeli would see it: as a filter placed between sovereign and people for absorbing all manner of good.

Bridgeman was loyal enough, in 1635, to arrange a ceremony of recantation in his cathedral for the Chester supporters of the Puritan lawyer William Prynne, currently passing through the city on his way to incarceration in Wales. A decade later, he fled the city as it faced a siege by Roundhead forces (Ellis Bradshaw among them). He died peacefully in 1652. His eldest son, Orlando, would be Lord Keeper (i.e., mouthpiece to Parliament) to Charles II, and his third son Henry (who had attended James Stanley to the scaffold) would be bishop of Sodor and Man, the semi-independent island state of which the Stanleys were hereditary "kings."[4]

Bolton faced two military assaults from Derby's men early in 1643. Despite the assistance and the cover provided by "the Bishop's house," both were repelled. As Broxap tells the story, by 20 April, the decisive encounter (though not the end) of the Lancashire Civil War had come about at Whalley, leaving Parliament set to win.[5]

It was the following October that, with typical irrelevance, King Charles commissioned Hewit, created doctor of divinity on his personal orders, to preach up loyalty in his native region. Hewit paid with his life for his own loyalty in June 1658, as Cromwell's Protectorship reached its nadir. William

Prynne prepared Hewit's case, linking Cromwell with Laud and Strafford as traitorous subverters of the "Fundamental Laws." The inference was clear. The Protectorship was not a viable alternative to monarchy. Indeed Cromwell's "High Court of Justice," which condemned Hewit after denying him trial by jury, was the kind of tyrannical innovation more likely to arise under the former. John Bradshaw, Cheshire cousin of the Bradshaws of Bradshaw and president of the court that condemned Charles I, had already announced his preference for a restoration of the monarchy over the establishment of a Protectorship. John Ashurst, who had repelled Derby's men from Bolton with great heroism in 1643, was soon to join those prepared to fight for Charles II.[6]

As the embodiment of the monarchy's constitutional credentials, Hewit had great charisma, and some sexual magnetism for pious aristocratic women. He had known poverty and reminded them of the trials of the poor. He spent his childhood in the Bolton vicinity and attended school there before going on to Merchant Taylor's, London, and Pembroke College, Cambridge, where he held the position of "sizar," or student menial to the gentry of the college.[7] He did not graduate. His family were weavers, and his portrait displays his own tendril-like version of weaver's fingers, in the act of spellbinding. He has an intense, rather childlike face.[8]

His first wife was the daughter of a merchant-tailor; his second was Lady Mary Bertie, to whose brother, the second earl of Lindsey, he was chaplain. In 1657 he married Cromwell's daughter (another strong-minded "Mary") to Lord Falconbridge, the absentee owner of Smithills Hall. He denied on the scaffold any complicity with Ormond, reminded his auditors that he was offering himself as a "State Martyr for the public Good" and the rights of Freemen, and added that many of the judges bullied into condemning him had personally assured him they knew he was "no meddler."[9] His London church—St Gregory's, by St Paul's—was almost certainly a focus for royalist "meddlers" more devious than he. With notoriety, came an interest in his sermons. Those accredited by his widow would seem to be drafts for the pulpit. As in the case of some of Pendlebury's sermons, this adds to their vividness. Some paragraphs are clearly "written up" with the graceful calculation behind any effortless performance. Here is a typically striking opening from "God and Man Mutually Embracing": "Love is the *punctum* or centre, about which the circumference of our thoughts doth move."

His appeal is understandable. It offers in chastened form, and as the path to heaven, the modes and longings of the masques of a vanished court: "Love's Triumph Through Callipolis," for instance, in which Charles himself had danced center stage, flanked by lesser exemplars of the same universal force. James Stanley, among these, had figured as "the Secure" Lover, so manly, graceful, and compelling was his deportment. Compare the drudgery of James Livesey (guilty of "Fourteenthly," on occasion) with the glancing

Dr Hewit: "Therefore not to detain you with reiteration." He was a tactful and sought after comforter in times full of grief:

> Be then the Word of God a Paradise to the faithful soul; but so, as among so many fruits of different taste and virtue, she may find one tree of life that may fully satisfy the hunger of justice, that she so seeks for: let the Scripture be her Orchard; but yet let there be one apple-tree whose shadow she desires sitting down under it, and the fruit sweet to her palate: let the truth of God be her garden of aromatic drugs; but let there be one *Rose of Sharon,* whose sweet smell may recover her fainting heart, and which she may put in her bosom, no otherwise than *a bundle of myrrh.*

With a fine exertion of negative capability, he reads verses from *Lamentations* and says: "I have now done with the parts of my Text, and you may expect I should apply them; but I forbear." Many a chastened cavalier (James Stanley among them) was compiling meditations from the same source. In the same sermon, however ("Zion in Sack-Cloth, and her Saints in Tears"), Hewit applies the story of Abraham's *divided* sacrifice, from which he drove the birds of prey. He reads this as an emblem for irremediable divisions in church and state, all of which in all their perplexity must be offered to God, not surrendered to atheism and despair.[10] This is the voice of a high church Anglicanism that ventures to speak for the whole people, though it knows itself, humanly speaking, to be heard only by a despised and envied few. Clinging to Donne's vision of the true Church as that which is "open to most men," Hewit sees the Sacrament and heaven as the fruition of *consent:* "to go with a multitude . . . where all comers are welcome." No man dare pray, or believe, of himself: "Many will prevail, where one alone can do but little good: *Woe unto him that is alone.*"[11]

The poignant tension in which Hewit functions—that of a precious clique that nevertheless almost uniquely retains the generosity of a coherent spiritual culture—would be explored in "Little Gidding," where it becomes, for the American poet, almost a definition of England itself. Meanwhile, it is worth recording what Hewit intended as his dying words: "I love and honour all Christians in the World, that love the same Lord Jesus in sincerity."

Like Marsh, Hewit ruffled authority by the continued use of a form of public prayer no longer officially sanctioned. Like Pilkington, he supplemented the text with a form of *group* confession too embarrassing to appear in any official prayer book. Pilkington gave godly Elizabethans words of contrition for having stood by while the Marian martyrs burned. Hewit urged cavaliers to repent of their arrogant and parasitical lifestyle of "honor" as a condition for the Restoration:

> By Theft, Rapines and Oppression: by vexatious suits much practised and countenanced; by Exactions; by unjust Gains in bargaining; by defrauding the Labourer

of his Hire; by want of due care in expending what we have, and of good Conscience in acquiring more, we have provoked and rebelled against thee.[12]

As Charles II put it, Presbyterianism was no religion for a gentleman. The
same might be said of this kind of charismatic high Anglicanism. Certainly,
it would be a rare gentleman who would compromise his pagan code of honor
by figuring as a lay elder with responsibility for the parish's morals. But
equally few gentlemen would care to wallow in expressions of corporate
revivalism like the above, however elegant. Hewit's alternative idea of
honor—reverence for views one cannot share—would become an important
code for certain Anglican clergy, but rarely for their lay patrons, least of all
in their parliamentary solidarity. Charles is said to have worn till his death
the ring Hewit sent to him from the scaffold. Hewit's impulse to tolerance
was by no means dead in his heart or in the actions over which he had
personal control. As the Governor of a church establishment at the mercy of
a political ascendancy, however, the sovereign's instincts in that direction
would never be given much play.

While Hewit was killed by the protectorship, Derby fell foul of the
"Rump" Parliament, which, till 1653, preceded Cromwell in power. Bent on
finding a scapegoat for the flight of Charles II after the Battle of Worcester,
in September 1651, they executed Derby at Bolton that October, as though
he (rather than Prince Rupert) had been responsible for the Bolton Massacre
of 1644. And so Derby, like Laud and Strafford and many others before him,
died for the faults of royalty, exactly as though the monarchy were still in
place. Neither could the earl himself learn new tricks. His speech on the
scaffold amounted to everything he knew: "I thank God I desire peace. I was
born in Honour, and I hope I shall die in Honour. . . . I have done nothing,
but as my Ancestors, to do you good."

He claimed the audience as his own, and indeed, the sigh that greeted
him as he mounted the scaffold gave way, before he was well into his speech,
to a reaction in his favor. This led to a more general brawl, which had to be
put down by Parliamentary troopers. There were "some cut, many hurt,"
records an eyewitness, "and one child was killed." It was a sort of rehearsal
for Peterloo.

Derby had to wait a little longer to die. He had the grace to abandon a
speech that now seemed too poor a thing to go on with. If there were any
ideas abroad in Bolton that day about the sovereignty of the people, they
would have been found among these same respectable troopers who had just
been compelled to butcher their own kind. Such men had no say in the
governmental arrangements to which they were indispensable. A Parliamentary vote, for such as them, was already a demand; yet already as fabulous
as "Manchester University": despaired of almost as soon as dreamed. No one
could have guessed that this earl's seventh successor (a convert from the

Whig party to Disraeli's Young England) would for the first time extend the vote to large numbers of the adult male representatives of the more respect-able "lower orders" in 1867, or that they would have to wait so long.

Secondhand accounts, notably that of his own chaplain, put elaborate apologies for the Stuart monarchy, the Church of England, and his own war record into Derby's mouth. But the report "taken in short-hand, as it was spoken" records much more convincing fragments of compressed contradic-tion. Significant is the final word he directed towards the crowd: "the Lord bless you all, the Lord bless this poor Nation."[13] Here, in its true, apocalyptic, context was something shared, below argument, by James Anderton the "loyal, and dutiful" Catholic, John Pym the "rebel" Puritan, and innumerable others: the conviction of a nation and a national constitution as something born, innate—forever, yet forever in process of becoming its true, original self. Evidence for the existence of such a thing is less likely to be positive than negative (as on the present occasion). Derby reminded his audience how the nation might cohere again: "God send that you have a King again, and Laws." His ancestor Lord Stanley might have said as much on the eve of Bosworth. That king and law were mutually sustaining, neither of them credible without the other, was a proposition many in his audience must have shared, their habits of thought firmly lodged in precedent. The king existed as upholder of law and as the fountain through which adjustments to its flow could be achieved. His function was not to subvert, but to realize, its "original" dynamic. Many Englishmen saw more danger in a new Con-queror like Cromwell than in a permitted human figurehead like Charles II. Only kingship sufficed to be a continuing talisman, a sacramental token not exactly "eternal" but, like the Sacrament, of divine institution and sufficient till the end of time.

Hobbes's Leviathan, published this same year (1651), posits an autocracy, constructed by consensus at an unspecified point in historical time. This is doubly blasphemous from the above point of view: it deprives the monarch of the divine force of his office and his subjects of the right to moderate its operations in practice. God's will is perennially open to reinterpretation, but Hobbes would saddle humanity with autocracy as the nonnegotiable consequence of its own will. Insofar as Charles I's innovations anticipated this godless theory, so far was he deemed impious as well as wrongheaded. His un-English attempt to go along with historical changes which elsewhere in Europe were producing a more autocratic style of monarchy might well be accounted a blasphemy in itself. The groans and sighs that greeted what many considered the blasphemy of his execution (echoed in the case of Derby, his lieutenant) may be perceived as expressions of tragic satisfaction. In Greek tragedy, the ultimate atonement for sin reconciles the sinner with his victims, as he joins them in the same inevitable destiny. Though availing itself of Christian icons, the cult of the martyr Charles (like the minor one of Derby himself) drew on much older roots. Unlike Hewit (on whom they may be said to rely) they are not martyr rebels; but martyr lords, not omens of transformation but a satisfaction to the people guaranteeing the continuity of their kind.

Four centuries after Bosworth the earls of Derby still had considerable political influence and still owned (as by then also did the Bridgeman family, as earls of Bradford) about a third of urban Bolton. Both earls maintained a landlord's veto on political and religious nonconformity. In 1882, newspaper readers were treated to the story of a locally cherished relic of the Civil War period, formerly the property of James Cockerele of the Man and Scythe, the market tavern that still displayed (as it does to this day) the arms of the Pilkingtons, Lord Derby's predecessors as lords of Bolton. The relic was an item of crockery believed to be the dish from which his lordship "partook of fish, as a sacramental offering" shortly before his execution.[14]

30

"God's Gifts . . . for Edifying the Body": Roundhead Soldiers

THE corner of the Salford hundred that included Bolton and Manchester was a marketplace of ideas. At least as much as elsewhere (given its geographical position), local strategies and resentments were part of the wider pattern of the four countries of the British Isles. More immediately, Bolton supplied fighting men for the Parliamentary side in various engagements and played a crucially damaging role, from Lord Derby's viewpoint, as the key to the survival of Manchester as a Roundhead stronghold, blocking communication lines between the king and the (very conservative) remainder of Lancashire and northwestern England.

In this context a solecism of Lord Derby's, uttered as he walked "up and down the scaffold" and recorded by the shorthand writers, becomes understandable: "the Son of God bless you all of this Town of *Bolton*, Manchester, and especially Lancashire." His bewildered geography implies a cruel truth: his ideal Lancashire is now diminished (yet more precious) in relation to its obnoxious parts. No longer simply the sum of its parts, "Lancashire" can be seen only by looking away from every part of it that suggests the unbearably victorious future: commercial, aggressively efficient, despising the past. Derby's scaffold is built by Parliament's orders literally at a crossroads— the crowd are downhill from him, in front and to left and right. The ancient tower of the parish church is behind him at the top of a rising street kept empty of civilians as an elementary precaution of crowd control. Exploiting the deference of his headsman—a local farmer[1]—Derby has the block turned round, so that he dies facing the church, with his assembled people now literally behind him. Kneeling between God and the crowd, he utters a battle cry that is also a prayer for earthly coherence, no longer imaginable except as the expression of divine totalitarianism: "Blessed be God's glorious Name for ever and ever, Amen: Let the whole Earth be filled with his Glory."

How guilty was Derby of the Bolton Massacre? Parliament found him guilty, though not convincingly, of having slaughtered a Roundhead captain in cold blood. Otherwise, he seems to have used his influence for moderation. Like William Hulton, the Bolton magistrate who presided over the Peterloo

Massacre of 1819, he was perhaps guilty only of being extinct. Hulton seems to have assumed that his mere presence and word of cool command would induce an outbreak of compliance.[2] And so it was with Derby.

More obviously at fault was Colonel Alexander Rigby, the Roundhead commander. He had left Bolton ungarrisoned for twelve months, and its defenses were out of repair. Rigby had concentrated his efforts on the siege of Lathom, but on hearing of the approach of Prince Rupert, retreated in some haste with his troops to Bolton, arriving on 27 May. The following day, Rupert, the earl, and thousands of cavalry (some Irish among them) arrived from the favored royalist direction, the southwest. The village of Deane was subjected to preliminary terror. The prince's first onslaughts on Bolton itself were repulsed, with much loss of life. The second attack was led by the earl. Somehow, he was able to enter his "own" town on foot, the first man in, as though carried through by the conviction that his own unmolested presence constituted order. But at that moment, chance or a traitor opened a breach for Rupert's cavalry. What should have been a sequel to "Love's Triumph through Callipolis" became an anticipation of Gallipoli, 1915, when thousands of Allied lives were thrown away for the fatuous pride of their traditional commanders. Colonel Rigby's strategy at this crisis was inspired. He mingled with incoming Cavaliers, learned their password, and used it to escape into Yorkshire with one attendant. Such behavior would find its reward six years later with the coming of the Commonwealth. Model Army standards prevailed for a season, and many of the gentleman-Roundheads in charge of the Lancashire militia—Alexander Rigby included—would be dismissed.[3]

How many died in the narrow streets trapped between the now useless barricades of mud? The current guess seems to be that between 1,000 and 1,500 in all were killed that day, perhaps half of them civilians of the town. Yet the Bolton parish register records only 78 civilian names: two of them women and two perhaps young boys. There is evidence of others. Whatever the total, scores of dead and dying with thousands of troops quartered among them for some days, consuming or removing every scrap of provision and commodity, left a scar never since forgotten. Cavalier gallantry, drunk, took its pleasures. All to help Alexander Rigby avoid the consequences of his class vendetta against Lathom House (an enterprise of little strategic value). All to get Rupert's cavalry to Marston Moor, where they were driven from the field at the first encounter. The relatively mild earlier campaign of 1643 induced pious reflections. But, typically, this pointless atrocity of 28 May 1644 reduced even Tilsley to temporary, if eloquent aporia: "Only this one thing they may boast of more in their bloody zeal for the worst of causes that ever was defended of English spirits, that they left almost three score poor widows husbandless and hundreds of poor children fatherless."[4]

The Rigbys prospered. George Rigby of Little Hulton, a younger brother

of Colonel Alexander Rigby, was one of Tilsley's most prominent parishioners. He ran, or helped to run, the local Roundhead spy system. He married
a daughter of William Hulton, an earlier avatar of that survivalist dynasty.
The approved bridegroom of their daughter and heir, Alice, was one Roger
Kenyon. After the Restoration Roger would use family connections to secure
his own appointment as deputy governor of the Isle of Man, under the ninth
earl of Derby. Roger's nephew, using the same connections, got to be court
physician to James III, the Catholic Old Pretender, at St. Germain. Theirs is
an example of a family network divided by politics and religion, but united
in opportunism.[5]

Another brother of George and Alexander was Joseph Rigby. All three
were the sons of Alexander Rigby senior, of Middleton, Goosnargh, near
Preston. Their Civil War record is the continuation, under circumstances of
greater risk and opportunity, of his peacetime investment policy. This included getting a new deal for smaller Protestant gentry at the expense of
older families. The campaign of 1643 left only two royalist strongholds of
any note in Lancashire: Lathom, which held out against Alexander junior
till December 1645; and Greenhalgh Castle, defended against Joseph till June
1644, when the death of its commander (an Anderton) led to its surrender.
More interesting than his war record, however, is Joseph's use of the peace.
Whereas Alexander senior had settled George in a new "Peel Hall," Little
Hulton, in crude challenge to an older establishment of the same name and
township, Joseph had been bought land in the temptingly anomalous township of Aspull.

Aspull was ripe for sequestration. It was dominated by recusancy to an
extant notable even for the conservative parish of Wigan, of which it was
the most easterly part. But for civil purposes it belonged, not to royalist West
Derby hundred, like the rest of Wigan, but to Roundhead Salford hundred
(it was taxed with Blackrod, Bolton). When the Commonwealth came in,
there was no question of Major Joseph Rigby's being dismissed from the
militia, like his brother Alexander. He was promoted Lieutenant Colonel.
He was also now a clerk of the peace, charged with securing the land of
local papists and delinquents. Among Aspull landowners who compounded
for their estates at this time was James Roscow. Aspull, hitherto a wilderness
of superstition, seemed set to become the Rigby bonanza farm. But Joseph
overreached himself. He was accused of "impeding profits" owed to Parliament by trying to extort lands for himself at less than the going rate. Given
his background, it is perhaps not very surprising that Joseph's son, a third
hopeful Alexander, chose to enlist with Lord Derby in 1651.[6] This act of
youthful rebellion (if such it was) anticipated the conservative position his
father would arrive at by 1656.

In that year, Joseph published a "Poem." Among recipients of dedicatory
verses by the author is Joseph's fellow Roundhead Richard Shuttleworth,

justice of the peace. But a more fulsome tribute goes to Ann, wife of the recusant cavalier James Anderton of Birchley. A social climber's tolerance is also extended to "the Right Worshipful, truly Noble, and his worthy Honoured Friend and Neighbour, Roger Bradshaigh of Haigh," head of the Catholic or at least pro-Catholic branch of the ancient Bradshaw clan. At the back of the book are complimentary verses to Joseph from humbler scribes: Presbyterian ministers Tilsley, Livesey, and James Rigby (a poor relation); and former army subordinates Humphrey Maulcbone and Charles Carr (these at least suggest real affection and admiration). There are verses by Charles Hotham, rector of Wigan, comparing Rigby to George Wither. The impression intended is of an establishment "visible and mixed," such as Livesey would argue for the following year. Citing Chrysostom's warning as to the provisional status of all theological ideas, Livesey urges flight from "pure negation."[7] People of the right sort, it seems, should abate their *odium theologicum* sufficiently to form a survivalist alliance.

What was to be the focus for consent? With a little help from the classics, Joseph enlightens the "Courteous and Judicious Reader":

> Experience teacheth that there's no one thing
> Can please each one; nor Parliament nor King.
> That each one's not pleas'd with a Protector;
> A wise Ulysses nor a valiant Hector.[8]

Like James Anderton senior, Rigby wants neither king nor Parliament alone. Nor does he want to see permanently institutionalized the makeshift tyranny of a Lord Protectorship such as blighted the child-kingships of Edward V and Edward VI. Like the earl of Derby on the scaffold he wants "a King again, and Laws." Yet, also like the earl, he places himself between God and the people, having (it follows) provided them with a king. What sort of king? After Bosworth, the Pilkingtons of Pilkington, the Stanleys' predecessors as local magnates, joined the doomed attempt to substitute the puppet of their faction, the serving man Lambert Simnel, for the obnoxious heir of John O'Gaunt. The Stanleys' successors as arbiters of the future (as this representative group seem to see themselves) have a more comfortable option. The victorious Cromwell has just refused the crown. Waiting on the continent is the legitimate duke of Lancaster, John Hewit's ring on his finger. To turn it into a coronation ring, Charles need only deploy the same array of precedents already invoked in Hewit's defense.

In this context, renovation and antiquarianism are indistinguishable. With an eye on Richard, Cromwell's son and likely successor, Prynne garnished Hewit's defence with strategically placed references to the "military" tyranny of "Richard the Second." Their significance was not hard to guess. Offering to follow Colonel Rigby wherever he may lead, Maulcbone deploys the same code. Let any deserter, he writes, "lose the love of John O'Gaunt" (the man whose son destroyed "Richard the Second").

While Rigby's associates have little difficulty in identifying Charles Stuart as the right heir of Lancaster and the United Kingdom, they do not want history to repeat itself. For one thing, such a group could never agree as to the definition of the Sacrament. They must define their new sovereign in a new way. Like the old Pilkingtons, they need to substitute Lambert Simnel for the sovereign, but they want to do this without removing the sovereign or extending sovereignty to Lambert Simnel. They are, literally and permanently, "interventionist." They assume—like Thomas Lever before them—their age-old right to manipulate events by speaking for the lower orders. They are in one respect all "Presbyterians": they regard it as their right and duty to exert moral management over their serving men and women. Preempting ideas current among these about the sovereignty of the people, Rigby provides his county "Neighbours" with an appropriate text: *An Ingenious Poem called the Drunkard's Prospective or Burning-Glass*. It will have many successors in the campaign against intemperance among the lower orders. Meanwhile, it affirms the right of the Rigby class to manage all the Lambert Simnels, and through them, the newly vulnerable sovereignty of kings. Disingenuously echoing the Twenty-third Psalm, Joseph assumes Bradshaigh will want the *Ingenious Poem* "to be read/Amongst your people when your Table is spread." In contrast to such divine shepherding, it is low tavern haunters (and not, one must infer, President Bradshaw, for instance) who have destroyed the monarch, being unworthy of the divine sovereignty residing within themselves, which (for their own good) the Rigby class will in future exert on their behalf:

> Oh, the prodigious fearful oaths they swear,
> As if that God were deaf, and could not hear
> The damned language which in drunken fit
> These Ruffians, monsters of the earth, do spit
> Out in defiance of his Majesty,
> And all subordinate authority.

Whose "Majesty," exactly? God's, or some future king's, or a blend of both to be defined by the "subordinate authority" of Rigby? Drink, the begetter of "riot and excess," has its own theology:

> Their Library's a large room, so full as passes
> Of Pots, Cans, Jugs, Tobacco pipes and glasses.

Such "learning" requires only the simplest rebuttal. Livesey supplies the inevitable American authority: "Ethnics abhor it." Tilsley concurs that "Flat

Atheism" is superior to this "Deity" of drink that dogs the people. As Rigby
sees it, there will always be such people and, obviously

> They have no voice in Commonwealth at all.

Only by special intervention of the Rigby muse, restringing the Spenserian
lyre, can such creatures be made members of the mystical Body of Christ:

> Send down thy heavenly Spirit, and thereby
> Those dead and stony hearts so mollify,
> That they henceforth all deadly sin may shun,
> And be made members of thine only Son.[9]

What is being constructed here is the Whiggish code of a set of power
brokers whose day will come with William III. Here is the "protective"
dominance over the people, and the proprietary tone in regard to the monarch, and the Sacrament, that will be normal for Zachary Taylor, curate of
Wigan, a Bradshaigh protégé and son of a Chetham protégé of the same
name. Like Hewit, he will become a gentleman by marriage: in his case the
bride (of 1685) will be Barbara, daughter of Sir Edward Stanley. Barbara's
nephew will in the most literal sense become Derby's successor, as the eleventh earl, by default of the direct male line, in 1736.[10]

To turn from Colonel Rigby to the Roundhead soldier Ellis Bradshaw is
to turn in the first instance from the springtime of the Whiggery whose
decadence Disraeli would satirize to the Eastertide of something that Whig
history, in its finest mood, could neither appropriate nor explain: an irreversible mental and spiritual development, released by but reaching far beyond
the impulse of transformative events.

At another level, Rigby and Bradshaw are not so very different. Both
share the peculiar self-consciousness, which is also a half-consciousness, of
an age in which "acting" and "playacting" are confused opponents. Regardless
of party or class, the moral heroism of the "Puritan" and the affectations of
the "Cavalier" are everywhere indivisible. On trial for his life, Hewit (as
fine an actor in his way as Charles Stuart or James Stanley) glances to right
and left, gathering the admiration of ladies who have crowded to his last
performance.[11]

In Rigby, too, hypocrisy is no simple matter. His "Poem" of 1656 appears
in partnership with the institution by Cromwell of the rule of Major-
Generals, satraps of the Protectorship locally responsible for licensing ale-
houses, purging the magistracy and promoting "virtue." One might guess
(and surely Rigby did) that their unpopularity would follow, and that this
would drive "a wedge between Cromwell's civilian and military supporters,"
making the Restoration every day more likely.[12] A foreseeable "setback" such

as this was merely an additional bonus anticipated, in the Rigby calculus. Yet his "Poem" is not "insincere." Here is a middle-aged man using for his own worldly security and advancement the genuine moral and personal virtues he has been raised in from youth and no doubt continues to enact.[13]

And so it is with Bradshaw. Of his eleven pamphlets, the first five, from 1649 to 1651, form a convinced body of real writing: the life expression of an intelligent and inquiring mind. But a piece of 1652 marks the end of inquiry. Symptomatically, it offers itself as an "Answer" to the ideas of John Goodwin. Goodwin, who was permissive by conviction, argued that men put their own souls in danger by "suppressing any way, doctrine, or practice concerning which they know not certainly whether it be from God or no." Bradshaw has to inform him that men cannot be safely left to receive the impression of faith or knowledge directly from creation. Sometimes they "must be content to receive knowledge at the second hand, . . . yea from base things in repute of the world and mean and contemptible." We are permitted the inference that these humble sources of enlightenment include Bradshaw himself, who has received the imprimatur of accredited divines. He has taken the fatal step from acting to playacting: a degrading step of which he seems proud, for he provides himself for the first time with an epistle dedicatory. It is addressed to "his Excellency Oliver Cromwell."[14]

With his naive and direct way of thinking, Bradshaw felt the force of law should follow the force of argument. He recognized that the abolition of tithes was an economic sine qua non of religious freedom. His "Downfall of Tithes no Sacrilege" of 1653 was in line with the current radicalism of "Barebone's" Parliament, which presided briefly over affairs after the fall of the "Rump."[15] But his hero Cromwell immediately dissolved it and became Lord Protector. Though tolerant for his period, Cromwell had no intention of alienating the gentry by abolishing tithes. This disappointment exemplified his general failure to deliver the sort of deal men like Bradshaw had risked their lives for. Something had to give. In Bradshaw's case it was tolerance, the first victim of unjust peace. He turned on the Quakers. By 1656, the self-forgetful "Husbandman" of Christ and eternity of 1649 had dwindled into a theological dandy, self-consciously complaining about how the Quakers, with their refusal of hat courtesy and their dubious grammar, had persistently misrepresented *him*.

These Quakers are "[u]ncivil, uncourteous, . . . brutish, . . . and dismal,"[16] writes Bradshaw in his new role as *arbiter elegantiarum*. According to him, they claim to have Christ but they deny the "means and Instruments to Christ." They scorn "God's . . .gifts unto men for edifying the body."[17] That is, they seek emancipation from the Sacrament as Bradshaw understands it. The Body of Christ, in seventeenth-century England, was also a chartered system of land-tenure. The Blood of Christ reached the faithful through a network of international diplomacy and trade. Groups like the Quakers, by rejecting "the outward observance of the Lord's Supper" altogether were registering their refusal to acquiesce in the right of all the Rigbys to manage and monitor God's gifts "for edifying the body" and nurturing the soul. Bradshaw cannot refuse.

Social historians tell us that one development of the Interregnum was that prosperous small men—alehouse keepers, drovers, husbandmen—started to call themselves "gentlemen" in emulation of their betters and to distance them from their inferiors.[18] In this and other ways, respectable soldiers of the Commonwealth all over England were getting the hang of the Rigby calculus.

It was not always thus. Bradshaw's pamphlets of 1649–50 comprise three which deal with nothing less than the Four Elements; a fourth that confronts the moral dilemma of history in the person of Prince Rupert; and a fifth that reads in a meteorological phenomenon a political future worth living and dying for.

His "New and Clear Discovery" about the "Ebbing and Flowing of the Main Sea" is eccentric but thought-provoking. Repelling with the sword of "Reason" and the buckler of "Scripture" any notion that the earth's globe is a mere spheral basin, a rigid ball of land slopped over with an alien watery element at the pull of the Moon, Bradshaw dares to speculate that the apparently solid land itself is equally fluid, a shifting substance that "never closeth" over its liquid core, but should rather be seen to "swim or float" in some indefinable way. This sense of dynamic flux and interchange appears crazy, insofar as Bradshaw belittles the influence of the Moon, but in its common-sense anticipation of a more sophisticated geology, of theories of continental shift and of late-twentieth-century interest in the chemistry of the deep ocean (about which less is currently known than about the Moon) Bradshaw is a reminder of the special dynamism of his own historical moment.[19]

His "Week-Day's Lecture" on "the Preaching of the Heavens" is all air and fire. One must imagine him pacing the green whaleback of Winter Hill, the local mountain of meditation, from which the westerly sea is not so much visible as palpable by the quality of the evening light, just as the stars come out. From its broad, high vacancy nothing seems nearer than the sky. Thomas Cole, "America's first great landscape painter," will often walk here in his boyhood and youth. Whitman's "Church" of British admirers will come here to read him and inevitably (though they will never tell this to their dying friend) to find him wanting.[20]

Bradshaw is meditating a remark attributed to Thales, one of the sages of ancient Greece, on the significance of "place." What matters is not the multiplicity of "things," but the immensity in which they cohere. It is not the calculus that counts, but the imagination to dare the great question that chills the bone and takes away the breath with its exhilaration, as this place does: "Yet there must of necessity, either be something, or nothing." Freed from the transubstantiationist obsession, he is obsessed by the new effort of

imagining how everywhere "place" and "substance," "emptiness" and "fulness" can fit together to make worlds within worlds; and worlds beyond:

> For, suppose we should Imagine, that above, and beyond (this starry Firmament
> that we daily see) there were never so many circumventing Heavens, and those
> also never so many miles, of distant circumference one above another, further, and
> further remote from us, and that on every side.

The roof has come off the world with the king's removal. For a moment, the
sovereignty of present imagination has replaced that of Rigby's manipulated
history and Livesey's empire of the dead. It is already the potential of humanity to "find place for further motion, . . . millions of times so far as they had
done before." Yet nowhere is foreign, for all is one, all is miracle:

> nor a grass on the Earth; nor a leaf, nor blossom nor flower whatsoever but his
> All-seeing, understanding Spirit is intent upon it: Yea, and not so only, but is
> intentively in it.

Yet the Word by which all worlds are made is so absolutely greater than
his creation that while everywhere is holy (so that, thinks Bradshaw, there
is no local hell, no local heaven) nowhere and nothing can hold out against
the transformation of boundaries and definitions that God perpetually
achieves:

> the glorious Splendor of the Majesty of God, being wholly intent, and that on
> every place . . . there is nothing able to endure the fervour of the heat thereof:
> but it would presently be consumed, as it must one day.

This being so, what of any exclusive claims to power or sanctity made on
behalf of particular persons or locations? Paraphrasing Christ's judgement on
the Temple of Jerusalem, Bradshaw annihilates before the event Derby's last
masque of power: "Are these the things that ye so seriously . . . set your eyes
on? How poor a business, and what poor things you stand to admire!" His
own version of divine totalitarianism needs no king, no earl, no bishop, nor
any substitute for any such persons.[21]

Another pamphlet brings him down to earth. This is his "Husbandman's
Harrow to pull down the Ridges of Presbyterial Government and to smooth
a little, the Independent." Like other soldiers of Cromwell, Bradshaw has
little time for professional theologians. No synod of theirs should dictate to
Parliament, he is sure. Like Marsh, he belongs to a "middling" class unim-
pressed by reversible extremes locked in mutual definition and denial. His
theology comes down to good-neighborliness. It feels right to him to deny to
any one at all the power to impose their definitions on others. He thinks a
little goodwill might yield "conclusions." Alas, when he comes down to

details, the aporia of the times reasserts itself: "where shall we find . . . consent?" asked Cromwell, speaking for all England. Bradshaw cannot find it. He breaks off in the time-honored manner: "I have more particulars to propose." He is too coy to tell us what they are.[22]

The "Dialogue between the Devil and Prince Rupert," published in 1649, was apparently written while Bradshaw was serving with Roundhead forces at Chester in 1645. In fustian verse like an old play, it nevertheless represents a moral recovery. Bradshaw stays firmly on the Roundhead side, while satirizing its management. He defeats Prince Rupert by attempting to understand him in terms of the antinomian zeitgeist with which Bradshaw himself must also wrestle. This is the provincial thought pattern Livesey abandoned, one that goes some way to reclaiming the moral balance of which Tilsley was for a while understandably bereft by the Bolton Massacre.

Promises of appropriate recompense worth nothing in the mouths of Roundhead paymasters are seriously reliable when Satan utters them:

> I need not budge, nor call a Parliament
> To furnish me with coin for my intent.

Rupert has nobler motives: "I am a Volunteer. . . . I serve for love of thee." Like the devil, he is a gentleman. God is both good and evil in his eyes. He evades both as long as he can, unable to endure the rumors that hell will bring no better resolution than that already forced upon the oppressed of earth, to suffer so long that one learns to rejoice in pain:

> I never yet regarded such reports,
> But chose to follow honour, wealth, and sports
> While this life last, and then let come what will,
> God hath they say decreed both good and ill.

But life does not last, Satan reminds him. Rupert turns away:

> Come let's to th'wine, I'll drink no cup so evil.
> Do thou thy worst, I'll 'scape thy gaping mouth,
> I can retire East, West, yea North and South.

No, says Satan, for my mouth is as wide as Marston Moor: "It's two miles wide, as 'twas at York i'th' battle." The prince has already embarked on an eternity of reentering it.[23]

On Monday, 25 February 1650, being market day, some "Apparitions" were "seen in the Air" over Bolton. Bradshaw's meticulous description makes clear these were a fine example of parhelia, or "false suns," such as sometimes appear in the winter sky by refraction of the sun's light on suspended crystals of ice. In this case, there were four such "bright places," set like circular posterns, "red and changeable" in a horizontal wall of light passing through the true sun and extending round the whole sky. Further curving streams of light came from these false suns to give the impression of a circular rainbow that had been arbitrarily broken in two, and the two halves set weirdly in the sky "with their backs together."

A rainbow suggests God's Covenant; broken rainbows, turned back to back, spell out to Bradshaw the fracturing of "mutuality" in "Church and State." He proceeds rapidly to a summary of divergent views obtaining. At one extreme, "One affirms that the oath of Allegiance binds us . . . to the person of Kings," which must therefore be defended even when the result would in practice be "to destroy his authority," which is not merely personal. At the other end of the spectrum, some think that to consult at all with the "Kings of the earth . . . is against the Lord." It is hard to resist the impression that Bradshaw himself is meditating a deeper view that lies between these poles.

An oath of allegiance works both ways, he thinks, or not at all. Allegiance is "relative" and "binds no further than the Laws of relations." All relations are "contractive," and men cannot be presumed to have lawfully contracted for their own "destruction." King and Parliament both have "not so much as their being, much less privileges, against the lawful rights and liberties of the subjects," Bradshaw suggests. In case of doubt, "we are bound to know neither King nor Parliament, but rather the people, who are the root of both":

Although Kingly Government in itself be lawful, yet to oblige a Nation to Hereditary Government, be they [any particular king] wise or foolish, can never be proved to be either wise or lawful in the sight of God, nor any rational man, if men once may choose and have power in their hands, through the providence of God.[24]

The extraordinary "Apparitions" with which the martyr town of Bolton has been favored are "admonitions of some great displeasure, and of wrath kindled." But "wrath" is to be averted, not by submission to the arrogations of government, but by reliance on popular intelligence. The "Nation" is no longer necessarily a hierarchy, based on precedent, but a sovereign people, governing themselves by reason. Before its appearance, Bradshaw and thousands like him have cast their permanent vote against *Leviathan*.

The encounter that Broxap calls the decisive battle of the Lancashire Civil War took place in a leafy lane near Whalley on 20 April 1643. Joseph Rigby's friend Colonel Shuttleworth was tentatively advancing with his troops on Whalley Abbey, the picturesque and valuable property of the Roundhead Ashtons, late of Great Lever. The earl of Derby had seized it and was currently in residence, surrounded by great numbers of the county's royalist gentry and their tenants. Almost more terrified of winning than of losing—

for the earl's defeat would change the balance of power in the region forever—the gentleman-Roundhead bade his men go back. But the men who,
under the Stanleys, had made the Tudors and destroyed the effective sovereignty of Scotland now "took matters into their own hands." They declared
they "would adventure themselves, see the enemy and have one bout with
them." The result was everything Shuttleworth most feared. The earl's forces
were shattered. The "real weakness of the royalist cause," dependent on
pressed men, was exposed for all to see.[25] The Abbey did not go unscathed.
But worst of all, the troops had won the war with a mutiny against every
kind of historical deference.

Here at last was the sequel to Marsh's demurral, pressed to better himself
by entering Derby's service: "I could not do that." Here were the grounds
of Bradshaw's conviction that a better world might begin in this world "if
men once may choose."

Lostock Hall Gateway shielded the Andertons, local Catholic apologists. *Photo by Gary Taylor.*

Kenyon Peel Hall Gateway screened the Rigbys, local Roundhead spymasters. *Bolton Museums.*

Among upland trees, the Puritan Chethams' Turton Tower held the northern skyline against Scots invaders. *Bolton Libraries.*

Amid meadows, Bishop Bridgeman's Great Lever Hall sheltered Irish and Cavalier insurgents from the south. *Bolton Museums.*

Lord Derby's Execution, 1651. From *A Description of the Civil War* (1785). *Bolton Libraries.*

Dog and Kennel Inn, Tonge Fold: Ellis Bradshaw's "local." Its annual rite
of spring for Charles II's Restoration (May 29) long outraged local Puritans.
Bolton Museums.

Oliver Heywood. Steel engraving by G. Parker. *By permission of The British
Library.* 492.f.21.1.

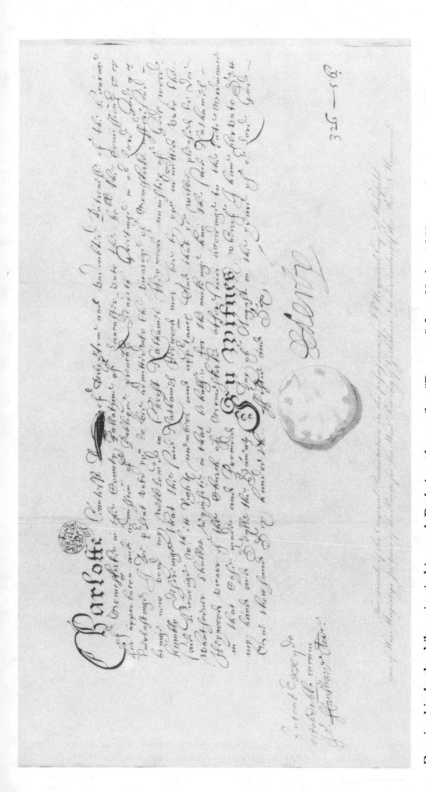

Denying his death while acting in his stead, Derby's widow strikes "Dowager" from Nathaniel Heywood's presentation document to Cromwell's Commissioners of 1656. *By permission of The British Library.* 492.f.21.2.

Hos oculos hæc ora pius Referebat Heuettus
  Gloria Rostrorum, Deliciæq Togæ.
Sed si Corda velis Cælestia, Confule Librum,
  Hosq Sacros verses sedulitate Sales.

Martyr Hewit's fingers conjure the return of monarchy. Frontispiece, *Repentance And Conversion* (1658). *Manchester Public Libraries.*

The Surey Impoſtor.

THE Reader is deſired to take Notice, That (through the Careleſsneſs of the Cutter) the Hand in Sir *Edmund Aſhton*'s Coat of Arms, mention'd *p.* 17. is left out.

Unhanded by Zachary Taylor's Whig manipulations, Richard Dugdale's muffled body argues for the Glorious Revolution of 1688–89. Frontispiece, *The Surey Impostor* (1697). *Manchester Public Libraries.*

'ΙΣΕΙΟΝ.

Penes Jacobum West de Interiori Templo Arm. F.R.S.

John Sturt's engraving of the androgynous Isis. The extreme delicacy of his rendering of her veiled features eludes reproduction. *By permission of The British Library.* 604.e.23 (2).

1880. Robert Lever's school awaits demolition in shadow of E. G. Paley's new St. Peter's. *Bolton School.*

PART SEVEN
Caroline Dissenters

Have I the Spirit?
—Nathaniel Heywood, *Christ Displayed* (1679)

31

Oliver and Nathaniel Heywood: Remaining Loyal, and Dutiful

In commending "to the Reader" his brother's *Christ Displayed,* Oliver Heywood takes the moment of death of an unnamed but exemplary martyr as the definition of the Christian Life. It is the whole of our brief function here to "cry out with the Martyr in the flames, 'None but Christ, none but Christ.'"[1] Simple confidence, however, can rarely be part of this experience: "mistakes are easy and dangerous," he warns. "[W]hat are you better for others' imagining, or your own conceiting that Christ is yours if it be not found so at the day of trial?" The same disquieting ambiguity is to be noted in the meditation on the story of Christ and the woman of Samaria with which Nathaniel's text commences. Christ takes his place by the well with an actorly expressiveness, "representing the gesture of a tired man." His role-playing is a foil to the underlying "secret of his Providence," which "had an intent to convert the people of that place."[2] Like Marsh, the Heywoods subordinate all things to the life of the spirit and are supremely concerned with an inner transcendency of personal assent and commitment to God, despite the world. For this very reason, they compel their readers, as he does, to measure a little the quality of their claims against the nature of what they aspire to transcend. It is here that they provide a contrast to Marsh, for world and transcendence have both become much more complicated things. No more than Joseph Rigby's hypocrisy (if such it is) can the sincerity of the Heywoods (for such it seems) be accounted a simple matter.

British Protestantism is more fragmented, and the British world is more elaborate and problematic. Ellis Bradshaw's last pamphlet, published in 1658, was addressed to "his Highness Richard the Lord Protector, together with the Parliament of the Common-wealth of England, Scotland, and Ireland, with the dominions thereunto belonging." Entitled *A Cordial Mediator for Accordance of Brethren,* it was a more mature version of his "Husbandman's Harrow" of 1649. One of many offers of the time to reconcile leading non-episcopalian Protestant groups, it makes poignant reading against a background dominated (not least in loyalist Lancashire) by schemes to restore a dynasty that had already declined to survive without bishops. It also makes an interesting match with Anderton's *Protestants' Apology* (1608). Anderton argued that attendance at mass could not in equity exclude Catholics from the political nation. Bradshaw now argues that access to the Sacrament can-not rightly be denied to those who happen not to be "politically incorporated into some Church or other."[3]

The Heywoods were stern, though not extreme, Presbyterians, yet never less than "loyal, and dutiful" monarchists. Circumstances, and a natural mel-lowing, led to considerable softening of Presbyterian peculiarities in the disci-pline of Oliver's Yorkshire conventicle by 1672. James II's Declarations of Indulgence, which were anathema to the Anglican hierarchy, prompted him to build a proper chapel in 1688. A triumphalist reading of his life would focus on the fact that he survived to see the Toleration Act of 1689. Less generous than the new king, William III, would have wished, it nevertheless secured freedom of worship (though not civil equality) to most Protestants. In the mood it helped to create, Heywood took a leading part in consolidating the "happy union" between Presbyterian and Congregationalist groups. Thus was apparently achieved the "accordance of brethren" Bradshaw and many others had seen as urgent since at least 1649.

There is of course a definite evolutionary shift in attitudes to monarchy from the beginning to the end of the Stuart dynasty. More and more the monarch is seen not as an initiator, but as the (often ambiguous or foiled) attestor to the validity of Parliament. In memorializing "the unparalleled murder of King Charles the first" or the malign influence of the "domineering prelates" over Charles II, Heywood contributes to the development of that "pathetical" way of writing about the monarchy, which his fellow Boltonian the Anglican Zachary Taylor will deploy against both Catholic and Protes-tant nonconformity. Meanwhile there can be no exaggerating the seriousness with which Heywood views Parliament, and the monarch as its God-given attestor. A godly Parliament (whoever the sovereign), he is convinced, is the only effective contemporary equivalent for Emperor Constantine. This stress on Parliamentary monarchy seems to have helped him accept the supplanting of James II by William III. At the same time, James Stanley's conviction that "king" and "laws" are mutually supportive remains an unnegotiable part of the Heywood credo, as do other convictions and deferences of the old regime. In 1657 Nathaniel Heywood is able to accept the living of Ormskirk from Cromwell's Commissioners, but only because James Stanley's dowager count-ess undertakes to present him to them.[4] William III was her kinsman—both were descended from William the Silent—no small scruple, perhaps, in the balance of Oliver's conscience during the events of 1688-9.

Deprived with two thousand others in 1662, the Heywoods are not con-verted into political radicals. Opening one of his soul-journals in May 1653, Oliver had undertaken to "act a spirit's part," which included using spiritual persuasion and a mild amount of civil disobedience to promote the gospel in a context of traditional social and political values. It absolutely forbade, however, lending one's voice to more obstreperous claims on behalf of one's conscience or the Holy Spirit. For the Heywoods, as for Anderton, unquestioning collaboration with a transformative god is uneasily matched with unquestioning loyalty to the snail-like evolution of a constitution based on centuries of precedent. Moreover, they are in the business of irritating this tension as a daily exercise in piety. Every day one is on the cross, "tortured between two thieves, my own corruptions and Satan's temptations." Yet the resolution is too absolute and simple to include Christ's clear denunciation of property, for example. Salvation no longer requires "as he once did of the young man, to sell all that thou hadst and give it to the poor, . . . but only requires that thou . . . open an empty hand and take Christ as thy saviour." Quite literally, one is constantly invited to perform a simple impossibility, to bend one's mind to a world beyond the world in which simple impossibilities are the normal currency. In "pathetical" strain, Oliver's ultrapiety (so near, as his favorite poet, George Herbert, might have warned him, to simple blasphemy) compels him to play-act the Holy Ghost (albeit a Holy Ghost that is timorous and fugitive): "'O that I had wings like a dove.' For then would I fly away and be at rest . . . and hide myself from my enchanting enemies."[5]

Inevitably, the problems of "England, Scotland, and Ireland, with the dominions thereunto belonging" continued to be inseparable from convulsions and disturbances, spiritual as well as material, in peace as in war. For the Heywoods' parents and other godly Boltonians, Charles I's (insincere) concession to the Scots in the matter of the Covenant was a source of spiritual rejoicing and a cause, even a fruit, of their personal conversion. In the same year (1641), the king's attempt to arrest the Five Members was a reason to form a "conventicle" (unlicenced prayer meeting). Events in the capital were perceived as a test, and inspirer, of particular local degrees of participation in gospel privileges. Almost simultaneously, there was an outbreak of rebellion in Ireland. Bolton's Merseyside colony of godly victuallers for Ireland, at Toxteth (which both Heywoods would continue to visit on their preaching journeys), was in the forefront of business and prayers.

And so it continued. When Ormond promised Ireland a parliament, in 1643, 5,000 Irish invaded north Wales and Cheshire. Hard fighting kept them out of Lancashire, where it was believed Prince Rupert had been promised the throne of Ireland as a base for the reconquest of England. South Lancashire suffered much in the wake of the "Battle of Preston" of 1648 (a messy and straggling engagement between Cromwell's forces and a Scottish army drawn to invade England by Charles I's worthless promise to tolerate Presbyterianism). Parliament was moved to devote collections from all English and Welsh churches to the relief of the county. In 1649 came the calamities in Ireland, when Cromwell's forces cruelly avenged, at Drogheda and Wexford, massacres perpetrated by Rupert and his Irishry at Bolton, Birmingham, and other Roundhead towns in England. In 1651 Charles II passed through Lancashire on his way to defeat at Worcester, backed by a mob of anti-Presbyterian Scots, armed refugees from their own country. He received an apathetic reaction in Preston, and, like the Young Pretender after him, steered well clear of Bolton, which on this occasion was cheered (or intimidated) by a grand parade of 12,000 of the Model Army's finest.[6]

After the Restoration for which they had so urgently prayed, the Heywoods would be victims of the cat-and-mouse "policy" improvised by a succession of English Parliaments for the containment of nonconformities at home and abroad. Neither their sufferings nor their persecutors were so grand, simple, and terrible as those of Marsh. Milton scarcely bequeathed *Paradise Lost* (1674) before mock epic became the order of the day. Oliver and Nathaniel were the middle pair of four surviving brothers. The eldest and youngest brothers, John and Josiah, charming scoundrels both, went to make fortunes in Barbados, and died there. Thomas, a half-brother, emigrated to Virginia, where the practice of employing African "servants" was already deemed as justifiable as it was profitable. Of Nathaniel's sons, Richard settled in Drogheda, as did a nephew, Benjamin, while Nathaniel junior founded one of the merchant dynasties of Liverpool,[7] a town whose (now mainly demolished) eighteenth-century elegance would be built in large measure on the slave trade. Truly, if this Swiftian world was "preposterous" (and Oliver Heywood enjoys using this fashionable word), it was not therefore less ghastly than Marsh's world.

Against this background, the Heywoods appear formidable. Acutely sensitive to the pressures of the world, they are truly heroic in their resistance. That such virtues as theirs (which include intelligence) should be exhausted in resistance marks the nature of their martyrdom. In terms of Plato's *Phaedo,* Marsh died for a Socratic reverence for the *logos*: the belief that knowledge is possible, without the trivial pretence already to know. But the Heywoods have moved on from epistemology to experiment. They are daily and hourly engaged in that "rehearsal for death," which in the *Phaedo* is the cost of dedication to truth. Like Thomas Lever, they renounce "security." They belong to a later generation, however, and the renunciation brings them no relief. Disowning mere formalities, they are perpetually extemporizing new forms with a craze for freshness and sincerity that already anticipates the Romantic movement their own movement helped to form. They are righteous, but they are beset by self-righteousness in others, and even in themselves. And, like the early monks (for whom Oliver nurses an admiration), they are righteous *on behalf of* others, though denying, according to their creed, the possibility of any but Christ bearing the sins of another.

An attempt to describe them might take as headings a pair of organically polarized terms of their own. First comes "Restraint," the beginning of conversion, which must be solemnly embraced and cultivated for the business of soul-making: "personal covenanting with God is the necessary and immediate product of the Holy Ghost in Believers."[8] Through this narrow gate, and by dint of earnestly applying the Word to daily experience—in Marsh's "Berean" manner—comes the power of "Scope," that is, of measured, conscious and available capacity and vision. All Christians have access to this, but it is the minister's "singular art": "comparing one Scripture with another, . . . shewing the main scope of the Holy Ghost therein, raising pertinent doctrines therefrom."[9] At the center of all is "Christ Displayed." It is here that assertion and erosion become inseparable. The pathology of monstrance and inquisition lapping deep into Lancashire from Counter-Reformation Europe does not leave Nathaniel Heywood untouched:

Well then, let every one of you be now inquisitive, and put such interrogatories as these to himself, 'Have I the Spirit? Is He given to me? Doth He dwell in my soul?' . . . let the search be deep and thorough, go to the bottom of your deceitful hearts. . . . If Christ be received, there will be a more earnest intent, desire and breathing of soul after Him.[10]

32

Restraint: The Poem of God

Above all things, Oliver Heywood desired to "observe ... the Pulses and impulses" of the Holy Spirit. In *Heart-Treasure* (1667), his first published book, written at a time when he faced imprisonment for daring to preach, he likens these "Pulses" to the pounding of a "Chap-man" on the door, an image that signals the most pervasive difference between George Marsh and Heywood himself. The Marian martyr's sense of perpetual "warfare" is replaced by a notion of continual "trade" as the typical image of the Christian's relationship with God-in-the-world. Marsh harkens to Christ as his true "Captain," despite appearances, but Heywood negotiates with the Spirit in his role as "God's great Factor in the World."[1] "Factor" is possibly ambiguous. Heywood's father was generous, trusting, and scrupulously honest. Unlike his cousin and London factor Nathaniel Hulton, he never became enormously rich.[2]

Doctrines of Son and Spirit inevitably match. Mildly claiming to follow, rather than to possess, the Holy Ghost, Marsh held with equally unruffled conviction the modest belief that Christ was "ever present with His sacrament." His calculated vagueness was just enough to burn him. But in Heywood vagueness has become chiaroscuro: for him, the quality of each reception of the sacrament depends on the quality of his own (primarily *esthetic*) condition at moment of reception. "I thought the shadow of Christ was delightful," he typically notes among occasional memoirs of his communions.[3] To the ambiguities of "trade," in describing Heywood's sense of the Spirit, must be added the ambiguities of a late-seventeenth-century esthetic.

Oliver and Nathaniel Heywood were "gentleman-commoners" of Henry VIII's swagger Trinity College, Cambridge. Such persons of quality (the great Isaac Newton, poor but of partly gentle birth, would be a mere "sizar," or student servitor, in the place) were meant to become great servants of the state, not poor country parsons. To say that Heywood "adored" the memory of George Herbert, an earlier alumnus of the same college, and the ultimate role model for gentleman-parsons, would be no exaggeration. Regularly, Heywood's own pen fails him, and he is glad to write, "Take yet a Verse from divine Herbert."[4] The quality of such deference is significant. The Puritan tradition of seeking influence at court through some Ganymede-Nehemiah—a Sidney, Essex, Buckingham—gifted with the royal ear, has been replaced by following the *example* of the unique Herbert, graced by King James with the same sinecure with which Elizabeth once favored Sidney, but proud to leave the court for a parsonage. "It's a personal affair," writes Heywood of religion. He thinks the world is transcended only through personal means.[5]

Heywood himself claimed no social grandeur. He knew he was only a distant "cousin" of the small-gentry Heywoods of Heywood. But in his ministry, and in addressing his readers, he relied on a *social* as well as a moral and spiritual leadership such as few of his successors (barred as they would be from English universities) would venture to assume. More important, he inherits not merely the ghost of Herbert's manner but his spirit of absolutely fearless sincerity, something that, in the end, also makes him close to Marsh. He does not want his flock to believe in him, but in the spirit they find in themselves. He uses the diction of his own relatively elevated status in order to tempt them to ennoble themselves. "Speculation will never make a man an Artist," he writes. "[Y]ou must (as the well-bred Bereans) try by Scripture what you hear."

These two strands—the idea of "trade" and the idea of a spiritual "art"—most naturally come together for him in the figure of his own grandfather and namesake, who trained as a carpenter and prospered in the textile trade. "A young Carpenter is long with a little. . . . 'Tis so in Religion," the Reverend Oliver writes. The bourgeois concept of "gain," and the notion—at once both more rarefied and more available—of a creativity that transforms perceiver and perceived, may issue in delightfully idiomatic clarity: "look about thee, make something of these objects," he urges (he is instancing the Yorkshire moorland landscape in the region of Haworth).

> [E]very Herb, Flower, Plant, spire of grass, Twig and leaf, Billow or Meteor, hath enough in it to puzzle the most profound Philosopher. . . . how much more the curious piece of man's Body . . . much more may I stand admiring the strange nature of my immortal soul.[6]

This is not the "Song of Myself," but it is one of its antecedents. No wonder Bolton Presbyterians took to Whitman "more fervidly than any," as the poet himself acknowledged.[7]

Sensitivity to the vital nuances of language may be fairly claimed as a leading asset of the tradition to which Heywood belongs. At the center of what "restraint" means for him is a word that occurs—as he delightedly notes—only once in the Greek New Testament. The word—ποίημα—is Paul's definition, writes Heywood, of a "gracious Christian." Literally meaning a "made thing," it transliterates into English as "poem." "For we are his *workmanship*," the King James version more prosaicly puts it.[8]

For Heywood, "Religion" was not only literally, but essentially and dy-namically a "Binding." Put under "restraint" by a challenging experience, the Christian enters a lifelong process of conversion, whose early and con-tinuing signs are "bitter cries of godly sorrow, and hearty groans for par-doning mercy," together with "self-examining and self-judging exercises." These expressions are drawn from Heywood's account of the conversion of his mother, Alice Critchlaw of Walmsley, in Longworth township, first put under "restraint" by the death of her own pious mother. Typically, she re-ceived encouragement from a well-loved brother and from some local gentle-women. She was unusually fortunate in her minister: James Horrocks, curate of Westhoughton chapelry, Deane. George Marsh's descendants were faithful members of his congregation. A charismatic and humorous Presbyterian of some genius, he deflected her aggression outwards into a dynamic of charity. A joyful admiration is the essence of Oliver's celebration of her.[9]

Such a conversion pattern was held to be the work of God, perfecting his creation in one redeemed soul. As Heywood wrote of St. Cyprian, "he per-ceived, and received what he felt, before he learned it, not by a series of study, but by a compendious act of divine grace."[10] Conversion was the art of God, and the converted soul the poem of God. Mere passivity was deemed insufficient, however. The rejection of "security," while it fomented anxiety, also encouraged a reconstructive—and destructive—dynamism. Indeed, even to seek a minister's help was often to transgress. Thus troubled residents of Bolton parish might need to stray into Deane for help, as Heywood's mother did, or adventure to Cockey Chapel, Ainsworth, a detached township of Middleton, in pursuit of conversion, as his father did. Parochial boundaries still reflected the land-tenure patterns of distant epochs and were often made nonsense of by new patterns of industrial settlement. Inevitably, the perfor-mance of spiritual duties and the spiritual development that grew from them were seen in terms of this new world, not in terms of the values of titled absentees. For the Heywoods, Lord Bridgeman, the Lord Keeper, was nothing more than a name on demands for money. But what is "preposterous in Naturals" cannot "hold in Spirituals," and an absent and nominal god is no god at all. "Trade with God in every performance," Heywood urges. "Rest not satisfied with . . . trudging in the common round of Formality. . . . [T]he Christian must travel far beyond the Indies." "Enlightenment," including a measure of intellectual enlightenment, was essential to maintaining such con-tact. In the idiomatically vivid expressions of the unsophisticated, "god" might dwindle from the main partner, to the evanescent product of internal bargaining, the poem not the poet of bewildered humanity. Heywood cites his own grandfather and namesake. Called to dinner by his wife from closet soul duty, he cried out, "thou hast robbed me of my god." Meditating in the fields one day, he "went about seeking, seeking, one came to him, asked him what he wanted, he said he had lost his god and was seeking his god."[11]

Mature Christians were under duty to enter into a personal covenant with God, not merely for themselves, but on behalf of their children. Heywood's parents did so. The obtaining of the best possible education for their children, for the promotion of true religion, was clearly part of that covenant. Oliver's series of books, copies of which he occasionally handed or sent to apt souls known to him, and his enormous round of preaching duties, were undertaken by way of fulfilment of this vow. Pledged to rescue souls from the extinct formularies of all episcopalian schools of religion, he was equally vehement that "God's Spirit is a Spirit of order." Order has its root within: "pertinent thoughts" fit for "seasonable use" cannot be learned, and are not to be mouthed, "like a parrot." Sincerity and the extempore are of the essence of the spirit, but if it is to be a divine spirit it must operate under censure. Having no respect for Erastian bishops, Heywood refers his readers to Fenner, Ball and Baxter for the general "common-place of Meditation." But he is sufficiently "loyal, and dutiful" to take authority from King James for this foundational restriction on Christian meditation:

> take the advice of a Royal learned Writer to his Princely Son, thus: "Censure yourself as sharply as if you were your own enemy. . . . [P]ray that God would give you grace so to live, as that you may every hour of your life be ready for death": thus he[12]

Thus also, and with rather more distinction, Richard Heywood. Having selected Trinity College on the grounds of personal contacts and its current reputation for godliness, he left the freshman Oliver at Cambridge in the summer of 1647 with some ground rules designed to forward his son's spiritual independence. Among these was the advice to compile "The meditations of my youth." Personal experience—and its development—were thus both restrained and induced. There is a technical—even technological—compulsion to align the soul with "the stupendous contrivance of free grace."

Few of the youth's own thoughts could have competed in vividness with his father's experience of three years before. He had traveled to Rotterdam to persuade Robert Park, a former vicar of Bolton, to leave his ministry among the English merchants there and return home. He was unsuccessful on that occasion. Coming in to port at Hull, he heard of the Bolton Massacre. Worse followed. He had to cross Marston Moor and "after the battle there, saw a lamentable spectacle of multitudes slain, stript, the saddest object that ever he beheld: he often mentioned it."[13] This was Ellis Bradshaw's hell. It is not surprising that in Oliver Heywood the military metaphors beloved of Marsh, and Horrocks, should be replaced by images of the journeying chapman and the trader in durable ware. They are more honorable and poetic, it seems, to him than anything that connotes of war. "Church-Divisions," like "Civil-Divisions," he regards as simply wrong. The "Spirit of Aemulation . . .

is contrary to the true Spirit," not the means of identifying it. A rival to such as Hewit in a number of points of theology, he shares Hewit's desire to belong to an establishment capable of accommodating difference. Exclusion, above all from education, creates the monsters it pretends to exorcize. Charles II's Declaration of Indulgence of 1672 was trumped in 1675 by Parliament's suppression of licenses for nonconforming preachers: "though the King's Majesty set them at liberty for a season, yet that was quickly retracted." Heywood recognized that damage was thus done, above all, to the theological balance of nonconformists, endangering the moral condition of the state. Under such a game of cat and mouse nothing serious could survive, only the vices of the "factious" and (which was nearly the same thing) the "illiterate." On all sides honest "experiment" *toward* doctrinal enlightenment, conducted on guidelines provided by Christ's moral law of love, was turned into forms of spiritual plagiarism designed to flatter or outrage an establishment pretending to have all the answers for no better reason than to silence all the questions. Excluded and included alike were going down a mud slide from "squibbling strictness, to open persecution of all that looks like seriousness."[14]

"I purposely waive the School-mens' voluminous disputes concerning grace," he writes, "and shall propound these seven directions to poor graceless souls; and they are plain and practical duties." In essence these amount to the fostering of an interplay between the private and the communal, between each of the faithful laying up "divine Discoveries, . . . a Diary of God's dealing with their souls" and the imitation of "such Tradesmen as miss no opportunity of getting gain" by converse with others "at home and abroad." While salvation is in essence "personal," not "federal," it can prosper only in a federal context.[15] Discussion, negotiation, an atmosphere of "seriousness," not the claptrap of the "parrot," in or out of the establishment, are what Heywood tries to keep alive in a marginalized and despised sect.

In many ways his books are a continuation of the "prophesying" movement stifled but not extinguished by Elizabeth in 1577. They are in the same tradition, going back to Lollard times, of an alert scripture debate, directed not at the formulation of abstractions, but at the building of moral resources ("Heart-Treasure," Heywood calls these). The textual reading is tested as well as enriched by the life experience of the readers. Not merely sold in London, but in local circulation as gift books and borrowed copies, his writings are also a substitute for the early Presbyterian conferences, such as that begun at Dedham, in Essex, in 1581. John Angier senior, who was Heywood's revered father-in-law, and whose *Life* he wrote, was a native of Dedham, reared in that local tradition, which owed much to the personal influence of Edmund Chapman—the name is suggestive—a fellow of Trinity College, Cambridge. At the outset of his ministerial career, Angier was on the point of leaving for America, doubtless feeling with Herbert that

> Religion stands a tiptoe in our land
> Ready to pass to the American strand.

But he received and responded to a "call" to the Salford Hundred of Lancashire, a region that had much in common with the area of Essex about
Dedham (and the area of Yorkshire about Northowram): "Protestantism was
an early tradition in these industrial villages, the successor to a strong lollard
strain in the early sixteenth century." Heywood's work continues the tradition of "preaching and education" in such townships.[16]

His own special characteristic is to minimize the Rome-Geneva divide
while fostering a high degree of self-analysis and self-consciousness in his
readers: "I hope we shall be so wise as to choose Bellarmine's *dying safe way,*
rather than his *Disputing politic way* to Heaven" is about the limit of his
engagement in the old controversies.[17] While phrases suggestive of morbidity
or exaggeration could be picked out, they are there to suggest a "pathetical"
reflection, not to carry a weak argument. *Closet Prayer, a Christian Duty,*
which ran to seven editions between 1671 and 1830, is perhaps his most
characteristic work. The *Advice to an Only Child* (1693, 1700, 1820) is a
rather dauntingly strict essay in godly heart searching for young people preparing for their first communion. His *Baptismal Bonds Renewed* (1687) sets
out a pattern for personal covenanting with God. A *Family-Altar* (1693,
1807) keeps alive the tradition of godly prayer and praise that had, for dissenters, been exiled from the established branch of the Reformed Church as the
price of the Restoration. "Loyal, and dutiful" to the anointed king of England,
no more than Anderton or Henry Bradshaw can Heywood accord soul homage to any king of earth: "Though the King of Tyre be as the anointed cherub,
and say he is God, yet shall he be brought down to the pit."[17]

But the trail leads forward as well as back. Refusing "calls" to York and
Preston, Heywood remained a traveling preacher centered at Northowram,
between Halifax and Bradford. His sons John and Eliezer began their education at nearby Hipperholme Grammar School, newly founded with a bequest
from Matthew Broadley, a local man who had been personal jeweler to
Charles I. They proceeded—in the nonconformist pattern—to Edinburgh
University. Both became ministers.[18]

By 1693 Heywood had established his own school in connection with the
new Northowram chapel. Its first master was David Hartley I, the founder
of a dynasty of intellectual Puritans of influence. They included his son
David Hartley II, whose *Observations on Man* (1749) helped to form the
mind of John Stuart Mill and was an enabling early influence on Coleridge
and Wordsworth. His son, David Hartley III, carefully educated by his father
by methods evolved from puritan disciplines, was not only a loyal subject
and personal friend of George III, but a consistent supporter in the House
of Commons of the American rebels, a friend of Benjamin Franklin, and
British signatory to the Treaty of Paris of 1783.[19]

Manically strenuous, they feel entirely passive. And in this bone-aching, sinew-tearing Gethsemane (their central icon of Christ) they can neither, like Lever or Pilkington before them, hope to address the political establish-ment as one of its members, nor, like their own more radical contemporaries the Quaker George Fox or his northern lieutenant Alexander Parker,[3] launch a campaign of renewal that breaks entirely from the past. Believing in intellec-tual education, they believe also that brain knowledge is not soul knowledge. From the height of their own privilege, they mediate fragments of the former in enforcement of the latter, while denying any causal connection between the two. They do this with great skill and very little condescension. By the nature of the exercise, however, neither writer nor reader can experience the emancipation from contemporary worldly conventions that would permit that radical identification with the gospel Jesus, across human divisions like class, sex, and race, such as George Fox was reclaiming. Reared to enact Christ's agony in the garden as a daily duty; compelled to seek him; warned against blithe hopes of finding him: against whom should they feel resentment if not him?

Only into the mouth of a dying woman—his own young wife, Elizabeth—can Oliver place the creed of such a womanish (neither "manly" nor "wom-anly") condition: "Choose the greatest affliction before the least sin," he reports as her last words. Denied expression of his own aggressive impulses, it is for him God, not Satan, who becomes that child's nightmare of all civil wars: an armed man standing by the bed, ready to kill. Most tellingly, the old vocabulary of "daily warfare," dear to Marsh and Horrocks, comes back into his language in *The Best Entail* (1693), a study of the immense, futile, restraint laid upon a doomed child by godly parents. Denying in their refined Calvinism any certainty for themselves, the Heywoods dared to guess at it in the case of others, for heaven or hell: "you must not be contented simply to have your child tormented, which is abhorrent to nature, but your Souls must be overruled with the divine pleasure," Heywood advises: "you must rest satisfied in that by which God thinks fit to Glorify himself." The spiritual abjection is matched by social courtesies. The work is dedicated to Philip, Lord Wharton: "A poor inconsiderable worm," writes the massive Hey-wood, "prostrates himself at your Lordship's feet." Such actorly self-consciousness is also a half-consciousness. Under the seal of marriage, a cou-ple might become one flesh at the expense of the bride's spirit. Elizabeth (John Angier's daughter) was subject to bouts of depression and self-loathing. She "could hardly get up to be married," her widower, with robust tender-ness, recalls, "yet the Lord had mercy on her, and not her only but on me also, lest I should have a sudden abatement of my comfort."[4] If a Puritan divine could thus be so "cavalier," so also could his hagiographer. Nathaniel Heywood died in 1677, and we are spared no improving detail by his biogra-pher, Sir Henry Ashurst. Nathaniel's wife died very soon after her husband.

Sir Henry makes no mention of this, but is careful to inform his readers that the lady was near kin to a bishop. Yet like his own dedicatee, Hugh, Lord Willoughby (cofounder with the Andrews family of the Presbyterian chapel at Rivington), Sir Henry has an objection (however selective in its operation) to bishops. During the Civil War, while the Willoughbys were annexing the Caribbean, the Ashursts were defending Bolton against ungodly powers, including those claimed by the parish's patron, John Bridgeman, bishop of Chester.[5]

Fox, a Leicestershire man (he hied from Drayton, hard by Marsh's Langton), found a great friend in Judge Fell, vice-chancellor of the Duchy of Lancaster, whose house near Ulverston was used for Quaker meetings from 1650. Fox was preaching in the Manchester region from 1652. It may indicate Bolton's reputation as "Geneva of the North" that he never seems to have ventured into the town, though his ideas spread there, as elsewhere.

Ellis Bradshaw's three anti-Quaker tracts all involve attacks on James Nayler. Unlike his highly individual earlier pieces they are part of a general pamphlet war. Pugnacious as ever, they now also display a self-conscious outrage (Nayler had dared to attack him in print). Bradshaw rarely stoops to be vicious, but the timing and title of the third pamphlet—*The Conviction of James Naylor* (1656)—has vicious connotations. Nayler, an eccentric whose behaviour was not typical of most Quakers, was currently undergoing trial and punishment by the state. Ironically, the king's removal had also removed the facility of a royal pardon, which would in effect have been Cromwell's prefered option.

Monarch or no monarch, the brutalization of Nayler symptomizes a communal risk in favor of repression, at the expense of a risk in favor of freedom, equivalent to Elizabeth's suppression of "prophesying" eighty years before.

As ever, the soul that feeds on resentment "is, whate'er she hates and ridicules."[6] The new posturing, self-conscious tone in Bradshaw is the mirror of its subject. Nayler was accused of play-acting Christ, even of going so far as to stage at Bristol Christ's Entry into Jerusalem, with himself in the principal role. Protestant England was clearly not so very different in its cultural atmosphere from contemporary Counter-Reformation Bavaria, which saw the institution of the Oberammergau passion plays. There, too, the new naturalism had its dangers. For if the actor seemed really to be Christ, why should not Christ be really an actor? The lowest, as well as the highest, motives were inevitably incarnated rather than examined in such a performance. By the end of the nineteenth century, the Bolton Whitmanites had caught the Anglo-Saxon fascination with these "blasphemous" dramas. They were moved, but they disliked the anti-Semitic elements in the script that would lead Hitler to cherish them. Was it the Jew in Christ or Christ in the Jew that was resented and expiated?

Similar confusions attended Nayler's story. He is said to have cultivated aspects of his personal appearance that recalled conventional images of Christ. Fanatics addressed him as "no more James Nayler, but Jesus." Above all, women adored him, singing "Holy, holy, holy" in his presence.

His punishment was sufficiently public and severe to suggest that it was indeed Christ who was resented in him. Pilloried and whipped, he was bored through the tongue with a hot iron like a voodoo doll and then branded on the forehead with "B" for "blasphemer." This was on 27 December, which (before Parliament abolished it) had been the day of St. John the Evangelist, the disciple whom Jesus loved. Yet it was Nayler's followers, predictably gathering round him to lick his wounds and pay him "other honours," who were accounted "ridiculous and superstitious."[7]

While being hot against any symptoms of excess or anarchy, it is typical of the Heywoods that they disdained to contend with Quakers as such. Nevertheless, Oliver's analysis of the Muncer rebellion in Germany of 1520–25 would seem to glance (if so, very unfairly) at contemporary Quaker "fanatics." It appeared in 1679, the same year, as it happens, that saw a spate of attacks on Quakers in Bolton.[8]

Richard Heywood, the well-to-do tradesman revolted to his core by military violence, proposed to his sons a self-discipline based on the continual verbalization of their own prayerful reflections, trained and monitored by his own supervision and that of his wife. They were sent to Henry VIII's Trinity College, Cambridge, an institution as Erastian as Julius II's Balliol, Oxford, had been papal and imperial. Begun as a *colonia conducta* from the obnoxiously radical St. John's, Trinity was constructed to attract, and foster, an élite, a continual succession of young men pledged to the renovation of the status quo, in particular their own status. Nathaniel matriculated in 1648 and Oliver in 1647. In 1646 George Fox, following the radical logic of his own "Inner Light," had announced "that a learned education at the university was no qualification for a minister, but that all depended on the anointing of the spirit."[9]

The young Oliver Heywood appears to have been an entirely typical Trinity undergraduate of the intellectual type: devoted to his own chosen studies and condescendingly selective in his attitude to the curriculum. In particular, his cool appraisal of his tutor, Akehurst, exemplifies a balance between arrogant "Puritan" individuality and an equally arrogant "Cavalier" suspicion of anything not quite *comme il faut*. Akehurst was popular enough to be almost too popular. "He had sometimes about thirty pupils, and, as I thought, was a gracious savoury Christian." But there was something not quite sound about him: "I have often taken notice of his inconstancy, and being singular in differing from grave and sober divines, and pride, which was too visible in his apparel, gesture and other outward tokens thereof." Thus speaks the new imperialist Englishman, alien to Pilkington, of the late seventeenth century: neither disciplined, exactly, but masked, nor humble exactly, but too complexly arrogant to condone in others any momentary betrayal of pride.

Akehurst, we learn, justified the condescending anxiety behind his pupil's scrutiny. He became a "common Quaker."[10] With his more complexly trained sensibility, Heywood shared Ellis Bradshaw's incapacity for abandoning the fetish of particular "outward tokens," and with them the inequalities of the world. In Heywood's case, the more rarefied the tokens, the more reliable they were likely to be. Freed from popish or Anglican formularies, one was under a duty to be exquisitely selective in one's recognition of the things that pertained to Christ. To share Christ and all life—as Lever had defined the Sacrament—was now too crude, or too politically embarrassing, even to be imagined.

And so the emphasis is on refined tokens, and on the minister's power to bring assurance of them: "some seal, some token, ... some kisses of his mouth." There is a new, womanish "naturalism" in such language, quite different from the artificial and symbolic mannerism of Richard Crashaw, for instance (who had left Cambridge for Rome not long before Oliver matricu- lated). Marsh burned because he could assure his flock only that Christ was "ever with" the consecrated bread, not transubstantiated "in form of bread." But in the Heywoods, language, and the claims of the clergy, run amok: "Oh, Sinners, we bring you Love-Letters from our Beloved." John Hewit, or Lawrence Anderton, could bring communion to the sick, and assure them that Christ was with them, without need to interrogate how. On a similar occasion, Oliver Heywood has a problem of the precise tuning of a spiritual sensibility to settle over the bedspread: the dying man "had great Fears upon him abut his sincerity." Once attained, however, and kept tuned like "the strings of an Instrument," we may enjoy "sweet reflections on our sincerity." Nothing imported from the bustling streets of Rome or Geneva can avail. The quality of assent to a fine thing must be of suburban delicacy: "If you accept of the Lord Jesus Christ, you are in the suburbs of Heaven, there is but a thin wall between you and the Land of Praises. ... When death digs a little hole in the wall ... you have no more to do, but set your foot down in the fairest of created Paradises." How different is the quality of the Heywoods' anxiety from that of their great contemporary, the Bedford tin- ker!: "Consider, that *this Devil, this Hell, Death and Damnation followeth after thee as hard as they can drive*. ... If they *seize upon thee* before thou get to the *City of Refuge*, they will put an everlasting stop to thy Journey: This also cries, *Run for it*."[11]

For Oliver Heywood, the "genuine motions of God's blessed Spirit" are "a delicate thing." One must "yield" to them, and never "grieve" it, or it will "deal with you as you deal with it." There is no pilgrimage, because no progression, only an unceasing round of equilibrations: "Thus thou dost spend thy days as in a circle," he confides to his diary. Yet he can teach another the way to go. Completing his *Advice to an Only Child,* he expresses the confidence "that you may smoothly and cheerfully walk in the way here chalked out before you, till you come to the Land of Glory." Nathaniel, a redoubtable pedestrian, circuits between two chapels, "Bickerstaff, . . . two miles south from Ormskirk, and Scarisbrick, two miles north." Robust of body, yet lean in the face, "his sweat hath dropped at his Hair-ends, . . . [and] Letters wet in his Pocket through linings, as if put in water." He is much sought after, an "experienced Casuist, resolving cases of Conscience with great satisfaction." As a result of his ministry, a Protestant heiress renounces her popish suitor for a godly bridegroom.

Nathaniel celebrates the Restoration of Charles II—who promised "liberty to tender consciences"—with a tactful sermon in his parish church at Orm-skirk, based on the Old Testament story in which the son of Saul welcomes his father's old enemy and successor, King David. This is remembered when the preacher is evicted in 1662. Mr. Ashworth, his Anglican replacement, is a Saturday-to-Monday parson who returns to teach school eight miles away during the week. Unsurprisingly, he is not much liked. Heywood remains virtually in "sole charge of that Town and Parish." The community colludes to evade the exclusion laws, for, earnest and (it is thought) a little "crackt," but also "cheerful" and given to "harmless Jests," Nathaniel is much beloved. Arrested, he is the subject of eulogy from the bench and dismissed. Workmen stop to joke with him in the street. From time to time, officers make a show of knocking on his door, but no one answering (though children are coming in and out of both doors), they go away again, disingenuously baffled. He spends one night in prison.

At last, 6 December 1677, a Sunday, "the day of his hard and sore labour," becomes the "day of his entrance into Eternal Rest." He is buried in the chancel of Ormskirk church. His Anglican supplanter attends. The local officer bears the mace before his coffin. A packed congregation interrupt the eulogy (by another banned minister) with sobs and echoes of assent.[12]

Ormskirk church contains the tombs of the Stanleys. The body of James Stanley, the beheaded earl of Derby, was brought there, his coffin filled with "seeds" (the waste of flax or cotton) to absorb the blood. In nominating Nathaniel Heywood as vicar in 1656, the dowager countess, Charlotte, a representative of leading Protestant dynasties of Europe, was maintaining in a recusant corner of Lancashire her destined battle with Rome. An almost equally powerful personality became Nathaniel's protectress after his eviction. This was the dowager Lady Stanley of Bickerstaff, born Mary Egerton. Her second husband—described as "consort" on the dedication page of Nathaniel's posthumous *Christ Displayed* (1679)—was Henry Hoghton, who had seized the opportunity to purchase part of Bolton manor after James Stanley's death. Her father, as General Egerton, had received the final surrender of Lathom. Her mother, the heiress Elizabeth Asshaw, was most likely kin to Bishop Pilkington's mother. Her first husband, Sir Thomas Stanley, fought against his relative, James Stanley, at Manchester in 1642, and afterwards. Sir Thomas died in 1653. His relationship to the earls of Derby was rather distant, but when the direct male line failed in 1736, it would be his and Mary Egerton's great-grandson who would succeed as eleventh earl. He brought to the title a middle-class fortune, inherited through his mother, Elizabeth Patten, daughter of a rich merchant of the manufacturing port of Preston. It was his successor who held the first "derby," which in Kentucky, Paris, and elsewhere still means a "horse race," and in England also means "a hotly fought local contest."

Such a pattern—from the quasi-feudal to the Whig-imperial—is a reminder that the political, military, and religious struggles of the seventeenth century were also biological contests from which dominant strains emerged. The highest aspirations, the lowest compulsions, God and Mammon, helped to form the pattern.

To clarify the pattern, and Nathaniel Heywood's place in it, it is necessary to broaden the chronology a little further. At the beginning of the Victorian age, with religious freedom, industrialization, and rocketing land values, the Scarisbricks of Scarisbrick commissioned their fellow Catholic A. W. N. Pugin to design a neo-Gothic mansion in the early-sixteenth-century style. After the death of her bachelor brothers, Anne Scarisbrick, last of the line, retired to her apartments in the high tower built for her by Pugin's son. The whole project was elaborated to a staggering degree of opulence such as they could never have aspired to when their dominance of the locality was last asserted, in the lifetime of Elizabeth Scarisbrick, heiress of Bickerstaff, who was born in 1516. Her marriage to a Stanley cadet, and the overthrow of the "old religion," brought the world she had once known to an end. This is the context against which must be set Ashurst's admiring account of Heywood's rescue of the souls of the dying from the clutches of popish priests, and of his anti-Catholic Gunpowder Plot sermon of 1672, delivered in Scarisbrick Chapel under the auspices of its current proprietor, Mary Egerton-Stanley-Hoghton. Her grandson, the new baronet of Bickerstaff, a child of two, her precious lifeline to the Protestant future, will be married to the all-important Patten fortune before reaching his majority.[13]

Again and again the pattern of powerful, frustrated women and manipulated, resentful men. This is not a sectarian matter. James Anderton, who owed his faith to a heroic mother, seems almost demented by Protestant developments tending towards a female presence in the ministry. It would be crude, however, to say that either he or the Heywoods, loving husbands both, and diligent preachers, disliked women, or hated Christ. Rather is their half-conscious resentment directed against that token of current human relationships, their inherited image of Christ. Him, beyond all their circling, they seek, and their own peace in the promise of him:

> It pleased the Father that in Him should all fulness dwell, . . . a fulness of suffi-
> ciency, and a fulness of redundancy; enough for Himself, and to fill all persons, all
> things; there is enough in Christ for every soul, and for the supply of every want
> . . . in Christ is not only, but dwells fulness.

To attain such plentitude, Christians must "see ye do nothing to the obedience of men, which is contrary to that which ye owe to Christ; and as
touching your soul and conscience, subject and enslave yourselves to no man
living."[14] The Heywoods lived by this law. Nathaniel suffered only continual
worry, harassment, impecuniousness. In Yorkshire, the impending succession
of James II (who had given hints of tolerance) was enough to put Oliver in
prison for eleven months from January 1685. At another time, he suffered
distraint of goods, down to the meal-chest. At the pleading of his second
wife, Abigail, the officers tipped out the unused meal onto an old curtain
not worth taking. As in Lancashire, people were better than the law: no one
could be found to buy the goods or to take them as a gift. Gifts of money
flowed in towards a new house.[15]

Yet "that which ye owe to Christ" had been shriveled away by these
means. Barely on sufferance from day to day, the remnants of Presbyterian
moral invincibity dare hardly challenge so much as the right to exist: "Laws
are committed to us, and must not be excogitated by us," warned Nathaniel.
Refrain from "thinking it a kind of happiness to be free" when "there is no
freedom but in sinning." Marsh walked a prisoner to Lancaster from Lathom,
but he walked unfettered. As being no rascal, the soldiers would not bind
him, he writes. A pettier cruelty now prevails, a stranger gulf between saint
and sinner. Snatched and brought to trial and briefly imprisoned in 1659, as
his wife bears and loses their child, Oliver is horrified and distraught to
spend a night "among the unruly soldiers . . . swearing and profanely talking."
No more are all men "God's good creatures," for it has somehow come about
that "there is no medium, all persons are either Saints or Brutes, like Angels
or like Devils."[16] Who can know which, behind the mask?

In such a universe, Christ can be no captain, and no king. He is partly an
item of womanish luxury, partly a tyrannical employer, partly a government
spy, and, in the end, an actor, resented and adored, utterly desirable because
utterly unknown:

> He is a delicate Banquet. The kisses of His mouth and hidden manna are most
> delectable to the spiritual touch. . . . He is a most knowing and discerning Lord.
> He observes the ways and works of his servants so narrowly, that the closest and
> subtilest among them cannot deceive Him; He spies them in every corner, nay
> every corner of their hearts. . . . He needs no informer. . . . The mask and veil on
> my Beloved's face fetcheth blood from me, yea murders me.[17]

34

Scope: The Lamentations of Saints

Destroyed by Nero the tyrant-poet of lies, Lucan the martyr-poet of uncomfortable truths is said to have blamed his mother for the crime for which he was ordered to commit suicide. That crime—as Lucan's fellow Spaniard Calderon would famously put it—was perhaps only that of "having been born." Oliver Heywood, too, felt all sin to be in essence Original Sin. As though to register his own predicament, he cites Lucan as he commences his biography of his father-in-law John Angier.[1] His inherited dream of a national religion seemed poised guiltily but helplessly to destroy itself somewhere between submission and evasion, between the traditions of Erastianism and classical scholarship. This division would be more openly realized between two of Heywood's distinguished successors: Zachary Taylor, the "Lancashire Levite," and Robert Ainsworth of the Latin *Thesaurus*. For Heywood (as for a third successor, Lawrence Fogg) the split is postponed by resort to Hebrew.

The relevant passage occurs in *Israel's Lamentation after the Lord* (1683). Before exploring its particular significance, it would be well to register the more general significance of Heywood's kind of intense textual probing. The contemporary context deserves a word, no less than the deeper background of Heywood's own development. As a source of consolation, such close reading concerns itself with scrutinizing the "scope" available to spiritual insights trained on the Bible (a technique whose great master, for Heywood, was John Angier). Since the consolation there offered awaits fulfilment at God's good pleasure, the intervening anguish expresses itself in forms of extempore "lamentation" such as would seem to be one of the many sources for the "blues" (a term that derives from English usage of c. 1550).[2] The unexampled performer of such "lamentation," for Heywood, was his first wife Elizabeth, Angier's daughter.

Israel's Lamentation was written at a time when the mortality of Charles II could no longer be ignored. The Catholicizing policies attributed to his brother and heir, the future James II, seemed to threaten persecution for Protestants and perhaps another civil war. In the event, James's reign was calamitous, but brief. In France, the revocation of the Edict of Nantes in 1685 would be the signal for massacres, but France would not set the pattern

for England, where there were more substantial responsibilities in place between the criminality of the monarch and that of the mob. Among these not
the least were the survival and development, from the reign of Edward VI
onwards, of a characteristically English mode of discourse that preferred an
unresolved contradiction of idea to an atrocious solution in fact. Apparent
opposites had much in common. It might have been predicted that a Presbyterian such as Nathaniel Heywood, strong for biblical sincerity, would dismiss
Henry of Navarre (author of the Edict of Nantes) as a "time-server."[3] But
equally notable is the recusant James Anderton's impatience with the degree
of personal power that Henry had at command and with the rhetoric devised
in its favor by revisionist French Jesuits. Catholic royalists who fought for
Charles I—James Anderton's nephew among them—and Presbyterian royalists who died on the other side—Nathaniel Heywood's uncle among them—
had something important in common. Neither wanted a king strong enough
to impose their own version of Christianity by decree. In the event, England's
new monarch—William III, grandson of Charles I and son-in-law to James
II—would be imported from Holland. In some ways, here was the dream of
Janeites and Marian sustainers fulfilled, a monarch tamed to a Protestant
constitution and Protestant alliances by his need to placate an expansionist
financial and commercial elite. But there was another sense in which the
Dutch connection represented resistance to the ideas of France. Louvain was
a center of neo-Stoic and neo-Thomist ideas, the legacy of resistance to ty-
rants down the ages. Such heritage inhibited any development in Holland
towards absolute monarchy. This conservative Catholic tradition—the tradition of James Anderton and of Lawrence Vaux, sub-prior of Louvain, before
him—implied an equitable balance between church and state, a balance out
of which might be generated (as was happening in Holland) the realization
that truth might be encountered through habits of tolerance at least as frequently as in systems of negation.

William's arrival therefore strengthened an English cultural tradition indebted to Catholics as well as to Protestants and to conservatives as well as
innovators. The tradition could live side by side with the rather different
Scottish tradition. Given the sort of conditions pioneered by Thomas Lever,
it proved able to travel further. But conditions could not be duplicated at
will. The seed was delicate. Those secular forces partly indebted to it for
their own success were in too much of a hurry to wait to see it nurtured in
Ireland or among "servants" brought over from Africa. Enlightenment became a source of darkness, and reason was turned against the moral inheritance that had first heeded its pleadings, in the days of democracy at Athens.
Irresponsibly in charge, a Protestant Whig elite endeavored to confine to its
own ranks virtues and benefits that the older Christian humanism had begun
to recognize as universal.

In refusing the Westhoughton curacy for that of Coley, in the West Riding, Oliver Heywood would seem to have wished to put space between himself and his parents. The Pennine border with Yorkshire was still a military reality, successfully garrisoned during the Civil War, regularly impassable in winter. Did he resent his parents and the local background they represented? An obscure resentment does seem to underlie much of his writing. Yet he palpably admires his parents' forceful commonsense; the generous moral energy promoted by Horrocks; and that whole Christian revival which locally owed as much to à Kempis as to Wycliffe. It is surely more likely that his resentment had an intellectual base, in the nature of the university education that represented for his innocent parents everything short of heaven for him. Drawing on techniques of the Angier family, Heywood evolved a style of "lamentation" capable of developing the inwardness of Herbert, the Trinity poet, not in order to shake off, but in an effort to maintain, his parents' legacy of human decency. Living through an age of polarity and exclusion, he desired to transmit to others a deeper synthesis than anything provided by the Trinity of his own day.

Thomas Hill, the college's current master and daily Bible expositor, outlawed any discussion of Arminian revisionism by "something here" (laying his "hand upon his breast" in the timeworn gesture of one refusing to engage in dialogue). Heywood's own arrogant selection drew him to prefer "Perkins . . . far above . . . Plato." He later regretted that he had not developed his talent for "natural philosophy,"[4] but this was not the "Manchester University" of his father's dreams. It was Cambridge, which would keep science off the curriculum after Newton, and even after Darwin.

It might be argued that the enclosed Calvinism of Perkins was not only insufficiently Trinitarian, but insufficiently transcendental, to serve as a guide to human life. It resolved the contradiction between the ideal and the real at the expense of the moral superiority of God. In such a tradition, the deity appears too often merely as "Father," pulling the strings of its "Spirit" within the human breast.[5] Its supporters tended towards a blasphemy antithetical to Nayler's. Far from identifying with God the Son, they could only block the discovery of the Logos within their own nature. Salvation was everything, yet salvation was a prelapsarian "contrivance" that reduced the Incarnation to a charade. The absolute denigration of the human followed from a view of divine behavior unrecognizable from gospel accounts of "the Word . . . made flesh." Here was a Christianity that sadly distorted Christ. Heywood died in 1702. His last works were concerned exclusively with heavenly fulfilment. A generation later, English Presbyterians had begun to turn their creed inside out, to rescue Christ from the ruins (as they saw them) of Trinitarian Christianity. Like the Heywoods, their intelligence was essentially moral. They abandoned an orthodoxy that had put their amiable predecessors in the grip of a scarcely tolerable strain: such a visceral loathing of doctrinal controversy; such an insupportable longing for the truth; such an incapacity for silence. Nathaniel was used, and (one might argue) worked to death by the local Whig-Presbyterian caucus. In 1683, under the shadow of the ambiguous "tolerance" proffered by Charles's heir, this same group found itself the target of a reactionary mob.[6] In the same year, Oliver turned to "Lamentation after the Lord."

Having for "almost three Apprenticeships" endured "divorcement from Public Places and Employments," he selects for comment a passage from the first book of Samuel, which mirrors his condition and his hopes. In this, the Philistines return the Ark of the Lord to Israel after twenty years. Eleazar ("God is helper," a variant of Eliezer, or "God is help," the name of Heywood's younger son) is consecrated as its new custodian. A bewildered and divided nation, long deprived of true worship, gives way to remorse, relief, repentance, and renewal: "the house of Israel lamented after the Lord."

Like his grandfather and namesake, Oliver dreads the withdrawal of God. He adduces from classical history a hateful and desolate image of this condition. The "Inhabitants of Tyrus, when Alexander besieged it," terrified that their god would leave them, took the "Image of Apollo," and bound it with a chain of gold to a post. It availed them nothing. Against such a background of metallic objectivity, the current Christian condition appears more spiritual, but also more "pathetical," and perhaps more desolate: "If anything fetch back a departing God, it must be a believing prayer."

The search for moral rightness is essential to Heywood's belief. One of the great sources of Johnsonian prose is the concise and accessible Bible commentary of interpreters trained in the classical languages. Heywood excels, as often, in his exposition of the story of the sons of Eli, Samuel's predecessor as judge of Israel. By "abusing the women that came to the door of the Temple," they polluted the shrine and destroyed its efficacy. No reader of the period of Charles II would require a gloss to parallel the "iniquity of Eli's house" with that of the House of Stuart. For Heywood, the ark of a national religion, under the Christian dispensation, is absolutely dependent for its effectuality on the spiritual dimension. A Christian is required to be "a Jew inwardly." The aspirations of old Israel are now duties: God "stops and halts, as in suspense what to do, that He may both alarm us, and afford us leisure to consider." In order to "reduce Him back to our Souls," we must deploy a lamentation that is truly "believing." Heywood explains:

> the same word in Hebrew signifies both to repent and to comfort, to mourn and to cease mourning, to lament and rejoice, for as true comfort belongs only to penitent Souls, so sorrow is the porch and inlet to joy

Here, based on a reading of the Hebrew *nahah* ("to become wailing"), is Heywood's definition of the oscillatory "scope" of the Holy Spirit as it operates within the individual to create the poem of God. In accordance with

English lyric convention, "scope," which rhymes with "hope," may be perceived by the very fact of that fated matching as its antithetical excluder. "The Church Porch" is of course the introductory poem to *The Temple*, by Heywood's favorite writer and model in the role of country parson, George Herbert. Subject not only to the general exclusion of 24 August 1662, but also to a series of personal excommunications (including one read out in Bolton Parish Church in 1663), Heywood went out from the porch of his own church for the last time more conscious than ever that the "Kingdom of Glory" which he inherited by baptism was also a "Kingdom of Grace." Only by entire subjection to the mysteries of grace could glory be won. And grace had taken hold of hope and split it asunder. Dwelling on the meaning of *nahah*, Heywood expands the three theological virtues to four. One cannot expect faith, hope and love for the asking. One must learn to live with "what he meets with in the Ordinance of God, Faith, Love, Desire, Joy."[7]

It is this oscillation between unfulfillable "desire" and insupportable "joy" that replaces the traditional Christian songs of "hope" with a new soul-song of lamentation, one that is mannerist, extempore, a kind of blues, having a similar relation to orthodox liturgy as jazz to the conventional ballad. This tune of life is not a matter of "pumping" for "Expressions and Affections," but, in a world where there is no liberty, a kind of predatory surrender to the "spirit of God, for where the Spirit is, there is Liberty." Heywood opens up the Lord's Prayer as a "Directory" for such variations. The whole Bible is a great series of headings for the variations of the heart, which in each Christian "sings him a merry tune." Such a soul "needs not to be prompted by men, that hath this lively Liturgy in his heart." Yet it is also, in both senses, "labour": "Dost thou feel the body of Sin within thee? . . . where are thy groans under it?" This is essentially a *moral* attunement, designed to "engage the poor guilty sinner to struggle with his own heart in the work of believing." Anticipatory of the "blues," it dwells on an obsessional affection. When love seems gone, "look again and rake in the ashes, and see if thou canst not find some spark of love."[8] Elizabeth Heywood excelled in such outpourings:

what a mighty spirit of prayer had she! . . . [S]he was able extempore to express herself to god in scripture phrases, and such suitable words as were no doubt both acceptable to god, and would have been discharged from incongruity, by the severest censurers of extemporary devotions.

Often, pain gave depth to her performance. Troubled about her brother, the scapegrace John Angier junior, "she trembled to inquire of him, lest she should hear what was evil . . . how did it rejoice her heart to read his penitential letters out of [New England]?" At root, a kind of nervous terror "dared" her to engage with and cultivate unspeakable anxieties from which only such performances could offer respite:

> she . . . would shut herself in a room and be long alone, though Satan often took advantage from her timorous nature to affright her in the dark night to hinder her in the performance by groundless fears.[9]

"Groundless" to her stalwart husband, at least. "There is neither Jew nor Greek, there is neither bond nor free, there is neither male nor female," wrote St. Paul in one of those bursts of generosity which occasionally sweep away his prevailing conservatism: "for ye are all one in Christ Jesus." Christians have since been left to debate whether the words imply a political program or merely a prospect for the afterlife. Unable to accept the right of Parliament to control the form of public prayer, Heywood rejected the Anglican Prayer Book of 1662 and its routine of conservative affirmations, but there remained for him a difference between parliamentary and monarchical authority. Parliament he sees as implying debate, consensus, enablement. To repudiate its decisions by cautious acts of civil disobedience is an extension and guarantee of the parliamentary process itself. But there is still that ghost of an unthinking reverence for consecrated royalty, a legacy from the royal Saxon saints, perhaps; maybe some pre-Christian taboo from an even remoter past. And just like Henry Bradshaw, he imagines these royal personages as archetypes of male and female characteristics as traditionally received. Here, at a scarcely conscious level, is to be found the deep subtext of his life assumptions, an atavistic monarchism below the life strategy that connotes with his conscious speculations about Parliament. And so, simply as king, James I, celebrating his entry into his English kingdom by printing *Basilicon Doron,* becomes an icon of masculine restraint and paternal censure; whereas merely as princess, the young Elizabeth, stainlessly surviving the reign of her Catholic sister, provides the leading example of the "advantages of a well-stocked Christian," drawing on the spiritual scope that is the gift of Bible study so as to endure affliction without sin. Citing *England's Elizabeth,* by his kinsman Thomas Heywood, Oliver appropriates the "Peerless Princess" as icon of lamentation.

The contrast with James is remarkable. The former is defined (without irony) as a "Royal learned Writer" before being quoted. The latter is briefly quoted, then rapidly assimilated into her gender-grouping: "How did silly women encounter and conquer the learned Doctors in the Marian days!"[10]

Masculization is a strange accompaniment to domestic retreat: from Werburgh's double cloister for men and women, via Elizabeth's ban on females and Bishop Bridgeman's hegira to Great Lever. In *A Family Altar,* Heywood adopts for his typical head of household—masculine and middle-class—the semimystical title "governor" Henry Bradshaw had assigned to Werburgh and Thomas Lever to Elizabeth. All are equal in Christ, but not yet. A

servant may take some leading part in domestic religious performances, provided only he "be humble, submissive, self-denying, and know his place."
The subject's "Relative Condition" is similarly enforced on the *Only Child*
(the original of whom is stated to be female): "Universal Obedience, . . .
Humility, . . . [and] Meekness" are prescribed, and cloying reponses are incul-
cated: "retire yourself into privacy for a little time, and ask yourself what
your demeanour was at the Lord's Table, . . . what meltings or softenings of
Heart? what glimpses of Love?" Such is the kind of "discipline"—an outlet
for the womanishness of the writer—that was trampled under foot by young
men like John Angier junior, and which trampled in its turn young women
like his sister:

> She was the mirror of patience and subjection in her relation, as a child as a wife,
> and of tenderness and care as a sister, and as a mother . . . if she offended any way
> it was through vehemency of affection.[11]

One finds in Heywood elements of a reasoned humanism that (like Pilkington before him) allows him to begin to acknowledge the separate contribution
of women. But one also finds a streak of falsified, antiquarian tribalism that
seeks to subordinate and appropriate that contribution.

Elizabeth died in 1661. Six years later, Heywood married Abigail Crompton of Breightmet. His relationship with her was less intense, perhaps more
comfortable, than with his "sweet Mistress Betty." There were no children.
She survived him by five years. An entry in Heywood's diary from May
1682 suggests that she facilitated rather than inspired his reflections and was
a dutiful companion rather than a charismatic consort. The passage also
exemplifies how the biography of royalty sustained the godly habits of journal
making and prophecy, providing a contemporary "text" alongside that of the
Bible and the working day for the exercise of spiritual "scope."

In Halifax to attend a funeral, Abigail hears that the bailiffs have warrants
to distrain her husband's goods. Nevertheless, she and Oliver spend Saturday
as usual in fasting and prayer, "god wonderfully helping my wife and me in
pleading with god in that and other affairs." Heywood ventures to "spend
the day after in my public work." There is a "numerous assembly, gracious
assistance." Then on Monday comes news about James, Duke of York,
Charles's brother and heir, "going to sea to Scotland and many of the nobility
with him." His design "was not good in that journey." It seems he intended
to appeal to Catholic malcontents in that country. On the Lord's Day, which
cost the Heywoods so much anxious prayer, however, there was distress of
weather, and the Duke suffered shipwreck, with much loss of life. The Duke
himself, "with 8 more," was saved, reserved no doubt for some other destiny.
But for the present, at least, his anti-Protestant intentions were foiled. "Lord
awake, humble—," Oliver scribbles into his diary, setting the note for an

appropriate lamentation; then adds: "The same day I had a letter from son Eliezer and he is perfectly recovered of his ague."[12]

The effect is of a patchwork. Political news, family affairs and Bible fragments are pieced together to create the vivid discourse of spiritual autobiography.

This habit—one of the cultural sources of Wordsworth's *Prelude*—has virtually disappeared, but the Duke of York's survival remains a misfortune for the British Isles and its peoples. Living to beget a male heir and a phantom dynasty, of great nuisance value to the French, James II failed to maintain any of his three kingdoms, but succeeded in providing the motivating force for a series of ethnic catastrophes—from the Siege of Derry (1689) to the Massacre of Glencoe (1692) to the Battle of Culloden (1746)—that has poisoned their relations ever since.

One may therefore in retrospect sympathize somewhat with the York authorities, who, anticipating anarchy and incendiarism, confined the dangerously nonconformist Oliver Heywood in York Castle for eleven months in 1685, arresting him on 26 January as Charles lay dying. The early months of a new reign were always difficult. York Castle had to be rebuilt, for instance, after being burnt to the ground early in the reign of the crusader king, Richard the Lion-Heart. The fire was either an act of suicide by the Jews who had fled there from the mob, or an act of piety by the mob, attempting to get at the Jews, with the royal connivance.

Inside, Abigail and Oliver quietly proceeded with their life's work of constructing an English conscience between the monarch and the mob. That conscience owed something to the legacy of humanistic rationality, something to barbarous new forms of antihumanist reaction. But there was also a Judeo-Christian tradition of male and female spiritual development, collaborative yet distinct. Heywood admired Salvian, the fifth-century ecclesiastical writer who pieced together a providential pattern from the strange vices of a decadent empire and the strange virtues of its barbarian successors. By consent, he and his wife lived apart, devoted to religious exercises. And so also Abigail and Oliver in their castle at York: she "in her closet" at "secret prayer alone," and he "in the chamber" with his two consolations: the Greek Testament and a pipe of Virginia tobacco. Occasionally, he must have thought of George Marsh, in his castle at Lancaster.[13]

PART EIGHT
Revolution and Thesaurus

I . . . declare my aversion to such Doctrines . . . wherein Success is produc'd for an Argument of the Divine Approbation. . . . But since Prophecy hath ceased, sure I am, that nothing but his Providence is Vocal to us.

—Zachary Taylor, *Obedience and Submission to the Present Government* (1690)

35

Revolution as Antiquity and Continuance

In January 1652 Francis, fifth baron Willoughby, governor of Barbados, acknowledged the sovereignty of Parliament. Later the same year, Oliver Heywood (though under the regular age) was ordained into the Presbyterian ministry. The governor's English estates had been sequestered on the king's death, but all his rights were now restored. His kinsman, the Roundhead major Thomas Willoughby, was resident at Horwich, where Catholic Andertons still held the manor. Heywood was tutor to the Willoughby children. As it turned out, the major lived to become the eleventh baron, and his son Hugh the twelfth. Here in a single moorland township was a reminder that the English Civil War was also a war for the New World, which by the same token was no longer to remain imaginary. At the same time, developments in the Bolton cotton trade were helping to destroy the mythical status of the biblical and classical lands of the Old World.

By the middle of King James's reign, England had achieved a translation of the Bible that, whatever its faults, remains incomparable. Also (with help from translations of ancient pagan authors), she had produced a native drama uniquely fit to challenge comparison with Hellenic masterpieces—"O'er picturing that Venus, where we see/The fancy outwork nature," as Enobarbus says of Cleopatra. Already, when those lines were written (by 1608), the commercial process had begun whereby (as the banker who wrote *The Waste Land* well knew) the cotton crop of Egypt, kingdom of Cleopatra and mystical site of the infancy of Christ, would be shipped direct to Bolton for manufacture. The "waste" proceeded to London to be turned into the world's paper currency. Already, within twenty years of *Othello's* printing, Lancashire was exporting *back* to Cyprus, birthplace of Venus and one of the sites of the Acts of the Apostles, finished goods bleached in Bolton and made up in Manchester, from Cypriot-grown cotton. The same applies to Rhodes, where the original of Enobarbus's "Venus" was once painted, by Protogenes.[1]

Old World as well as New became a new world under pressure of such commerce: the world Eliot would know; no longer the world of Dante. The English "rebellion" against King Charles; the "revolution" that substituted William III for Charles's son James II: these events were no small part of a more enormous change. Oliver Heywood was born in 1630. It is perhaps symptomatic that his father, having made a failure in cotton, reverted to the native trade in wool, of which the parish of Halifax (where Oliver spent his ministry) was the great northern center. Robert Ainsworth, a Protestant nonjuror and compiler of the *Thesaurus Linguae Latinae . . . or . . . Dictionary of the Latin Tongue* (1736), was born thirty years later, the conventional limit of a generation. The difference is one of two worlds. Zachary Taylor, whose clever pen would help to write the Whig legend that the "revolution" of 1688–89 was of divine inevitability and beneficence, was just seven years older than Ainsworth. His style of argument (for it is mainly style) is of one levitated between two polarities that are pulling him apart, and the Church of England with him.

In the tradition inherited by Dante, Christians have dual citizenship. De-riving from the Greeks the duty to make a fairer world, they must also acknowledge that only in the third heaven, the heaven of Venus, are to be found those "heavenly Princes" by whose "understanding" the desires of humanity for justice, happiness, and peace are rightly directed. Oliver Hey-wood's political vision is directly derived from this tradition, yet from Dante's viewpoint it errs by the fervor with which it embraces its own "solitariness":

> when my soul is taken up into those third Heavens, and looks down on this empty world, I am ready to say, Oh, poor Princes that see not the King of Heaven's face! there is no third person can interpose to be a witness betwixt my Lord and my heart.

Such effusions, from Dante's viewpoint, risk the blasphemy of despairing of Providence, as though God were altogether invisible in the world. The Heywoods spent their lives wrestling against this, in them, deeply engrained "Calvinist" tendency, which is indeed as old as history. Zachary Taylor ac-knowledges his own "Anglican" tendency towards the opposite blasphemy, that of equating one's own party with the workings of Providence. So far, his experience and theirs merely complement each other. What is new in Taylor is something that seems to move his imperialist generation altogether out of Dante's scope. In his third heaven, the Florentine is reminded that it is especially important never to expect too little, or too much, of nature; always it is necessary to observe and reverence the genius of a particular person or place: "Always, if nature meets with fortune unsuited to it, like any kind of seed out of its own region, it has ill success."[2] The Heywoods lived by this quintessence of Christian humanism. Summarized in one of their favorite Latin tags—*nil invita Minerva*[3]—it was the idea of city-states like Athens and Florence as long as they remembered that everywhere is its own center. Boltonians, the Heywoods followed each his own bent, and indeed allowed themselves to become exaggerations of their individual characters. Nathaniel went west to lend himself to the comparative "craziness" of delightful Ormskirk, and Oliver went east to learn to love, and be loved by, the apparent "dourness" of Halifax. Each developed an individual strain of Presbyterianism. Yet they were never less than Little Leverites, and themselves.

Taylor was dubbed the "Lancashire Levite," an official priest of a county notorious for its polarization between Catholic and Protestant scorners of the official religion. His father, of the same name, was a graduate of Trinity College, Dublin. At one time a chaplain to the Royalist army, he was Presbyterian minister at Cockey Moor, Ainsworth (the Heywood chapel), and "learned Master" of Bolton Grammar School by 1653, the year Zachary junior was christened in Bolton Parish Church. He had the privilege of teaching Humphrey Chetham junior. He renounced his Rochdale curacy in 1662 yet later conformed enough to teach again in Lancashire schools. Family tensions, as well as crises of conscience, may have lain behind such changes. His wife Abigail was an Anglican. Calamy calls him a "very good scholar, a useful schoolmaster, a solid orthodox preacher, and a pious man."[4]

Whatever compromises it may have cost his father, Zachary junior was able to study at Jesus College, Cambridge. He was vicar of Ormskirk from 1680 to 1693 and then became curate of Wigan, whose rich rectory was held in plurality by the bishops of Chester. It was as vicar of Ormskirk that he found arguments to trump that declining star William Sancroft, archbishop of Canterbury. Sancroft opposed the religious policy of James II, the monarch he had crowned and anointed. But he could not be induced to withdraw his allegiance from him, and in 1689 he gave his imprimatur, in the interests of allegiance to James, to the record of a convocation of the Church of England, dating from the early years of James I, which had been drawn up in manuscript under the supervision of John Overall, the prolocutor of its lower house.[5] The reason it had never been published before was that James I regarded it as lacking in enthusiasm for the royal prerogative.[6] The reason Sancroft published it was its consistent support for the idea that kingship was a divine, patriarchal institution not ultimately dependent on the will of the people. As the summary of what seem to have been rather lively debates, it was far too volatile an instrument to serve the turn Sancroft desired: theological support for unwavering allegiance to the person of a monarch rightfully crowned. Taylor showed his forensic skill by removing the personal element and reducing the argument to matters of abstraction. In doing so, he was promoting a potential for liberalism and enlightenment, freed from "personalities," and at the same time helping to further the kinds of anonymity of place and person under which the most egregious or convenient atrocities could be perpetrated and ignored. Flinging aside any puritanical definitions of good and evil he may have inherited, the Lancashire Levite truly emerges as an "early modern." At the same time, his *Obedience and Submission to the Present Government Derived from Bishop Overall's Convocation Book* (1690) represents a substantial draft upon the moral capital of the seventeenth century.

Rather than transcribing the pamphlet war of 1690,[7] in which Taylor cut so fine a figure, it would seem more useful to focus on one central issue: the question of the succession. For Taylor's nonjuror opponents, James II had a "right" of blood to assert his "authority" as king. This "Right" and "Authority" were both held in trust for the future in the person of his legitimate child by his second wife, Mary of Modena. Were it not for this new male heir, it might have been convenient to regard James's flight as a form of abdication, leaving the throne vacant for his elder daughter Mary and her husband (who was also her cousin), William of Orange. Gossips sought release from the dilemma by concocting the tale of a supposititious child smuggled into Mary of Modena's bed in a warming pan. The better class of casuist—Taylor included—ignored this canard.

The alternative was simplicity itself. In place of the baby, a supposititious Providence must be slipped into the bed of state. The "patriarchal" *authority* of kings must no longer be regarded as descending by heritable *right*. In distinguishing mere "right" from all-important authority, the Anglican Taylor relies on Presbyterian patterns of thought about the transmission of Christianity. It suits his convenience, however, to turn their implied value system inside out. Ellis Bradshaw's *Husbandman's Harrow* sketches from the Independent viewpoint the local (and national) debate about baptism, arguing that while the metaphysical reality of God's indwelling—"justifying faith"—cannot be inherited, a more carnal "historical Christianity" can be transmitted. Parents not openly ungodly, who have themselves undergone the rite of baptism, may bring their children to be christened, since it is not for us to judge their state of grace. Presbyterians, by contrast, insisted that only those indubitably qualified—in the eyes of the elders—could claim initiation for their children.

Given Heywood insistence that faith is nontransferable, and granted Heywood dominance at Cockey, it seems likely that Zachary Taylor senior preached this latter view, which, in any case, closely approximates to the view taken by Zachary junior of that all-important nonentity, James II's son. Accepting the son's legitimacy, Taylor nevertheless implies that the father's "defection" from the kingdom (as it might be, from Cockey Chapel) renders the babe unacceptable in the eyes of Parliamentary "elders." The element essential to acceptance—whatever it is—cannot be inherited.

Now, Ellis Bradshaw and Zachary Taylor senior would agree that it is the *metaphysical* element that is both essential and nontransferable. Zachary junior, having imitated his father by turning Bradshaw's argument round (it is also the usual Anglican argument), now goes one better by turning it inside out, degrading the theory of Providence in the process. True, James's son might inherit some merely notional "metaphysical Right" of blood descent. But this is worthless without concrete "Authority": pragmatic effectuality is the only acceptable mark of divine favor. For the purposes of this argument, Taylor's god has no metaphysical reality, and is merely the impression of external force, albeit mitigated by the "consent of the people." There is a balancing trick being maintained here, which is central to the Whig pattern of control. Something obviously carnal—physical begetting and conceiving— is dismissed as a "metaphysical Right" and reduced to a notion. This is virtu- ally to say that inconvenient materialities are notional. Meanwhile, some- thing largely notional—William III's supposed "Authority"—which is by no means universally conceded, and for which as a matter of fact he will have to go to war—is asserted as stable, concrete. It is to be absolutely justified by results, even though these results cannot actually follow unless we now pledge belief in them.[8]

Faith in the universal and unseen has been replaced by faith in selective aspects of the seen. By the same token, brute fact, which is to be observed everywhere, is now to be shuffled out of the line of vision (like the servants in neoclassical houses) wherever its presence is inconvenient. "What be- comes of the poor Irish men?" asks Taylor's antagonist, not rhetorically: "what can be said to justify a war there . . . against a Prince who hath both Right and Authority?" Irish arrangements "will prove as Thorough a Settlement now," replies the son of the Ascendancy, alas not inaccurately, "as was in Queen Elizabeth's, and some other reigns."[9] Providence appears to be a very conformable organ. The sovereign is clearly going to be kept in check by the "consent of the people," but the consent of the people is to go only so far as Zachary allows. Checkmate. Any serious challenger will need to redraft the rules.

36

"A Dissuasive from Contention"

TAYLOR is much more fun to read than any of his antagonists. It is a grim realism that gives him the edge. A surface of elegance, effrontery, compulsive readability, glides over issues which (he realizes) are too terrible and desperate not to be so veiled. Containment, and a balance of power, are going to be the best things on offer. It is only in the conviction that any alternative would be worse that he disports himself so diligently in their favor.

Underlying everything he wrote are the arguments, and anxieties, that produced *A Dissuasive from Contention,* his offering as a king's preacher during 1682, when it was feared Charles might die and his brother bring in an unholy alliance of Jesuits and Covenanters. Dedicating the piece to Lawrence Hyde, earl of Rochester, James's brother-in-law, "we are exposed to as much danger," writes Taylor, "from the sword of the Lord, in the hands of the Saints, as that of Peter's in his degenerated successors."[1] It is the *style* of such remarks, in their calculated flippancy and familiarity, that proclaims the right to centrality and control. In asking for a measure of practical financial clemency and fairness for Catholics, Taylor anticipates Hyde's policy as James's first lord treasurer. This involved moves to relieve the pressure on Catholics without conceding their claims for "equity" or emancipation. Having no concept of "gradualism" and incapable of distinguishing between private convictions and public necessity, James dismissed him. This was more than a personal failure: it was the failure of personal monarchy itself.

In 1682, with one eye on James and another on his own position in the recusant West Derby hundred of Lancashire, Taylor chose to claim that the threat came rather from the Papists' opponent-allies in zealotry and infatuation, the Calvinists. Incapable, as he blithely demonstrates, of construing their own articles aright, they are currently panicking themselves into a repetition of a former injustice. Already, to allay the "groundless fears" of sectarians, "one Prince was brought to the *Block.*" The same zealots later gave their allegiance to the present king, doubtless intending, in their sober constitutional wisdom, that he would inherit his father's scaffold when the moment came.

Pledged to hold the center against equivalent extremes, Taylor is anxious to prove how futile must be the prayers of both (and they have only prayers) to harm the essential rightness of the Anglican state. Whereas Anglican clergy and people share the form of worship provided, the Dissenters' cult of extempore prayer is a form of Romanism "in Presbyterian weeds." Like the Latin Mass, it is a Babelized jargon in which only the clergy are adepts. Having no rational language, but only variants of the same vagary which he dubs "Romancing," how can either set of infatuates claim power? Their spells will not help them: "there is no *Inchantment* against the Church: neither is there any *Divination* against the State." For the information of both,

> Providence is a Book, and though the Characters be so mystical, that none but God can teach us how to read them: the Language often such, that we must go to Heaven for to learn it: Yet where the Providence quadrates with the Promise, we may conclude, the Lord has spoken.[2]

Truth to tell, the negligent alliterations and pseudomathematical insertions ("quadrates") come to no more than the claim— which James Nayler or the pope himself might make—that readings of contemporary events may be "squared" with readings of the textual tradition to produce *quod erat demonstrandum*. In Zachary's case, this amounts to the proposition that the status quo makes sense, while any opposition is madness.

But Taylor's weakness is his strength, and he knows the meaning of both. Laying his cards on the table to show how desperate they are, he invites his opponents (rivals of each other) to consider the advisability of allowing him to win. As in the best mock epic, there are terrors Homer never knew behind this childlike arbitration. As a representative of the establishment, Taylor holds the card that, by the rules of the peculiar game that is the English monarchy, gives the right to win to its holder *because* it has already been declared the losing card. It is the sickly king himself. His patriarchal power is absolute and can brook no veto, ergo it must be allowed to operate in any way his subjects choose. Zachary proceeds to educate rival wings of nonconformist extremism in the politics of choice. The king twirls in the hand of the king's preacher like a baby's windmill. At one twirl, Charles is a conquering pagan emperor, confident in his clemency: "Caesar's gracious connivance being grown to a Privilege of the People, no less than Parliament." In plainer language, the Crown is at the mercy of Parliament. Another twirl: Charles is the abject female sinner from the gospel story: "And how can you, that are not without Sin yourselves, dare to throw a Stone at the Head of Majesty?" In plain language, the king's army, the king's justices (and, let it be said, the church-and-king mobs) will revenge any disturbance of the current balance between church and state. Papists and Dissenters are always claiming that the establishment is vulnerable to their "Plea of Conscience" in favor of toleration. But toleration is something only the Anglican establishment can grant them. Heaven, in its mercy, is deaf to their mutual anathemas, declines to grant either group the final chance to "wrest the Infamy" out of the other's hands, nor (in case they thought so) "dare Hell itself pretend to patronise an insurrection." As a matter of fact, the Anglican establishment is already as defenseless as its detractors ought to wish. Its traditions are only "reserved . . . unabrogated"—not imposed, but merely "suffered to continue." As long as it continues, its generous atmosphere supplies the medium for the evolution of all the nonconformities that subsist in relation to it, as the alternative to suffocating each other.[3]

Superficially convincing, the sermon collapses into a childish contrivance on closer inspection. It is only when we have all the pieces on the floor that it becomes possible to appreciate the statesmanlike mastery with which they have been put together. Somehow, between the veil and the abyss—the claims of Anglicanism and the threat of anarchy—Zachary has rigged the promise of a safety net. Faithful or otherwise to the plans of the Hydes, this takes the form of clues as to the possibility of real future progress in tolerance and security for such as are "kind to friends and charitable to Brethren."[4]

There is a solid humanist project under the tricks of Taylor's style, a primitive Christian decorum under his theological arabesques. Like many a child of divided parents, he longs above all for the security of an even keel. Unfortunately, in achieving it, he cannot retain either his mother's Anglicanism or his father's Presbyterianism, nor is it possible to combine both. Instead, he retreats to a chilly remove where at most what is to be found of faith (from a sermon of 1695) is some such parcel of personal and public symmetrications as the following: "That there is a Reward for Righteousness, and a Recompense for Virtue, is such a necessary Article of Faith, that Religion can by no means subsist without it."[5] He can find no miraculous fishes nor can he return to shore. From 1695 to his death (which seems to have been in May, 1705), he held the rectory of Croston, some twelve miles away to the northwest, in plurality with his Wigan curacy. Yet one does not get the impression that he considered himself very amply rewarded for his efforts on behalf of William and Mary. His last recorded work was on *The Decency and Moderation of Christian Mourning* (1703).[6]

It is now possible to take up his quarrel with the nonjuror wing of his own communion, after the "Revolution" of 1688–89. His opponent virtually concedes Zachary's main point without recognizing it. Taylor has twisted Church of England principles to defend the regicide President Bradshaw, he rages; he has accommodated himself to Jesuit arguments; last but not least he has conceded the claims of the "Rebels in the year '42." And what for? Simply to pretend that there is an extraordinary providence whereby we can get ourselves a new king *without* the "Extinction or Submission of the Right Heirs."[7] Taylor's answer is not hard to summarize: "By all means let us use any argument tending to show the redundancy of war or assassination, or judicial murder, as the means to get a new government; let us by all means claim an extraordinary providence that lends government some authority superior to cruelty and superstition." Ever the modernist, Taylor risks effacing providence altogether in his efforts to burnish it and risks abolishing the grounds of morality to make morality reasonable. If it is possible to walk the tightrope on the side of the angels, he will do it.

The three betrayals alleged above may be placidly acknowledged as the sine qua non of Zachary's (and perhaps the nation's) continued survival. They involve a new view of the sacramental tradition and of scriptural authority and a new criterion operating *beyond* both.

As to condoning the career of President Bradshaw in the interests of a "thorough settlement," no one seems to have objected when, in 1694, the Regicide's nephew, Henry Bradshaw of Marple, purchased his family's ancestral seat, Bradshaw Hall, Bolton. He thus became the effective head of his clan and the leading "balance" in the parish to Sir Francis Anderton, whose brother was a Jesuit at St. Omer. Whether one considers the matter at a national, European, or parochial level is all one. To condone the "new" Henry Bradshaw was to condone the extinction of the claim that a sovereign was a sacred "person," comparable to the "presence" of Christ in the Sacrament. A "person" of whom it could continue to be said that he was "legally" done to death has forfeited any such claim. Taylor keeps his arguments abstract. He refuses to reopen the trial of Charles I, preferring to point out that it is only the rightists, with their anarchic death wish, who want to do that. Read as the sequel to the "old" Henry Bradshaw's *St. Werburgh,* Taylor's *Obedience and Submission* severs the last link between the royal person and the presence of miracle in the world, discountenancing both. Such were the means, at last, by which the old monk Henry's fear of the future was overcome. The sovereign was now merely the permitted head of government, and "Government is only an Administration of Societies."[8] The metaphysical or moral dimension—as dear to Bishop Pilkington as to the monk Bradshaw, as eagerly scanned by Oliver Heywood as by Lawrence Vaux—has been discarded from the citizen's contract with the state.

Whether survival on such terms for "royalty" or "gentry" could be accounted nominal or real is a matter of opinion. That Taylor's antisentiment is the coming thing is undeniable. Parliament could settle the kingdom on the children of the Princess Anne, but could not make any of them survive. The Hanoverian succession, created by Act of Parliament, casts a slur of inauthenticity and a taint of alienation on the English monarchy to this day. The new Henry Bradshaw was also the last of a line, as old as the kingdom of England itself. His daughter and sole heir would marry Nathaniel Isherwood, a Bolton fustian tradesman. His surname is a reminder that in leaving behind the monastic scriptorium we have opened the dossier on *Goodbye to Berlin.*[9]

As to the need to accommodate oneself to arguments of the kind called

"Jesuitical," Taylor was curate of recusant Wigan, and had many good reasons to flatter the sensibilities of the Bradshaighs, a leading family of that
parish. They represented the proCatholic wing of the Bradshaw clan. Indeed,
one of their number, Richard Bradshaigh (alias "Barton"), had been Jesuit
provincial of the English province during the Protectorship.[10] Taylor is to be
found exercising every kind of discretion—with frequent resort to the Roman
Vulgate—in mediating textual authority to these people. The note of expedi-
ency is set by his treatment of "Bishop Overall's Convocation-Book." He
argues from it, since Sancroft has set it up, but meanwhile notes that it has
no validity, since it never received the royal sanction.[11] Thus he achieves the
circuit he requires for his own perfect liberty of movement. Convocation—
the communal conscience of the established church—can have no "rights"
without the express sanction of the monarch. But the monarch—as already
demonstrated—can have no "right" to impose any such sanction, which
would tend to exclude other human "rights." The convocation-book is therefore not the sacred text of Zachary's opponents, but Zachary's own play-
thing, to do with precisely as he requires.

He dares to extend this "freedom" to Scripture itself. In doing so, he
abrogates the learned tradition of such as Pilkington and the Heywoods,
who with prayerful urgency mediated the ancient texts to the faithful in
vivid contemporary English. This is a joke to Taylor. Here is a typical throwaway in reference to the attempted "Usurpations of Princes": "θεὸς ἀπὸ
μηχανῆς. He is a present God in trouble."[12] In gleefully approximating the
God of the sublime Forty-sixth Psalm—the refuge of the persecuted in all
ages—to the deus ex machina of the pagan stage, and not translating the
Greek, Taylor provides a deliciously subversive joke for the initiated, while
leaving hoi polloi where he clearly thinks they belong—in the dark. The
chronicles of monarchy present themselves, in such a setting, as a theatrical
plot, to be written and rewritten to serve a turn. It is worth noting in this
context that one of Taylor's recurrent jokes is at the expense of his opponent's
efforts to glean a message for seventeenth-century Britain from the brief and
murderous reign of Queen Athaliah, Jezebel's daughter, dating from the ninth
century B.C. What makes her funny—and endlessly manipulable—for Taylor
is the fact that she is female, an implement in Taylor's project to feminize
sin, suffering and (as malleable exemplar of both) monarchy itself.

An exact contemporary of Obedience and Submission is the biblical tragedy
Athalie. It is no coincidence that the incomparably meticulous stylist, the
Jansenist Jean Racine, chooses to end his play with the word that pins the
audience's attention to its central problem and aspiration. It is God the "Father" who is left in our minds as the ultimate source of power beyond the
monstrous ineptitudes of all the dynasties. He is an aspiration, implying hope
of redress from such as Athaliah, yet also a problem, as the creator of Athaliah, that typical figure of Racinian tragedy—a frustrated female dynamism

(like Racine's patron Madame de Maintenon) with whom the patriarchal arbiters of Olympus and Sinai seem incompetent to deal.

It is this whole debate—at a crucial moment in European and British history—that Taylor chooses to trivialize in the interests of commonsense. His is a peculiarly Anglo-Saxon method for postponing tragedy.

At last we come to the "rebels of '42." In Lancashire these were chiefly enemies of James Stanley. It was possible—and common—to hate the seventh earl of Derby (as he became in that year) and "honor" the king. National politics was also a family feud. Truer to motivation than fact, legend records that the first three shots of the Civil War were fired in Manchester in July 1642 by Sir Thomas Stanley, all of them aimed at his "cousin" James. To condone the ultimate "success" of such a rebel was merely to consent to biology. The Stuarts themselves were hardly rewarding people to die for. During the reign of the last of them—Queen Anne—the eccentric tenth earl, last of his own line, provided Knowsley (scene of Margaret Beaufort's educational project for the redemption and governance of England, later extended to receive her son Henry VII) with a further new wing. Its inevitable style of hyper-aristocratic understatement made a gracious foil to the centerpiece of the composition: a "memorial stone" denouncing in detail the sordid ingratitude of Charles II to "the Family" of the owner. His own successor, the eleventh earl, was a distant "cousin." This was Edward Stanley, great-grandson of Sir Thomas and nephew (by marriage) of Zachary Taylor.[13] It is this connection that justified Zachary in the adoption of his airy, "gentlemanly" style, which stops always just this side of the supercilious. Such a style is more than a vehicle. It is the success which is in turn also his argument.

Despite his murmurs of extenuation; despite his reliance on "loyal, and dutiful" traditions that are the product of a sterner morality than his own; despite his own genuine passion for a freer, saner, kinder world, the criterion that for Taylor effectively replaces the old challenges of scripture and the sacraments is externally apparent "success." Once a Churchill had destroyed the armies of the Sun King in Europe, it seemed to be the voice of Providence itself that called into being that British imperial mission to the remaining continents for which Taylor and his kind had set free the Anglo-Saxon conscience. Unresolved, the problem of multiple kingdoms and frustrated regions that had prompted the Civil War blossomed into an expansionist dynamic. Financing the enterprise, while it lasted, was the "seed out of its own region," the imported cotton of the Middle East and North America, with all its "bitter fruit." A set of accounts having reference to this trade (together with a sample of cloth) came out of the wainscot of Hacken Hall, Darcy Lever, when the house was demolished in 1917. It had been compiled while Overall was compiling his convocation book (no later than 1610). As a precedent (for it is the earliest such document known), it is the Hacken Hall account book whose implications would seem to be the more momentous.[14]

37

Contention and Continuance

NOTING that Taylor rejects the image for the construction and transmission of authority provided by Hobbes's *Leviathan,* one might ask what model can be inferred form his own writings. Hobbes envisaged an irreversible transference of power from the many to the one. At some (necessarily unre- corded) moment in prehistory, the human species recognised and pledged itself to a pattern of subordination and interdependence as the means of survival. Taylor dismisses this foundation myth as "metaphysical" nonsense.[1] His own model, the reflex of his Whiggish pragmatism, is makeshift and unacknowledged. Against Hobbes's "Leviathan," or gigantic body politic with but one kingly "head," we have a "body" of working men (so many Lambert Simnels) *cut off from* a sometimes bewildered "head" of decision- taking gentry. The "head's" adornment, cincture, and source of power is the Crown in Parliament, the abstraction to which they are in process of reduc- ing their new Henry VII: no gothic reincarnation of Arthurian chivalry and the *sagesse* of "time-honour'd Lancaster," but a bisexual Stadtholder from brick Holland whose sole emotion is implacable resistance to France. While offering itself as the astute disciple of historical Providence, and as robustly masculine in its administrative efficiency, this curious figure is in fact wanting in life or the means of reproducing itself. Absolutely dependent for its exis- tence on the female principle it exploits and excludes, it is dependent for its *mode* of being on three contending sets of necromancers who compete for the privilege of fitting body to head. Romish priests (in Taylor's view) would produce a puppet of truly awesome malignity, jerked by the fingers of the Sun King, and Calvinist sectarians could manage something clumsily vicious after the pattern of New England Puritans. Only Taylor himself, as the wizard of the establishment, can bring the figure to serene, harmonious, and rational life. Such a pattern is to be inferred from Zachary's contributions to a pamphlet war of the 1690s on the subject of the "Surey Demoniac," a tragic and farcical phenomenon that first came to the notice of the people of Whalley, Lancashire, in April 1689.

The same month saw the double coronation of William and Mary. Hers was the stronger claim by "right" of blood, but actual "authority" for the

266

administration was vested in him, subject to parliamentary controls that would one day provide a precedent for those limiting the American presidency and that would evolve, in the United Kingdom, to the point where the role of the personal sovereign would become almost entirely passive and symbolic. William would evolve into an executive dependent on popular suffrage (Franklin Delano Roosevelt, William Ewart Gladstone), while Mary would survive as "First Lady" (Eleanor Roosevelt, Queen Victoria). This is the pattern already envisaged in Taylor's habit of feminizing the purely royal. A "king" like Edward III—warrior, statesman, the Lord's anointed—was simply not convincing anymore.

On 11 April 1689 the sacred ceremony was delayed for two hours while conference was held about the news of James II's landing in Ireland. The way from palace to abbey was lined with Dutch soldiers. Bishop Compton of London (suspended by James) performed the ceremony, Archbishop Sancroft having refused to attend.[2] Soon after, Richard Dugdale, a young gardener of Martenhall, Whalley, began to exhibit signs of "possession." Currently the residence of Ashtons from Great Lever, Whalley Abbey and its setting retained much of the magic and prestige of the "old religion," that pre-Reformation state of mind that had room for pagan folk legends as well as the lore of monks. Opportunism, or superstition, drew connections between the two troublous events. Sectarian lines of battle were drawn. Dugdale's rantings and caperings, his eye-rollings, scalp-waggings, his ventriloquism in snatches from the three learned languages, were as anxiously studied as if it were indeed the soul of England that was in travail in his haunted body. Oliver Heywood showed signs of interest, then he thought better of it. Crasser Presbyterians—Thomas Jolly, John Carrington—held well-attended and career-enhancing "exorcisms" of Dugdale in a Whalley barn. "Popelings from Stoneyhurst," and elsewhere, tried to take advantage. Zachary Taylor, champion of the establishment, decided to resolve the matter. Closely identified with the horrors—real and imaginary—of the "Lancashire witches," the setting was not without its possibilities. London printers needed little encouragement to set up their type.[3]

The details of the episode are a fascinating source for social and religious historians. It must here suffice to summarize Taylor's "resolution" in terms of the pattern it offers of the Whig uses of religion. With all his playfulness, Taylor offers himself as *more* serious than his rivals. The claim may be biased, but it is not contemptible. His faith is in the wit of the biblical Jesus, for whom the sabbath was made for man, not vice versa. He is sincerely delighted to follow the promptings of the Holy Spirit in opening Dr. Willis's *Pathology of the Brain,* while consigning to the dustheap Increase Mather's *Account of the Trials of the New England Witches.*[4] Above all, he interprets his own role as spiritual father to be as one who seeks and saves rather than persecutes and anathematizes. All it remains to say against him is that he does all this with a little too much enjoyment of his own panache. And there is a sting in his tail.

Zachary almost never spells out the conclusion he requires us to reach. He prefers the method of the "useful schoolmaster," laying a train of clues that lead all one way. Here, it becomes captivatingly easy for readers to convince themselves that doltish Calvinists *really believe* in witches. It is certainly an acknowledged fact that Jolly and his crew rounded up old women who appeared not to be able to say the Lord's Prayer correctly. Taylor turns substantial evidence about Calvinists into a comic foil for his own sinister hints about Romanists. At a stroke, the popish threat becomes a gigantic menace, the Protestant delinquents shrink to their own notions, and—for this is a part of the world where recusancy is still formidable—no Catholic gentry need be named. *Some* wily Romanists, it seems, are prepared to exploit the peasants' *real belief* in witches. It is all part of a plot—surely— to turn this half-demolished setting of the Pilgrimage of Grace into a ro- mancer's backdrop for an uprising in favor of James II or his "Prince of Wales." Why not? Delusion is the Jesuits' raison d'être, after all, as it is also the Calvinists' preferred fodder and Louis XIV's current coin. In the person of his recusant sister, it whispers to Dugdale through the wattle and daub partition of the ancient barn, controlling his antics with scraps of that semiob- scene theology that treats of "the different Sexes and various relations that [sundry unclean] spirits stand in, one to another." Her source may be some monkish treatise or Richard Baxter's *World of Spirits Evinced by Apparitions*. Either way, it "is all over popery."[5]

Calvinists—another fact of record—have persuaded some working men to swear affidavits before local magistrates, tending to suspicion of witchcraft and putting a number of decent women in danger. Papists, on the same hand, expect to subvert the minds of our establishment gentry through their suggestible womenfolk, hereabouts still hankering after their priests. Dug- dale's unruly young body lusts after a recusant maid, it seems, who has the ear of her equally unreliable mistress. Our observant friends among the deserving poor of Whalley are inclined to identify an old, splayfooted Quak- erwoman who shows an unhealthy interest in Dugdale's exhibitions with a Romish priest in disguise. Zachary, while not pressing the point home—a typical technique of his—manages to denigrate both popery and Quakerism by his suggestive toying with this image.[6]

He leaves his readers to make the conclusion that nonconformity is all one: vicious, cruel, dangerous, and ignorant. Any tolerance—such is the nature of things—can only be of intolerance. Mild and rational as we are, our Anglican tolerance must therefore take the form of a mild and rational repression. Things ignorant and vicious by definition can no longer have any share in any charitable or educational endowments they may have initiated. There must be no access to Whalley Grammar School or Bolton Grammar

School, for instance, for any species of dissenter. That is—is it not?—the only alternative to the savage repression with which our satanic rivals would destroy all things?

Taylor (just as he reports his rivals) deploys the feminine principle to make his own particular connection between the male "body" and the male "head" of that decapitated Gulliver, the British state. But his Anglican brand of wizardry is all rational, all benign. Not merely demons, but all traces of Lancashire dialect, relinquish their prey at his approach. In constructing his own tableau, Zachary, just like Dugdale, knows how to "throw" his own voice:

> But there is no satisfaction like that which is personal; I therefore went myself to the old woman (whom they would have the world to think a witch) and desired her to repeat, if she could, the Lord's Prayer. *I thank God* (saith she) *I can say it, and do say it perhaps as often as those do that accuse me I cannot:* which I believe may be true enough, for upon this she kneeled decently down, and repeated the Lord's prayer, and was as perfect in the last Petition as any one of the rest.[7]

"Dugdale the mother" is also "required" to undergo this test, to clear herself from Carrington's insinuations. At the beautiful feet of Zachary, she sails through with no trace of difficulty. Reason returns to the community. The "head" gentlemen club together to purchase, for the disturbed "body" of Dugdale the gardener, the medical attention it requires. A local Anglican curate, who is also a capable physician, diagnoses epilepsy and a growth on the stomach.[8] As to whether the patient now has a future, or ever had a mind of his own, readers are left hintless.

Taylor is in the same tradition (in this context, no bad one) as John Bridgeman, bishop of Chester and rector of Wigan, successor to the Ashtons as lord of Great Lever. Ordered by Charles I's council in 1633 to reopen the cases of seventeen "witches" from the Pendle district (which includes Whalley), who had been condemned to die at Lancaster, the good cynic made sure they were all acquitted.[9] Next to such an achievement, it seems fair to require Catholics and Presbyterians to modernize their theology a little before being granted access to the full benefits of the British state. To demand equity from Protestants in the same breath as defending all the actions of Mary Tudor (as James Anderton did) might have been honest, consistent, and pious, but was it humane, rational, or Christian? Not, happily, in the arena of language in which Taylor performs. Neither are the frightful certainties that the Heywoods inherited, and that maimed for them the image of Christ himself.

There remains the slightly desolate reflection that what Taylor offers is not freedom of conscience but suspension of persecution; not the sword of justice, but the sword of Damocles; not "the doing of miracles" or real belief therein, but only that other and lesser of those "two marks by which together, not asunder a true Prophet is to be known," according to Hobbes's *Leviathan*. Simply and brutally, it is "not teaching any other Religion than that which is already established."[10]

It is worth remembering, however, that Taylor's objective target was the Jacobite succession; that the Stuarts had a record of murderous unreliability in pursuit of their own "honor"; and that their claim to rule by blood-right represented a veto on the future, which lay with an ever-broadening constitution. James II's "Prince of Wales," also variously known as "James III" and the "Old Pretender," provoked a rising in his favor whose main forces were defeated at Preston, on the Ribble, on 13 November 1715. Strategic failure assured, he made a brief personal appearance in Scotland the following Christmas, relevant to nothing but his own "honor," before slipping back to the continent in a French ship.

Leading aristocrats among the rebels were dealt with in London, most of the rest being tried at Lancaster, where many were executed. The new regimes in Britain and France concluded an alliance, joined by the American colonies. The world, and Lostock, was no longer safe for Jacobites.

The Ribble was anciently the boundary between lands held by the Scottish king under the feudal system and the English royal appanage of south Lancashire. The threat of insurgents becoming visible from Turton Tower provoked the "honor" of those Boltonians who still held this antique map in their heads. In the case of the Andertons, it was the troops on the Hanoverian side who constituted the enemy. They could no more have stood aside than the traditional schoolboy or Don Quixote. Doubtless they enjoyed their "day's out with the rebels," but the Old Pretender's defeat meant that Lostock was taken from them. Lands and title went briefly to a relative—Sir Laurence Anderton—a former Benedictine whose conscience permitted him to make a show of conformity. Then the estate passed to the Blundells of Ince, nonresidents, as most local landowners had now become. Former mass sites in Bolton and Deane—Lostock Hall, Heaton Hall, Turton Tower and (finally, in 1721) Smithills Hall—ceased to function as such.[11]

The way was cleared for John Johnson, founder of the Johnsonian Baptists, a native of Lostock and joint minister of a chapel there from 1726, before moving to Liverpool. The Anderton theology of a God substantially present in the mass, a vulnerable miracle to be personally fought for, was replaced by a high-supralapsarian abstraction. Scarcely deigning to refute theories of spiritual tuition by wafer, Johnson was aiming at the Quaker "inner light" in its opposition to ministerial exclusivity when he asserted that "[t]he gift of God . . . is a sovereign commission: not conveyed by man: but immediately coming down from the Father of lights." The commissioned minister, set apart from all other mortals, was the cynosure of an exclusively transcendental quest. Religion, and this life, were quite different things, for the former consisted solely in developing an *understanding* of "the Fulness of Grace, from God the Father, in the beloved Son, by the Holy Ghost: Abstracted from all other things." In such a scheme, the Anglican tradition of "honoring" other views, as Hewit, or of modernizing theology for the sake of a more rational morality, as Taylor, could have no place. "Charity," for Johnson, when it means acknowledging non-Johnsonians as "Brethren in Christ," is a baneful "weed in the Professor's garden" to be plucked out. Disclaiming any of the pedagogical duties of an establishment, he refuses that connection between the gospel and morals that was central for James Anderton and Oliver Heywood alike. Johnsonian ministers (eventually amounting to about half of the Apostolic dozen) were ordered to reject the temptation to "admonish Sinners . . . in the regulation of their lives."[12]

In 1745 the Jacobites tried again. Charles Edward Stuart, the "Young Chevalier" or "Young Pretender," got as far south as Derby in pursuit of his patrimony As he approached Bolton, a Hanoverian mob laid siege to Walmsley Chapel, Longworth, hard by the former home of Oliver Heywood's mother. Barricaded within, Presbyterian farmers had their muskets and pitchforks ready.[13] But the Jacobites took another route to Manchester, then still a center for nonjurors of many kinds of religious persuasion. Presbyterianism, in England, was already dying from within. At Bolton as elsewhere, the belief prevailed among them that worship was to be offered only to the Father. Outlawed as non-Christians, the "Unitarians" (as they came to be called) were merely obeying the same instinct that sent Christ himself into the wilderness—the necesity of renewing tradition from the deep wells of conscience. To pray with Christ, instead of to him, and to be imbued with the Spirit, instead of racking it for a definition, set many free from the disabilities exemplified by the Heywoods. As for other groups, innovation, no less than antiquity, became a source of continuance.[14]

Charles II, a wiser and better king than his father, had set a precedent for a patchwork of tolerance that would eventually prevail. John Bossy aptly cites Voltaire. In England, there came to be "thirty" religions, which came to approximate to a peace.[15] Charles's policy can be seen in miniature in Bolton and Deane. Leaving the mass centers undisturbed, he used his prerogative to appoint as vicar of Deane Richard Hatton, an intransigent Covenanter. He did this in the teeth of the high church bishop of Chester, Dr. Pearson, who had just appointed the orthodox John Lever as vicar of Bolton. The year was 1673.[16] James, duke of York, married Mary of Modena that November.

Human tolerance is always partial, and the Quakers were the scapegoats, at Bolton as elsewhere. In 1674 the Friend James Harrison suffered "distress" of goods for holding meetings (like Marsh before him) in his Bolton house. Five years later, he was fined for preaching there. Phineas and Phoebe Pemberton, who ran the local grocery store, were fined for attendance. Witnesses

against them were not eager: "in order to convict," states the report, "Inform-
ers" and others "drank in ine [sic] afternoon as much as 50 shillings." One
under-bailiff, exceptionally dutiful, died of excess the following day.

In 1682 a colony of Quakers followed William Penn across the Delaware.
Phineas and Phoebe Pemberton joined them and were able to purchase a
large plantation along the river bank.[17] James Harrison and one Roger Longworth, also of Bolton, "great travellers at Home and Abroad in the service
of Truth," came thither from Barbados and are buried there.[18]

Contention, without which there is no continuance, proved to be something more profound than a mere reaction to external force. In 1743 the
Friends Jane and James Wardley moved to Bolton from Manchester and
joined the meeting house at Acresfield, in the town. Dissatisfied, in due
course, they seceded to form an exuberant new group of "Shaking" Quakers.
In 1758 they were joined by Ann Lee. She came to believe that God was
both male and female. Whatever of the divine nature had been revealed in
Christ was equally present, Lee was sure, within herself. The Wardleys
balked at her doctrine of celibacy, and after the group's move to Manchester
in 1760, were excluded. In 1774 Ann Lee and eight of the faithful sailed to
America to found the first Shaker settlement at Waterfield, near Albany,
New York, in the territory granted by Charles II to his brother James, duke
of York, and named after him ever since.[19]

38

Antiquity and Continuance: A Reinterpretation

For James Anderton, "antiquity" and "continuance" are a seamless garment. Everything is to be seen *sub specie aeternitatis*. Rome is the true Church of Christ, and the types of Christ began with time and Adam. Christ's true followers, under his "vicar," await the end of time, when, at Christ's return to judgment, heaven and earth "as a vesture . . . shall be changed."[1]

The difficulty is in the details. Innocent III (1198–1216), the first pontiff to style himself "vicar of Christ," came nearest to converting theory into practice. Anderton fully shared Ockham's view that it was "heresy" for a pope to claim temporal power. As Newman would put it, such a claim tended to favor "the tyrannous use of his spiritual power." He felt one should not make a permanent fetish out of what historical research suggested was no more than a temporary expedient, "destined to fall." More fervent in his outlook, Anderton rejects, "for salvation," any claim implying that King John, for instance, could be said to have set a precedent for the future when in 1213 he was compelled by the success of Innocent's "heretical" pursuit of temporal power to place England and Ireland under the suzerainty of the popes in perpetuity. Yet Anderton happily embraces a precedent that was a consequence of this same humbling of John—the signing in 1215 of Magna Carta, the fount of English liberties. And of course the metaphysical linchpin of the whole policy, by which Innocent claimed for the hierarchical pyramid of which he was the apex a veto on the presence of Christ in the world—the doctrine of transubstantiation, formulated in 1215—is for Anderton of the very essence of his faith.[2]

The pinching legalism of Latin—a language that in its heyday had produced no philosophy worth the name—had shrunk to an abstract jargon as much at odds with the nascent English empiricism of particularity and precedent at one end of the old Mediterranean world as it was with the humane delicacy and technical finesse of the Greeks (to whom is owing even the codification of Roman Law) at the other. In smashing their way into the Greek capital of Constantinople in 1204 and cutting down the imperial bodyguard of Englishmen and Danes, the "crusaders" of Innocent III were doing their best, not only to make final ruin of that governmental project to which Constantine had set his hand at York nine centuries before, but to obliterate the very language of the gospels. Further triumphs of the Roman will—the institution of the Inquisition by Frederick II in 1232, the sanctioning in 1252 by Innocent IV of torture in the interests of breaking the accused—involved in practice an onslaught on the humanity of Christ in the persons of his people the Jews (since 1215 ordered to wear a distinctive badge), among many thousands of others. As the sceptical English Hellenist A. H. Clough noted of the "great Coliseum," a structure having these ambitions may be "grand and capacious and massive, . . . but tell me, is this an idea?"[3]

William of Ockham (1300–49) eventually conformed to the doctrine of transubstantiation, while arguing for an interpretation of it that opposed, or complemented, that of Aquinas. One might lament this as an example of the contradictory spirit that above all things James Anderton regretted. In reviewing the Protestant writers of Deane and Bolton, however—he was lay rector of both—it becomes easier to see how impossible it was for them to retain without radical reinterpretation the legacy whose local guardian he was certain he was. For them, dialogue had become of the essence of truth. To read Lever, Marsh, and Pilkington is to encounter, not indeed any abstract "Plantonism" or "theory of ideas," but a certain atmosphere of the *Phaedo*. Marsh cannot quite agree with his inquisitors, yet will not pretend to know better than they. It is not a fixed dogma he dies for, but the right to pursue inquiry and to believe for oneself, not as a catechized child. Lever insists, with enabling pedantry, that one chooses to join the Church with each saying of the creed, not repeating words "as" the Church demands, but each time recovering their deep mystery, in company "with" the Church of all ages. Touched by the Greek tragic spirit, Pilkington cannot manage without two contradictory glimpses into the mystery of the godhead. Both Dionysus and Apollo are to be encountered at Rivington, at Golgotha.

While there is no tracing the map of influence, Ockham's presence at least must be added to that of Plato, even if only as exemplifying a "Britannic" spirit alongside Plato's "Hellenism." Ockham's stance allies itself with Pela-gius's fifth-century doctrine of self-dependency and Roger Bacon's irascible thirteenth-century experimentalism. Sustaining many kinds of nonconfor-mity in all times and places, this universal spirit is the confidence of Abraham: better to risk God and the desert than the conventions of Ur. Ockham is confident of God when he claims that the church of which Christ in heaven is head need not fail on earth, even though the papacy itself become extinct. He does not recognize an abstract entity called "the papacy," only a succes-sion of popes. Popes differ (later there would be rival popes), but none is utterly deprived, or totally apprized, of the whole wisdom of God. Holding fast by the claims of Judaic monotheism, Ockham affirms in one breath a sense of God's omnipotence and a sense of the multiple possibilities of the world. On earth, the "papacy" is supremely important in spiritual matters, but beside the absolute, unknowable God it is as grass.[4]

Claiming for themselves a share in the Catholic tradition, all the Protestant writers we have reviewed in any detail may be best described—in contrast to Anderton—as "doing without the Pope." This is for all of them a temporary necessity for the survival of the eternal truths of the faith. Contrary to Anderton's fears, they are not concerned, either severally or as a group, to construct any substitute for the dogmatic authority of the papacy. Only John Johnson, risen from the Andertons' own peasantry, sets out to do that. Like Anderton himself, he is at the mercy of translations. For all the other Protestants (including Taylor), access to the Greek testament is an imperative. Having no Greek, and detesting the Calvinist Bible's assertion that "wives" were present with the apostles at the approach of Pentecost, Anderton relies on the Latin Vulgate, and various English, versions, as "proof" of the all-important "celibacy" of the apostles. Copying without understanding the relevant Greek word, he happily accepts the clinching translation—"women." In fact, like the French *femme,* the Greek word is used for both "wife" and "woman," hence the difficulty.[5] As so often, the real truth of the matter is that the biblical writer has not anticipated, and cannot be racked to satisfy, our curiosity on this secondary question, which (in this of all contexts) is a matter not of absolute significance but of relative insignificance. Pilkington breathes in this atmosphere of "not knowing" as though it were the fresh air of Rivington. The Heywoods submit to it with a little more ambiguity. While it frees them for personal "experiments" with the Spirit, it also reduces them to a stressful dependence on their results. Pilkington's twin luxuries—silence, and the Anglican Liturgy he helped to compile—are denied them.

At odds with the "Platonism" and "Aristotelianism" concocted by medieval scholastics out of their fragmentary knowledge of Greek writings, Ockham is in the tradition of all healthy philosophy in his refusal of forms of authoritarian bullying—as practised against him by Pope John XXII, for instance—and in his realization that language can never be made to mean exactly what we choose. Refusal and realization alike rely on the patience needed to await eternity, as the alternative to preempting it. The two elements—never to forget the distinction between the human and the divine, and never to remit the impossible task of evolving an adequate language that refuses to rely on abstractions as closures of debate—run through all the writers who might (if only literally) be described as of the Bolton "school." Due partly to its eighteenth-century decline, knowledge of the early Bolton Grammar School—the one almost constant institution—is at present extremely scarce. As in the case of Ockham's God, we can only dimly infer its character from the manifest evidence of its creativity. We might, in both jest and earnest, and with a sense of Ockham's distrust of the foisting off of "groups" as though they were enforcing entities, venture to summarize the various surviving writings of its alumni as constituting a "school" of thought. As a literal school, it represents more readily than some theoretical schools the Ockhamite reminder that "Christ's mystical body consists of real persons." Our inferences are effects of causes that require always to be reconsidered, not prescriptions for "an end to translating."

An inquiry into the printed legacy of "real persons," in their effort of will to transcribe their deepest being, is very liable, not least in an English context, to encounter what has been called that "whole tendency of Ockham's thinking," which is "against what is fixed and inviolable."[6] For each of the writers of the Bolton "school," as for Ockham, the tendency was a consequence, not a denial, of their belief in a Father Omnipotent. Omnipotence, they feel, is not to be preempted by any little intermediary abstractions of our own. In this view, they are entirely typical of much English writing.

A subject matter of that writing was the peculiar relation of English monarchs—from Henry VIII to William and Mary—to church and state. Given the nature of its treatment, it was not a subject matter whose pretensions were likely to be sustained. Performing the work of an anarchist mob in the same instant as he snatched at the dual supremacy, Henry VIII obliterated the shrines of England's royal saints. With or without the promptings of Henry's new professor of Greek, it was never likely that an English tradition of profound reverence for the power of God, and lively scepticism about the powers of men, would reverse itself in favor of royal theologians like James I, or Henry himself. A primate of mental and moral substance like Archbishop Grindal could earn the respect of a Spenser in his opposition to Elizabeth. A Whitgift or a Laud—martinets of limited brain, the chosen and futile tools of Elizabeth, or Charles I—were candidates for the respect of nobody. As offering to succeed where Innocent III had failed, they hardly rose to the level of the absurd. Any dignity they retain is of an entirely private character.

And so the royal authority became the "subject" of its own writing "subjects." James Anderton demands from his royal master the right, as of "equity," to remain loyal to his secular authority. His spiritual allegiance is owed elsewhere. Ellis Bradshaw ponders Greek philosophers and the stars above Bolton. He can find no divine right of kings either in the one, the other, or both together. Brought to the block, Hewit dare not proclaim a doctrine— only "Jesus Christ," and an "honoring" of all who believe him. Repenting into common sense, Oliver Heywood adjusts the tradition of Leviticus with the help of Athenian customs and his own observations of John Angier junior. Such a man's tacit acceptance of William III tells more than all of Taylor's arguments against the metaphysical "right" of James II. Yet there is something noble, after all, even in Taylor, when (making a nosegay, as it were, of Ockhamist nominalism and the Platonic dialectic) he offers us his conclusion that, while all governments whatever that are permitted by God are variants of his own "theocracy," one must concede that his Providence has been especially "vocal" on this occasion in permitting William to reign by consent of a Parliament that will continue to argue for the maintenance and extension of the "liberties" begun in Magna Carta.

The monarch as "subject" of a special discourse, in which personal conviction, political allegiance, and questions of ecclesiastical government and foreign relations were all implicated, has ceased to exist.

39
Thesaurus

DESPITE the hopes and fears that gathered in the word, the arrangements of 1688–89 were not so much a "revolution" as a notable incident in a continuous revolution. Taylor's claim that a "settlement" had been achieved proved to be a highly relative statement. To imply that the established Church of England—and its grip on the magistracy and endowed institutions—provided the best chance of tolerance, survival, and the development of "liberties" was also to imply that such an arrangement could be transitional only. The age of revolution was due to be upstaged by the age of reform. The enforceable abstraction of a "Crown in Parliament," operating as a depersonalized "defender of the faith" and thus serving to ration access to education and public office on sectarian grounds, was overtaken by events. Political disabilities to which Protestant and Roman Catholic nonconformists were subject fell away in 1828–29. The first Parliamentary Reform Act followed in 1832—only then was slavery outlawed in the British Empire (1833). Finally, during midcentury, even Oxford and Cambridge were unshackled. The forces of complacency exulted in the fall of "superstition." Economic exclusions of course remained.

The Bolton that was volatile and vocal under the Tudors continued to be so. It would be impossible to give any indication of its output in a few words. The importance of printing, the connection between religious and economic revisionism, and the sub-Ockhamist opportunism that pervaded all levels may be indicated.

The "sustainers" of the Marian exile had their successors. The town was a printing and publishing center from 1785. Its first known book includes an account of the beheading of Lord Derby. In a cotton center, the aspirations and rivalries of the English and American civil wars naturally commingled, whether we are considering Southern plantation owners and their Bolton friends, relatives, and house guests or noting that the first printer of *The Leaves of Grass* was cousin by marriage to the socialist Dr. Johnston, Whitman's Boltonian disciple and memoirist. The printing and publishing empire of Tillotson & Son, financed from the sale of pawn tickets by a kinsman of William III's archbishop of Canterbury, would only be the largest such enterprise in the parish. The influence of Mrs. Tillotson (her brother was the soap king, philanthropist, art collector, and exploiter of the Niger, W. H. Lever) was naturally strong. Hardy's *Tess of the d'Urbervilles* was among the novels commissioned, but rejected as improper.[1]

The double legacy of economic and moral "Puritanism" may be indicated in another way by making mention of John Brown, D.D. (Yale), Bolton printer's devil, minister of Bunyan's chapel, Bedford, and author of a still valuable biography of him. His grandson, the economist John Maynard Keynes, was reared from the cradle by his mother, Brown's daughter and disciple, in the responsibilities of moral stewardship. Never, to his mind, could problems of applied mathematics and problems of cultural value be resolved in isolation. The brains behind Roosevelt's New Deal, Lord Keynes remains suspect in some quarters as personally "degenerate." His brother, Sir Geoffrey Keynes, is remembered for another aspect of "revolution": the revival, or rather founding and codifying, of the study of William Blake.[2]

Finally, what Eliot chose to call the "formless" and "homemade" philosophy of "Minute Particulars," so essential to Blake, and so typical of English radicals in general, is also the "philosophy" of the British imperial system. That contempt for abstraction that, for better and worse, is so marked in Locke, the great influence of the 1690s, would continue to prevail. Resources were not thrown away on "prestige." Government did not commission John Bowring to invade China, for instance. But middle-class voters approved when, as plenipotentiary to the Celestial Empire, this editor of Bentham, M.P. for Bolton and prolific hymn-writer ("In the Cross of Christ I glory") bombarded Canton to guarantee Hong Kong. The earl of Derby protested his high-handed conduct. By 1867, however, Derby himself was prime minister, and his son, Lord Stanley, was foreign secretary. The invasion of Abyssinia was arranged; 10,000 men were dispatched from Bombay under the command of Sir Robert Napier. It was nothing like Napoleon's Russian campaign. A triumph for the details of the commissariat, it struck hard, fast, and effectively, not for "empire" or "England" but for Bolton's cotton profits from the Sudan, for Derby's Bolton rents, for the survival of the Conservative party in south Lancashire, and (no less vulnerable and crucial) for the investment network linking the City of London to the arms trade and other interests. Yet another poetic subject had become a modern topic:

> It was an Abyssinian maid,
>   And on her dulcimer she play'd,
> Singing of Mount Abora.[3]

It is as providing, together, evidence for the continuity of a deep spiritual and intellectual reworking of, and protest against, the sort of mechanistic "development" sketched above, that a final pair of writers deserve to be mentioned. If the events of 1688–89 inaugurated the subject matter of modernism, they did not destroy less obvious forces already engaged in constructing its aspirations.

Lawrence Fogg (1623–1718), William III's dean of Chester, and Robert Ainsworth (1660–1743), the nonconformist and nonjuror who compiled the Latin *Thesaurus,* provide our terminus. Either of them deserves fuller notice than can be given here. To mention both is to leave unmentioned a number of fellow parishioners whose printed efforts, from now on, begin to proliferate well beyond the scope of a study such as this. The same would of course be true of many parishes. Two things are to be observed of them, each with an important reservation. First, neither of them can be said to discuss the monarchy, yet the configuration provided by "William-and-Mary" is a vital emblem of what they represent. It is as though the influence exerted downwards on the minds and bodies of their subjects by earlier monarchs as personalities has been replaced by an *ambience* or *zeitgeist* (English, in its "Minute Particulars," lacks even a term to define it) that includes monarchs and subjects together in a single complex of variables. Secondly, Fogg is purely a professional theologian, while nothing that can be called contemporary "Christianity" is to be found in Ainsworth's published writings at all. Yet, while they seem to exclude, they also permit each other. They do not merely "coexist," but rather corroborate each other. Educated at the "same" school, though a generation apart, both are accomplished Hellenists and write with reverence for the silence as well as the word. They never knowingly collaborated nor is there reason to believe either was aware of the work of the other. They simply exemplify that quality in the culture that Engels (not usually a very generous observer) so admired in the Lancashire and Cheshire Volunteers: extraordinary success in performing the maneuver known as the "advance in line," an advance made simultaneously by individuals acting, as though by instinct, together.[4]

T. S. Eliot, the sharply sympathetic outsider already invoked in this context, provides a useful beacon on the horizon. Ainsworth's practice of a continuously revised modernity that engages in a punctilious collation of the past is something that is now almost impossible to describe without gesturing towards *The Waste Land.* What they share, as though for salvation, is a policy of disengagement and objectivity. On the other hand, Fogg's Anglican heeding of the idiom, his refusal of entrapping formulae, and his devotion to the search for the right word because words are too much and never enough make him one of innumerable anticipators of *Four Quartets.* What they share is a rooted commitment to "real persons," to the observed genius of actual places. To say these things is not to make a bid for the relative position of any of the three in some imaginary literary hierarchy, but simply to observe aspects of the culture they all share, of which the most significant may perhaps be summarized by noting that *The Waste Land* and *Four Quartets* are distinct productions of the same mind (always understanding "production" and "mind" as, in a deep sense, "collaborations") and could never have existed otherwise.

The configuration of William and Mary was not a repetition of Mary Tudor and Philip of Spain. Both were crowned and hallowed, yet while hers was the nearer "right," actual "authority" was vested in him. Yet he was the foreigner, the unloved, while she was the first monarch since Elizabeth who could claim to be English. Her affability softened the military single-mindedness and the socially embarrassing atmosphere of repressed sexual peculiarity that surrounded her husband. Their joint monument is the new Hampton Court, the brick palace in a green garden, with its king's staircase to one side and queen's staircase to the other. It was designed by Wren.

On 1 July 1690, near the River Boyne in Ireland, William defeated his father-in-law and destroyed the chances of a Catholic succession. In commemoration of this victory, which some have never ceased to celebrate, the "Protestants of the Empire"[5] were eventually able to erect an enormous obelisk, emblem since the days of Egypt of masculine supremacy springing from a divine source. The site chosen was Drogheda, the scene of the Cromwellian massacres. The date was 1736.

Mary died in 1694. There was genuine popular mourning: not till the funeral of Queen Victoria would monarchy be so gifted. The obsequies remain one of the most memorable and significant of all royal occasions, if only because the specially commissioned music was by Henry Purcell, marginalized in his day as a Catholic and now recognized as a great and abiding influence in English music, not least for his celebration of the defeated Dido, the Semitic queen of Carthage reborn in Virgil as a type of Cleopatra.

The configuration of William and Mary suggests the inescapable connection, and the absolute distinction, between cultural dominance and cultural achievement. It suggests also that masculine power, in isolation from the female, is bleak and deadly and that female power has a more mysterious source and an influence of an altogether more permanent—because more personal—kind. Their strange conjunction connotes with something modernists like Virginia Woolf would understand and that is the most noticeable feature of Ainsworth: an aspiration to androgyny.

Like the Drogheda obelisk, the first edition of Ainsworth's Thesaurus was ready in 1736; and it shares some of its confidence. "Designed for the use of the British Nations," it would continue to offer access to Latin, in all its uses, to English speakers worldwide. As a two-way dictionary it also permitted continental scholars to read English books, "liberating" in particular the "minority" languages from dependence on French or German, and indeed providing Europe with an "English" escape route from the "Latin culture" itself. But in other respects it is quite different from the monolith.

For Ainsworth, a discussion like Taylor's of such things as the "right" of

James II becomes entirely a matter of what Ockham calls *voces*, that is "terms." Writing in Latin, he reminds us of the supreme importance of expression and would have us recognize verbal *"proprietatem"* to be the source of all accuracy and influence; adding that to provide that source is the definition of a lexicon. His own gives, as the first definition of *proprietas*, "the *right* of a thing." No longer a metaphysical entity, "right" has become a matter of verbal precision. His English preface makes clear this priority is now also to obtain in morals. The "bad influence" students should fear is *not* (as his predecessors from Richard Pynson and Thomas Elyot onwards have believed) the moral threat of dubious "expressions not of the politest sort" in pagan texts, but rather intellectual stultification at the hands of precisely such forbidders of adolescent curiosity, who purge their dictionaries of vast numbers of commonly used Latin words in an attempt to shield the young. Ainsworth impishly regrets their obfuscation: after all, "the difficulty of translating the more vulgar expressions is so much greater." Clearly, for such a mind science *is* morality. Duty connotes with honesty and honesty with habits of intellectual rigor.

Obsession with eternity has been replaced by a continuously revised modernity that engages in a punctilious collation of the past. "Antiquity" and "continuance," Ainsworth clearly perceives, are mutually destabilizing, a perpetual challenge to the intellectual will. At outset he announces that "dictionaries are of great service" precisely *because* they "are capable of continual improvements." A Latin *Thesaurus* must keep up with the newest English words: "alert" and "dupe" and "stockjobber." It is never merely a matter of vocabulary lists, but of "adjusting the said two languages the one to the other." Each generation finds new things in ancient texts, transforming, and transformed by, series of inferences drawn from the vulnerable material of a manuscript tradition about which final certainty is never to be had. If "right" has become a prize of intellectual endeavor, then "authority" is now open to continual revision.[6]

The first of our writers to learn his own Latin in the new Cromwellian stone-built Bolton Grammar School, Ainsworth taught a private school of his own in Bolton for some years before moving in about 1698 to London, where he found pupils and patrons among a class that combined a Puritan background similar to his own with a level of expenditure—and an appetite for collecting—rarely equaled since the days of Renaissance Italy or imperial Rome itself. His educational treatise of 1698 (reprinted 1699 and 1736) is virtually a spoof of Thomas Lever's *The Right Way*. Entitled *The Most Natural and Easy Way*, it concedes that "a Reformation is necessary" while disowning any pretence that its author's "Diminutive Name should stand in the catalogue of Reformers." Solemnity is disavowed in the aim—"a taste of all Arts and Sciences," for their own sake or as a preliminary to vocational or university study—and in the method. Play is to be used as much as possible in teaching, and a "hundred harmless inventions" may be used to engage the juvenile mind. Yet at the same time he claims a more serious set of priorities than traditional schoolmasters. He prefaces by supporting proposals of Sir William Hustler, M.P., "against General Maltreatment of children." He believes his own method of light but constant monitoring—a pair of masters to every dozen boys—has more success in taking "care of morals" than the flogging system. He is certain his Socratic approach of stimulating pupils to make their "own" discoveries is more likely to breed true scholars than is that dismal "Hydra that never dies," the catechizing system. His attitude to young beginners anticipates modern methods as applied to adults: constant oral practice, and all the grammar you need to begin enjoying an author reduced to "half a sheet of paper." In spectacular defiance of the "public school" system (for which he announces his contempt), he weans young students, not on the military grind of Livy or Caesar, the middle-aged sententiousness of Horace or the sour rantings of Juvenal, but on the playful young satirist Persius—he died before he was thirty—who takes us directly into the fashionable gossip of Nero's Rome. With deft brevity he creates a "divine" (Ainsworth's term) impression of delightsome garrulity. Simply because he is so stylish and idiomatic, schoolmasters have usually deemed him "obscure," while conceding that he was "read with pleasure and with avidity by his contemporaries." It all sounds far too much fun to suit the traditional father's idea of discipline for its own sake. Ainsworth's educational approach may reflect his own upbringing. Both his parents died young, and he and his two brothers were brought up at Bolton by their well-to-do paternal grandmother.

A binary pattern of wilfulness and responsiveness runs through him, governing his choice of influences. As the philosopher of the Revolution settlement of 1688–89, Locke was steadily winning converts. Ainsworth readily acknowledges Locke's *Thoughts upon Education* of 1693 as a supreme influence, but he supplements it from the example of the Abbé Fleury, tutor to the royal princes at the court of Louis XIV. Rich in insights, which he plunders, Lockean notions as to the unformed nature of young minds are for Ainsworth clearly only half a theory. The tabula rasa is a useful image, not an enforceable abstraction. As though his charges were princes, a teacher must heed the "particular motives . . . in every particular scholar." The "knowledge of his scholar's temper must be the *Theory,* and the proceeding by that knowledge the *Practick.*"[7]

A handful of years previously, Oliver Heywood had chosen David Hartley I as schoolmaster at Northowram. This man's son, David Hartley II, would draw from Locke a theory of the absolute impressionability of young minds, which contributed to his own influential system of necessitarian materialism. Coleridge named the doomed child of "Frost at Midnight" after him. He was soon bored with both of them. Any educator, the good Yorkshireman was sure, could make what he would of a child's mind. He proceeded to raise

David Hartley III on a diet of classics from which any hint of immorality had been removed. Thanks to great strength of character and affection on both sides, it seems to have worked. But mass produced at economy rate in the Victorian "Gradgrind" system (Hartley was also translated by a Lutheran rector for the enlightenment of Prussia), the theory of pupil passivity had less happy results.[8] What Ainsworth calls the "soft and moist clay" of the scarcely formed child implies the tragic unpredictability of *self*-realization. The mind cannot bear the impression of its own absolute passivity. Brought to the stake and ordered to "know" what it is told to "know," it can only murmur "I know not." Behind Ainsworth's wilful affectations is a legacy of meditated "otherness," the challenge of the divine βρέφος to which Pilkington also in part responded.

Indeed, the "degenerate" suburban tutor may be accounted no less serious than the prince-bishop. There is a blank contradiction between Pilkington the tender and witty biblical commentator and the icon of enforcement adopted after his death as the official seal of Rivington Grammar School. This exhibited a bearded master, book raised in one hand, birch rods in the other. Generations of boys were being offered the harsh choice Pilkington had defined as futile. Moreover, there is reason to believe the magnificent, intimidating figure bears a personal resemblance to himself. By such means he is dissociated from the female nurturing image he had developed (with a hopeful eye on Elizabeth) to define aspects of the role of Christian leaders. Even in his own writings, an occasional lapse into sentimentality—on the subject of the Marian martyrdoms, for instance—makes up the gap between innovative scholar and founding father.[9] In Ainsworth, a similar ambiguity surfaces as an androgynous tone. In the interests of consistency, and in the absence (insisted on by Ainsworth) of any actual educating *"woman,"* masculine authority acquires a female aspect. From intellectual as well as moral conviction, there are no punishments whatever in his school, only rewards.

The paradigm is particularly clear in his beautifully printed and bound J. *Casa His Galateus* of 1701. It is a "Treatise of Manners" written originally in Italian, then put into Latin, and now rendered into English by "the pretty lisping Translators" of Ainsworth's private boys' school in Hackney. Charmingly inconsequential, it is the perfect corpus on which to test Ainsworth's semi-Lockean theory of seriously beneficial consequences following from just such means. Youth should work, he says, with "plaster of Paris." There is time enough for "our Divines" and their grinding-machinery of "Flints and nether Millstones." His mocking phrase renders their solemnity *un*serious. A decade before *The Rape of the Lock,* one nonconformist, excluded from the responsibilities of any public office, is helping to form the style of another.[10] Ainsworth would address the *Thesaurus* to his friend Richard Mead, Pope's physician, one of a circle of engaging notables to be sculpted by Roubiliac.[11]

Obliquely, in his spoof epistle dedicatory to *Galateus,* part school report and part prospectus, addressed to one of the "merchant" fathers, Ainsworth reveals a good balance between encouragement and restraining good sense. A sympathetic reader would conclude him a good teacher. The traditional paterfamilias, however, would recoil from the captivating manner in which he confides his advice.

Some fathers—including one with the good old Puritan name of "Cart-wright"—withdrew their boys. Distressed, Ainsworth appealed (in 1707) to the Reverend John Strype, an Anglican clergyman and one of the influential contacts he relied on for recommendations and advice.

The presence of Strype brings to full circle any account of relations be-tween Tudor humanism and the English Reformation. His *Life of Sir John Cheke,* Henry's professor of Greek and a suspected propagandist of the Mar-ian exile, had appeared in 1705. The first volume of his *Annals of the Refor-mation and Establishment of Religion* would appear in 1709. The implication of the title—a consistency between soundness of reformation and security of establishment—has since been more often questioned than confirmed. Manu-scripts in the British Museum reveal Strype as mildly interested in Ains-worth as a living curio from a regional collection he does not quite understand. Bemused by Ainsworth's claim to be a nonjuror, he wonders whether he is not rather more likely to be a dissenter.[12] The whole tradition of royalist Protestant nonconformity—of Tilsley, Heyrick, the Heywoods, and so many more—seems too illogical to the annalist ever to have existed. It may now seem that Ainsworth's partly personal, partly inherited, eccen-tricity was essential to providing the national and international language of English with a document of adaptation. The *Thesaurus,* which he began to compile in earnest in 1714, was still going into revised editions in the 1880s. It outlasted the grammar school building that had been new when Ainsworth attended it. It was itself still "new" when the "other" Thomas Eliot was born, in St. Louis, in the cotton state of Missouri.[13] For him, too, "degeneracy" was a serious project, even a striving towards salvation.

Meanwhile, in amassing the documents of its own and other people's history, that "English" culture was entering a phase of disengagement (or, if preferred, of "objective emancipation") from the root ideologies of everything it amassed. An embarrassment of riches may be gleaned without passing our parish boundaries. The bachelor fifteenth and last baron Willoughby of Parham, for instance, was interred in the family vault at Horwich, Deane, in February 1765. The huge "commemorative tablet" that was then reared within the tiny nonconformist chapel his family had helped to build at Riv-ington, Bolton, is hardly big enough to compile his compilations: chairman of the committees of the House of Peers; president of the Society of Antiquar-ies; vice-president of the Royal Society and of the Society for the Encourage-ment of the Fine Arts; trustee of the British Museum; commissioner of longitude—the list is global as well as prescriptive. Other examples may be found in the footnote, which is not exhaustive.[14]

To open Ainsworth's *Monumenta Vetustatis Kempiana* of 1720 is to enter the world of which Pound and Eliot would be the poets. Recorded here are statues, inscriptions, and gemstones; the embalmed bodies, or urns, of the dead; Charon's fee, placed under the tongue of the dead (the coins, once paltry and invaluable, now merely of a certain market value, are the subject of a special catalogue by Professor Ward); the lamps and the vases of mourn-ers' tears placed incomprehensibly in the grave for an eternal light and conso-lation. Here are not merely Roman and Hellenistic remains but the remains that Roman or Hellenistic virtuosos amassed. The objects themselves were auctioned at the Phoenix Tavern during March 1721 and dispersed. As a collection, they exist only as an edition by Ainsworth. On the title page, he confesses the essentially circular nature of the ritual with which he is en-gaged. The collection is to be "illustrated from the ancient writers whom it illustrates."[15] It is as though his acutely modern mind—revisionist, "alert," and wilful—were simultaneously driven back upon itself in search of some unreachable archetype.

He was able to make out something in embryo. The only work of his that can be called "religious" is an elegant Latin miniature of 1729 whose Greek title transliterates as *Iseion*. The subject is a *delubrum* ("idol") of the Egyptian goddess Isis. A line from Lucan is cited as the "text" of the discourse. We are in another region of sensibility from the male obelisks of Karnak or the Lostock maypole (the latter only very recently defunct at Ainsworth's time of writing). Of this divinity—*"Dea, sive Deus,"* that is, "whether God-dess or God"—one can say little except that *it* (for the term is neuter) is "Ἀνδρογύνον," an androgyne.

Even the particular variant of the Greek term chosen for the title is se-lected with care. The mysterious and unusual *Iseion* more readily suggests some link with *ison* ("an equality") than would the more ordinary and com-prehensible *Isieion*. Needless to say, Ainsworth does not descend to spell out this signpost to a pervasive technique which is of essence esoteric. His vis à vis is the collector James West, forty years his junior, son of a rich merchant of Warwickshire and London. In the style of the times, we are privileged to overhear a private lucubration meditated between two individuals who re-gard themselves as in a measure public men. Already a member of the Inner Temple and fellow of the Royal Society, West would eventually become treasurer of the first and president of the second.

A frontispiece is provided by a suitably distinguished and eclectic work-man, John Sturt, the miniaturist calligrapher, who on other occasions illus-trated Anglican prayer books, *Pilgrim's Progress,* and the *Rules of Perspective* of Andrea Pozzo, the virtuoso of Counter-Reformation trompe l'oeil. Here he shows us an "idol . . . invested with the robe of paternal dignity." His or her head is fenced about by rays "somewhat more languid" ("*languidioribus*") than those of "her" brother and consort Osiris. If we consult Ainsworth in his capacity as lexicographer, we find that for "*languidus*" he gives mood words like "faint, weak, . . . enervated, [and] . . . faded," but that the only example offered of the comparative is *languidiora vina*, of "racy, mellow wine," in Ainsworth's phrase. As both Ceres and Bacchus, Isis draws in towards a central repletion, relaxed and dangerous: at once life-enhancing and life-draining. Hence the perennial fascination of Cleopatra, the self-styled "second Isis." In such a context there can be few biblical touchstones. Demetrius, the fashioner of the many-breasted Diana of Ephesus, goddess of childbirth and inexplicable death, is glancingly mentioned. There is a polite nod to another scholar's possible deduction linking Isis with "Eve, mother of generation." We are reminded that, in that capacity, Isis stands guardian over a pair of children: male to her right, female to her left. The whole thing is done with extreme lightness of touch, and is only eight pages long.[16] It is a pilgrimage of the imagination to the court of Hadrian, with its preference for Greek, its eclectic iconography, its ambiguous friendships, its fascination with Egypt.

Aspects that are now commonly given the epithet "fin de siècle" are apparent. Not least significant is the containing mode of exquisite miniaturization itself, as though the very constriction involved were a narrow entrance to an alternative world. The layers of the Judeo-Christian, and the Greco-Roman, cultures are peeled away. Isis does not belong in a world where any pair of males must define themselves as opponents in a civil war for the approval of a divine father (Cain and Abel, Romulus and Remus), or where any new knowledge must be a criminal-feminine innovation (Eve, Pandora). The acquired masculine "instinct" that equates the feminine with weakness and evil, the male with righteousness and power, has been banished to the very edge of the reader's consciousness. Ainsworth makes clear at outset his mood of delicate reverence: these are matters of "light and faith," if only someone else's. True to his roots in the tradition of Ockhamite nominalism, the unfathomable Calvinist God of Ainsworth's childhood has been translated into something rather unexpected.

The most curious aspect of this product of a hypersensitive classical sensibility first trained in Bolton Grammar School is that it may be held to "prophesy" the sorts of personal conviction about the double gender of God that would seize hold of Ann Lee and her Shaker companions in Bolton's backstreets a generation later.[17]

If only in embryo, Ainsworth may surely be called a "religious writer." The topics he raises will be raised again in the parish and the world. In 1795, in the wake of the French Revolution, as a collapsing Turkish Empire entices Napoleon and his British rivals towards the conquest of Egypt, James Pilkington of Horwich, the bishop's namesake and kinsman, will give a new lease of life to the Lollard tradition of "commonweal." His title announces his intent: *The Doctrine of Equality of Rank and Condition, examined and supported on the authority of the New Testament, and on the principles of Reason and Benevolence.*[18] A century later, in the wake of *Das Kapital* and imperial disaster at Khartoum, Bolton begins to stir to the activities of collaborators of Whitman, Tolstoy, and Edward Carpenter as well as of the suffragette Pankhursts and other turbulent females with a background in the Salford hundred, such as the socialist Beatrice Webb and the Irish nationalist Countess Markievicz. Recovering their own past in the attempt to rewrite its future, such "degenerates" joked that Rivington was "our property," which meant (they would explain) "proper to us." Bold but not threatening, softly wooded but never insipid, lit at evening by a magical light from the invisible western sea, Rivington would now be called a fair balance of yin and yang. Fired by summer soirees in its old Lollard preaching hollows and its manse garden, initiates propagated what they considered to be slogans of spiritual renewal: "A man has a feminine as well as a masculine nature"; "The refusal to 'look up' or 'look down' will be the end of war."[19] In 1900 the Rivington estate became the legal property of the world-capitalist Lord Lever (W. H. Lever, later Lord Leverhulme). Many of his aims were a liberal version of their own; they detested him. The 1990s have seen a similar outbreak and polarization. The Anglican Synod, for example, has voted for women priests, and moves are being made that outrage some as excessive and others as inadequate to allow ancient and modern celebrations of gender difference to restructure the intervening legacy of spiritual repression, starting from Genesis.[20]

In his own context as one enabled by the Revolution of 1688–89, Ainsworth corroborates the miniature "religious work" *Iseion* with a tiny essay on secular power. To find it, we must look up *rex* in the *Thesaurus*. The first definition listed: "A *king*, under which also *a queen* is included."

Cultural dominance, it seems, begets cultural achievement, which in turn threatens its parent with radical renewal. The empowerment to fix and prescribe precipitates new discoveries that compel all prescriptions to be rewritten and the terms of dominance to make an unpredictable shift. Raised and educated in Bolton, for instance, Edward Whitehead emigrates to the Hapsburg Empire and revolutionizes the balance of naval power by the invention of the self-propelled torpedo. Most of the world's rival empires purchase it, including Japan, but not Russia. Hence the destruction outside Port Arthur in February 1904 of the whole czarist fleet by a few Japanese destroyers. Back in Bolton, Charlie Sixsmith, the parish's leading Russia merchant and third in the semi-blasphemous "Holy Trinity" of which Edward Carpenter is the apex, rejoices in this reversal of the victory of Salamis, which long ago gave hegemony to the West.[21]

The world of which Eliot became the poet—the world that had

Whitehead and Sixsmith in it—was a world whose meanings were being compiled in the 1690s. The leading foundation of the decade, which would become second in significance only to the Crown in Parliament itself, was the Bank of England. The London of 1698 would be too preoccupied with the presence of Czar Peter ("the Great"), supposedly incognito, learning book-binding and naval engineering, with King William's open approval, to pay much heed to such a thing as Ainsworth's *Most Natural and Easy Way,* of the same year, for instance. Yet both events were strands in the same weaving.

After his victory at the Boyne, William could "settle" the Church. In 1691 John Tillotson replaced Sancroft at Canterbury, and John Sharp, of a Puritan and scientific family, neighbors of Tillotson in the Yorkshire Pennines, became Archbishop of York. Lawrence Fogg was made dean of Chester, heir to the abbots of St. Werburgh. As a deeply conscientious member of this new establishment, he was preoccupied with the responsibility of evolving, in such a world, a discourse for the survival and propagation of Christian belief. His massive *Theologiae Speculativae Schema, e variis systematibus mod-ernis . . . excerptum* appeared, after a long gestation, towards the end of a long life that had begun under James I and would not end before the Han-overians were settled. He was born in Darcy Lever, where his forebears had waited for letters from their imprisoned friend George Marsh. Like Hewit, he had bravely continued with the Anglican liturgy under Cromwell (as rector of Hawarden, in Flintshire, north Wales). Somewhat more remarkably, he resigned in 1662 in protest against the Act of Conformity. He apparently found it impossible to continue under compulsion a course he had gladly undertaken at his own risk. Charles's Declaration of Indulgence of 1672 won him to a vicarage and, soon after, a prebend's stall at Chester. His theology is at one with his life.[22]

The terms "speculative" and "modern" alert to salient aspects of his *Schema.* Also important is *"excerptum,"* which admits the need to "select" and denies the pretense of a complete knowledge. For him, as for Ainsworth, our notions of "the right of a thing" depend on series of inferences drawn from a forever imperfect textual tradition. Oliver Heywood resorted to the spiritual strengths of Hebrew. Fogg draws comfort from its limitations. Eras-mus (*De Libero Arbitrio* [1218]) chided Luther for not recognizing God's "attempering" of Old Testament language "to our sense," but *An Entrance* reduces the whole supralapsarian myth of an evil-inspiring deity to a factor of Hebrew syntax, which puts "*Actives* for *Passives,* and Transitives for Im-personals." Inferences must at every step be tested with an eye to the "Repre-sentations of God" to which they lead. The transubstantiationist formula—insofar as it suggests a priest may in any sense "make God"—he dismisses as "a conceit." He begs to prefer some "Notion as the Mind of a sober Christian may acquiesce in." As for the supralapsarians' image of a God who damns from all eternity, they must excuse him for not recognizing the divinity of what is so evidently a "Monster" the "Production" of which, as in all such cases, is a function of God's willingness to accommodate himself even to our defects. Such an image is by no means "a perfect Effect," yet God remains perfect, and our Redeemer, beyond all human imagining. Like the *Thesaurus*, the *Schema* is now only of antiquarian interest insofar as it is merely an encyclopedia of contemporary scholarship. But, like the *Thesaurus*, it is lifted right out of that category by the quality of the intellectual will whose exercise it invites. All theological speculation is as a labyrinth within a labyrinth. Lawrence claims to offer only the "ingredients" for each reader to make an individual choice. The functional *effect* of that choice is what matters. No one may presume, or have reason to despair. "A thread twisted of these Ingredients, will lead us out of those Labyrinths," is his nearest approach to the dogmatic.[23] The titles of his short pastoral works in English indicate his style of thought: they are offered as *A General View* and *An Entrance* into what remains a mystery.[24] In both, he endeavors an "Agreeableness with the Condition of his Flock, and possibly with the Genius of some others also." The elision between "Condition" and "Genius"—external circumstance and individual will—is deliberate.

Analytical pressures in the material itself have compelled this account of our parochial "religious writers" to stress first one, and then another, of the persons of the Trinity, when reporting Protestant opinion. For the first time, in the *General View*, the tradition of disengagement from the more paltry certainties of the human mind permits a Protestant to draw up his own deeply meditated personal tribute to the whole Trinity. Its most striking difference from the official Article "Of Faith in the Holy Trinity" is its reliance on the distinction between what is "Infinite" and what can be "represented." This alert humility makes it praise infinite "wisdom" before "infinite power," the Hagia Sophia before the seraglios of enforcement.[25] Like Marsh, he shuns a word-spinning that begets moral nihilism, and like Lever he steps over squabbles about what the eucharist "is" in order to celebrate, with Paul, its *dynamic* (we need the Greek word), whereby "We being many are one Bread and one Body." Contrary to what John Johnson will soon be preaching across the water in Liverpool, he postpones any "understanding" of the holy mysteries beyond the enactment of the intellectual will required to make sure that "*Malice* . . . be *cast* out . . . and *Charity* . . . be *Put* on."[26]

To initiate his own meaning, he places on the title page of the *Schema* a quotation from the Greek of Paul's second letter to his beloved Timothy. Writing at the time when "only Luke" ("the beloved physician") is with him, the apostle reminds one he does not expect to see again in this life of their former conversations and begs him to remain faithful to the general intention behind them. The key word transliterates as *hypotyposis*.[27] As invariably in living language, there is a distinction to be noted here that is both elusive and vital. Very approximately, in Latin or English terms, it is not a rigid or prescriptive "form" (forma) but rather a vaguer, more enabling "foreshadowing" (adumbratio) that is at issue. There is a suggestion, refined but not prissy, in the accompanying phrase and larger context, of early pregnancy. Hypotyposis is a sort of diminutive, or softened and somewhat metaphorical, form of typosis, used in medical contexts to imply "a foetus of 35 days."[28] This "just recognizable embryo of the future," as Paul calls it in his first letter to Timothy, is the opposite, he explains, of "logic chopping." He suggests his meaning in a sort of prose poem that makes clear it is Christ, not any particular system of doctrine, that is not to be denied: "If we cannot be faithful, He remains faithful."[29] As always, the precise quality of the vagueness of the term is important. The translator faces the dilemma of either developing a suggestion beyond the point of proper delicacy or (disastrously) stifling it altogether with a dead formula, incapable of development or surprise. Faced with hypotyposis, the Authorized Version abandons responsibility, shuns any suggestion "not of the politest sort" and opts for transliterating the Vulgate. Whereas the original implies something like: "Keep hold of that sort-of-embryo of healthy expression you heard when you were with me," we are given the prescriptive order of a Roman centurion to a potentially insubordinate recruit: "Hold fast the form of sound words thou hast heard of me." This is St. Jerome's best shot, the best the "Latin culture" and its limping replicants can offer. It is a catastrophe of the first order, since it constructs the replacement of the apostle by his executioner.[30]

Imaged above the western door of a Byzantine church to inspire communicants moving out into the world (in the place where the Latin culture, in the purity of its celibacy, delighted to portray the torments of the damned), may be seen the Mother of Jesus, asleep in death, her new soul life emerging from her in the aspect (to the Greek traditional) of a newborn child. There is more than one way of sacking Byzantium. The kidnappers and suffocators of the cultural heritage are invariably the enemies of the people. One thinks of Colonel Fletcher, who as treasurer-governor of Bolton Grammar School managed its scholarship fund for the exclusive benefit of his own relatives. Walking up and down at Peterloo, prodding the unmanageable people with his walking cane, like bullocks, he relied on his fellow magistrate and cogovernor, William Hulton, esquire (who had been awarded an M.A. by Oxford in 1807 by mere right of being a gentleman), to invoke the unanswerable argument of the yeomanry, should need arise. It is in carrying out their duty to the vital integrity of language that Fogg and Ainsworth exemplify an alternative to the yeomanry. For the dean, all duties begin with that; for the lexicographer, they perhaps end there.

T. S. Eliot is at loggerheads with St. Paul when he sets out, in his Notes towards the Definition of Culture, to prescribe a "limitation" to things that are living and unpredictable. Indeed, his effort may serve as a useful illustration of everything Paul (and Fogg) do not mean, since the very particular term *hypotyposis* is regularly used in *opposition* to the term *horos,* which implies just that prescriptive kind of "setting of bounds" Eliot was anxious to inaugurate in the *Notes*.[31] He is sometimes a little too willing to cringe to the supremacy of the imperialist "Latin culture" and to forget that accompanying all empires is that centrally Jewish experience for which a Greek term is used (though it applies to all cultures whatsoever, including the Latin): *diaspora*.[32] In the far more deeply meditated "Little Gidding" he is much further from fantasies of cultural domination and much nearer to the cost of cultural achievement as exemplified (for instance) by the real persons of our Bolton "school." The following lines might have been commissioned as reminders of Ainsworth, Fogg, the Heywoods, Hewit, and Marsh as a representative group. Without Dante's (and Anderton's) sense of spiritual and civil law, connected but distinct, the dialectic behind the lines would have no meaning at all:

> Every phrase and every sentence is an end and a beginning,
> Every poem an epitaph. And any action
> Is a step to the block, to the fire[33]

While Fogg's *hypotyposis* exemplifies the vital, vulnerable "beginning" of that first line, it is Ainsworth who looks towards the "end" that may never be finally brought to birth. On the title page of his *Thesaurus* he places a birthing image from the pagan esthete Longinus that exactly complements that in Paul. Roughly speaking, this may be rendered as "[t]he issue of words is the final birthing of much experience." Here, the key word is *epigennema* ("final birthing") which an eighteenth-century Latin translation by the Welshman Zachary Pearce gives, unambiguously and enablingly, as *"ultimus foetus."*[34] All our words are dying words, the dying words of a mother which give her newborn child a name.

Later research would reinterpret the evidence in detail, but for eighteenth-century scholars, Paul and Longinus were complementary. Apostle and esthete, provincial Jew and Athenian Greek, the servants respectively of Christ and of Zenobia (who claimed the inheritance of Cleopatra), both men were butchered, unarmed, by the Roman state, Longinus some two centuries after Paul. When they wrote the word "Rome" in Greek, they were using a term which also defined "Rome" from their own experience. For "Rome," in Greek, means, literally, "brute force." One is reminded of the monk Bradshaw's reading of "brutes and Welshmen," synonymous with barbarism and each other, and of the Tudor policy of cannibalizing the Roman tradition to which Werburgh's dynasty had been so faithful, of deriving "British" from the Latin "Brutus" and annexing the destiny of the "brute."

The legacy exemplified by Ainsworth and Fogg (and Zachary Pearce) is quite other than that. The copy of the papercovered 1714 edition of Fogg's

General View[35] that has reached the British Museum was at some time provided with a commentary in the shape of a cutting from a nineteenth-century
American newspaper. This is now glued meticulously over the inner surface
of the outer paper cover, its text running at right angles to that of the original
pamphlet, all the way (as far as one can guess), under the spine. Whether
the intention was simply to strengthen the older booklet, or simply to bring
the two texts together, the effect is of both. It describes the incident, which
so moved Whitman, of Queen Victoria seizing pen and writing, unprompted
by her government, to offer a woman's sympathy to the widow of the mur-
dered Lincoln. The journalist's comment occupies a line of text that rims the
left edge of the dean of Chester's title page: "The revenge of martyrdom is
never fulfilled but by the conversion of the world."

This mysterious material connection no doubt admits of some quite banal
explanation. It remains nonetheless a connection, a bridge across civil wars,
which is equally recognizable as a miracle of the princess Werburgh or as an
epiphany of George Marsh. One is reminded of all that global unity in diver-
sity implied by a "Passage to India." One thinks of J. W. Wallace, reading
Whitman's poem of that title on the Rivington moors and finding the representation in his hand inadequate to the realization around him. Like Ainsworth he was raised in the Cromwellian Bolton Grammar School. His loving
memoir of Whitman delighted Virginia Woolf. He remembered sitting in
Whitman's chair facing the portrait of Lincoln and the poet's remark about
the painter who attempted innumerable portraits of Cleopatra, none of them
the same, none satisfactory. The theme would be a leitmotiv in *The Waste
Land* for the attempt to represent "vilest things" transposed "in her" into
"themselves," a fallen universe redemptively identified and united in "infinite
variety." Distinct as that poem is from *Four Quartets*, both are achievements
of the same culture. Despite chronology, to be able to write

> April is the cruellest month, breeding
> Lilacs out of the dead land, mixing
> Memory and desire

—is already to have taken this to heart:

> We die with the dying;
> See, they depart, and we go with them.
> We are born with the dead:
> See, they return, and bring us with them.[36]

Notes

PREFACE

1. Michel Foucault, quoted in J. V. Harari, *Textual Strategies* (London: Methuen, 1980), p. 158.
2. Homer, *Iliad*, 22.347

CHAPTER 1. HENRY BRADSHAW: LAST OF THE OLD CATHOLIC ORDER

1. Henry Bradshaw, *The Life of Saint Werburge of Chester*, Englisht A.D. 1513, printed by Pynson A.D. 1521, and now reedited by Carl Horstmann (London: published for the Early English Text Society by N. Trübner & Co., 1887), ix.
2. Ibid., 131. Spelling modernized.
3. Ibid., 199.

CHAPTER 2. "PLACE SPIRITUAL": THE REAL PRESENCE OF CHRIST

1. Bradshaw, *Saint Werburge*, 149.
2. Ibid., 35.
3. Ibid., 187.

CHAPTER 3. "GHOSTLY TUITION": THE DISCIPLINE OF THE HOLY SPIRIT

1. Horstmann follows Anthony à Wood, *Athenae Oxonienses* (1691) to the effect that Bradshaw studied at Gloucester College, a Benedictine house at Oxford.
2. Bradshaw, *Saint Werburge*, 108.
3. The term *filioque* ("and the Son"), added after the words "the Holy Ghost . . . proceedeth from the Father" in the so-called Nicene Creed, was an interpolation sanctioned at Rome from the early eleventh century, but never in the East. Belief in transubstantiation was declared *de fide* by the Lateran Council of 1215. The Latin *transubstantiari* demands allegiance to a notion of purely miraculous transformation of substance as the binding definition of the relationship between Christ and the consecrated elements, whereas the word selected by the Eastern Church at the Jerusalem Synod of 1672—μετουσιοῦσθαι—expresses the idea of the spiritual recognition of a participation in being as the key to that relationship. See F. L. Cross, ed., *Dictionary of the Christian Church* (Oxford University Press, 1963), 722.

4. Bradshaw, *Saint Werburge*, 34.
5. Ibid., 197.

CHAPTER 4. "LIFE HISTORIAL": THE TRANSMITTED AUTHORITY OF THE FATHER

1. Ibid., xxix.
2. Ibid., 118.
3. Evidence on Henry Bradshaw's family background is not very firm. *See*, Henry Bradshaw, *Holy Lyfe and History of Saynt Werburge*, ed. E. Hawkins (Manchester: The Chetham Society, 1848); and Thomas Boston Johnstone, *The Religious History of Bolton* (Bolton: S. J. Blackley, 1887), 352. The Bradshaws were an ancient, prolific gentry clan of Lancashire and Cheshire. The monk Henry may have been a son of John Bradshaw of Haigh Hall, Wigan, and Bradshaw Hall, Bolton, who succeeded to his estates in infancy, 1427.
4. Bradshaw, *Saint Werburge*, 190.

CHAPTER 5. THOMAS LEVER: SEEKING THE PLACE SPIRITUAL

1. Edmund Sandys to Matthew Parker, 30 April 1559, in *Correspondence of Matthew Parker*, ed. John Bruce (Cambridge University Press, 1853), 66: "Mr. Lever wisely put such a scruple in the Queen's head that she would not take the title of supreme head".
2. F Walker, *Historical Geography of South-West Lancashire before the Industrial Revolution* (Manchester: The Chetham Society, 1939), 33–49.
3. For Thomas Lever and his Heaton relatives, *see* Christina Hallowell Garrett, *The Marian Exiles* (Cambridge University Press, 1938, reprinted 1966); and the *General Index to the Publications of the Parker Society* (Cambridge University Press, 1855). "Heaton" is the modern spelling, but the old family spelling seems to have been "Heton;" and "Eaton" is also found. John Lever succeeded as a minor in 1501, his guardians being Richard Heaton of Heaton and Hugh Oldham (later Bishop of Exeter), Clerk of the Hanaper and a native of Manchester parish. An ancient farm called "Oldhams" near Smithills suggests some possible closer connection. For Richard Heaton's chantry and his (unfruitful) complaints to the chancellor of the Duchy of Lancaster against seven men called Greenhalgh and their companions who smashed up images of the Holy Trinity and St. Anne and cast them "out of the churchyard" (probably down the steep slope of Deane Clough, which falls away close to the west door), *see* James Boardman, *Records and Traditions of Deane Church, Village, and Parish*, 2 vols. (privately published, 1904), 134–6 and Public Record Office, *Duchy of Lancaster Pleadings*, Henry VIII, Vol. 21, H. 24.
4. Johnstone, *Religious History*, 490. Deane Church survives. For a telling photograph of old St. Peter's, Bolton, during demolition in 1868, see W. E. Brown, *Bolton as it Was* (Nelson: Hendon Publishing, 1986), 6.
5. For details on the sixteenth-century Bolton Grammar School, *see* W. E. Brown, *The History of Bolton School* (Bolton: Bolton School, 1976), 11–38. By a will of 3 April 1516, John Barton of Smithills, a widower and Observant Friar, set aside money for a priest to "teche gramer at Bolton." In 1525 James Bolton was one of the trustees

of the grammar school, and his name comes third in a list made 1573 of trustees of "about xl years now past" which is headed by John Lever (Thomas's father) and seconded by Alexander Orrell, most likely a relative of John, whose mother was an Orrell of Turton. Leading members of this family would become notable recusants. It was John Lever who seems to have been responsible for the crucial initiative of acquiring land through a trust "towards the maintenance of a schoolmaster," in 1525. It was, however, Orrell land, and tensions between Levers and Orrells make the early history of the school.

6. Robert Bolton, *A History of the County of Westchester* (New York: Alexander S. Gould, 1848).

7. Garrett, *The Marian Exiles*, 52.

8. Laurence Vaux, *A Catechisme or Christian Doctrine*, reprinted from an Edition of 1583; with an Introductory memoir of the Author by Thomas Graves Law (Manchester: The Chetham Society, 1885), xxv.

9. H. C. Porter, *Reformation and Reaction in Tudor Cambridge* (Cambridge University Press, 1958, reprint, Hamden, Conn.: Archon Books, 1972), 259.

CHAPTER 6. THE EFFECTUAL BODY OF CHRIST

1. Porter, *Reformation*, 68.

2. Thomas Lever, preface to *The Meditations of Bradford*, and "Meditation on the Tenth Commandment" (1567), reprinted in John Bradford, *Writings*, vol. 1, ed. Aubrey Townsend (Cambridge University Press, 1848), 565–71.

3. Garrett, *The Marian Exiles*, 219.

4. Thomas Lever, prefatory epistle to a sermon delivered at Paul's Cross (originally published December 1550), reprinted E. Arber, *English Reprints*, no. 25 (1870), 94. Spelling modernized.

5. Thomas Lever to Henry Bullinger, Berne, 12 May 1556, *Original Letters relative to the English Reformation*, trans. and ed. Hastings Robinson (Cambridge University Press, 1846), 162.

CHAPTER 7. MANIFESTO CONTRADICTED BY REVOLUTION

1. Arber, *English Reprints*, 67–8, 95.

2. S. T. Bindoff, *Tudor England* (Harmondsworth: Penguin Books, 1975), 130.

3. Arber, *English Reprints*, 65.

4. Arber, *English Reprints*, 46–7.

5. William Shakespeare, *King Lear*, 2.4.267–8; 3.4.32–3, 100–7.

6. Hugh Latimer, *Sermons*, ed. George Elwes Corrie (Cambridge University Press, 1844), xvi, 120, 128.

7. Arber, *English Reprints*, 64–5. *See also* F. R. Raines, ed., *The Visitation of the County Palatine of Lancaster, made in the year 1567* (Manchester: Chetham Society, 1870), 9. I cannot improve on Garrett's statement (p. 182) that Thomas and George Heaton were "in some sort" cousins to Thomas Lever.

8. John Lyly, *The Anatomy of Wit, Euphues and his England*, eds. M. W. Croll and H. Clemons (New York: Russell & Russell, 1964), xlix.

9. Bindoff, *Tudor England*, 140.

10. Fecknam, Mary's "abbott of Winchester." *See* John Foxe, *Actes and Monuments*, 2 vols. (J. Daye, 1583), 1419. A clue to the ethical and theological partisanship

of the editors of the Parker Society series, which led them to reprint a volume of dry Anglo-Zwinglian sermons by Edmund Sandys and to omit to reprint Lever's sermons or his treatise, is provided by their Index, in which (unlike her sisters) Lady Jane Grey is listed under her Christian name, a glaringly discreet way of reclaiming her as Queen of England.

11. Porter, *Reformation*, 66.

12. Ralph Lever, *The Arte of Reason* (London: H. Bynneman, 1573). R. Lever delights to use "Witcraft" for "Reason". *See also The most noble, ancient and learned playe, set forth by R. Lever and augmented by W. F.* (London: printed by Rouland Hall for James Rowbotham, 1563). There is a dedication to Lord Robert Dudley, and the preface informs the reader that the invention of this "battle of numbers" is "ascribed to Pythagoras." During 1563 Elizabeth allowed the impracticality of any marriage to Dudley to be realised, and a hint seems to be implied that he now has leisure for and need of philosophic recuperation. R. Lever disclaims this work on **3r of *The Arte of Reason*. The *Short-Title Catalogue* identifies "W.F." with W. Fulwood, whose name is an acrostic on a8r. The *Dictionary of National Biography* identifies "W.F." with William Fulke, R. Lever's fellow-Johnian. This particular confusion may be described as understandable enough to have been intended as part of the mystification involved in the compilation of *The most noble*. See W. A. Jackson, F. S. Ferguson, Katharine F. Pantzer, *A Short-Title Catalogue of Books Printed in England [etc.]* 1475–1640 (London: The Bibliographical Society, 1976), 2.60; Thomas Cooper, "Ralph Lever", in *The Dictionary of National Biography*, ed. Leslie Stephen and Sidney Lee (Oxford University Press, 1917), 11. 1020–21.

13. Porter, *Reformation*, 75.

CHAPTER 8. NEGOTIATION PREVENTED BY THE NEEDS OF POWER

1. Patrick Collinson, *The Elizabethan Puritan Movement* (Oxford University Press, 1990), 232.

2. *Original Letters*, 154.

3. Thomas Lever to Henry Bullinger, Coventry 10 July 1560, *Zurich Letters*, trans. and ed. Hastings Robinson, 1st series (Cambridge University Press, 1842), 84 (English), 50 (Latin).

4. John Strype, *Annals of the Reformation* (1725), vol. 1, 337.

5. "Examination of Certain Londoners", in Edmund Grindal, *The Remains*, ed. William Nicholson (Cambridge University Press, 1843), 205–7. The Londoners seem to have a realistic sense of Lever's status as cat's paw:

Bishop: No? how say you to Sampson and Lever, and others? do not they preach?

White: Though they preach . . . the law standeth in force against them still, howsoever you suffer them now.

6. *Zurich Letters*, 1st series, 51: "*non astringimus neque ego illis, neque illi cives mihi.*" Coventry was not, however, a *civitas* in the Swiss or Ciceronian sense, but *Camera Principis*.

7. Hugh Simonds, vicar of St. Michael's, Coventry, was deprived for marriage in 1553. The next vicar to be inducted was William Ireland, 22 September 1577. John Blithe, archdeacon of Coventry, died in 1558. Lever compounded for first fruits as Archdeacon in 1560. The Calvinistic William James became archdeacon of Coventry, 27 August 1577. The man who succeeded to both appointments, Dr. William Hinton, was in 1611 brought to order for suffering Communion to be received without kneel-

ing, etc. The neighboring church, Holy Trinity, had an ordinary succession of vicars, culminating in Humphrey Venn, or Fen (inducted 21 February 1577), who was in 1584 suspended for refusing to subscribe to the Articles and in 1591 removed for subscribing to the Book of Discipline. Details in B. Poole, *Coventry: Its History and Antiquities* (Coventry, 1869); Browne Willis, *A Survey of the Cathedrals,* 3 vols. (London: T. Osborne, 1742), 3.414; Collinson, *Elizabethan,* 327.

8. Collinson, *Elizabethan,* 51.

9. Coventry details from Poole, *Coventry;* and from Frederick Leigh Colville, *The Worthies of Warwickshire* (Warwick, 1869); R. W. Ingram, "Production of Medieval Drama in Coventry," in *The Elizabethan Theatre; 5,* ed. G. R. Hibbard (University of Waterloo Press, Canada, 1975), 20; Frederick Smith, *Coventry: Six Hundred Years of Municipal Life,* (Coventry, 1945–46).

10. The three Englishmen helping to defend Malta: Sir Oliver Starkey, last English Hospitaller and secretary to the Grand Master; and John Smith and Edward Stanley, Catholic runagates of their respective dynasties. Parker nevertheless referred to the defenders of Malta as "christians" in the official Form of Thanksgiving. *See* Ernle Bradford, *The Great Siege* (London: The Reprint Society, 1962), 151 and William Keatinge Clay, ed., *Liturgical Services of the Reign of Queen Elizabeth* (Cambridge University Press, 1847), 524.

11. Arber, *English Reprints,* 4–5; Thomas Lever, *A Treatise of the right way frō danger of sinne and vengeance in this wicked worlde unto godly wealth and salvation in Christe* (London: H. Bynneman, 1575), chapter 8 (original edition, Geneva 1556).

12. Garrett, *The Marian Exiles,* 220; Porter, *Reformation,* 61; Collinson, *Elizabethan,* 61.

13. R. Lever, dedication to the Rt. Hon. Lord Walter, earl of Essex in *The Arte of Reason* (1573): "nine years ago . . . ye made me your reader: and used at sundry times to conferre with me in that kind of learning." Other information from Thomas Baker, *History of St. John's College, Cambridge,* ed. John E. B. Mayor, 2 vols., (Cambridge University Press, 1869).

14. Porter, *Reformation,* 119–35. *See also* Richard Longworth, *Answer to Articles exhibited against him* (Cambridge University Press, 1569). Thomas Longworth appears as eldest son of George, eldest brother to Richard, in Raines, *Visitation,* 23.

15. Grindal, *Remains,* 205.

16. Grindal, *Remains,* x.

CHAPTER 9. THE REPUBLIC OF CHRIST

1. J. R. Green, *History of the English People* (London: Macmillan, 1890), 2. 430.

2. Porter, *Reformation,* 171, 373–74. Burleigh thought the Articles "might cause men to be desperate," Elizabeth that they were "dangerous to weak ignorant minds."

3. Laurence Vaux, *A Catechisme,* 11, 94. *See also* A. C. Southern, *Elizabethan Recusant Prose, 1559–1582* (London: Sands & Co., 1950), 532–36, and Boardman, *Deane,* 134–36.

4. Christopher Haigh, *The Last Days of the Lancashire Monasteries* (Manchester University Press, 1969), 9–27. Gross superstition and immorality are quite absent: an agreeable lifestyle, supported by sharp financing, is ripe for annexation.

5. Alexander Nowell, *A Catechism written in Latin, together with the same Catechism translated into English by Thomas Norton,* ed. G. E. Corrie (Cambridge University Press, 1853), 113. Official ambiguity about "Discipline" at the time of the catechism's first appearance in 1570 is suggested by the fact that Nowell's title page

includes the word *Disciplina* in large print, a term Norton discreetly renders "Learn-ing" in the English edition.

6. Thomas Lever, *A Treatise,* chapter 5. Original Spelling.

7. Mark 9.24.

8. James Pilkington, *The Works of James Pilkington,* ed. James Scholefield (Cam-bridge University Press, 1842), 619.

9. Brown, *Bolton School,* 24. In 1563 Carter published *Annotationes in Dialectica Ioan Setoni* (an earlier alumnus of St. John's and a Catholic), dedicated to the earl of Derby. This was reprinted several times until 1639. He left college by August 1564. He had Whalley connections, and is perhaps referred to by Pilkington (*Works,* vii) in a letter of 1564 to Archbishop Parker: "Whalley hath as ill a vicar as the worst: and there is one come thither, that hath been deprived or changed his name, and now teacheth school there, of evil to make them worse."Carter was not long at Bolton, though he was apparently there in 1578. He became the first (recorded) headmaster of Wigan Grammar School in 1579. His Bolton connections were the (recusant) Orrells, though Carter married.

10. Porter, *Reformation,* 151.

11. Details in Garrett, *The Marian Exiles.*

12. A. F. Scott Pearson, *Thomas Cartwright and Elizabethan Puritanism* (Glouces-ter, Mass.: Peter Smith, 1966), 58–62.

13. *Mutare vel Timere Sperno.*

14. One version of a recurrent legend: "Their family crest includes a man with a scythe and the motto 'Now Thus—Now Thus,' which is an allusion to one of the family who, in order to escape his enemies, disguised himself as a mower" (M. D. Smith, *Leverhulme's Rivington* [Chorley: NB Colour Print, 1992]), 11. Bolton's an-cient market inn, "The Man and Scythe," displays a mower in Pilkington livery. The Pilkingtons of Pilkington (of which the Rivington Pilkingtons were a cadet branch) held the lordship of Bolton during the fourteenth century.

15. *Zurich Letters,* 1st series, 287, 292.

16. Collinson, *Elizabethan,* 191.

17. Collinson, *Elizabethan,* 172, 193.

18. Collinson, *Elizabethan,* 196.

19. Collinson, *Elizabethan,* 184. Lever would doubtless have been a key figure in Grindal's efforts, thwarted by Elizabeth, "to subject prophesying to the more effective oversight of bishops and archdeacons" (Collinson, *Elizabethan,* 195).

20. R. G. Usher, *The Presbyterian Movement in the Reign of Queen Elizabeth* (London: Historical Society of Great Britain, 1905), xix–xx.

21. Arber, *English Reprints,* 3.

22. Edwin Sandys, *Sermons,* ed. John Ayre (Cambridge University Press, 1841), 88; Thomas Lever, *A Treatise,* chapter 6; Alexander Nowell, *A Catechism* (transla-tion), 206, 212: the sacraments are "tokens"—the Lord's Supper has "two parts. . . . The one part, the bread and wine, . . . the other part, Christ himself."

23. Mark 16.15, 20.

24. Collinson, *Elizabethan* (p.233), dates the beginning of formal Presbyterian con-ference in Warwickshire from 1583. J. A. F. Thomson, *The Later Lollards,* dates attempts to suppress processions and plays, and the outlawing of maypoles, etc., by Coventry magistrates from the same period.

25. Quotation and details from Garrett, *The Marian Exiles,* 52–53, 221. Garrett sees Lever's Aarau Colony as a prototype "of corporate colonization in New England" and notes that it represented a "geographical epitome of England."

26. "The town was a splendid stage for an adolescent romance. Set at the end of

the magnificent Jura mountains, its old centre with its maze of narrow streets rises in terraces from the river Aare" (Roger Highfield and Paul Carter, *The Private Lives of Albert Einstein* [London: Faber & Faber, 1993]), 24–25).

27. *Original Letters,* 169.

CHAPTER 10. GEORGE MARSH: FOLLOWING GHOSTLY TUITION

1. *Zurich Letters,* 2nd series, 16, n.
2. Foxe, *Actes and Monuments,* 1408.
3. Foxe, *Actes and Monuments,* 1410.
4. R. C. Richardson, *Puritanism in North-West England: A Regional Study of the Diocese of Chester in 1642* (Manchester University Press, 1972), 89.
5. M. M. Knappen, *Tudor Puritanism* (Chicago University Press, 1970), 106.
6. Foxe, *Actes and Monuments,* 1567, 1571. On Philip Melanchthon: *see* Clyde Leonard Manschreck, *Melanchthon the Quiet Reformer* (New York: Abingdon Press, 1958), 235: "Melanchthon regarded transubstantiation . . . and Zwingli's memorialism as late developments. . . . 'I will not be a starter or defender of any new dogma,' Melanchthon wrote to Brentz. . . . 'I earnestly wish the Church would decide the matter without sophistry or tyranny.'" On Socrates *see* Plato, *Crito,* 50–52.

CHAPTER 11. EARL AND YEOMAN

1. Brown, *Bolton School,* 19.
2. *Original Letters,* 150–52. See also Pilkington, *Works,* iv.
3. Strype, *Ecclesiastical Memorials,* 1.576, quoted in Porter, *Reformation,* 84.
4. Porter, *Reformation,* 84.
5. John Bradford, *Writings,* vol. 2, 51–54, 188–89. Garrett, *The Marian Exiles,* 8, n., calls "George Heton" a "refugee."—perhaps a confusion with Guy Heton (pp. 181, 383).
6. Local details in Boardman, *Deane.*
7. Haigh, *Lancashire Monasteries,* 139.
8. Details in Nathaniel Hawthorne, *The English Notebooks,* ed. Randall Stewart (New York: Russell & Russell, 1962), 638, n.
9. Walker, *Historical Geography,* 49–50.
10. Michael Bennett, *The Battle of Bosworth* (Gloucester: Alan Sutton, 1985), 153. See also pp. 105, 116–18. "The position of the Stanleys . . . could be, indeed was, interpreted in a number of ways: they were maintaining a common front with Richard III; . . . they were waiting to effect a juncture with rebel allies; or they were intending to sit on the side-lines to come in on the winning side. . . . [T]hey could even divide their forces and pursue several strategies at once. . . . Henry Tudor . . . knew that he owed his deliverance to Sir William Stanley, who had at long last committed his troops. . . . Richard, . . . unhorsed and over powered, . . . was hacked to death . . . by low-born Welshmen." Bennett, ibid., 164, quotes *The Great Chronicle of London,* ed. A. H. Thomas and I. D. Thornley (London, 1938), 237–38: "And incontinently, as it was said, Sir William Stanley which won the possession of King Richard's helmet with the crown being upon it came straight to King Henry and set it upon his head saying, "Sir, here I make you King of England.'" William Stanley was exe-cuted for treasonous talk in 1495, and later accounts (including Shakespeare's) have

Henry crowned in more decorous fashion by William's elder brother, Thomas Stanley, first earl of Derby.

11. Welsh, in this instance; but Scots (including, apparently, highlanders, Bennett, *Bosworth,* 162) were already among the Tudor guard at Bosworth, and of course the Irish were to provide an increasingly numerous presence in the British war machine.

12. Haigh, *Lancashire Monasteries,* 72, recounts how at the dissolution, Derby was granted Burscough Priory, near Lathom, but did not venture to remove the lead from the roof. Under Mary, the Earl took good care to avoid sending Bradford home to Manchester to be burned (Bradford, *Writings,* 2. xxxvii–viii).

13. The Levers, Bradshaws, Cromptons, and Foggs of Darcy Lever; to be distin-guished, e.g., from established gentry like the Levers of Little Lever and the Brad-shaws of Bradshaw. *See* William Farrer and J. Brownbill, eds., *Victoria County History: Lancashire,* volume 5 (University of London Institute of Historical Research, 1966), 263–66.

14. Richardson, *Puritanism,* chapter 4.

15. Foxe, *Actes and Monuments,* 1563.

Chapter 12. Royal Lancaster

1. Knappen, *Tudor Puritanism,* 95.

2. Foxe, *Actes and Monuments,* 1564.

3. Bill Naughton, *Saintly Billy: A Catholic Boyhood* (Oxford University Press, 1988), 109.

4. Garrett, *The Marian Exiles,* 321. Ellen Warburton, possibly a descendant, became the mother of the lexicographer Robert Ainsworth (1660–1743).

5. Foxe, *Actes and Monuments,* 1568. It is possible the gloss implied by the phrases beginning, "I mean", and, "to wit," is the work of transcribers, eager to emphasise what Marsh may only have hinted at.

6. Johnstone, *Religious History,* 358, notes several "Hetons" among donors of land to Furness Abbey and mentions the tradition of a connection between the Deane Heatons and that part of north Lancashire.

7. Foxe, *Actes and Monuments,* 1570.

Chapter 13. Visitors

1. *See* Foxe, *Actes and Monuments,* 1564–65. However affected by transmission, Marsh's account provides a convincing sense of comparatively mild bustle and debate, at all levels. There is a general feeling that the community will manage to avoid burning anybody. The irruption of the alien and pedantic Cotes into this local deco-rum has a ghastly resonance, in contrast with the procedures of Bishop Tunstall of Durham, the natural leader of his own very different community. His moderation helped to ensure no heretics were burned in his diocese (*see* Gladys Hinde, ed., *The Registers of Cuthbert Tunstall and James Pilkington, Bishops of Durham* (Durham and London: Surtees Society, 1952), xxvi–vii).

2. Walker, *Historical Geography,* 50, notes that because of south Lancashire's status as a royal demesne, it never saw the development of the usual manorial plan dependent on bond-labor. John O'Gaunt's gesture was therefore essentially a confir-mation of what, in much of the county, was simply the status quo: landlords controlled by economics, not feudal law. There was a unique development of "difficult ...

intermediate" classes (p. 31), together with greater marital mobility. There were no nunneries in the county, and to that extent no facility whereby well-to-do fathers could "protect" their daughters from "unfortunate" alliances.

3. Foxe, *Actes and Monuments*, 1474–75.

CHAPTER 14. FROM THE MONASTERY TO THE CITY

1. For a summary of Oxford College histories, *see* A. R. Woolley, *The Clarendon Guide to Oxford* (Oxford University Press, 1963), 30–31, 97–100.

2. Foxe, *Actes and Monuments*, 1564.

3. For brief history of Pope Paul IV, *see* F. L. Cross, *Dictionary of the Christian Church*, 1032–3.

4. Thomas Becon (Cranmer's chaplain and minister of St. Stephen's, Walbrook in the city of London, 1548–54) cited Ambrose as arguing that the flesh of Christ is offered for the salvation of the body and the blood for the soul, a line of reasoning possibly recalled by Marsh at Lathom: "The commixtion of the Body and Blood of Christ was health both of body and soul." Thomas Becon, *Prayers and other pieces*, ed. John Ayre (Cambridge University Press, 1844), 413.

5. Robert Ashton, *The English Civil War: Conservatism and Revolution, 1603–1649* (London: Weidenfeld & Nicolson, 1989), 95.

6. Foxe, *Actes and Monuments*, 1485.

7. M. Hardman, *Six Victorian Thinkers* (Manchester University Press, 1991), 96–97, 125.

8. Foxe, *Actes and Monuments*, 1675.

9. Felipe Fernandez Armesto, *The Spanish Armada* (Oxford University Press, 1988).

10. T. W. Moody, F. X. Martin, and F. J. Byrne, eds., *A New History of Ireland* (Oxford University Press, 1991), 3.77–79: "The removal of the Gaelic landholders into narrow confines . . . was now authorised. The remaining two thirds was allocated for plantation 'by Englishmen born in England or Ireland.'" Hans Claude Hamilton, *Calendar of the State Papers relating to Ireland . . . 1509–1573* (London: Longman, 1860), 134, 137, 143, 145.

11. John Brown, *The History of Great and Little Bolton* (Manchester, 1825), 265–75.

12. Richardson, *Puritanism*, 17.

13. Philip Melanchthon, "Baccalaureate Theses" (delivered September 1519), *Selected Writings*, trans. Charles Leander Hill (Minneapolis, Minn.: Augsburg Publishing, 1962), 17–18. Marsh also knew of E. Sarcerius.

14. Richard Hooker, *The Works of Richard Hooker*, ed. John Keble (Oxford University Press, 1845), 3.543.

15. During the first ever papal mass in England—Westminster Cathedral on the morning of 28 May 1982—the Jesuit commentator for BBC Radio 4 explained that while communion in both kinds had recently come to be expected by the laity, it was "not convenient" on this sensitive and historic occasion.

16. Foxe, *Actes and Monuments*, 1498. Gardiner refers to the Donatists, whose independent African Church was destroyed by the Saracens in the 7th–8th cent. *See* F. L. Cross, *Dictionary of the Christian Church*, 415.

17. Foxe, *Actes and Monuments*, 1565.

CHAPTER 15. MATURE TUITION

1. Boardman, *Deane* (p. 472) cites the manuscript of Dr. Cowper, mayor of Chester in 1745.

2. Nikolaus Pevsner, *Cambridgeshire* (Harmondsworth: Penguin Books, 1954), 140: "wholly Gothic [although] . . . erected in 1555–64, . . . [its] windows . . . have only the most elementary panel tracery. . . . The roof . . . is flat and has very shallow arched principals."

3. Porter, *Reformation*, 55–57.

4. William Keatinge Clay, ed., *Liturgies Set Forth in the Reign of Queen Elizabeth* (Cambridge University Press, 1847), 13. *See also* Joseph Ketley, ed., *Liturgies Set Forth in the Reign of King Edward VI* (Cambridge University Press, 1844), 101, 233.

5. Boardman, *Deane*, 434 (quoting Burnet).

6. Foxe, *Actes and Monuments*, 1567.

7. Tacitus, *Annales*, XV.44.18–25.

8. Boardman, *Deane*, 471.

9. Pilkington, *Works*, 197–98. More impressive is the prayer of confession that follows: "we . . . consented to the persecution of our brother."

10. Thomas Lever, *Treatise*, chapter 11.

11. Brown, *Bolton School*, 25. Boardman, *Deane*, 515–16. The Deane school apparently existed from 1590, but intermittently. Giles Marsh of Marsh Fold, in his will dated 9 September 1615 set aside "£10, desiring Mr. Barton and the rest of the worships in the said parish to labour for a free school there." In 1624 Ralph Barton of Grays Inn and Ralph Heaton of Heaton, gentlemen, jointly donated land worth 40 shillings a year.

12. Bradford, *Writings*, 2.119. Foxe, *Actes and Monuments*, 1623.

13. Foxe, *Actes and Monuments*, 1496.

14. "Propositions on the Mass" (1521), 62, 63: "All of us are priests. The priesthood is nothing more than the right to pray." Hill, *Theses*, 67.

15. Foxe, *Actes and Monuments*, 1573. The Latin original: William Keatinge Clay, ed., *Private Prayers Put Forth by Authority . . . of Queen Elizabeth* (Cambridge University Press, 1851), 373. The English translation that Marsh used daily and perhaps made noticeably modifies the Calvinistic tendencies of the original: *Confidentes de tua singulari in nos bonitate et gratia summatim tibi exponinus putrem et corruptam arborem nostram* ("Confident of your singular goodness and grace to us, we briefly expose to you our putrid and corrupt tree"), which becomes "trusting in thy gracious goodness, [we] do briefly open to thee the evil tree of our heart."

16. Foxe, *Actes and Monuments*, 1561–62. Boardman, *Deane*, 438–43.

17. Hill, *Selected Writings of Philip Melanchthon*, 17–18; Keble, *Works of Richard Hooker*, 3.543; Foxe, *Actes and Monuments*, 1569, 1570: "the true justifying faith, which is never idle, but worketh by charity . . . we must serve our neighbours by all means we can."

18. Foxe, *Actes and Monuments*, 1568: "as the godly Thessalonians did, search ye the scriptures daily, whether those things which be preached unto you be even so or not" (Acts 17.10–13). Coincidentally, Thessaly was the utopia of exile to which Crito hoped to win Socrates (Plato, *Crito*, 53).

19. Fred Wild, *Sketch of the Life of J. W. Wallace* (Bolton, 1932). Wild and Wallace were at school in the 1860s, when the grammar school was still adjacent to

the parish church. The tag game "King of the Castle" or (at classical schools) "Caesar!" is as old as any.

20. *See* Thomas à Kempis, *De Imitatione Christi*, 3.43–4, in *The Following of Christ*, trans. Richard Challoner (York and London: C. Croshaw and M. Andrews, 1829), 294.

21. Strype, *Annals*, 1.357–60.

22. Foxe, *Actes and Monuments*, 1573.

23. Foxe, *Actes and Monuments*, 1563.

24. Pilkington, *Works*, 329.

25. Foxe, *Actes and Monuments*, 1563.

26. Sandys, *Sermons*, ix–xii.

27. Clyde Leonard Manschreck, *Melanchthon: The Quiet Reformer* (New York: Abingdon Press, 1958), 237: "With the bread and wine the body and blood of Christ are truly and substantially present, offered and received."

28. Boardman, *Deane*, 199.

CHAPTER 16. JAMES PILKINGTON: MEDITATING THE LIFE HISTORIAL

1. Porter, *Reformation*, 89.

2. Pilkington, *Works*, 44.

CHAPTER 17. SURVIVAL

1. Garrett, *The Marian Exiles*, 1, 7–8.

2. Quoted in Vaux, *Catechism*, xiii.

3. Henry Stanley became the fourth earl of Derby on the death of his father in 1572 and was one of the commissioners who tried Mary Queen of Scots. His brothers Edmond and Thomas were in 1571 implicated in the attempt to release her from Tutbury.

4. Sir John Harington, *A Briefe View of the State of the Church of England . . . to the Yeere 1608* (London, 1653), 76–81. Harington cites a saying about financial corruption in the relations between "Crown and Mitre": "Marr or Mart or Martin Eeely".

5. Johnstone, *Religious History*, 361.

6. Peter Northcott Dale, *Many Mansions: The Growth of Religion in Bolton, 1750–1850* (Bolton: P. N. Dale, 1985), 56.

7. Andrew Pettegree, *Emden and the Dutch Revolt: Exile and the Development of Reformed Protestantism* (Oxford University Press, 1992). A case is made for the impact of the Marian exiles in helping to determine the form of Protestantism that Emden would subsequently be instrumental in spreading to the Dutch homeland.

8. Grindal, *Remains*, 462.

9. Christopher Hibbert, *The Virgin Queen: The Personal History of Elizabeth I* (London: Viking, 1990), 209, citing Henry III's ambassador to Elizabeth on Mary's "privilege common to all kings."

10. *Pilkington brothers in Durham diocese:*
Richard Pilkington of Rivington (1484?–1551) married Alicia Asshaw of Heath Charnock on 20 October 1505. They had five daughters: Katherine, Janet, Margaret and

two others, of whom one probably died young; and seven sons, of whom one (Charles) died young and without issue, and another (George) succeeded to the estate. The others—all except Francis members of St. John's College, Cambridge—were:

3. James (1519–76) Marian exile. Consecrated bishop of Durham, 2 March 1561; enthroned 10 April 1561; d. 23 January 1576.

4. Francis (d. 1597). James's steward. Later Leonard's factotum at Whitburn.

5. Leonard (1527?–99) Marian exile. Rector of Middleton-in-Teesdale, 1560–61. (Succeeded James as Reguis Professor of Divinity—resigned within a year—and as master of John's, resigned 1564). Rector of Whitburn, 1563; canon and prebend of Durham, 1567; joined Dean Whittingham of Durham in refusing Archbishop Sandys's visitation, 1578, excommunicated and in a few days absolved; Treasurer of Durham, 1592

6. John (1529?–1603) called "learned" by Ascham; deputy for Grindal as master of Pembroke College, Cambridge, also prebend of St. Paul's, 1559–62; chaplain to James and canon and prebend of Durham, 1561; archdeacon of Durham and rector of Easington, 1563–1603.

7. Laurence (d. 21 March 1583). Vicar of Norham, 1565; rector of Kniblesworth, 1572.

Lever brothers in Durham diocese:
John Lever of Little Lever died in 1540. He played an active part in helping to establish Bolton Grammar School, 1516–25. He and his wife, Elenor, daughter of Richard Heaton of Heaton, had two daughters, Jane and Helene (their youngest children), and a number of sons, of whom six survived to maturity. Of these, it is known that Roger (the third) had three sons and Gilbert (the fourth) four sons. A little more is known of John and Elenor's eldest son, Richard. He married Catherine, daughter of Robert Bolton of Little Bolton. They had five daughters and three sons. Of these, the second son, Thomas Lever junior (nephew to the famous preacher) married Jenett, sixth child of Thomas Longworth of Longworth. Jenett's brother (their parents' third child) was Richard Longworth (1533–77), Elizabethan master of St. John's College, Cambridge. Heth, daughter of Thomas Lever junior and his wife, Jenett, married Nicholas Andrews of London, who bought Little Lever manor, 1624. Their son, John, married Jane, daughter of Robert Lever senior, of Darcy Lever. Robert Lever junior (second son to Robert senior) was a London merchant and a bachelor. In 1620 he inherited some of the Pilkington lands at Rivington purchased by his father in 1612. By his will of 1641, Robert junior refounded Bolton Grammar School.

The three remaining sons of John Lever of Little Lever and his wife, Elenor, were all clergymen:

Thomas (1521–77). Preacher to Edward VI; master of St. John's College, Cambridge, 1551; led pioneering colony to Aarau, Switzerland, during the reign of Mary; Elizabethan archdeacon of Coventry; canon and prebend of Durham, 1564; deprived in favor of Richard Longworth, 1567; master of Sherburn Hospital, Durham, 1563–77. He married a widow with three children, 1559. The couple had a daughter in 1560. In 1567 this Thomas Lever is listed as having two sons.
Ralph (d. 1585). Marian exile; tutor-reader to the Devereux family, from 1563; chaplain sacellanus (i.e., secretary) to Bishop James Pilkington; rector of Washington, 1565 (resigned, 1577); archdeacon of Northumberland and rector of Howick,

1566 (resigned both, 1573); canon and prebend of Durham, 1567; rector of Stanhope, 1575; exercized episcopal jurisdiction in Durham, 1576–77; master of Sherburn Hospital, 1577; D.D., 1578; completed incorporation of Sherburn, 1585.
John. Marian exile. Founder-headmaster of Tonbridge Grammar School, 1559–74; rector of Washington, 1577.
Note: Among alumni of Tonbridge may be mentioned the novelist E. M. Forster (1879–1970).

Sources: R. G. Pilkington, *Harland's History and Pedigrees of the Pilkingtons*, 4th. ed. (Dublin, 1906); Gladys Hinde, ed., *The Registers of Cuthbert Tunstall and James Pilkington, Bishops of Durham* (Durham and London: Surtees Society, 1952); F. R. Raines, ed., *The Visitation of the County Palatine of Lancaster, made in the year 1567* (Manchester: Chetham Society, 1870).

11. Pilkington, *Works*, 663–72; J. Whitaker, *The Statutes and Charter of Rivington School* (London, 1837); M. M. Kay, *The History of Rivington and Blackrod Grammar School* (Manchester University Press, 1966); Brown, *Bolton School*, 25–26. William Orrell, John Bradshaw, Ralph Ashton, Esquires, and Richard Lever and George Longworth, gentlemen, were trustees of Bolton Grammar School in 1584. They claimed there were "six score scholars, many of them very poor." Blackrod Grammar School was founded by will of John Holme, dated 18 September 1568. Among its emoluments was a £5 exhibition to Pembroke College, Cambridge. Early trustees included Alexander Rigby of Arley, Edward Norris of Blackrod, Roger Bradshaigh of Haigh, John Brown of Westhoughton, Christopher Anderton of Lostock, William Anderton of Anderton, William Brown, and Peter Longworth.

12. Hibbert, *Virgin Queen*, 175.
13. *Zurich Letters*, 1st series, 260. Pilkington, *Works*, ix–x.
14. Sophocles, *Oedipus Tyrannus*, ll. 49–57. Present author's translation.
15. *Zurich Letters*, 1st series, 218, 222.
16. Pilkington, *Works*, 379, 450, 405, 38.

CHAPTER 18. STABILITY

1. Stanley Sadie, ed., *The New Grove Dictionary of Music and Musicians* (London: Macmillan, 1980), 14. 122–23.
2. Otto Clemen, ed., *Luthers Werke* (Berlin: de Gruyter, 1966), 3.101.
3. Plato, *Phaedrus* 247.c; *Symposium*, 201–12. Lever, "Preface," in Bradford, *Writings*, 1.568: "embracing and using the goodness of God in every thing, so as may allure, move and draw thee most comfortably towards the fulness, pureness, and perfection of all things in God himself." Cf. Pilkington, *Works*, 642.
4. Pilkington, *Works*, 213, 317.
5. Pilkington, *Works*, 355.
6. Porter, *Reformation*, 288–313. Cf. Pilkington, *Works*, ii, 168, 445: God has chosen to save those who will "put their good wills" to well-doing; and foreknows who they will be; but does not create individuals for certain salvation or damnation.
7. Horace, *De Arte Poetica*, 224: *Spectator functusque sacris et potus et exlex* ("the spectator and celebrant of sacred things drunk and disorderly"). Pilkington, *Works*, 673–78, 682.
8. *Zurich Letters*, 1st series, 321 (English), 189 (Latin). Pearson, *Thomas Cartwright*, 158–59, cites an example of Horne aiding and abetting Guernsey Presbyterians, within his diocese, in their efforts to exert the discipline (1575–76).

9. Hinde, *Registers,* xxxiv–v. In the Middle Ages, women were allowed into the "Galilee" Chapel, as it is called, placed west of the main door, and might only venture a few yards into the main building, to a line of grey marble that is still to be seen set into the pavement. Contrary to the normal arrangement, this west chapel held the Lady Altar, but also served as the bishop's consistory court.

10. Fuller narratives may be read in R. G. Pilkington, *Pedigrees* and Bennett, *Bosworth.* The original manor of Pilkington was on the Irwell, just north of Manchester. Members of this family fought at Hastings and as crusaders and were implicated in the murder of Piers Gaveston, favorite of Edward II. They, and the Yorkshire branch were very prominent under Richard III. Sir Thomas Pilkington of Pilkington died 16 June 1487, at the Battle of Stoke, fighting for Lambert Simnel. Two of his six granddaughters, the residual heiresses of the estates of the Verdon barony, married Bolton merchants. The Rivington branch emerged during the thirteenth century on lands acquired by marriages with de Rivingtons and de Andertons.

11. Garrett, *The Marian Exiles,* 251. Collinson, *Elizabethan,* 72. Strype, *Annals,* 1.1.263.

12. F. L. Cross, *Dictionary of the Christian Church,* 1349.

13. Hibbert, *Virgin Queen,* 77, 212–13.

14. Pilkington, *Works,* 589.

15. Pilkington, *Works,* 381.

16. Pilkington, *Works,* 489. Pilkington preached at Paul's Cross, 8 June 1561, on the burning by lightning of St. Paul's steeple. The sermon was never printed, but Morwen printed *Addicion* (i.e., a refutation) to which Pilkington replied in his *Confutacion* (1563).

17. Foxe, *Actes and Monuments,* 1966–68. Pilkington, *Works,* 574, 656–57. Pilkington's references to Paul III (1468–1549) are almost maliciously bland. Born Alessandro Farnese, this pope promoted colloquy with the emperor, and with German Protestants, and made moderate statements about marriage, as Pilkington says. But he also denounced Henry VIII, and restored the Inquisition. His private life was scandalous. *See* F. L. Cross, *Dictionary of the Christian Church,* 1032.

18. Porter, *Reformation,* 105, 109–10. Pevsner, *Cambridgeshire,* 122. Lever, and again Pilkington, removed altars at John's. Lever took down the rood, which was put up again under Mary, at a cost of 2d.

19. Pearson, *Thomas Cartwright,* 8–9.

20. Pevsner, *Durham,* 168.

21. *Registers,* xxvii–xxx.

22. Parker, *Correspondence,* 146; Grindal, *Remains,* 327; Pilkington, *Works,* 586.

CHAPTER 19. RESTRAINT

1. Pevsner, *Lancashire: The Rural North* (Harmondsworth: Penguin Books, 1979), 209.

2. D. M. Palliser, *The Age of Elizabeth: England under the Later Tudors, 1547–1603* (London: Longman, 1983), 268.

3. Pilkington, *Works,* 497. Clay, *Liturgical Services,* xii. Parker, *Correspondence,* 237, 292–93.

4. Collinson, *Elizabethan,* 474.

5. John Bossy, *The English Catholic Community, 1570–1850* (London: Darton, Longman & Todd, 1975), 90–91. Quakers, rather than Roman Catholics, reaped the "benefits of Anglican incapacity in the northern uplands." Pilkington's stress on the

uses of silence, and his dislike of dogmatic brittleness of any kind, might be said to make him one of the natural fathers of Quakerism.

6. Pilkington, *Works*, 331, 361.

7. *Original Letters*, 135.

8. Pilkington, *Works*, 562, 579.

9. Foxe, *Actes and Monuments*, 1495: Saunders refuses to change his "uncorrupt religion . . . though an angel out of heaven should preach *another* gospel." Cf. John Bradford to George Heaton, 8 February 1555: "if an angel should come from heaven, and preach *otherwise*, the same were accursed" (Bradford, *Writings*, 2.188–89). The reference is to Galatians, 1.8: "if we or an angel from heaven preach a gospel to you *beyond* (παρά) what we have preached to you, let it be anathema" (my translation and italics). Pilkington's point is far from trivial. Typically, he presses towards reconciliation by insisting on the most scrupulous reading of the context. Paul is arguing against the claims of rival preachers that all Christians, including those born outside the Jewish community, must take on the *additional* burden of the whole Jewish Law.

10. Pilkington, *Works*, 326, 523. "Ockham's razor" is a philosophic term having reference to the English nominalist philosopher William of Ockham (c. 1300–c. 1349), one of whose main principles it was to resist the multiplication of entities without necessity. Denying the separate existence of universals, he held it impossible to prove either the existence or the attributes of God. Pilkington, along with other Protestants of his generation, shows the influence of Ockham's contempt for any pretence of certain or elaborate knowledge of spiritual or philosophic matters.

11. Pilkington, *Works*, 588.

12. Hibbert, *Virgin Queen*, 94. Pilkington, *Works*, 120, 146, 252, 540, 564. Pilkington got under Elizabeth's skin again by assigning large doweries to his two surviving children, Deborah and Ruth.

Chapter 20. Measure

1. Pevsner, *Durham*, 166.

2. William Shakespeare, *The Tempest*, 4.1.148–50. Cf. Thomas Lever, *Treatise*, chapter 5.

3. Pilkington, *Works*, 546. See F. L. Cross, *Dictionary of the Christian Church*, 544: "Gelasius of Cyzicus (fl. A.D. 475) . . . wrote a 'Syntagma,' or collection of the *Acta* of the Nicene Council (A.D. 325) [that] . . . made use of good sources . . . but . . . has little, if any, independent historical value."

4. Pevsner, *Durham*, 198. Dean Hunt's "altar" dates from c. 1626.

5. Pilkington, *Works*, 53, 546.

6. Nicholas Tyacke, *Anti-Calvinists: The Rise of English Arminianism, c. 1590–1640* (Oxford University Press, 1990), 214.

7. Charles Carlton, *Archbishop William Laud* (London: Routledge & Kegan Paul, 1987), 117.

8. Luke 6.36–38.

9. Plato, *Phaedo* 60–61, 69. Dante, *Inferno* 1.31–39. Pilkington, *Works*, 92.

10. Pilkington, *Works*, 57. *See also* pp. 50, 230, 366–67.

11. Pilkington, *Works*, 50. Luke 4.23.

12. Collinson, *Elizabethan*, 169.

13. Hibbert, *Virgin Queen*, 133.

14. Sandys, *Sermons*, 144. Pilkington, *Works*, 670. Both prayers are very revealing of their authors.

15. Luke 1.46–55.

16. Euripides, *Bacchae*, ed. E. R. Dodds (Oxford University Press, 1960), lv, 14 (line 289).

17. Luke 2.16–18: καὶ ἀνεῦραν τὸ βρέφος ἰδόντες δὲ ἐγνώρισαν καὶ πάντες οἱ ἀκούσαντες ἐθαύμασαν.

18. Pilkington, *Works*, 445, 456. See J.-P. Guépin, *The Tragic Paradox: Myth and Ritual in Greek Tragedy* (Amsterdam: Hakkert, 1968), xi: "In its most extreme form Dionysiac sacrifice consisted of the mothers tearing apart their own babies, who represented the god, and eating them raw."

19. John K. Walton, *Lancashire: A Social History, 1558–1939* (Manchester University Press, 1987), 13.

20. R. G. Pilkington, *Pedigrees*, 12–13; Johnstone, *Religious History*, 363; Bernard Burke, *A Genealogical History of the Dormant . . . and Extinct Peerages* (London, 1883; reprint Baltimore Genealogical Publishing, 1978), 278–80. Gossip possibly known to James Pilkington: Robert Holland, a poor knight of Breightmet, favorite of Edward II, baron 1314, beheaded after betraying Thomas, earl of Lancaster. His second son, Thomas, commanded the van at Crécy (1346) and married Joane, heiress of Edmund, earl of Kent, thus acquiring that title. After his death, Joane married the Black Prince. Their son Richard II (king 1377–99) was thus half-brother to Thomas Holland junior, earl of Kent, and John Holland, earl of Huntingdon (1387) and duke of Exeter (1397). Thomas was beheaded by Henry IV for treason and John by "the common people" for his extravagance and crime. In 1393 Robert Pilkington of Pilkington served as seneschal to Lord Halton, in the retinue of John Holland. Constance Holland, Mrs. Oscar Wilde, was of this lineage.

21. Pilkington, *Works*, 125. The first two lines are attributed to Richard Rolle de Hampole, 1290–1349, and were quoted by John Ball in his famous sermon at Blackheath in the Wat Tyler Rebellion of 1381. A Gilbert Pilkington (who flourished about 1350) was the copyist/author of *The Tournament of Tottenham*, a burlesque in verse on the "parade and fopperies of chivalry." Thomas Holland senior became Knight of the Garter in 1353. See Gilbert Pilkington, *The Tournament of Tottenham . . . Taken out of an ancient MS, and published by W. Bedwell* (London: J. Norton, 1631). Along with other armigerous Puritans, the Pilkingtons of Rivington did not present themselves for accreditation by Norroy in his Lancashire visitation of 1567 (Raines, *Visitation*, iii). However, in 1561 James Pilkington had an addition made to his personal arms (a cross patance voided gules, a crescent gules on dexter chief) as follows: on a chief vert three suns or. The crest, inherited from his father—on a helmet, a mower with his scythe, proper—was replaced by a bishop robed, in the act of preaching (R. G. Pilkington, *Pedigrees*, 93).

22. Pilkington, *Works*, 354, 378.

23. Pilkington, *Works*, ii, 100–1. M. D. Smith, *Rivington*, 63. Kay, *Rivington Grammar School*, 102, 123.

Chapter 21. Entourage

1. Solomon Partington, *Winter Hill Right of Way*, five pamphlets (Bolton: Tillotson and Sons, 1899 [1–3]; Bolton: Robert Lee, 1900 [4]; Bolton: William Robinson, 1901 [5]). Other pamphlets by Partington, socialist and cooperator, include *George Marsh, the Bolton Protestant Martyr* (Liverpool, 1898).

2. "Discovering Bolton," in *Metropolitan Bolton Guide* (Bolton: Metropolitan Council, 1980), 16.

3. A. L. F. Rivet and Colin Smith, *The Place Names of Roman Britain* (New Jersey: Princeton University Press, 1970), 310.

4. Boardman, *Deane*, 1. *See also* Whittaker, *History of Manchester* (1773), 1. 159.

5. The following is a useful map with commentary: James Graham-Campbell, *Saxon and Viking Britain*, London: Council for British Archaeology, 1978.

6. The "Marsh" letter exonerating "Leiver, Pilkinton" by name is surely spurious. It first appears in John Foxe, *Actes and Monuments newly enlarged* (London: J. Day, 1570), 1572. Cobbling phrases from genuine letters, to the detriment of rhythm and sense, it allots Marsh a place among a martyr-elect, with second-class redemption by association for his coreligionists, who are warned off martyrdom: a parody of the pattern in Bradshaw as between the "elect" Werburgh and her humble faithful. Nothing else in Marsh supports such an attitude. While none must court martyrdom, none must evade it, if called, according to another letter (Miles Coverdale, *The Letters of the Martyrs*, ed. E Bickersteth (London, 1837), 522): "Wherefore, my dear brethren . . . jeopard ye your lives, if need shall so require." Marsh's brother-in-law Jeffrey Hurst insisted on doing so.

7. Franklin Baker, *The Life and Times of Rev. James Woods, Commonly Called "General Woods": A Discourse Commemorative of the Centenary of his Death* (Bolton: Robert Kenyon, 1859). The Andertons of Lostock took the Jacobite side.

8. Joshua Dobson, *Religious Gratitude Explained: and religious and civil liberty, reformed Christianity and loyalty to the present government recommended: in two sermons with a large appendix* (London, 1747). Dobson was Presbyterian minister at Cockey Moor (locally believed to derive its name from the Roman Coccium). A battery of sources is marshaled to argue that a Roman Catholic monarchy is irrational, unscriptural and un-British, because "where the true Fundamentals of Government are understood . . . the Imperial, or Regal Power is Authority in Trust, to be managed for the Good of the Community" (p. 29).

9. Robert Walmsley, *Peterloo: The Case Reopened* (Manchester University Press, 1969).

10. R. G. Pilkington, *Pedigrees*, 88.

11. Brown, *Bolton School*, 12, 27–28; Pevsner, *Lancashire: The Rural North*, 210; Partington, *Winter Hill*, 7.

12. Boardman, *Deane*, illustration opposite p. 632. "This James died in 1870, at the early age of thirty-seven much lamented, and descendants of his are still found residing in Deane (p. 634)."

13. Philip Sidney, cupbearer to Elizabeth, 1578 and joint master of ordnance (with Ambrose Dudley), 1585. Robert Devereux reappeared at court, 1584; "general of the horse" in Leicester's expedition in aid of the states general, August 1585.

14. E.g., "Does not some chronicle tell, that Joseph of Arimethea came hither and preached here?" (Pilkington, *Works*, 511). "The rude Saxon overran this realm, and destroyed all learning and religion, with help of the Pope and his creatures" (pp. 584–5). "Let us amend, or we shall be given up to the Spaniards, Scots, Flemings, or Frenchmen, as we were then to the Saxons" (p. 189).

15. Pilkington, *Works*, 283, 285, 461–62.

CHAPTER 22. REINTERPRETATION

1. Pilkington, *Works*, 454.

2. Grammar School at Farnworth near Widnes, on the Mersey (not to be con-

fused with Farnworth, the Bolton township), founded by William Smyth of Prescot, protégé of the Lady Margaret Beaufort, Bishop of Lincoln, 1496, chancellor of Oxford 1500–3, cofounder of Brasenose, Oxford, 1509.

3. Tyacke, *Anti-Calvinists*, 114–15.

4. Pilkington, *Works*, 42. Confession: pp. 131–32 (both from *Haggai*). Slaves to superstition versus true children of belief: p. 335 (*Nehemiah*).

5. Pilkington, *Works*, 98. Cf. ibid., p. 308 (*Nehemiah*): "Take in good part, O Lord, our simple good will: that that wanteth in us . . . thy Son . . . hath fulfilled for us." Reciprocal goodwill between God and man is the basis of well-being for Pilkington. His paraphrase of Nehemiah's prayer (pp. 299–300)—"O Lord, correct us after thine own good will. . . . Our judges, rulers, and lawyers, have sought their own gain more than justice to their people"—involves notions of social justice entirely contradicted by the proposition of Whitaker that was the basis of the Lambeth Articles, since that postulated a god incompatible with any conceivable notion of good will; one who "from eternity has predestined some men to life, and reprobated some to death." Delighted, Whitgift found this "agreeable to the Articles of Religion established by authority". (Porter, *Reformation*, 365).

6. Pilkington, *Works*, 523.

7. Porter, *Reformation*, 164

8. *Sermons or Homilies, Appointed to be Read in Churches in the Time of Queen Elizabeth* (London: Prayer-Book and Homily Society, 1817), 292. Phrases almost identical to some in *Haggai* (Pilkington, *Works*, 55–56) occur on pp. 286–7: "he that ruffleth in his sables, in his fine furred gown, corked slippers, trim buskins, and warm mittens, is more ready to chill for cold, than the poor labouring man, which can abide in the field all the day long, when the north wind blows, with a few beggarly clouts about him." Universal foppery requires "one gown for the day, another for the night; one long, another short; one for winter, another for summer; one through furred, another but faced; one for the working day, another for the holy-day; one of this colour, another of that colour; one of cloth, another of silk or damask. We must have change of apparel, one afore dinner, and another after; one of the Spanish fashion, another Turkey: and to be brief, never content with sufficient." Foreigners despair of our absurdity: "a certain man, that would picture every countryman in his accustomed apparel, when he had painted other nations, he pictured the Englishman all naked, and gave him cloth under his arm, and bade him make it himself as he thought best; for he changed his fashion so often, that he knew not how to make it." The Homily notably reduces the approving references to the laborer in the *Haggai* passage and (almost inevitably) omits the latter's approbation of the beggar, "healthful, strong," and blessed by God because more content with poverty and hardship than the rich are with excess.

9. Pilkington, *Works*, 172.

10. *Sermons or Homilies*, 22, 561. Pilkington (p. 172) denies the term "christian" to the Romish use of "conjuring" at baptism (which for him does not, however, invalidate the baptism), but that is a very different matter from publicly denying the term to hundreds of unnamed victims of the monarchy. Pilkington's unfinished *Nehemiah* was published with "A Preface of M. John Fox, to the Christian Reader."

11. Pilkington, *Works*, 420: "Those bloody marriages in France of late."

12. Porter, *Reformation*, 315, 320–21.

13. For example, B. C., *Puritanisme the mother, Sinn the daughter . . . wherein is demonstrated that the fayth of the Puritans doth forcibly induce . . . the perpetrating of sinne, etc.* (Birchley Hall secret press? 1633).

14. Porter, *Reformation*, 349–50.

15. Robert Some, "A Godly Treatise against the Foul and Gross Sin of Oppression," in Pilkington, *Works*, 475.

16. Pilkington, *Works*, 464.

17. Pilkington, *Works*, 414.

18. Plato, *Laws* 906, in *The Dialogues of Plato*, trans. B. Jowett (Oxford University Press, 1875), 477: "there is . . . an immortal conflict going on among us, which requires marvellous watchfulness. . . . Injustice and insolence and folly are the destruction of us, and justice and temperance and wisdom are the salvation of us."

19. Richard Bancroft (1544–1610), archbishop of Canterbury, son of the small Lancashire gentleman John Bancroft and Mary Bancroft née Curwen, niece of Hugh Curwen, bishop of Oxford. "At the Hampton Court conference (January 1604) . . . when . . . a well-sustained proposal was made for a new translation of the Bible, Bancroft petulantly observed that 'if every man's humour should be followed, there would be no end of translating.' See J. B. Mullinger, "Thomas Bancroft," in *The Dictionary of National Biography*, ed. Leslie Stephen and Sidney Lee (Oxford University Press, 1917), 1.1030.

20. Pilkington, *Works*, 426, 441–42.

21. Pilkington, *Works*, 433, 436.

22. Martini Lutheri *De Servo Arbitrio* (1525), in reply to Desiderii Erasmi *De Libero Arbitrio* (1524), in *Luthers Werke*, 3.129: "captivus, subiectus, et servus est, vel voluntatis Dei vel voluntatis Satanae." Pilkington's position seems closer to Melanchthon's notion of *causa concurrens*—"God draws, but draws him who is willing." See Clyde L. Manschreck, ed. and trans., *Melanchthon on Christian Doctrine Loci Communes 1555* (New York: Oxford University Press, 1965), xiii.

23. Hinde, *Registers*, xix. Pilkington apparently ordained "deacons" and "ministers" (not "priests"). Records are "haphazard"; about 47 "ministers" can be traced. He regarded the term "bishop" as "a name of office . . . rather than of dignity," yet the office was by "tradition of the apostles" (Pilkington, *Works*, 494, 605).

24. Pilkington, *Works*, xii–xiii.

25. George Ormerod, *The History of the County Palatine and City of Chester* (London, 1882). The current Bishop's throne is Victorian, the Henrician *bricolage* having been regrouped by Blomfield to form part of a "restored" shrine in the Lady Chapel.

26. Pilkington, *Works*, 251: "The Scots invading England . . . played at dice for all the . . . great cities" (a memory of Flodden, in which Boltonians were among the Stanley forces); pp. 380–81: "But I fear me, that if, after the order of this discipline which is so greedily sought . . . their consistory of seniors were set in their seats with their pastor in every church . . . they should find many proud peacocks, that would not bend their necks under the yoke of such simple silly woodcocks."

27. Pilkington, *Works*, 452–53. Ashton, *Civil War*, 286.

CHAPTER 23. JAMES ANDERTON: CLAIMING EQUITY FOR THE VISIBLE CHURCH

1. Anderton family details in William Farrer and J. Brownbill, eds., *The Victoria County History of England: Lancashire*, 5.295–99 (London: Constable & Co., 1911, reprint Dawson Publishing, Kent, for the University of London, 1991) (hereafter *VCH: Lancashire*); A. F. Allison, "Who was John Brereley? The Identity of a seventeenth-century Controversialist," *Recusant History*, 16 (1982–83), 17–41.

JAMES ANDERTON (1557–1613), who wrote under the pseudonym "John Brereley Priest," was eldest son of Christopher Anderton I, a comparatively self-made lawyer whose ancestry is uncertain, and a lady who was an Anderton of Anderton. Christopher I bought Lostock in 1562 and acquired many other properties, both locally and also at Clitheroe and in Essex. James extended the estates after inheriting in 1592. He was never officially cited for recusancy. Dying childless, he bequeathed money for the support of priests. He was succeeded by Christopher II, his younger brother, who died in 1619. The heir was this man's son, Christopher III. In 1615 two-thirds of the estates were sequestered for recusancy. Christopher III was forced to surrender the remainder to Parliament and had not regained them at his death in 1650. His heir Francis conformed, regained the estates, and was created a baronet (in 1677). He died the following year at Paris and was buried in the chapel of the English Benedictines. His son, Sir Charles, remained in possession and was buried, as lay rector, under the communion table of Bolton Parish Church, but without memorial. Finally, his heir Francis was dispossessed for participation in the Jacobite Rebellion of 1715.

2. ROGER ANDERTON, fourth son of Christopher I. When James Anderton died in 1613, Lostock was raided by officials of the bishop of Chester. Birchley (over the border in the more "Catholic" West Derby hundred, though still in Chester Diocese) was now held by Roger Anderton from Christopher II and became a recusant printing and propaganda center. Roger died in 1640. His son, James Anderton II, of Gray's Inn, officered Cavalier troops against Bolton during the Civil War. He died in 1673.

3. Caroline Hibbard, "The Contribution of 1639: Court and Country Catholicism," *Recusant History,"* 16 (1982–83), 42–60.

4. VCH: *Lancashire,* 5.298 and illustration. The shiplike effect was originally enhanced by an octagonal turret with weather vanes. The house (demolished in 1816) had an overhanging, half-timbered, upper floor with gables, and a stone lower part.

5. James I to his first English Parliament, 19 March 1604, in J. R. Tanner, *Constitutional Documents of the Reign of James I* (Cambridge University Press, 1930), 24–30.

6. LAWRENCE ANDERTON, baptised at Chorley, Lancashire, 12 August 1575; died in Lancashire 1643. Educated Blackburn Grammar School, Christ's College, Cambridge and the English College, Seville. Worked in England as a Jesuit from 1604. Superior of the Lancashire District, 1621. A leading figure in Jesuit London headquarters from 1627. His father, Thomas Anderton, was a younger brother of Christopher I and held the manor of Horwich, in Deane parish, from James Anderton I, from 1593.

7. [Lawrence Anderton], "The Epistle Dedicatorie to M. Doctour Morton," *The Progenie of Catholikes and Protestants* (Rouen, Widow of N. Conrant, 1633). The phrase quoted is in the final paragraph of the epistle, over the pseudonymous initials "N. N."

8. James Anderton [John Brereley Priest, pseud.], "The Conclusion to the Judges and Counsell of England," *The Protestants Apologie for the Roman Church* (S. Omer, English College Press, 1608), 715: "Priority of Possession receiving also this favour in our Law, that to the party disseysed of such his possession, you afford special remedy by writ of Assyse." Compare with "Wee do most humbly now hereupon appeale to your Majesty concerning the equity of this our present Apologie" (p. 639).

9. J. Anderton, *Protestants Apologie,* title page and p. 675.

10. Ibid., title page.

11. [James Anderton], *Sainct Austines Religion* ([Birchley Hall Press?] 1620), 339.

12. J. Anderton, "Preface to the Reader," in *Protestants Apologie,* vi, notes that he is reclaiming from the Calvinist "M. Whitaker" (Dr. William Whitaker, master of St. John's College, Cambridge, who died 1595) this method of "argument, [which

is] taken from confession of the adversary." Thomas Whitaker, who taught school at Burnley (about 20 miles northeast of Lostock) till his death in 1626, was the master's relative, perhaps his son (see Porter, Reformation, 201).

13. J. Anderton, Protestants Apologie, 699. [J. Anderton], Sainct Austines Religion, 47.

14. J. Anderton, Protestants Apologie, 662, 665. By contrast the anarchic "Calvinists of Embden" reduce their Lutheran magistrate to worship in his own house (p. 652). Taking possession of Heaton Hall in 1593, Anderton clearly saw himself as rescuing it for loyalty as well as for the Mass from a family tainted by connections with Emden.

15. J. Anderton, Protestants Apologie, 668, 675.

CHAPTER 24. "THE MARKS OF THE TRUE CHURCH"

1. Brown, Bolton School, 28–29.

2. J. Anderton, Protestants Apologie, 656.

3. Gilbert Gerard of Ince, Lancashire, died in 1593. Treasurer of Gray's Inn (with Nicholas Bacon), 1556. M.P. for Wigan, 1553 and 1555. Attorney-general, 22 January 1558–59; master of the rolls, 1581. M.P. for Lancaster, 1584. His wife was Anne Ratcliffe of Walmsley (Longworth township, about 4½ miles northeast of Lostock Hall). Their daughter Katharine (d. 1617) married Richard Hoghton, sheriff of County of Lancaster and M.P. for Lancaster, 1599; baronet, 1611. He entertained King James at Hoghton, 1617; died in 1630. James Anderton, as a duchy of Lancaster official, would have a duty to wait on King James during his triumphant sojourn at York, the ancient northern capital, in 1603. The epistle to the king that prefaces Sainct Austines Religion describes how the King's "ever honoured memory with me remaineth . . . enfolded within the purest findon of my loyal heart," which suggests some personal contact.

4. J. Anderton, Sainct Austines Religion, 15.

5. VCH: Lancashire, 4.85 (Birchley, a former Heaton property); 5.8 (Horwich); 5.11 (Heaton manor: James Anderton buys out the last Heaton claimant, Richard Heaton of Westmeath, Ireland, 1593; of Christopher Anderton I it is stated that in 1572 "the mortgage money was offered to him by the Heatons just after the expiry of the term, and, to the great scandal of the neighbours, he refused it and kept the manor").

6. Brown, Bolton School, 23, 27–28.

7. J. Anderton, Protestants Apologie, 3, 539, 581, 676; Sainct Austines Religion, 60.

8. James Anderton [John Brereley Priest, pseud.], The Lyturgie of the Masse ([Birchley Hall Press?] 1620), 163–64; James Anderton, Protestants Apologie, 6. Compare with Thomas Lever, "Preface" to The Meditations of Bradford (1567) reprinted in John Bradford, Writings (Cambridge University Press, 1848), 1.565–71.

9. J. Anderton, Protestants Apologie (1608), vii; preliminary address "To the Right Honorable Lords and other the Knights and Burgesses, Assembled in the High and most Honorable Court of Parliament," in The Apologie of the Romane Church, devided into three severall tractes ([unidentified English secret press] 1604).

10. J. Anderton, Protestants Apologie, xxxix–xl, xlvii, li–lii, lv.

11. J. Anderton, Protestants Apologie, xi, xlvii. Anderton equates papal claims to depose monarchs with the "error . . . our Church of old condemned for hereticall in Wyckcliffe."

12. J. Anderton, *Protestants Apologie*, xlvii, lii. *See also* "Advertisement to the Reader": "I must needs acknowledge, that a good part of this labour was the collec-tions of a Worshipful and reverend Priest, gathered together some few years before he entered into holy Orders." Clearly, behind the symbolic soubriquet "John Brereley Priest" a personal influence is commemorated. The surname remained a characteristic local one. (The 1843 *Bolton Directory* lists five Brierleys—a dressmaker, a shopkeeper, an auctioneer, and two furniture brokers—and two Andertons: a surgeon and a schoolmaster.)

CHAPTER 25. "LOYAL, AND DUTIFUL"

1. *An Act for the better discovering and repressing of Popish Recusants* (1606), reprinted in Tanner, *Constitutional Documents,* 86–94. *An Act for administering the Oath of Allegiance* (1610), reprinted ibid., 105–9.
2. J. Anderton, *Protestants Apologie,* lv.
3. Père Coton, *Lettre Déclaratoire à la Reine mère* (Paris, 1610), 7 ff., quoted and discussed by Thomas Clancy, S.J., in "English Catholics and the Papal Deposing Power," part 2, *Recusant History,* 6 (1961–62, reprint 1966), 217–18: "An English version . . . was included in Thomas Owen's *A Letter of a Catholike Man* of the same year." Compare with J. Anderton, *Protestants Apologie,* li, lv–vi. Clancy mentions among Catholic priests supportive of the Stuart regime "the Benedictine Thomas Preston (who wrote under the alias of Roger Widdrington)" in "English Catholics and the Papal Deposing Power," part 3, *Recusant History,* 7 (1963–64, reprint 1966), 4. Christopher Anderton III was married to Agnes, daughter of John Preston, by 1619. Neither was yet twelve. See *VCH: Lancashire,* 5.297. Clancy's reference ("En-glish Catholics," part 2, 208) to Anderton's "half-hearted attempts to edulcorate the deposing power" of the papacy is relevant only to his sense that it was *comparatively* less dangerous in practice than Anabaptist theocracies.
4. J. Anderton, *Lyturgie of the Masse,* ii. Compare with *Summa Theologica* 3 83.1.
5. J. Anderton, *Protestants Apologie,* xlviii, liv. Compare with Luke 23.2 where Christ is arrested for apparently "forbidding to give tribute to Caesar."
6. J. Anderton, *Protestants Apologie,* xlii.
7. Ibid., xxviii.
8. James Anderton [I.B.P., pseud.], *The Reformed Protestant, Tending Directly to Atheisme and all Impietie* (Printed at Colen [*sic*], 1621), 31, 66, 81ff. "Colen" is maybe a piece of jocular mystification by Roger Anderton for "Cologne" (in Catholic Germany) or "Colne" (in the Catholic west Pennines) or, in any case, "Colonia," a "Colony of the Roman allegiance." Roger's Birchley Hall, which housed the secret press, might well be called a "colony" of the Anderton headquarters, Lostock Hall.

CHAPTER 26. "ANTIQUITY AND CONTINUANCE"

1. J. Anderton, *Sainct Austines Religion,* 4.
2. G. M. Hopkins was at Leigh in 1879 for the centenary of its Catholic chapel, opened immediately after the first Catholic Relief Act. Earlier priests of Leigh in-cluded Fr. Ambrose Barlow, executed at Lancaster, 1641. For local collieries, *see* Crompton's dedication to his *Saint Austins Religion* (edition of 1624), "To all Seduced Papistes [who] neither know what they do, or should believe: much like the colliar, that told the devil, he beleeved as the Romane Church did." Compare with G. M.

Hopkins, Advent Sermon, Bedford Leigh, 30 November 1879, in *Sermons and Devotional Writings*, ed. C. Devlin, S.J. (Oxford University Press, 1959), 39: "you . . . that work in the pit go where all is darker than night." Bolton's merchants, pursuing markets for cheap cloth goods, forged early links with Lutheran Germany. Prominent in this line of business were the Isherwoods, from whom the novelist Christopher Isherwood was descended.

3. William Crompton (1599?–1642), son of Richard Crompton, counsellor-at-law. Educated Leigh Grammar School and Brasenose College, Oxford. Works include *Saint Austins Religion. Wherein is Manifestly proved out of the Works of that Learned Father, that he dissented from Popery* (London: A.M[athewes,] 1624); *Saint Austins Religion . . . Whereunto is newly added, Saint Austins Summes, in Answer to Mr. Iohn Brereley, Priest* (London: John Marriott, 1625) [Dedication to George, duke of Buckingham]; *A Wedding Ring Fitted to the Finger of every Paire that have or shall meete in the Feare of God* (London: Eliz. Allde for Edward Blount, 1632).

William Crompton (1633–96), son of the above. Educated Merchant Taylors' School and Christ Church, Oxford. Ejected from the living of Collumpton, Devon, in 1662. Preached in conventicles.

4. *VCH: Lancashire*, 5.297.

5. J. Anderton, *Sainct Austines Religion*, 59. Compare with Crompton, *Saint Austins Religion* (1624), 71. King James died 24 March (the last day of 1624, old style).

6. Richard Pilkington (1568?–1631). Educated Rivington Grammar School and Emmanuel College, Cambridge. Archdeacon of Carlisle, 1597–1600, and of Leicester, 1625–31, besides other preferments. Works include *Parallela, or the grounds of the new Roman Catholic and of the ancient Christian Religion out of the holy Scriptures compared together* (London, 1618). Answered by Anthony Champney (1569?–1643?), *Mr. Pilkinton, his Parallela disparalled* (St. Omer, 1620), with a prefatory epistle to George Abbot (archbishop of Canterbury, who died in 1633), referring to Pilkington as "a minion of yours." Champney, like Anderton, was a Catholic controversialist who advocated secular loyalty to the Crown.

7. Thomas Morton (1564–1659). Educated at York and Halifax Grammar Schools and St. John's College, Cambridge. Distinguished himself by courageous acts of charity during plague at York, 1602. Bishop of Chester, 1615. Assisted King James to draw up a *Declaration of Sports* for Lancashire, 1617. Bishop of Coventry and Lichfield, 1618. Bishop of Durham, 1632. Fled from Durham in 1640 before the invading Scottish army. Works include *Apologia Catholica* (London, 1605–6); *A Catholike Appeale for Protestants* (G. Bishop & J. Norton, 1609); *Causa Regia . . . adversus R. Bellarmini tractatum* (London, 1620).

8. "Originated" in a special sense. The founding of the see of Canterbury by Pope Gregory provided for Protestants and Catholics alike the one unavoidable piece of evidence about early British Christianity. Its late date (A.D. 596) allowed Protestants to construct an earlier British Church, alternative to Rome; its primacy as a stable piece of evidence allowed Catholics to give it absolute teleological status, nullifying all British deviancies, including any that may have preceded it. *See* J. Anderton, *Protestants Apologie*, 57. Inconveniently for this latter view, a bishop of York was mentioned in the acts of the Conference of Arles, summoned by Constantine in A.D. 314. After centuries of controversy, the witty Pope Innocent VI (1352–62) recognized the inconsistency by dubbing the York prelate "Primate of England" but his brother of Canterbury "Primate of All England," titles their Protestant successors still hold.

9. J. Anderton, *Sainct Austines Religion*, 13.

10. Montague Rhodes James, *A Descriptive Catalogue of the MSS in the Library of*

Sidney Sussex College, Cambridge (Cambridge University Press, 1895), 74: *Epistolae quaedam Reverendi patris Roberti Grosthead quondam Lincoln. Episc. prout repertae sunt in libro imperfecto manuscripto in bibliotheca Dunelmensi: lviii. 1-50.* James comments, "I think it possible that the whole volume is written [i.e., copied] by John Pilkington."

11. Lawrence Anderton [A Catholike Priest of the Society of Jesus, pseud.], *The Nonentity of Protestancy or A Discourse, Wherein is demonstrated, that Protestancy is not any Reall thing, but is in it selfe a Platonicall Idaea; a want of all Positive Fayth; and a meere Nothing.* ([S. Omer, English College Press,] 1633).

12. Thomas Morton, "Preface to the Christian Reader," *Catholike Appeal,* B. Cf. ibid., 9 ("*Transubstantiation is . . . a non-ens* in the doctrine of *S.Gregorie*"); [Lawrence Anderton,] *The Progenie of Catholicks and Protestants* (Rouen: The Widow of Nicolas Courant, 1633), D.

13. J. Anderton, *Protestants Apologie,* 541–42, note d.

14. Pilkington, *Works,* 353.

CHAPTER 27. CIVIL WAR BOLTON: CLAIMING THE MARKS OF THE TRUE CHURCH

1. Conrad Russell, *The Causes of the English Civil War* (Oxford University Press, 1990), 26–57.

2. Brown, *Bolton School,* 35–45. John Amos Comenius (1592–1671), the Moravian educator, was in England in 1641–42. His advanced ideas, in favor with Puritan trustees, were blocked in practice because rent could not be raised from unsympathetic occupiers of school trust land.

3. Ernest Broxap, *The Great Civil War in Lancashire,* 2nd ed. (Manchester University Press, 1973), 38.

4. G. M. Ramsden, *A Responsible Society: Bank Street Chapel* (Bolton, Lancashire, 1985), 63. Among other applications, Bolton developed as a center of bleaching. See also Broxap, *The Great Civil War,* xiv–xv, on the chemical laboratories of Pilkington Bros., currently (1973) encroaching on the site of Lathom House.

5. M. Hardman, *Ruskin and Bradford* (Manchester University Press, 1986), 111.

6. *The Petition of divers His Majesties faithfull Subjects, of the true Protestant Religion, in the County Palatine of Lancaster . . . With His Majesties Answer, June 6, 1642* (London, Robert Barker [1642]).

7. Broxap, *The Great Civil War,* 43, 107, 147, 202–3. G. M. Trevelyan, *England under the Stuarts* (London, 1947), 191.

CHAPTER 28. "A LITTLE TICKET OF LEAD": PRESBYTERIAN DIVINES

1. Tilsley married Margaret Chetham, niece of the great Humphrey, in January 1643. Boardman, *Deane,* 2.544–64. John E. Bailey, *Rev. John Tilsley, M.A.* (*Leigh Chronicle* Printing Works, 1884). John Tilsley (1614–84), *A true copie of the Petition of Twelve thousand five hundred and upwards of Well-affected Gentlemen, Ministers, Free-holders and others of the County Palatine of Lancaster . . . Together with a Paraenetick to Lancashire . . . Together with the Answer of the Right Honourable the House of PEERES* (London: John Macock for Luke Fawn, 1646), 2, 8.

2. J. Horsfall Turner, ed., *The Rev. Oliver Heywood B.A., 1630–1702, His Autobiography, Diaries, Anecdote and Event Books,* 3 vols. (Brighouse: A. B. Bayes, 1882), I.28; Graham Pendlebury, *Aspects of the English Civil War in Bolton and its Neighbourhood* (Manchester: Neil Richardson, 1983); B. T. Barton, *Historical Gleanings of Bolton and District* (Bolton, 1881), 138.

3. The church of All Saints North Street, York, has fine (and rare) examples of fourteenth- and fifteenth-century glass.

4. Barton, *Historical Gleanings* (1881), 373. Accounts of Mr. Alexander Norres, 1 June 1658–25 June 1660. The "old school" was mended with "strawe woode nayles witeninge" and in 1660 rethatched by Roger Thornley for fourteen shillings. For the "new" stone school, a handsome chapel-like building of 1658, photographed (interior and exterior) before demolition in 1880, *see* W. E. Brown, *Bolton as it Was* (Nelson: Hendon Publishing, 1986), 7.

5. George Herbert, "The Church Porch," stanza 29.

6. I am preparing an account of Bolton Whitmanites from unpublished material in the Bolton Archive.

7. Ramsden, *A Responsible Society,* 12, 67. Ron Smith, *Duke's Alley Independent (Congregational) Chapel, Bolton* (Bolton and District Family History Society, 1987). Peter Northcott Dale, *Many Mansions: The Growth of Religion in Bolton, 1750–1850* (Bolton: Peter Northcott Dale, 1985), 16.

8. Henry Pendlebury, *A Plain Representation of Transubstantiation* (London: J. Johnson), 1687.

9. W. H. Auden, "In Memory of W.B. Yeats," 2.9.

10. Henry Pendlebury, *Sacrificium Missaticum, Mysterium Iniquitatis, or a Treatise concerning the Sacrifice of the Mass* (London: W. Griffin, 1768), ix.

11. H. Pendlebury, *A Plain Representation,* 5, 9, 27, 39, 41. H. Pendlebury, *Sacrificium Missaticum,* xxxviii–ix. [John Chorlton], "A Brief Account of the Life of the Author," in Henry Pendlebury, *Invisible Realities The Christian's Greatest Concernment* (London: Printed by J. D. for Ann Unsworth of Manchester, 1696), viii.

12. John Johnson, born in Lostock, 1706, and died in Liverpool, 1791. Baptist minister at Lostock, 1726; at Dale Street, Liverpool, 1741; at Stanley Street, Liverpool, 1750–91. Archibald Sparke, *Bibliographia Boltoniensis* (Manchester University Press, 1913), 88a (annotated copy, Bolton Archive). *See also* James Gardner, *Faiths of the World,* (New York: Fullarton, n.d.), 2.249.

13. Henry Pendlebury, *The Barren Fig-Tree, or A Practical Exposition of the Parable* (London: Printed by R. Janeway, Jun for Ed. Giles, 1700).

14. [James Livesey], "Epistle Dedicatory," in ΨΥΧΗΣΗΜΙΑ [sic, for ΨΥΧΗΖΗΜΙΑ, "Life-loss" *or* "Soul-harm," the ambiguity being part of Livesey's theme?] *or The greatest loss . . . a short Discourse Occasioned By the doleful loss of an eminently pious and learned Gentleman, viz. Mr. Humphrey Chetham, who died at Turton Tower, Feb. 13. was interred at Manchester the 18. 1658/9 Aged twenty three years seven months* (London: Printed by J. D. for Tho. Parkhurst, 1660).

15. James Livesey, *Enchiridion Judicum or Jehosaphats Charge to his Judges . . . Together with Catastrophe Magnatum or King Davids Lamentation at Prince Abners Incineration. In a Sermon meditated on . . . the Right Worshipful John Atherton of Atherton Esq; High-Sheriffe of the County Palatine of Lanc. By James Livesey, Minister of the Gospel at Atherton, alias Chow-bent* (London: Printed by R. I. for Tho. Parkhurst, 1657), 177.

16. Ibid., 19, 66, 174.

17. As n. 14, above.

18. [James Livesey], *Series Decretorum Dei Causarumque et Mediorum Salutis*

nostrae (London: Printed by R. Ibbitson for Thomas Parkhurst, 1657). The work, a Latin treatise on various views on Election, is dedicated to John Tilsley of Deane and Leonard Clayton of Blackburn. Under "Errata" at the end, Livesey writes (play-fully citing Stobaeus on Theodoctes) that men have ever desired two things "'which when they had obtained, they were quickly with them tyred, viz old age and wives', I may add a third, to bee in Print."

CHAPTER 29. "I HOPE I SHALL DIE IN HONOUR": ROYALIST MARTYRS

1. G. Pendlebury, *Aspects*, 6.
2. Ibid, 15.
3. J. D. Alsop, "Bishop John Bridgeman and the Lancashire Ship Money," *Northern History* 24 (1988): 212–14.
4. Barton, *Historical Gleanings* (1881), 327–30.
5. Broxap, *The Great Civil War*, 69–70. George Ormerod, *Tracts Relating to Military Proceedings in Lancashire during the Great Civil War* (Chetham Society: Manchester, 1844), 76, 129.
6. J. P. Earwaker, *Notes on the Life of Dr John Hewytt*, reprinted from the *Manchester Courier* (Manchester, 1877). [William Prynne], *Beheaded Dr. John Hewytts Ghost Pleading . . . Against The . . . Court of Justice, sitting in Westminister Hall* (London: Printed in the Year of our Lord, 1659). B. G. Blackwood, *The Lancashire Gentry and the Great Rebellion, 1640–1660* (Chetham Society: Manchester University Press, 1978), 113. Conrad Russell, *The Crisis of Parliaments, 1509–1660* (Oxford University Press, 1992), 387.
7. Brown, *Bolton School*, 30–32. John Hewit (1614–58) was a native of Eccles parish, of which Deane was anciently the northern half.
8. Frontispiece to John Hewytt, *Repentance and Conversion* (London: Printed by J. C., 1658). There is a portrait of Hewit at Lyme Park, Cheshire, where may also be seen part of the cloak worn by Charles I on the scaffold.
9. The DNB attributes verses from *Eikon Basilike* to Hewit, but there is no evidence for this. John Hewit, *Prayers of Intercession for Their Use who Mourn in Secret . . . with an Anniversary Prayer for the 30th of January . . . Together with the Manner of his Execution on Tower Hill, and his last Dying Speech.* (London, 1659), 81–88.
10. Hewytt, *Repentance and Conversion*, 55, 160, 185–86, 217. Cf. F. R. Raines, ed., *The Stanley Papers* (Chetham Society: Manchester, 1853), 55.
11. *Dr Hewit's Letter to Dr Wilde on Monday, June 7, 1658 being the day before he suffered Death*, Thommason Tracts 669.f.21 (6), British Library. Cf. John Donne, *Holy Sonnets* 18.14.
12. Hewit, *Prayers of Intercession*, 31, 86.
13. All quotations from *The Earle of Derby's Speech on the Scaffold Immediately before his Execution at Bolton in Lancashire, on Wednesday, October 15. 1651 Exactly taken in short-hand, as it was spoken* (London: Printed for Nathaniel Brooks, 1651). Less convincing, however, are *The True Speech Delivered on the Scaffold by James Earl of Derby* (London: Printed for Robert Eles [1651]), and the version by Rev. Humphrey Bagaley, Derby's chaplain, printed in J. G. Cumming, *The Great Stanley* (London, 1867), 230, 274.
14. B. T. Barton, *Historical Gleanings*, 2nd series (Bolton: *Daily Chronicle* Office, 1882), 171. Hints are dropped that the Earl's dish is a talisman of longevity and

wealth. James Cockerele, the original owner, died aged 106 in 1700. The husband of the 1882 owner, Mrs Wrigley, née Schofield, is a kinsman of Bury's millionaire paper manufacturer, Thomas Wrigley!

CHAPTER 30. "GOD'S GIFTS . . . FOR EDIFYING THE BODY": ROUNDHEAD SOLDIERS

1. Whewell, who had a small farm on Edgeworth Moor. By turning the block, Derby might also hope to elude the relic-ghouls. If so, his taste was shared by the wife of Edward Robinson, a commonwealth Justice of the peace, of the Haulgh, Bolton, who is said to have buried the block "where the malignants shall never obtain a single chip." Barton, *Historical Gleanings* (1881), 111, 207.

2. William Hulton (1787–1864), chairman of the special committee of Lancashire and Cheshire magistrates, 1819. *See* Robert Walmsley, *Peterloo: The Case Reopened* (Manchester University Press, 1969). Walmsley's detailed evidence suggests this conclusion and also that Hulton was elected by his colleagues as dispensable.

3. Broxap, *The Great Civil War*, 115–25. Ormerod, *Tracts*, 188–98.

4. G. Pendlebury, *Aspects*, 9–17. Blackwood, *Lancashire Gentry*, 3. Barton, *Historical Gleanings* (1882), 115. Of "All these 78 of Bolton slayne the 28th of May, 1644" listed in the parish register, none is called a "soldier"; all are male names except the wives of "Wm Isherwood" and "Arthur Seddon." Entries include "Edward Haslam, with his sonne" and one "Tilsley Grundy," possibly named after John Tilsley and so perhaps very young?

5. Barton, *Historical Gleanings* (1881), 14–15. *VCH: Lancashire*, 5.31.

6. *VCH: Lancashire* 4.118–21. "James Roscow" was the name of one of the shorthand writers of *The Earle of Derby's Speech* (the other name is not given). A "Ralph Roscow," churchwarden of Bolton, signed the "National Protestation" against papists in 1641 and sympathised with the Heywood campaign against the leaden "tickets" (Boardman, *Deane*, 538).

7. James Livesey, *Series Decretorum Dei*, 325.

8. Joseph Rigbie, *An Ingenious Poem called the Drunkards Prospective, or Burning-Glasse* (London: Printed for the Author, 1656), ix.

9. Rigbie, *Ingenious Poem*, vii, 9, 11, 24.

10. *VCH: Lancashire*, 3.278.

11. Earwaker, *Notes*, 24, citing *Mercurius Politicus*.

12. Russell, *Crisis of Parliaments*, 395.

13. B. G. Blackwood, "Catholic and Protestant Gentry," *Transactions of the Historical Society of Lancashire and Cheshire* 126 (1976): 14.

14. Ellis Bradshaw, "Epistle Dedicatorie," in *A Compendious Answer to a Book called a Brief Survey of the Judgement of Mr. John Goodwin* (London: Printed by H. Hills, 1652). Cf. John Goodwin, ΘΕΟΜΑΧΙΑ; *or the grand imprudence of men . . . in suppressing any way, doctrine, or practice, concerning which they know not certainly whether it be from God or no* (London, 1644).

15. Ellis Bradshaw, *Downfal of Tythes No Sacriledge* (London: H. Cripps and L. Lloyd, 1653).

16. Ellis Bradshaw, *The Quakers Quaking Principles Examined and Refuted* (London: Lodowicke Lloyd, 1656), 1 [with an epistle dedicatory to Cromwell].

17. Ellis Bradshaw, *The Conviction of James Naylor* (London: Printed by M.S. for Lodowicke Lloyd, 1656), 31.

18. Blackwood, *Lancashire Gentry*, 10, 30. There was, and is, strong surname-

solidarity in south Lancashire, but there is no evidence that Ellis Bradshaw was any near relation of the gentry Bradshaws.

19. Ellis Bradshawe, *A New And cleer Discovery of the True and Proper, Natural Cause, of the Ebbing and Flowing of the Main Sea* (London: Printed by Gartrude Dawson for Thomas Brewster, 1649).

20. Thomas Cole, born in Bolton 1801, emigrated 1819, and died in Catskill, N.Y., in 1848 (Cole Papers, New York State Library). Cole lived for some years at Heapey, north of Bolton, across the moors. Cf. J. W. Wallace to John Johnston, 7 September 1890, on reading Whitman's poem, "Passage to India" while walking over the moors to Heapey (Whitman Papers, Bolton Public Library). The natural surroundings "transcended it, and mocked it."

21. Ellis Bradshawe, *A week-daies Lecture, or Continued Sermon to Wit, The Preaching of the Heavens* (London: Printed by Gar: Dawson for Tho: Brewster and G. Moule, 1649).

22. Ellis Bradshaw, *An Husbandmans Harrow to pull down the Ridges of Presbyteriall Government and to smooth, a little, the Independent* (London: Printed for E. B., 1649).

23. E. B., *A Dialogue between the Devil & Prince Rupert, Written at the Leaguer before Chester upon Ruperts coming to relieve the said City* [April 1, 1645] (London: Printed for T.B., [1649]).

24. Ellis Bradshaw, *A True Relation of the strange Apparitions Seen in the Air, on Monday 25 February, in and about the Town of Bolton in the Mores in the County of Lancaster, at mid-day, to the amazement of the Beholders. Being a Letter from Ellis Bradshaw of the Same Town, to a Friend in London* (London: Printed for Tho. Brewster and Gregory Moule, 1650), 6–7.

25. Broxap, *The Great Civil War*, 82–84.

CHAPTER 31. OLIVER AND NATHANIEL HEYWOOD: REMAINING LOYAL, AND DUTIFUL

1. Oliver Heywood, epistle dedicatory, in Nathaneel [sic] Heywood, *Christ Displayed As The Choicest Gift and Best Master.* (London: Tho. Parkhurst, 1679).

2. N. Heywood, *Christ Displayed*, 2.

3. Ellis Bradshaw, *A Cordial-Mediator for Accordance of Brethren That Are of different Judgment and ways of Administration in things that concerne the Kingdome of God* (London: Lodowick Lloyd, 1658), 17.

4. Oliver Heywood, *A Narrative of the Holy Life, and Happy Death of . . . Mr. John Angier* (London: Tho. Parkhurst, 1683–84), 31. J. Horsfall Turner, ed., *The Rev. Oliver Heywood B.A., 1630–1702; His Autobiography, Diaries, Anecdote and Event Books*, 3 vols. (Brighouse: A.B. Bayes, 1882), 1.215. Oliver Heywood, *Israel's Lamentation After the Lord* (London: Tho. Parkhurst, 1683), 75, 95. *The Whole Works of the Rev. Oliver Heywood . . . with Memoirs of His Life* [edited by Richard Slate], 5 vols. (Idle: John Vint, 1827–25), 1.607.

5. O. Heywood, *The Whole Works*, 1.385, 390. N. Heywood, *Christ Displayed*, 49.

6. Turner, *Oliver Heywood*, 1.49. Broxap, *The Great Civil War*, 93, 159, 171–73, 181–83.

7. Turner, *Oliver Heywood*, section 1 (prefatory genealogy).

8. [Oliver Heywood], *Baptismal Bonds Renewed* (London: Tho. Parkhurst, 1687), 88.

9. O. Heywood, *John Angier*, 35.

10. N. Heywood, *Christ Displayed*, 61.

CHAPTER 32. RESTRAINT: THE POEM OF GOD

1. [Oliver Heywood], *Heart-Treasure or, an Essay Tending to fil and furnish the Head and Heart of every Christian . . . to help him in Meditation, Conference, Religious Performances, spiritual actions* (London: Printed by A. Ibbitson for Thomas Parkhurst, 1667), 204. Cf. James H. Longworth, *The Cotton Mills of Bolton, 1780–1985* (Bolton Museums and Art Gallery, 1987), 10: "'chapmen' would buy raw cotton [or other] yarns for distribution to rural spinners whose resulting earnings provided a valuable addition to their smallholding subsistencies."

2. B.T. Barton, *Historical Gleanings*, 3rd series (1883), 21.

3. O. Heywood, *The Whole Works*, I.416.

4. E.g., O. Heywood, *Heart-Treasure*, 214.

5. O. Heywood, *Baptismal Bonds*, 133.

6. O. Heywood, *Heart-Treasure*, 19, 293, 315–25.

7. Walt Whitman, Camden, N.J., to Dr. John Johnston, Bolton, Lancashire, 18 July 1891, in Walt Whitman, *The Correspondence*, ed. Edwin Haviland Miller (New York University Press, 1969), 5.231.

8. O. Heywood, *Heart-Treasure*, 236, citing Ephesians 2.10.

9. O. Heywood, *Baptismal Bonds*, 1. Turner, *Oliver Heywood*, 1.41–57. Barton, *Historical Gleanings* (1883), 57.

10. O. Heywood, *Heart-Treasure*, 133.

11. Turner, *Oliver Heywood*, 1.19–20, 24. Heywood, *Heart-Treasure*, 34, 134.

12. O. Heywood, *Heart-Treasure*, 213 (citing James I, *Basilicon Doron* (1603), 16–17), 229, 288.

13. Oliver Heywood, *Life in God's Favour A Seasonable Discourse* (London: Printed for Dorman Newman, 1679), 43. Turner, *Oliver Heywood*, 1.83. Robert Park(e), vicar of Bolton, 1625–30, Gosnell Lecturer, Bolton, 1645–62.

14. O. Heywood, *Israel's Lamentation*, 37, 46, 52. That historical chestnut, the campaign by Saxon King Ethelbert (d. 616), Augustine's convert, against the British monks of Chester and north Wales, predictably glossed in opponent, sectarian ways by Pilkington and Anderton, Heywood sees as simply a recidivist act of barbaric *paganism*. Just as his kind of scrupulous introspection anticipates Coleridge and Wordsworth, so his kind of equation between "Christianity" and "tolerance," and "tolerance" and "progress," anticipates the "Whig" history of Macaulay, J. S. Mill, and Matthew Arnold.

15. O. Heywood, *Heart-Treasure*, 93, 137, 181. O. Heywood, *Israel's Lamentation*, 84.

16. Patrick Collinson, *Elizabethan*, 222, 239. O. Heywood, *John Angier*, 1, 9, 13, 15, 16. Dr. Thomas Hill, master of Trinity when Oliver Heywood studied there, was an early mentor of Angier during his time as assistant to the Reverend John Cotton, minister at Boston, Lincolnshire, where he also met and married Ellen Winstanley, of Wigan, niece to Mrs. Cotton. The Winstanley connection brought him to preach at Bolton, and he was soon "called" to Ringley, two miles from Great Lever, where he occasionally ministered to Bishop Bridgeman's wife. Fearful for his sons' careers, the Bishop helped to prevail on the embarrassing nonconformist (who had episcopal ordination) to move to Denton, Manchester, where he continued his ministry unmolested till his death in 1677. The "so much noted verses" from Herbert's *The Church*

Militant were at first rejected by the Cambridge censor, but allowed under pressure from Nicholas Farrer (Isaak Walton, *Walton's Lives* (London: Henry Washbourne, 1858), 341).

17. O. Heywood, *Heart-Treasure*, 71. O. Heywood, "The Epistle to the Reader," in *Life in God's Favour*, iv.

18. Turner, *Oliver Heywood*, 108. Mark Pearson, *Northowram: Its History and Antiquities with a Life of Oliver Heywood* (Halifax: F. King, 1898), 57. Ironically, the "Heywood Chapel" was probably indebted for its survival during the eighteenth century to the leading local weaving masters, a family of incomers from Lancashire by name of Anderton.

19. Theodore Huguelet, introduction to David Hartley, *Observations on Man His Frame, His Duty, and His Expectations* (1749), ed. Theodore Huguelet (Gainesville: Scholars' Facsimiles, 1966). Hardman, *Ruskin and Bradford*, 99–101, 113–14. Dorothy Wordsworth spent formative years with paternal relatives near Halifax.

CHAPTER 33. CHRIST DISPLAYED

1. *Hinc lucem et pocula sacra*, the motto of Cambridge University.

2. Albert Peel, ed., *Tracts Ascribed to Richard Bancroft* (Cambridge: Cambridge University Press, 1953), 10.

3. W. C. Braithwaite, *The Beginnings of Quakerism*, 2nd ed., revised by H. J. Cadbury (Cambridge University Press, 1961), 178: "Alexander Parker, from the Bowland district [was] convinced in 1653 [when] twenty-five years old [and became] one of Fox's closest personal friends." Parker died in 1689. By 1660, Oliver Atherton of Ormskirk and James Harrison (a shoemaker from Kendal, active in Bolton) joined in monitoring meetings for Fox. Thomas Walters, a Bolton Quaker, was imprisoned 1663. See Braithwaite, *Beginnings*, 392; Dilworth Abbatt, "Alexander Parker," *Journal of the Friends' Historical Society* 8.1 (1911), 30.

4. O Heywood, *The Whole Works*, I.405. Turner, *Oliver Heywood*, 1.64, 67. [Oliver Heywood], *The Best Entail or, Dying Parents Living Hope for their surviving children* (London: Tho. Parkhurst, 1693), v, 88. Pearson, *Northowram*, 92, notes that Oliver Heywood weighed 18 stone (252 pounds).

5. Mrs. Nathaniel Heywood, née Elizabeth Parr, kin to Dr. Parr, bishop of Sodor and Man. Sir Henry Ashurst (or Ashhurst), first baronet. His mother was a Bradshaw of Bradshaw, and his father, Henry Ashurst senior (1614–80), a justice of the peace and London treasurer of the Lancashire Relief Fund, 1648; his uncles were William Ashurst, M.P. for Newton and Major John Ashurst, Roundhead commander at Bolton, 1643. During this period Bishop Bridgeman's grant to his own heirs of the Bolton Rectory (of which he was patron) was temporarily set aside. As governor of Barbados, Francis, fifth Lord Willoughby (1613–66), proclaimed King Charles II on 7 May 1650. Succeeded as governor of Barbados and "Caribee" (with estates in Antigua and Surinam) by his brother William, who recaptured Tobago. Hugh, twelfth Lord Willoughby, and John Andrews of Little Lever were leading trustees of Rivington Chapel, 1703. See J. Holding and C. D. Rogers, *The Nonconformist Chapel in Rivington* (Manchester: Shorrock & Davis, 1988).

6. Alexander Pope, "Epistle to a Lady," l. 120; in *Epistles to Several Persons*, edited by F. W. Bateson (London: Methuen, 1961), 60. Ellis Bradshaw, *The Quakers Whitest Divell Unvailed . . . In Answer to a Letter subscribed Iames Naylor* (1654); *The Quakers Quaking Principles Examined and Refuted In a briefe answer to . . . James Naylor in his Answers to Mr. Baxter* (London: Lodowicke Lloyd, 1656); *The Convic-*

tion of James Naylor . . . In answer to a Book of his called Wickednesse weighed . . . writ in answer to . . . The Quakers quaking Principles (Printed by M. S. for Lodowicke Lloyd, 1656). The first London Synagogue also dates from 1656.

7. Daniel Neal, *The History of the Puritans*, 3 vols. (London: Th. Tegg & Son, 1837), 2.663, 665. Braithwaite, *Beginnings*, 241–78. John Johnston, *To the Passion Play and Back* (Bolton: Tillotson, 1900). The plays, founded by vow of 1633, admired by Hitler for depiction of "muck and mire of Jewry": H. R. Trevor-Roper, ed., *Hitler's Table Talk 1941–1944* (Oxford University Press, 1988), 563.

8. O. Heywood, *Life in God's Favour*, x–xiii. Dale, *Many Mansions*, 18.

9. Neal, *Puritans*, 2.573.

10. Joseph Hunter, *Rise of the Old Dissent exemplified in the Life of Oliver Heywood* (London, 1842), 21.

11. O. Heywood, *Life in God's Favour*, xvii–viii; Epistle "To Mr. John Denton," in *Job's Appeal . . . Funeral Discourse . . . Upon . . . Death of Mr. Johnathan Denton* (London: B. Aylmer, 1695); *A Family Altar*, 119. See also O. Heywood's epistle in his *Baptismal Bonds* and N. Heywood, *Christ Displayed*, 91. Cf. *The Heavenly Footman*, in *The Miscellaneous Works of John Bunyan* ed. Graham Midgley, vol. 5 (Oxford University Press, 1986), 166.

12. O. Heywood, *Heart-Treasure*, 204; *The Whole Works*, 1.401. Sir Henry Ashhurst, *Some Remarks upon the Life of . . . Mr. Nathanael Heywood* (London: Tho. Cockerill, 1695), 11, 14, 16, 19, 26, 33–34, 36, 39–40, 63, 68–70. Mr. Starky preached the funeral sermon.

13. VCH: *Lancashire*, 3.278, 5.111. Phoebe Stanton, *Pugin* (London: Thames & Hudson, 1971), 28–33. Further details from the late Peter Fleetwood-Hesketh.

14. N. Heywood, *Christ Displayed*, 16–17, 215.

15. Pearson, *Northowram*, 78, 87.

16. N. Heywood, *Christ Displayed*, 213, 219. Pearson, *Northwram*, 69–71. O. Heywood, *Baptismal Bonds*, 91. For "there is no medium," cf. Turner, *Oliver Heywood*, I.49 (Heywood's mother, "demolishing the relicks of superstition"). Surviving medieval figurework at Deane Church may represent polarized didactic pruning of this kind. Externally, there is only a Clough Boggart (local devil), with souls in his bag, by the south entrance. On entering, a small, lovely fifteenth-century angel is visible. Some agreeably humorous human maskheads also survive.

17. N. Heywood, *Christ Displayed*, 29, 199; O. Heywood, *Life in God's Favour*, 145–46.

CHAPTER 34. SCOPE: THE LAMENTATIONS OF SAINTS

1. O. Heywood, preface to *John Angier*. Cf. J. Lemprière, ed., *Classical Dictionary* (London: T. & J. Allman, 1829), 363–64. (The first edition of this standard work was published in 1788.) Lemprière was then appointed head of the Bolton Grammar School, but was forced to reign, 1792, after a flogging incident (Brown, *Bolton School*, 72–73).

2. *See*, e.g., C. T. Onions, ed., *The Shorter Oxford English Dictionary* (Oxford University Press, 1959), 1.193. "*Blue . . . 3.fig.* Affected with fear, discomfort, anxiety, etc: low-spirited; esp. in *To look b.* 1550."

3. N. Heywood, *Christ Displayed*, 225–26.

4. Hunter, *Rise*, 21 ff.

5. Porter, *Reformation*, 288–313.

6. Michael Mullett, "'A Receptacle for Papists and an Asilum': Catholicism and

Disorder in Late Seventeenth-Century Wigan," *Catholic History Review* 73 (1987): 391–407.

7. O. Heywood, *Israel's Lamentation*, Epistle, "To All the Mourners in Zion" [p.x], 28, 31, 33, 128, 131. O. Heywood, *Heart-Treasure*, 11. Cf. 1 Samuel 7.2. Information on Hebrew from Robert Young, *Analytical Concordance to the Holy Bible* (London: Lutterworth Press, 1952), 293, 294, 583, 1029.

8. O. Heywood, epistle in *Job's Appeal; Heart-Treasure*, 22, 27; *Life in God's Favour*, 109, 123, 133; *Whole Works*, 3.94–98, 115.

9. Turner, *Oliver Heywood*, 1.60–67.

10. O. Heywood, *Heart-Treasure*, 213, 243. Cf. Galatians 1:28.

11. Turner, *Oliver Heywood*, 1.61. Cf. O. Heywood, *Family Altar*, 131–32; *Advice to an Only Child*, 27, 54, 58, 169; "Mr. Angiers Dying Speeches," in O. Heywood, *John Angier*, 118: "For my Son that hath greatly played the Prodigal, hedg [sic] up his way with thorns, and make a stone-wall, bring him into such straits, that he may begin to bethink himself."

12. Turner, *Oliver Heywood*, 4.71.

13. Pearson, *Northowram*, 87. Salvianus Massiliensis (c. 400–c. 480). His *De Gubernatione Dei* is quoted by Oliver Heywood in, for example, titlepages of *Family Altar* and *Christ Displayed*.

CHAPTER 35. REVOLUTION AS ANTIQUITY AND CONTINUANCE

1. William Shakespeare, *Antony and Cleopatra* 2.2.204–5. For Protogenes's Venus, See Pliny 35.10 Cf. Lemprière, 566. For Oliver Heywood on the dreadful death of Dr. William Anderton of the Horwich branch (1675), *see* Turner, *Oliver Heywood*, 3.211. On the early cotton trade, *see* W. E. Brown, *Bolton as it Was* (Nelson, Lancashire: Hendon Publishing, 1986), 39; H. B. Heylin, historical preface to *Buyers and Sellers in the Cotton Trade* (London: Ch. Griffin, 1913); Longworth, *Cotton Mills of Bolton*, 10.

2. *Paradiso* viii. 139–48, *The Divine Comedy of Dante Alighieri*, trans. J. D. Sinclair (Oxford University Press, 1961), 122–25. Cf. O. Heywood, *Life in God's Favour*, 146.

3. O. Heywood, *John Angier*, 4 (with reference to the sacred and secular vocations of Angier senior and his brothers): "*nil invita Minerva*, that which is attempted without heart . . . goes on heavily . . . wisely therefore did the Athenians" in allowing children to choose a calling. Cf. Sinclair, *Paradiso*, 125: "you wrest to religion one born to gird on the sword, and you make a king of one that is fit for sermons."

4. James Livesey, in the epistle dedicatory of his ΨΥΧΙΙΣΗΜΙΑ, mentions young Humphrey's "learned Master M. Zachary Taylor . . . pious and painful tutor Mr. Sam Birche." Edmund Calamy, junior, *The Nonconformists' Memorial*, ed. S. Palmer, (London: T. Hurst, 1802–3), 2.377. The author's wife was Ann Lever of Darcy Lever, niece to Robert Lever (d. 1644), the re-founder of Bolton G.S.

5. *Bishop Overall's Convocation-Book MDCVI, Concerning the Government of God's Catholick Church and the Kingdoms of the Whole World* (London: Walter Ketilby, 1690; reprint, Library of Anglo-Catholic Theology, Oxford: J. H. Parker, 1844).

6. James sought his clergy's advice as to whether he should recognize the emerging Dutch Republic. Their support for any government "thoroughly settled" offended him as antimonarchical. Taylor is amused by his opponents' efforts to deduce context and significance for this phrase from the "express words of the Convocation-Book"

instead of from history, which shows the dithering monarch and his advisors over-taken by worldwide developments in favor of Holland.

7. Among others (in sequence): (1) [Zachary Taylor], *Obedience and Submission To the Present Government, Demonstrated from Bishop Overall's Convocation Book* (London: Randal Taylor, 1690); (2) [Thomas Wagstaffe], *In Answer to a late pamphlet entituled Obedience and Submission to the present government demonstrated from M. Dorrall's Convocation-book,* (London: 1690); (3) William Sherlock, *The Case of the Allegiance due to Soveraign Powers . . . with A more particular Respect to the Oath lately enjoyned, of Allegiance to Their Present Majesties, K. William and Q. Mary,* 3rd ed. (London: W. Rogers, 1691); (4) [Zachary Taylor], *A Letter to Dr. Sherlock, In Vindication of the part of Josephus's History, which gives an Account of Iaddus the High-Priest's Submitting to Alexander the Great while Darius was living Against the ANSWER To the Piece Intituled Obedience and Submission to the Present Govern-ment* (London: Thomas Jones, 1691); (5) [Zachary Taylor], *The Vindication of a Late Pamphlet (Entituled Obedience and Submission to the Present Government Demon-strated from Bp. Overall's Convocation-Book) From the False Glosses, and Illusive Interpretations of a Pretended Answer* (London: Ric. Baldwin, 1691); (6) William Sherlock, *A Vindication of the Case of Allegiance . . . In Reply to an Answer To a late Pamphlet, Intituled, Obedience and Submission* (London: W. Rogers, 1691); (7) [Thomas Wagstaffe], *An Answer to Dr. Sherlock's Vindication of the Case of Alle-giance due to sovereign powers, which he made in reply to an Answer to a late pamphlet intituled: Obedience and submission to the present government* (London, 1692).

8. Bradshaw, *Husbandman's Harrow,* 72; Taylor, *Obedience and Submission,* 5–6. In *Vindication of a Late Pamphlet,* Taylor writes that "plainly the opposition is be-twixt Right, as that implies a Civil Title amongst Men which excludes the pretences of all other Human Rights, and Authority [which] is nothing else, but that divine Power, which . . . instructs a Person . . . to act and execute with Equity and Mercy, the Administration of a Government," (pp. 11–12), that "[T]here was never such a thing as transferring a Right, but only in the Metaphysical Head of Mr. Hobs," (p. 20), and that William III's is "a Revolution upon an Appeal to God for Justice and Equity," (pp. 22, 30). Wagstaffe, *An Answer,* alleges Taylor claims "those only who followed the several Revolutions . . . acted according to the Principles of the Church of England," (pp. 13, 22) and that Taylor claims the "Permission of Providence is . . . sufficient warrant to act contrary to the Rule of Right," (p. 23).

9. Wagstaffe, *An Answer,* 15. Taylor, *The Vindication of a Late Pamphlet,* 27.

CHAPTER 36. "A DISSUASIVE FROM CONTENTION"

1. Taylor, Dedication to *A Dissuasive from Contention being a Sermon Preached and Designed for the last Itineration of the King's Preachers in the County Palatine of Lancaster* (London: Printed by John Gain, for William Cadman, 1682).

2. Taylor, *Dissuasive from Contention,* 31.

3. Ibid., 4–8, 11–14, 20.

4. Ibid., 20. Taylor occasionally draws on writings of Edward Hyde (1609–74), first earl of Clarendon, Charles II's lord chancellor, who took a lead in extending and legislating for colonial dominions and was equally opposed by Catholics and Presbyterians. He was exiled in 1667. His children were Anne, who was born in 1637, married James, duke of York, in 1660 (Queens Mary and Anne were her children), and died (of cancer of the breast) in 1671; Henry, born in 1638, second earl of Clarendon 1674, denounced (with brother Laurence) as favoring Catholics by

Commons, January 1681, served as lord-lieutenant of Ireland 1685–87, admitted some Roman Catholics as councillors and army officers, and died in 1709; Laurence (Taylor: "Lawrence"), who was born in 1641, was created Earl of Rochester and became Lord Treasurer in 1685, made efforts to alienate the king from Queen Mary (of Modena) and the court Jesuits, was dismissed 1687, and was compensated with forfeited Irish estates.

5. Taylor, *The Death of the Righteous ... Delivered at Wigan, April 18, 1695, At the Obsequies of the ... Lady Elizabeth Relict of Sir Roger Bradshaigh, of Haigh, Knight and Baronet* [London]: Printed by O. Jones, for Sam. Lowndes, 1695), 1.

6. Zachary Taylor, who was baptised at Bolton Parish Church on 24 April 1653, was the son of Zachary and Abigail (Ward) Taylor. He became vicar of Ormskirk on 9 March 1680 and resigned in 1693. Afterwards he was curate to the bishop of Chester in his plurality as rector of Wigan (surely a galling position). On 12 July 1685 he married Barbara, daughter of Sir Edward Stanley of Bickerstaffe. (She died in 1689). With a subsequent wife, Anne, Taylor had several children. The date of his death is not clear. Richard Harrison, History Department, Lancaster University, tells me Taylor last drew income from his Wigan curacy in 1704. Sparke (*Bibliographia Boltoniensis*, 139) describes him as "Curate of Wigan, 1693–1705; Rector of Croston, 1695, till his death in 1705, probably in May."

7. Wagstaffe, *An Answer*, 3.

8. Taylor, *The Vindication of a Late Pamphlet*, 21.

9. *VCH: Lancashire* 5.270. The novelist Christopher William Bradshaw Isherwood (to give him his full name) was a descendant of this family. His *Goodbye to Berlin* (London: Hogarth Press) appeared in 1939.

10. Richard Bradshaigh (*alias* "Barton"), was born in Lancashire in 1601, served as Jesuit provincial of English province from 1656 to 1660, and then became rector of English College, St. Omer, until his death in 1669.

11. Taylor, *Obedience and Submission*, 2.

12. Taylor, *Obedience and Submission*, 17. Cf. Psalms 46.1 (*Deus noster refugium*): "God is our hope and strength: a very present help in trouble." Taylor represents a generation that has clearly lost the sense of the spiritual profundity of Athenian drama shared by early humanists like Pilkington. This sense would be recovered by twentieth-century scholars, e.g., E. R. Dodds, *Euripides Bacchae* (Oxford University Press, 1944).

13. Pevsner, *South Lancashire*, 133. Barton, *Historical Gleanings* (1881), 206. *VCH: Lancashire*, 3.278. Robert Ashton, *The English Civil War* (London: Weidenfeld & Nicolson, 1989), 174.

14. Dante, *Paradiso* 8.93, 140–41. Brown, *Bolton as it Was*, 39.

CHAPTER 37. CONTENTION AND CONTINUANCE

1. Taylor, *Vindication of a Late Pamphlet*, 20. Cf. Thomas Hobbes, *Leviathan*, Pt. 1. ch. 14, in *Hobbes's Leviathan* Reprinted from the Edition of 1651 (Oxford University Press, 1962), 99–109; Jonathan Swift, preface to *A Tale of a Tub* (1704, written 1696–97): "Hob's *Leviathan*, which tosses and plays with all other Schemes of Religion and Government." See Jonathan Swift, *A Tale of a Tub*, edited by Herbert Davis (Oxford: Basil Blackwell, 1965), 24.

2. A. P. Stanley, *Historical Memorials of Westminster Abbey* (London: John Murray, 1868), 94–96.

3. In sequence: (1) [Thomas Jolly and John Carrington],*The Surey Demoniack,*

or an Account of Satan's Strange and Dreadful Actings in and about the body of Richard Dugdale of Surey, near Whalley in Lancashire: And how he was Dispossesst by God's Blessing on the Fastings and Prayers of Divers Ministers and People: The Matter of Fact attested by the Oaths of several Credible Persons, before some of His Majesties Justices of the Peace in the said County (London: Jonathan Robinson, 1697). (2) Zachary Taylor, *The Surey Impostor being an Answer to a late Fanatical Pamphlet entituled The Surey Demoniack* (London: John Jones . . . and Ephraim Johnson Bookseller in Manchester, 1697). (3) [Thomas Jolly and John Carrington], *The Lancashire Levite Rebuk'd or, a Vindication of the Dissenters from Popery, Superstition, Ignorance and Knavery, unjustly charged upon them by Mr. Zachary Taylor* (London: Printed by Rich. Janeway . . . and sold by Richard Baldwin, 1698). (4) Zachary Taylor, *Popery, Superstition, Ignorance and Knavery, very unjustly by a letter in the general pretended: but as far as was Charg'd very fully Prov'd upon the Dissenters that were concerned in the Surey Imposture* (London: John Jones, 1698). (5) Zachary Taylor, *Popery, Superstition, Ignorance and Knavery Confess'd, and fully Proved on the Surey Dissenters From the Second Letter of an Apostate Friend to Zachary Taylor. To which is added A Refutation of Mr. T. Jollie's Vindication of the Devil in Dugdale; or the Surey Demoniack.* (London: W. Keblewhite and J. Jones, 1699).

Also relevant is Zachary Taylor, *The Devil Turn'd Casuist; or the cheats of Rome laid open in the exorcism of a despairing devil, at the house of Thomas Pennington in Orrel, in the Parish of Wigan* (London, 1696).

4. Jolly and Carrington, in the preface to *Surey Demoniack,* recommend "Mr. Baxter's The World of Spirits Evinced by Apparitions [printed as the appendix to] Mr. Increase Mather's A Further Account of the Trials of New England Witches, 1693." Dugdale is described as a middle-size nineteen-year-old handyman gardener at time of his "possession" (29 April 1689). After dancing and drinking at a Rush-Bearing on 25 July 1688 and contracting pain in his side after a fight, he was "heard" to offer himself to the devil. ("Rush Bearing," in former days, was in effect a new-year festival of high summer, when churches and other buildings had their floor coverings of rushes renewed). In *The Surey Impostor* (3, 27–40), Taylor corrects the Dissenters' Greek; regrets that Carrington picks up gossip about his betters by hanging about kitchen doors; determines that Dugdale is partly diseased, partly a recusant, and partly given to repeating tricks he developed in search of popularity at Whalley Grammar School; and alerts readers to the *Pathologiae Cerebri et Nervosi Generis Specimen* (Oxford, 1667), by Dr. Thomas Willis (1621–75), Sedleian Professor of Natural History, Oxford, and to the practical work of Dr. John Radcliffe (1650–1714), court physician and endower of the Radcliffe Infirmary and Observatory, Oxford.

5. Jolly and Carrington, *Surey Demoniack,* 49; Taylor, *Surey Impostor,* 38, 56 ff.

6. Jolly and Carrington, *Surey Demoniack,* 51. A husbandman, skinner, saddler, and woollen weaver, swore affidavits before Hugh, Lord Willoughby, and Ralph Egerton, esq., at Holcomb on 29 July 1695. Carrington, a Cheshire man, was promoted to Lancaster soon after exorcizing Dugdale. Taylor wonders how "the violence of the convulsions distorting his body," clearly requiring medical attention, could be alleged as terpsichorean "dexterity" purchased at the price of a soul (*Surey Impostor,* 3).

7. Taylor, *Surey Impostor,* 21.

8. VCH: *Lancashire* 6.381 names the curate as Henry Crabtree of Todmorden. Dugdale also received help from a Mr. Chew.

9. Barton, *Historical Gleanings* (1881), 327.

10. Hobbes, *Leviathan,* Pt. 3, chap. 32, para. 7 (*Hobbes's Leviathan,* 288).

11. *VCH: Lancashire* 5.297–98. Dale, *Many Mansions,* 56. Smithhills ceased to be a mass center on the death of the third Viscount Fauconberg/Falconbridge in 1721.

12. John Johnson (1706–91), born in Lostock and ministered thereabouts from 1726; Dale Street, Liverpool, 1741; and Stanley Street, Liverpool, from 1750. At the time of his death there were six or seven Johnsonian bodies in England. *See* John Johnson, *An Occasional Review of the Prebendary of Litchfield's Sermon and Address to the People called Quakers* (London: Printed for the Author, 1762), 46; *The Faith of God's Elect* (Liverpool: Printed by E. Owen, 1754). The obnoxious prebendary was Matthew Pilkington, who was appointed in 1748, and died in 1765. He was the author of *A Rational Concordance, or an Index of the Bible* (Nottingham, 1749) and *Remarks upon Several Passages of Scripture* (Cambridge and London, 1759).

13. Barton, *Historical Gleanings* (1881), 175.

14. At Bank Street, Bolton, the final break came during the ministry of Thomas Dixon junior, who was ordained in 1753, and died in 1754. He was the son of Thomas Dixon senior, M.D., minister 1723–29, during whose time the Cumberland Presbyterian Academy transferred to Bolton. Ramsden, *A Responsible Society,* 66–67.

15. John Bossy, *The English Catholic Community, 1570–1850,* v.

16. Boardman, *Records and Traditions of Deane,* 2.572. Both vicars were "conformable" in 1689. The vicar of Bolton (d. 1691) made a point of walking "up and down the town arm in arm together" with *another* John Lever (no known relation, but perhaps a schoolfellow at Bolton), son of the "papist" Adam Lever and his wife Margaret Isherwood and evicted from Cockey Moor in 1662. He was Presbyterian minister at Bolton in 1689–92. James Johnston, *Mawdsley Street Congregational Chapel 1808–1908* (Bolton, 1908), 29.

17. Dale, *Many Mansions,* 18.

18. [John Whiting], *Persecution Expos'd* (London: J. Sowle, 1715). Longworth arrived from Barbados in March 1687 and was buried on 8 June 1687; Harrison arrived in 1681–82 and died and was buried on 8 August 1687.

19. Dale, *Many Mansions,* 109.

CHAPTER 38. ANTIQUITY AND CONTINUANCE: A REINTERPRETATION

1. Psalm 102.26. Cf. John 19.23.

2. Gordon Leff, *William of Ockham* (Manchester University Press, 1975), 634–36; Wilfrid Ward, *The Life of John Henry Newman* (London, 1912), 2.380; J. Anderton, Preface to *Protestants Apologie,* 48, 54.

3. A. L. P. Norrington, ed., *The Poems of Arthur Hugh Clough* (Oxford University Press, 1968), 178. See also Cross, *Dictionary of the Christian Church,* 118–19, 1040, 1462–3.

4. Leff, *Ockham,* 596–613, 637–39; Etienne Gilson, *La Philosophie au Moyen Age* (Paris: Payot, 1944), 653.

5. James Anderton, *The Apologie of the Roman Church, devided into three severall tractes* (1604), 143. Citing Acts 1.14, Anderton notes that Calvin's translation of 1573 (*cum uxoribus*) gives the apostles "wives," and alleges against this "our English translators" of 1576 and 1580, who give "women," as the *cum mulieribus* of the Vulgate. He appends the Greek γυναιξι [sic].

6. Leff, *Ockham,* 497, 639, 642.

CHAPTER 39. THESAURUS

1. Edwin Haviland Miller, ed., *Walt Whitman: The Correspondence* (New York: New York University Press, 1969), 5.63. The wives of Johnston and Andrew Rome were first cousins. A reading of Frank Singleton, *Tillotson's 1850–1950* (Bolton: Tillotson, 1950), suggests the illness and death of her husband, William Frederick Tillotson (1844–89) preoccupied Mary Tillotson's energies while reaching a negative decision about "Too late beloved," the draft of the early part of what would be *Tess* (1891). The story of a wronged, virtuous working girl was a standard Tillotson plot. Tess's apparent *consent* was the problem.

2. Christopher Hill, *A Turbulent, Seditious, and Factious People: John Bunyan and His Church, 1628–1688* (Oxford University Press, 1988), vii: "There is the never-to-be-forgotten biographer John Brown." Cf. J. M. Keynes to Virginia Woolf, 1934, quoted in Robert Skidelsky, *The Economist as Saviour: 1920–1937*, vol. 2 of *John Maynard Keynes* (London: Macmillan, 1992), xx: "Our generation—yours and mine . . . owed a great deal to our fathers' religion." *See* also Geoffrey Keynes, *Blake Studies* (Oxford University Press), 1971.

3. S. T. Coleridge, "Kubla Khan," ll. 39–41. The commercial Xanadus of each industrial parish were independent space stations exploiting rival compilations of the same imperial galaxy. Sundered from Bury to the east by two miles of country road, Bolton's suburbs included Khartoum. For sideways views on this piecemeal culture, *see* T. S. Eliot, *The Sacred Wood* (London: Methuen, 1932), 156 (Blake); Nathaniel Hawthorne, *The English Notebooks*, ed. Randall Stewart (New York: Russell and Russell, 1962), 6: "The Doctor is a brisk man . . . not exactly a gentleman; and indeed what Englishman is?" (Dr. Sir John Bowring, 1792–1872).

4. F. Engels, "A Review of English Volunteer Riflemen," *Volunteer Journal of Lancashire and Cheshire*, 14 September 1860, reprinted in W. O. Henderson, ed., *Engels: Selected Writings* (Harmondsworth: Penguin, 1967), 348: "the English appear . . . to have quite an exceptional talent for this movement."

5. Benjamin Vincent, *Haydn's Dictionary of Dates* (London: E. Moxon, 1876), 110.

6. Robert Ainsworth, *Thesaurus Linguae Latinae Compendiarius or, a Compendious Dictionary of the Latin Tongue, Designed for the Use of the British Nations: In THREE PARTS* (London: Printed for J. J. and P. Knapton, 1736). Both double and triple in form, the *Thesaurus* is a pair of volumes, English-Latin word lists in one, Latin-English in the other, with an encyclopedia relevant to both cultures divided between the two. Ainsworth lists predecessors from Richard Pynson, *Promptorium* (1499), the *Ortus Vocabulorum* (1516), and Thomas Elyot, *Bibliotheca* (1542) to the Cambridge Dictionary of 1693.

7. Robert Ainsworth, *The Most Natural and Easie Way of Institution* (1698). The 1699 edition was issued anonymously. Persius: Lemprière, *Classical Dictionary*, 504. Robert Ainsworth (1660–1743) had an elder brother, John, and a younger brother, William. Their parents—Rodger Ainsworth, probably a "chapman," or middleman between weaver and merchant, and Ellen Warburton Ainsworth—died aged 40 and 38, respectively. *See* John Keelan, *The Ainsworth Family* (Bolton: Friends of Smithhills Hall, 1993), 3–4. A Thomas Warburton was married at Aarau in Lever's time. Another (or possibly the same) "Warburton" was Marsh's companion at Lancaster.

8. Hardman, *Ruskin and Bradford*, 99–101. David Hartley, *Observations on Man*

(1749) appeared in an annotated version by the Reverend H. A. Pistorius, rector of Poseritz, Rugen, Pomerania (Rostock and Leipsig, 1772).

9. See Smith, Rivington, 62–68, and cf., Pilkington, Works, 355, 642.

10. Robert Ainsworth, epistle dedicatory to "S. N., merchant" to J. Casa His Galateus or a Treatise of Manners (London, 1701).

11. Richard Mead, M.D. (1673–1754), was the son of an ejected minister of 1662. He had large private means, was a renowned classicist, and was physician to royalty and Alexander Pope. Ainsworth, in addressing him, mentions as "mihi amicissimus" Edmund Chishull (1671–1733), chaplain to the Smyrna factory from 1688, traveler, writer, and antiquarian. The manuscripts in his collection were purchased for the British Museum in 1785. Sir Hans Sloane (1660–1752), whose collections of books, manuscripts, and specimens of natural history were part of the original British Museum of 1759, was another patron. See British Museum, Latin Manuscripts Collection, 4050, f.98.

12. See British Museum, Additional Manuscripts Collection, 5853, ff. 502, 505–7. Reared (like his kinsman, the novelist William Harrison Ainsworth) in a Calvinist tradition, Robert Ainsworth attended Wesleyan sermons in old age. Charles Wesley records their meeting on 12 May 1738, in his diary: "I was much moved to see Mr. Ainsworth, a man of great learning, above seventy, who, like old Simeon, was waiting to see the Lord's salvation." Ainsworth was buried on 2 May 1743 at the East India Company's chapel, Poplar, London. His memorial tablet, designed by himself, was placed just inside the south door. He left £12 to buy burial linen for the Bolton poor, with further bequests to Bolton relatives. See Keelan, The Ainsworth Family, 4.

13. E.g., An Abridgement of Ainsworth's Latin Dictionary Materially Improved by Thomas Morell. New edition. London: Ward Lock and Co., 1882.

14. M. D. Smith, Rivington (Chorley, Lancashire: Nelson Brothers, 1988), 198. Also: John Lodge (d. 1774), deputy-keeper of the muniments of Ireland, Bermingham Tower, Dublin, The Peerage of Ireland, 4 vols. (London 1754); The Uses of Holding Parliaments in Ireland (Dublin, 1770); Desiderata Curiosa Hibernica, 2 vols. (Dublin, 1772); various manuscript compilations in the British Museum; Dorning Rasbotham, justice of the peace (1730–91), high sheriff of Lancaster, 1769, "retired" to Birch House, Farnworth, Bolton, aged 32 to compile a (never completed, but to others valuable) "History of Lancashire", published Codrus, an Athenian tragedy moralizing the injustices of monarchy, in 1774, A Dissuasive from Popular Rioting directed against Mechanical Improvements (1779); Sir Ashton Lever, baronet, died by his own hand in 1788 (trustee of Bolton Grammar School by kinship with the seventeenth-century endower, Robert Lever of Darcy Lever), rented Leicester House, London to house his Leverian Museum; Sir William W. B. Hulton, baronet (1844–1907, descendant of the chief magistrate at Peterloo) conserved medieval charters and Elizabethan letters, including fifty-two by earls of Leicester and Essex to Elizabeth (Bolton Journal, 30 June 1900), wrote Lancashire, Our Own County (privately printed), collection dispersed by auction 1947, house demolished 1962–63.

15. Robert Ainsworth, ed., Monumenta Vetustatis Kempiana (Londin: Daniel Bridge 1720). John Kemp (1665–1717), fellow of the Royal Society 1712; died unmarried; his collection realized £1,090 8s. 6d.

16. Robert Ainsworth, ΙΣΕΙΟΝ . . . Penes Jacobum West de Interiori Templo Arm. FRS Sturt sc. (London, 1729). James West (1704?–1772), treasurer of the Inner Temple and president of the Royal Society from 1768; large private income; M.P. as client of the duke of Newcastle; envied by Horace Walpole; left manuscripts to the British Museum and his books to the Bodleian Library, Oxford. In allusion to West's "Temple" connections, Ainsworth "amends" busto to Templo in the Lucan line cited

(9.158). John Sturt (1658–1730), was a calligraphic engraver of an elegy on Queen Mary done small enough to fit on a finger ring.

17. Dale, *Many Mansions*, 109.

18. James Pilkington, *The Doctrine of Equality* (London: J. Johnson, 1795). The Horwich Pilkingtons derive from Richard Pilkington (a descendant of the Bishop's parents) and his wife Mary, the daughter of Richard Hardman of Great Lever (will of 1623).

19. Whitmanite Collection, Central Library, Bolton; Sixsmith manuscripts, John Rylands Library, Manchester. Relevant publications include C. C. Coe, *General Gordon in a New Light* (Bolton: Tillotsons, 1885); C. A. Clarke, *The Effects of the Factory System* (London, 1899) (the Russian edition was prefaced by Tolstoy); J. Johnston, *Wastage of Child Life*, Fabian Socialist series 7 (London, 1909); J. Johnston and J. W. Wallace, *Visits to Walt Whitman in 1890–91* (London: Allen & Unwin, 1917). A review of *Visits* (by Virginia Woolf) appeared in *The Times Literary Supplement*, 3 January 1918. See M. D. Smith, *Leverhulme's Rivington* (Chorley: NB Colour Print, 1984). British Medical Association building (1906) by modernist Bolton architect Charles Holden (1875–1960) was a Whitman memorial: A. Service, ed., *Edwardian Architecture* (London: Architectural Press, 1975), 386–92.

20. E.g., minister for prisons Ann Widdecombe, "first MP to leave the C of E to become a Roman Catholic in protest at the ordination of women . . . co-founder [of] Women and Families for [Nuclear] Defence" apologized on 15 January for misleading Parliament by denying that Whittington Hospital authorities had protested her department's policy of shackling female prisoners undergoing birth pangs; Angel Koyanti, "modern Lady Godiva," who staged nude protest on 17 January at Coventry Cathedral before Prince Michael of Kent and 1,000 other worshippers offering "thanksgiving for . . . benefits" and "penitence" for the misuse of automobiles over a hundred years. Painted on her body the slogan "The Goddess is the Mother of Creation." The bishop's comment was that her "protest was 'unnecessary but understandable.'" *Sources: The Observer*, 14 January 1996; "5.00 PM," news program, BBC, 15 January 1996; *Daily Star*, 18 January 1996; *Private Eye*, 9 February 1996. Meanwhile, "John Fogg, of the Scout Association, defended its new open-door policy with quiet dignity: 'Our policy is firmly that no young person or adult should receive less favourable treatment because of their sexuality'" (*The Guardian*, 25 March, 1997).

21. Robert Whitehead (1823–1905) attended Bolton Grammar School from 1829 to 1839. During his last year, he declaimed from Quintus Curtius's history of the conquests of Alexander the Great. He created the Austrian naval port of Fiume, near Trieste, where he evolved a self-propelled torpedo by 1866. In 1867 Derby appointed his friend Charles James Lever, M.D., LL.D (1809–72), the Irish Ascendancy novelist (of the Levers of Little Lever) vice consul to Trieste, by then a very sensitive post.

22. Lawrence Fogg, *Theologiae Speculativae Schema, e variis systematibus modernis magnam partem excerptum . . . Cui accessit Brevis . . . Discussio . . . in opem et subsidium Tironum collecta* (London: H. & G. Mortlock; Chester: R. Minshull, 1712). Fogg was curate of Prestwich in 1666–72, at a time when the Presbyterian tradition was tolerated in the parish (at Ringley) and nearby at Denton (John Angier senior). On the Sharps, see Hardman, *Ruskin and Bradford*, 102.

23. Lawrence Fogg, *God's Infinite Grace in Election and Impartial Equity in Preterition Vindicated: or an Antidote against Offences, occasioned by . . . Parties unwarily contending* (Chester: Printed by E. Ince, for the Author, 1713).

24. Lawrence Fogg, *Two Treatises I. A General View of Christian Religion . . . II. An Entrance into the Doctrine of Christianity* (Chester: Printed by E. Ince, for R. Minshull, 1712).

25. Lawrence Fogg, *A General View of Christian Religion* (Chester: James Holland, 1714), 3: "There is a God Infinite in Wisdom, Power and Goodness, the Creator and Governor of all things, one in Essence, yet by certain Properties and Actions, represented to be Father, Son, and Holy Ghost." *Cf,* the first of the "Articles of Religion" of the Anglican *Book of Common Prayer* (all editions): *"Of Faith in the Holy Trinity.* There is but one living and true God, everlasting, without body, parts, or passions; of infinite power, wisdom, and goodness; the Maker and Preserver of all things both visible and invisible. And in unity of this Godhead there be three Persons, of one substance, power, and eternity; the Father, the Son, and the Holy Ghost." In upholding the monarchy, Parliament retains a veto on "Established Church" doctrine, and this Elizabethan formula, to the dismay of many Anglican theologians, remains official.

26. Lawrence Fogg, *An Entrance,* 225–38.

27. 2 Timothy 1.13: ὑποτύπωσιν ἔχε ὑγιαινόντων λόγων ὧν παρ' ἐμοῦ ἤκουσας. H. G. Liddell and R. Scott, editors, *A Greek-English Lexicon* (Oxford University Press, 1958), 750, 1841–42. ἔχω may be used to mean "fall pregnant" and παρά may mean "by" in that context. ὑγιαινόντων (Cf. Eng. "doing nicely" in medical idiom) is present participle of an active verb, implying greater *intellectual vivacity* than would equivalent form of the simple adjective ὑγιής ("wholesome"), which appears in, e.g., Titus 2.8 to imply *moral purity.* Cf. 2 Timothy 4.11, Colossians 4.14.

28. Hippocrates, *Nutriment,* 42. *See* W. H. S. Jones, editor and translator, *Hippocrates* (London: Heinemann, 1923), 1.356.

29. 1 Timothy 1.16; 2 Timothy 2.13–14. Paul reminds Timothy he has his lively faith from his mother and grandmother, Eunice and Lois (2 Timothy 1.5) and that a contentious faith is γάγγραινα, "a cancerous ulcer" (2 Timothy 2.17).

30. 2 Timothy 1.13, Vulgate: *Formam habe sanorum verborum, quae a me audisti.* παρ'ἐμοῦ is rather *chez moi* than *a me;* ἤκουσας implies a more active and consentful "listening" than the relatively passive *audisti* ("you have finished hearing").

31. T. S. Eliot, *Notes towards the Definition of Culture* (London and Boston: Faber and Faber Limited, 1979), 3: "Definition: 1. The setting of bounds; limitation (rare)—1483—Oxford English Dictionary." To clarify the distinction mentioned, Liddell and Scott (p. 1900) cite H. von Arnim, *Stoicorum Veterum Fragmenta* (Leipzig, 1903), 2.76; and as an example of ὅρος (p. 1256) cite Aeschylus, *Agamemnon* l. 485 (Chorus of Old Men on Clytaemestra): "θῆλυς ὅ. *the boundary* of a woman's mind." A superb example of the Byzantine iconography mentioned, in the Cari Cami, Istanbul, dates from the period of revival between the Latin sack and the Ottoman Conquest. Cf. William Shakespeare, *Antony and Cleopatra* 5.2.307–8.

32. On Fletcher, Hulton, and the literal diaspora ("scattering") of the Peterloo crowd on 16 August 1819, *see* Brown, *Bolton School,* 75, 81; Walmsley, *Peterloo,* 165–68. Dr. Robert Eveleigh Taylor (1773–1827), Bolton physician, Unitarian, protested Fletcher spy system; died in Kaskaskin, Illinois.

33. T. S. Eliot, "Little Gidding," 5.11–13, in *Collected Poems* (London: Faber and Faber Limited, 1965), 222.

34. *Dionysii Longini De Sublimitate Commentarius quem nova versione donavit . . . Zacharias Pearce.* (London: J. and R. Tonson, 1762), section 6, 33: *"multae experientiae ultimus foetus."* Ainsworth: Ἡ τῶν λόγων κρίσις πολλῆς ἐστι πείρας, τελευταῖον ἐπιγέννημα.

35. Lawrence Fogg, *A General View of Christian Religion . . . Primarily intended for Persons within the Author's peculiar Curacy at Plemstal [sic] near Chester* (Chester: Printed by E. Ince, for James Holland, 1714). The author addresses Sir John Bridgeman, baronet, patron of Plemstall, and reminds him that forty years earlier his

grandfather Orlando Bridgeman, lord keeper to Charles II, came to an arrangement with Bishop Wilkins (Oliver Cromwell's brother-in-law and a founder of the Royal Society) to provide a "peculiar" for him.

36. T. S. Eliot, "The Waste Land," 1.1–3; "Little Gidding," 5.15–18; Virginia Woolf, *Granite and Rainbow* (London: Hogarth Press, 1958), 229–31; Shakespeare, *Antony and Cleopatra* 2.5.240–43.

Bibliography

Religious Writers of Bolton and Deane and the English Monarchy,
1521–1689
Titles are listed chronologically under each author.

Anderton, James (1557–1613).

The apologie of the romane church, devided into three severall tractes. [English secret press,] 1604. (Issued under the pseudonymous initials "I.Br.", without James Anderton's consent.)

The protestants apologie for the roman church. By J. Brereley. [S. Omer, English College Press], 1608. (Enlarged and revised edition.)

[Another issue, with title page replaced by new prelims,] 1608.

Apologia Protestantium pro Romana ecclesia . . . per Ioannem Brerleium sacerdotem anglum vulgari idiomate composita, et per Guilielmum Raynerum Latine versa. Paris: J. Ducarroy, 1615. (Translation.)

[Another issue of this translation.] 1617.

The protestants apologie. (S. Omer, 1608.) Facsimile edition. No. 75 in the English Recusant Literature series. Menston: Scolar Press, 1971.

The lyturgie of the masse. "Colen" [Lancashire? Birchley Hall Press?], 1620.

The lyturgie of the masse. ("Colen", 1620). Facsimile edition. No. 184 in the English Recusant Literature series. London: Scolar Press, 1974.

Sainct Austines religion. Collected from his owne writings, and from the confessiõs of the learned protestants. [Lancashire? Birchley Hall Press?] 1620.

Sainct Austines religion. (1620). Facsimile edition. No. 30 in the English Recusant Literature series. Menston: Scolar Press, 1970.

The reformed protestant, tending directly to atheisme. By I. B. P. "Colen" [Lancashire? Birchley Hall Press?], 1621.

Luthers life collected from the writings of him selfe, and other learned protestants. S. Omer, [C. Boscard] for J. Heigham, 1624. (Distinctly cruder than any of the above works.)

Luthers Life. (S. Omer, 1624.) Facsimile edition. No. 172 in the English Recusant Literature series. Ilkley and London: Scolar Press, 1973.

ANDERTON, Lawrence (1575–1643).

One God, one fayth. Or a discourse against lukewarm-christians. [S. Omer, English College Press,] 1625. (Issued under the pseudonym "W. B., Priest".)

The non-entity of protestancy. [S. Omer, English College Press], 1633. (Issued under the pseudonymous initials "W. B.")

The progenie of catholicks and protestants. Rouen: Widow of N. Courant, 1633. (Issued under the pseudonymous initials "N. N.")

335

The triple cord or a treatise proving the truth of the roman religion. [S. Omer, English College Press] 1634. (Issued under the pseudonymous initials "N. N.")

Miscellanea or a treatise contayning two hundred animadversions. [S. Omer, English College Press], 1640. (Issued under the pseudonymous initials "N. N. P.")

BRADSHAW, Ellis (d. 1678?).

A dialogue between the devil and Prince Rupert: For T. B. London, [1649].

An husbandmans harrow to pull down the ridges of the Presbyteriall government and to smooth, a little, the Independent. London: The author, 1649.

[Another edition] London: For E. B. to be sold by Giles Calvert, 1649.

A new and cleer discovery of the . . . ebbing and flowing of the main sea. London: By Gartrude Dawson for Thomas Brewster, 1649.

A week-daies lecture, or . . . the preaching of the heavens. London: By Gar: Dawson for Tho: Brewster and Gr: Moule, 1649.

A true relation of the strange apparitions seen in the air. London: For Tho. Brewster, and Gregory Moule, 1650.

A compendious answer to a book called A brief survey of the judgement of Mr. John Goodwin. London: By H. Hills, to be sold by. T. Brewster, 1652.

Downfal of tythes no sacriledge. For H. Cripps, and L. Lloyd, 1653.

The Quakers whitest divell unvailed. 1654.

The Quakers quaking principles examined . . . in . . . answer to . . . James Naylor in his Answers unto Mr. Baxter. Lodowicke Lloyd, 1656.

The conviction of James Naylor . . . in answer to a booke of his called Wickednesse weighed . . . writ in answer to . . . The Quakers quaking principles examined . . . by Ellis Bradshaw. By M. S. for Lodowicke Lloyd, 1656.

A cordial-mediator for accordance of brethren. Printed, and . . . sold by Lodowick Lloyd, also by Henry Crips, and by Thomas Brewster, 1658.

BRADSHAW, Henry (d. 1513).

Here begynneth the holy lyfe and history of saynt Werburge. [London]: Richarde Pynson, 1521.

[Another edition] *The holy lyfe and history of Saynt Werburge.* Edited by Edward Hawkins. Manchester: Chetham Society, 1848.

[Another edition] *The Life of Saint Werburge of Chester.* Edited by Carl Horstmann. London: Early Texts Society, 1887.

HEWIT, John (1614–1658).

Baptised Eccles (of which parish Deane was anciently the northern half), 4 September 1614; believed to have attended Bolton Grammar School before his family's removal to London; beheaded Tower-Hill, 8 June 1658. All publications are (probably) posthumous, mostly of 1658. Nathaniel Hardy of St. Dyonis Backchurch, in Hewit's funeral oration (St. Gregory's, 13 June 1658) denounced the *Select Sermons* (offered as short-hand transcripts) as inauthentic, some being "translations out of French Authours."

Certain considerations against the vanities of this world. London: Edward Crouch, 1658.

[Another edition.] 1658.

Dr. Hewit's letter to Dr. Wilde on Monday, June 7. 1658 [London, 1658].

Nine select sermons. London: Henry Eversden and Tho. Rookes, [1655?]

[A reissue.] London: Henry Eversden and Thomas Rookes, 1658.

[Another edition.] [1658.]

[Another edition.] [London]: John Williams, 1659.

Repentance and Conversion. (With portrait.) [London]: J. C. to be sold by Samuel Speed, 1658.

(Contains disavowal by G. Wild and J. Barwick of *Nine Select Sermons.*)

[Another edition.] Sam. Speed, to be sold by William Thorpe, 1658.

The speech and deportment of John Hewyt, D.D., on the Scaffold on Tower-hill, June 8. London, 1658.

The true and exact speech and prayer of Doctor I. Hewytt ... immediately before his execution. June 8, 1658. [London, 1658].

[Another edition] [London,] 1658.

[Another edition] [London, 1658?]

Prayers of Intercession. 1659.

See also:

The Tryals of Sir Henry Slingsby Kt, and John Hewet, D.D., for High Treason ... With the substance of their Speeches on the Scaffold. London, 1658.

[William Prynne], *Beheaded Dr. John Hewytts Ghost pleading ... in the New High Commission ... in Westminster Hall.* London, 1659.

HEYWOOD, Nathaniel (1633–77).

Christ displayed. Edited by O. H. [Oliver Heywood]. London: Tho. Parkhurst, 1679.

[Reprinted] *The whole works of the Rev. Oliver Heywood,* Volume 1. (1827). [See below].

HEYWOOD, Oliver (1630–1702).

Heart-treasure. London: By A. Ibbitson for Thomas Parkhurst, 1667.

The sure mercies of David. 1670. (Part 2 of *Heart-treasure.*)

[Another edition.] 1671.

[Another edition.] [London:] By R. W. for Tho. Parkhurst, 1672.

Closet-prayer, a Christian duty. London: Thomas Parkhurst, 1671.

[Another edition.] By A. M. for Tho. Parkhurst, [1671?].

[Another edition.] Thomas Parkhurst, 1687.

[Another edition.] 1700.

[Another edition.] London, 1794.

[Another, revised, edition] *with a short sketch of his life.* Edited by J. Kerby. [London,] 1816.

[Another edition.] 1830.

A narrative of the holy life ... of ... Mr. John Angier. 1677.

[Another edition.] London: Tho. Parkhurst, 1683.

[Another edition.] 1685.

[Another edition.] Edited by Ernest Axon. Manchester: Chetham Society, 1937.

Life in God's favour. London: Dorman Newman, 1679.

[Another edition.] Halifax: Brearley Hall, 1796.

Meetness for Heaven. [London,] 1679.

Israel's Lamentation after the Lord. London: Tho. Parkhurst, 1683.

Baptismal bonds renewed. London: Tho. Parkhurst, 1687.

Advice to an only child. London: Tho. Parkhurst, 1693.

[Another edition.] 1700.

[Another edition.] 1820.

The best entail. For Thomas Parkhurst, 1693.

A family altar erected to the honour of . . . God. London: Tho. Parkhurst, 1693.

[Another, revised, edition] *with an account of his life [and] Seven familiar discourses on the Lord's Prayer.* Edited by Charles Atmore. Liverpool: Nuttall & Co, 1807.

Job's appeal. London: B. Aylmer, 1695.

A new creature. Discourses. London: Tho. Parkhurst, 1695.

Heavenly converse. Manchester: By J. Back for Ephraim Johnston, 1697.

The general assembly. London: Tho. Parkhurst, 1700.

A treatise of Christ's intercession. London: Printed by T. Whitworth, Leeds, for T. Parkhurst, 1701.

[Selections.] *Memorials of Providence in the remarkable providential supplies of . . . Oliver Heywood.* No. 1 in the Cottage Library of Christian Knowledge series. [1810?]

Select Nonconformist Remains: being original sermons of Oliver Heywood, Thomas Jollie, Henry Newcombe, and Henry Pendlebury. Edited by Richard Slate. London, 1814.

[Collections.] *The whole works of the Rev. O. Heywood with a Memoir of his life by Richard Slate.* [Edited by Richard Slate.] 5 vols. Idle, 1827–25.

Nonconformist Register of Baptisms, Marriages and Deaths, compiled by O. Heywood & T. Dickenson . . . known as the Northowram or Coley Register. Edited by J. H. Turner. Brighouse, 1881.

J. Horsfall Turner, editor: *The Rev. Oliver Heywood . . . autobiography, diaries, anecdote and event books.* 4 vols. Brighouse: The Editor, 1882–85.

LEVER, Christopher (before 1587–after 1627?)

Stuart writer on monarchy. Educated, Christ's College, Cambridge, but did not graduate. Given Durham and Cecil aspirations, perhaps an example of the Lever-Pilkington *diaspora;* and as such beyond the scale of the present study. Cited here as representing a viewpoint otherwise omitted. John Lever, vicar of Bolton (d. 1691) was of similar churchmanship.

A Crucifixe: or a meditation upon repentance and the Holie Passion. London: By V. S. for John Budge, 1607.

Queene Elizabeth's Teares; or her resolute bearing the Christian Crosse. London: By V. S. for Mathew Lownes, 1607. (Dedication to Robert [Cecil], earl of Salisbury.)

[Both the above reprinted.] A. B. Grosart, *Miscellanies of the Fuller Worthies' Library.* Blackburn: Printed for Private Circulation, 1872.

Heaven and Earth, Religion and Policy. Or the maine difference betweene Religion and Policy. [London,] 1608.

The Holie Pilgrime leading the way to Heaven. London, 1618. (Dedication to "the worshipful Master Newton, tutor to the Prince and Dean of Durham; Master Murray, tutor to the Duke of York and Master of Sherburne House." Epistle to Archbishop Richard Bancroft.)

The Historie of the Defendors of the Catholique Faith. London, By G. M. for Nicolas Fussell and Humphrey Mozeley, 1627. (Dedication to Charles I. The work is as by one used to tutoring aristocratic families. Analyses its subjects from Henry VIII to James I under three headings: "Divine," "Politic," and "Moral." Typical comment: Mary Tudor, in her excessive zeal for the divine, confounded her political position and as a result subverted morality. Concerns close to Thomas Lever and James Pilkington are discussed in a manner somewhat reminiscent of Ralph Lever and to conclusions that anticipate Zachary Taylor junior. Conclusion reached (p. 370): "And let never a Caesar of this Empire, incline their favour to either of these crucified thieves [Romanists, Presbyterians], for though they hang with Truth, yet are they not true.")

LEVER, RALPH (d. 1585).

The Most ancient and learned playe, called the philosophers game. Set forth by W. F. London: R. Hall for J. Rowbotham [1562–63]. (Disclaimed by R. Lever in *The Arte of Reason.* W. F. is W. Fulwood, though in the context the initials (perhaps intentionally) suggest "William Fulke.")

[Another issue] *The most Noble, auncient and learned playe, called the Philosophers game* ... Set forth ... by Rafe Lever and augmented by W. F. London: R. Hall for J. Rowbotham, 1563.

The Arte of Reason, rightly termed, Witcraft, teaching a perfect way to argue and dispute. Made by Ralphe Lever. London: H. Bynneman, 1573.

LEVER, Thomas (1521–77).

A fruitfull sermon made in Poules churche at London in the shroudes the seconde daye of February. [London:] J. Daie and W. Seres, 1550.

[Two further editions, which have "Februari" in the title.]

A sermon preached the thyrd Sonday in Lent before the kynges maiestie. [London:] J. Daie and W. Seres, 1550.

[Another edition.] *A sermon preached the thyrd Sondaye in Lente before the kynges maiestie.* London: J. Day, 1550.

[Another issue, with corrected title.] *A sermon preached ye fourth Sudaye in Lente before the kynges maiestie.* London: J. Day, 1550.

[Another issue, with quires D-E reset.] J. Daie and W. Seres, 1550.

A sermon preached at Paules crosse, the .xiiii. daie of December. London: J. Day [1551.]

[Another edition] [London: J. Day, 1551.]

[Another edition.] [Worcester: J. Oswen, 1551?] (Has "Poules" in title.)

Three fruitfull sermōs, made by T. Lever. Anno domini 1550. Now newlie perused by the aucthour. London: J. Kyngston, for Henry Kirckham, 1572.

[Another edition] *Sermons.* Edited by E. Arber. London: English Reprints Series No. 25, 1870.

[Another issue] London: Constable, 1895.

A meditacion upon the Lordes Prayer, made M.D.Li. at Saynete Mary Wolchurche in London. London: J. Daye [1551].

[Another edition] *A meditacion upō the the lordes praier.* London: J. Kyngston and A. Kyngston [1551].

A treatise of the right way fro danger of synne nowe newly augmented. London: H. Bynneman for G. Byshop, 1571. (First edition, Geneva, 1556.)

[Another edition] *A treatise of the right way frō danger of sinne and vengeance in this wicked worlde unto godly wealth and salvation in Christe.* London: H. Bynneman for G. Byshop, 1575.

[Another issue, which also contains *A meditation uppon the Lordes prayer.*]

"A Preface, shewing the true understanding of God's word, and the right use of God's works and benefits, evident and easy to be seen in the exercise of these Meditations" and "A meditation on the Tenth Commandment." In John Bradford, *Godly Meditations uppon the ten Commaundementes.* London: William Seres, 1567. (Lever's Edition comprises extracts with additions, tending to palliate supralapsarian tendencies.)

[Another edition in] *The Writings of John Bradford.* Edited by Aubrey Townsend. Vol. 2., 565–71. Cambridge: Parker Society, 1848.

LIVESEY, James (1625–82).

Enchiridion judicum; or Jehosaphat's charge to his Judges . . . together with Catastrophe Magnatum, or, King David's lamentation at Abner's incineration . . . preached at the funeral of . . . J. Atherton, Esq. By James Livesey, Minister of the Gospel at Atherton, alias Chow-bent. London: By R. I. for Tho. Parkhurst, 1657.

(Another title page omits "alias Chow-bent" and the two quotations, and misprints Livesey's Christian name as "John." A separate titlepage also exists for *Catastrophe Magnatum* alone. In 1562 the Athertons had been compelled to sell their manor of Lostock to Christopher, the father of James Anderton.)

Series decretorum Dei causarumque et mediorum salutis nostrae. London: Printed by R. Ibbitson for Thomas Parkhurst, 1657.

ΨΥΧΗΣΗΜΙΑ : *or the greatest loss . . . a short Discourse occasioned by the doleful loss of . . . Mr. Humphrey Chetham.* London: By J. B. for Tho. Parkhurst, 1660.

ΠΝΕΥΜΑΤ-ΑΠΟΛΟΓΙΑ. *Or, an apology for the power and liberty of the Spirit, as at first to give a being to, so still to give a blessing by his ordinances. In three sermons.* London: By A. M. for Robert Clavel, 1674.

The spirit of the Lord. London: By F. M. for Robert Clavel, 1674.

LONGWORTH, Richard (1533–79).

Answer to Articles exhibited against him. Cambridge, 1569.

MARSH, George (1515?–1555).

"George Marsh writeth his own examination" and other letters. In John Foxe, *Actes and Monuments of matters most speciall in the church. Newly revised.* 2 vols. London: [J. Daye,] 1583.

(The spurious "An Other Letter," p. 1572, first appears in *Actes and Monuments newly enlarged.* London: J. Day, 1570.)

[Letters] Miles Coverdale, *Certain most godly, fruitful and comfortable letters . . . of holy Martyrs.* London: J. Day, 1564.

[Further editions include:] *The Letters of the Martyrs: Collected.* Preface by M. Coverdale. Introductory remarks by E. Bickersteth. London: John F. Shaw, 1837.

ORMEROD, George, editor. *Tracts relating to the Military Proceedings in Lancashire during the Great Civil War. Commencing with the Removal by Parliament, of James Lord Strange, afterwards Earl of Derby, from his Lieutenancy of Lancashire, and Terminating with his execution at Bolton.* Manchester: Chetham Society, 1844.

PENDLEBURY, Henry (1626–95).

A plain representation of transubstantiation. By a Countrey Divine. For J. Johnson, 1687. (Published at the insistence of John Tillotson.)

The books opened. Manchester: J. D. for Ann Unsworth, 1696.

Invisible realities. Edited, with a life of the author, by J. Chorlton. J. D. for Ann Unsworth. Manchester, 1696.

[Another edition.] [1815.] Bury, Lancashire.

The barren fig-tree. Norwich: R. Janeway, Jun. [London] for Ed. Giles, 1700.

Sacrificium Missaticum, Mysterium Iniquitatis, or a Treatise concerning the sacrifice of the mass. London: W. Cooke, 1768.

[Selections.] *Select Nonconformist Remains: being original sermons of Oliver Heywood, Thomas Jollie, Henry Newcombe, and Henry Pendlebury.* Edited by Richard Slate. London, 1814.

PILKINGTON, James (1519–1575/6).

Aggeus the prophete declared by a large commentarye. [London]: W. Seres, 1560.

[Another issue, with type reset.]

[Another issue, with quires A, B, Ee, Ff reset.]

Aggeus and Abdias prophetes, the one corrected, the other newly added, and both at large declared. London: W. Seres, 1562.

An exposition upon Abdias [1562] (Second part of above).

The burnynge of Paules church in London in the yeare of oure Lord 1561 ... AN ADDICION [by John Morwen] *... A CONFUTACION of an Addicion, with an Appologye Written And Cast In The Stretes of West Chester, Agaynst The Causes of Burnyng Paule's Church In London, Whych Causes, The Reverend Byshop Of Duresme Declared at Paule's Crosse 8. Junii. 1561 ... Also Certaine Questions ... Fullye Althoughe Shortly Aunswered.* London: W. Seres, 1563.

Homily against "Excess of Apparel." In *The seconde tome of Homelyes* [Edited by J. Jewel?] [R. Jugge and J. Cawood], 1563.

[Another edition, adding Homily 21: against rebellion.] [R. Jugge and J. Cawood] 1571.

(Among many other editions, a Welsh edition of the first and second book of Homilies appeared 1606.)

The Statutes and Charter of Rivington School. Edited by the Rev. J. Whitaker. London: Whittaker & Co., 1837. [The school was founded by letters patent of 13 May 1566.]

A godlie exposition upon certeine chapters of Nehemiah. Newlie published. In the latter end, because the author could not finish that treatise of oppression ... is added that by R. Some. Cambridge: T. Thomas, 1585. [Contains also "A Preface of M. John Fox, to the Christian Reader."]

[An extract] *Two godlie and fruitful treatises of oppression. The one taken out of the Exposition uppon the fift chapter of Nehemiah.* By J. Pilkington. The other by R. Some. Cambridge: T. Thomas, 1585.

The Works of James Pilkington. Edited by the Rev. James Scholefield, A.M., Regius Professor of Greek. Cambridge: Parker Society, 1842.

RIGBY, Joseph (d. 1671).

An ingenious poem, called the drunkards prospective, or burning-glasse. For the author, 1656.

J. Crossley, editor. *Observations and instructions divine and morall in verse by Robert Heywood.* Manchester: Chetham Society, 1869. [For Rigby's verses on "Repentance."]

SPARKE, Archibald, editor. *The Township Booke of Halliwell* [Deane]. Manchester: Chetham Society, 1910. (Gives details of the calamitous impact of the Civil War on a single township.)

STANLEY, James, seventh earl of Derby (1607–51).

The Earle of Darby's speech on the scaffold . . . exactly taken in short-hand [by James Roscow and another]. London: Nathaniel Brooks, 1651. (Like Marsh's Lathom examination in Foxe, this suggests unfakeable immediacy.)

The true speech delivered on the scaffold by James Earl of Derby. London: Robert Eles, [1651]. (Like Marsh's Chester examination in Foxe, this suggests partisan wish fulfilment.)

De laetste Reden van den . . . Grave van Derby [Amsterdam?] 1651. (Derby's widow Charlotte was granddaughter to William the Silent.)

Private Devotions and Miscellanies of James, seventh Earl of Derby. With a prefatory memoir and an appendix of documents. Edited by F. R. Raines. 3 vols. Manchester: Chetham Society, 1867.

TAYLOR, Zachary (1653–1705?).

A dissuasive from contention. London: By John Gain for William Cadman, 1683.

Obedience and submission to the present government demonstrated from Bishop Overall's Convocation Book. London: Robert Clavel, 1690.

[Another edition] London: Randal Taylor, 1690.

The vindication of a late pamphlet (entituled Obedience and submission). London: Ric. Baldwin, 1691.

The death of the righteous. [London]: E. Jones for Sam. Lowndes, 1695.

The devil turn'd casuist. London: E. Whitlock, 1696.

[Another edition] London: Peter Buck, 1696.

The Surey Impostor. London: For John James, and Ephraim Johnson Bookseller in Manchester, 1697.

Popery . . . superstition . . . unjustly . . . pretended. London: John Jones and Ephraim Jonston . . . Manchester, 1698.

Popery, superstition, ignorance . . . confess'd. London: Printed for W. Keblewhite and J. Jones. 1699.

The decency and moderation of Christian mourning. London, 1703.

TILSLEY, John (1614–84).

A true copy of the petition . . . of the county . . . with some true and materiall observations . . . Together with a Paraenetick to Lancashire. London: John Macock for Luke Fawn, 1646.

The true relation of the taking of the town of Preston by colonell Seatons forces from Manchester. London, 1642.

VAUX, Laurence (1519/20–85).

A catechisme, or a christian doctrine necessarie for chyldren and the ignorant people. [Louvain: J. Fowler, 1568.]

[Another edition] *A catechisme, or a christian doctrine. With an instruction newly added of the laudable ceremonies used in the catholike church.* Antuerpiae, ap. J. Foulerum, 1574.

[Another edition] Rothomagi [G. L'Oysselet,] ap. H. Mareschalum, 1580.

[Another edition, with the title] *A catechisme or christian doctrine . . . with an addition of the ceremonies. Whereunto are adioyned certayne briefe notes of dyvers godly matters.* [Rouen, Fr. Parson's press?] 1583.

[Another edition.] *Whereunto is adioyned a brief forme of confession* [Rouen, G. L'Oyselet], 1583.

[Another edition.] [Rouen, G. L'Oyselet,] 1590.

[Another edition.] [English secret press,] 1599.

[Another edition.] "Roan" [i.e., English secret press], 1605.

[Another edition.] Revewed and amplified in this edition by J. Heigham. S. Omers. [C. Boscard], 1620.

[Another issue, c. 1670?, repeats 1620 date.]

[*See also*] Laurence Vaux. *A Catechisme or Christian Doctrine.* Reprinted from an Edition of 1583, with an Introductory Memoir of the Author by Thomas Graves Law. Manchester: Chetham Society, 1885. Law argues that the Louvain catechism first appeared in 1567, though no copies survive.

Index

Italicized page numbers refer to illustrations.

Aarau, 38, 62, 87, 88, 96, 129, 299–300 n;
St. Ursula's church, 87, 98
Abbot, George, 174
Abyssinia, 279
Abraham, 274
Act of Conformity (1662), 173, 185, 188,
226, 242, 249, 257, 289
Adam, 193
Adrian IV (pope), 99
Aeschylus, 333 n
Africa, 302 n; Congo, 165; Niger, 279
African slave trade, 228, 246, 278
Agincourt, 128
Agricola, Cnaeus Julius (Roman gover-
nor of Britain), 99
Ainsworth: chapel, 257; chapelry and
township, 232. See also Cockey Moor
Ainsworth, Rodger, 330 n; sons of, John,
Robert, and William, 330 n (see also
Ainsworth, Robert); wife of, Ellen
(née Warburton), 301, 330 n
Ainsworth, Robert (1660–1743), 281–
87; and the androgynous Isis, 220, 286.
Works: J. Casa His Galateus, 284–85;
Monumenta Vetustatis Kempiana, 286;
The Most Natural and Easie Way,
282–83, 289; Thesaurus Linguae Lat-
inae . . . or . . . Dictionary of the Latin
Tongue, 245, 256, 280–82, 285,
287–88, 290, 292
Akehurst, Mr., 240–41
Alexander the Great, 150, 248, 332 n
Alfred the Great (king of England), 145
All Hallows, Bread Street, London, 77,
88, 98
Alva, duke of, 183
Ambrose, Saint (bishop of Milan),
96–98, 101, 130, 302
America, 38, 99, 186, 188, 234–35, 265,
267, 272, 278; as source of reconcili-

ation, 293; as source of stereotypes,
188
American colonies, 270
American Indians, 186, 190–91, 205
Amiens, 37
Amry, 103, 105
Anabaptists, 86, 106–7, 171, 315 n
Anacletus (pope), 105
Anderton family, 203, 323 n
Anderton, James (1557–1613), 159–77,
190–91, 199, 204, 243, 246, 269, 335;
impropriator of Bolton, Deane, and Eccles, 162, 176, 185, 273–75, 312–13 n;
protonotary of common pleas, 159;
pseudonym "John Brereley Priest,"
166–67, 176, 315 n. Writings: Apologie of the Roman Church (1604),
159–60, 175; Lyturgie of the Masse,
161, 168–70, 172, 187; Protestants
Apologie (1608), 159, 161, 163–64,
166, 168, 175–77, 226, 292; Reformed
Protestant, 162, 171–72; Sainct Austines Religion, 162, 173–74
Anderton, Lawrence (1575–1643), 165,
174, 241, 313 n, 335–36; Jesuit superior of the Lancashire district, 160.
Writings: Non-entity of Protestancy,
176; Progenie of Catholicks, 176
Anderton (of Anderton) family: 307 n,
313 n; William, 306 n
Anderton (of Birchley) family: Ann, 204;
James (nephew of James Anderton of
Lostock), 159; 246; 313 n; Roger,
159–60, 164, 174–76, 313 n; secret
press, 152, 311 n, 313 n, 314 n, 315 n,
335
Anderton (of Horwich) family: Thomas
(father of Lawrence), 164; William,
325 n. See also Anderton, Lawrence
Anderton (of Lostock) family: Agnes

(née Preston), 315 n; Charles, 313 n; Christopher, I, 159, 306 n; 312–13 n; Christopher, II, 313 n; Christopher, III, 173, 184, 313 n; Francis, I, 185, 263, 313 n; Francis, II, 313 n; James (son and heir of Christopher, I), 159 (see also Anderton, James); Laurence (baronet and benedictine), 270; Margaret (née Tyldesley), 159

Andrews family: Heth (Mrs. Nicholas, née Lever, of Little Lever), 182; Jane (Mrs. John, Sr., née Lever, of Darcy Lever), 37, 165, 182, 236–37; John, Jr., 239, 323 n; John, Sr., 165, 182; Nicholas, 305 n. See also Lever, Richard, of Little Lever

Angier family: Ellen (née Winstanley), 322 n; John, Jr. (vicar of Deane), 185, 188, 249, 251, 276, 325 n; John, Sr. (minister at Ringley, then at Denton), 185, 187, 234, 238, 245, 332 n

Anglezarke moor, 145

Anne (queen of England), 265, 326 n; her children, 263

Anselm, 136

Antony, Saint, 136

Antwerp, 36

Apollo, 133, 135, 139–41, 248, 274

Apollo (in Acts), 143

Aquaviva (Jesuit general), 168

Aquila (in Acts), 143

Ariadne, 140

Arianism, 96

Aristotle, 166, 176–77, 275

Arminianism, 138–40, 149, 171, 174, 185, 247

army preachers, 153, 257

Arthur (legendary king of Britain), 145–46, 266

Arthur (prince of Wales), 146

articles of belief, 31, 55, 134, 152, 298 n, 311 n

Ascham, Roger, 80, 176, 305 n

Ashton family, 56, 92, 145, 165, 211, 267, 269; Hugh (archdeacon of the West Riding), 92, 131; Ralph (trustee of Bolton grammar school), 306 n

Ashurst family: Henry, Jr., 238–39, 242–43, 323 n; Henry, Sr. (J. P., of London), 323 n; John (Roundhead major at Bolton), 196, 323 n; William (M.P. for Newton), 323 n

Ashworth, Mr. (vicar of Ormskirk), 242

Askew, Anne, 30, 40–41

Aspull township: an administrative anomaly, 203; recusancy in, 203. See also Rigby (of Aspull) family

Athalia (daughter of Jezebel), 264

Athens, 246, 256, 292

Atherton, 109

Atherton, Oliver, 323 n

Atherton (of Atherton) family, 340; John, 192, 318 n; Mrs. John, 192

Augustine, of Canterbury, Saint, 136, 148; and British "heretics," 310 n, 322 n

Augustine, of Hippo, Saint, 96–97, 169, 173, 192; De Civitate Dei, 96, 98

Avignon, 131

Bacchus. See Dionysus

Bacon, Nicholas, 314 n

Bacon, Roger, 274

Bagaley, Humphrey, 319 n

Bale, John, 30, 40, 41, 60

Ball, John, 309 n

Ball, Thomas, 233

Bancroft, Richard: archbishop of Canterbury, 148, 153, 175, 236, 312 n, 338; bishop of London, 83

baptism, 151, 236, 258, 263, 265, 311 n

Baptists, 191

Barbados, 228, 255, 272, 323 n

Barlow, Ambrose, 315 n

Bartholomew's Day (massacre of), 124, 151

Barton (of Smithills) family: Andrew, 82; John, 295 n; Ralph, 303 n

Basle, 62

Bavaria, 239

Baxter, Richard, 233, 323 n; World of Spirits, 268

Beaconsfield, Benjamin Disraeli, earl of, 195; satire on old-Tory and Whig duopoly, in Coningsby, 206

Beaufort, the Lady Margaret, 78, 80, 92–94, 148; school of, at Knowsley, 80, 190, 265

Becon, Thomas, 302 n

Bedford, Francis Russell, earl of, 121

Bedford Leigh, 173, 315–16 n

beggars, 311 n

Bellarmine, R., 190, 235; *Disputationes de Controversiis Christianae Fidei* (1581–82), 175

Bentham, Jeremy, 279

Bentham, Thomas, 50, 60

Bernard of Clairvaux, Saint, 127

Berne, 62

Bible, 87, 89, 107, 110–11, 135–36, 138, 148, 152, 170, 188, 237, 245, 252; Authorized (King James) Version, 174, 231, 255, 291; Vulgate, 130, 264, 275, 291. *For individual books of the Bible, see* New Testament; Old Testament

Bickerstaff, 242; chapel, 242

Birche, Samuel, 325 n

Bird, John, 90

Birmingham (civil war massacre at), 228

Bishop Auckland, 134, 153

Bismarck-Schonhausen, Karl Otto, Prince von, 99

Blackburn: grammar school, 313 n; Presbyterian minister at, 319 n

Blackrod, 36, 39, 56, 144, 203; grammar school, 306 n

Blake, William, 140, 279

Blithe, John, 297 n

blues, 252

Blundell (of Ince Blundell) family, 270

Boardman, William, 186, 191

Bolholt, 39

Bolton, 78, 91, 144, 211; Acresfield Quaker Meeting, 272; Bank Street Presbyterian Chapel, 188–89, 329 n; cotton trade, 255, 278–79; Duke's Alley Independent Chapel, 318 n; "Geneva of the North," 239; grammar school, 58, 66, 78, 80, 94, 111, 121, 164, 181, 187, 189, 196, 221, 236, 257, 268, 275, 282, 287, 291, 295–96 n, 318 n; lectureships, 164, 191; manor, 194, 299 n; Man and Scythe tavern, 200, 299 n; market, 84, 183, 194, 210; massacre (May 1644), 161, 183, 201–2, 210, 228, 233, 320 n; Moor Lane chapel, 189; parish, 15, 36–37, 82, 108, 145, 162, 185, 232, 270, 285; parish church (St. Peter's), 37, 64–66, 188–89, 200, 221, 236, 249, 257, 295 n, 313 n; as parliamentary stronghold, 36, 181–212; as printing and publishing center, 278; Quakers and

"Shaking" Quakers in, 240, 271–72, 287, 323 n; river Croal, 38, 66, 189; river Irwell, 38–39, 307 n; river Tonge, 38; Winter Hill, 208, 309 n. *See also* commerce and industry; *names of individual townships*

Bolton (of Bolton) family: Catherine (marries Richard Lever of Little Lever), 37–38; James (vicar of Bolton), 37, 295–96 n

Bombay, 279

Bonner, Edmund (bishop of London), 130

Book of Homilies, 150–51, 311 n, 341; "Homily against Disobedience," 151. *See also* Grindal, Edmund; Pilkington, James

Bossy, John: *The English Catholic Community,* 271

Boston (Lincolnshire), 322 n; (Massachusetts), 107

Bosworth (battle of), 80, 83–84, 128, 199, 204, 300–301 n

Bowes, Martin: lord mayor of London, 40, 119; M.P. for London, 81

Bowring, John (M.P. for Bolton and plenipotentiary to the Celestial Empire), 279, 330 n

Boyne (battle of the), 281, 289

Bradford, 235

Bradford, earls of, 200. *See also* Bridgeman family

Bradford, John, 77–78, 79, 81, 82, 86, 91, 106–7, 136, 150, 301 n

Bradshaigh (of Haigh) family: Elizabeth, 327 n; Richard, alias "Barton" (Jesuit provincial), 264; Roger, Jr., 204–5, 327 n; Roger, Sr., 306 n

Bradshaw, 36, 39; hall, 73, 263

Bradshaw, Ellis (d. 1678?), 186, 188, 195, 206–12, 239, 241, 336. Works: *Compendious Answer to . . . John Goodwin,* 207; *Conviction of James Naylor,* 207, 239; *Cordial-Mediator,* 225; *Dialogue between the Devil and Prince Rupert,* 210, 233; *Downfal of Tythes,* 207; *Husbandmans Harrow,* 209, 258; *New and Cleer Discovery,* 208; *True Relation,* 210; *Week-Daies Lecture,* 208–9, 276

Bradshaw family, 295 n, 320–21 n

Bradshaw, Henry (d. 1513), benedictine of Chester, 23–32, 35–36, 37, 40, 41,

47, 79, 85, 101, 111, 129, 144, 187, 250; *Holy Lyfe and History of Saynt Werburge*, 23–32, 61, 160, 162, 187, 263, 292, 336

Bradshaw (of Bradshaw) family, 31, 35–36, 39, 196; John, 306n; Robert, 36, 37, 182, 184

Bradshaw (of Darcy Lever) family, 91, 301n

Bradshaw (of Haigh) family. *See* Bradshaigh (of Haigh) family

Bradshaw (of Marple) family: Henry, buys Bradshaw Hall, Bradshaw, 263; John ("the Regicide"), 36, 196, 205, 262–63. *See also* Isherwood family

Breightmet, 142, 251, 309n

Bridgeman family, 194, 200, 322n; Henry (bishop of Sodor and Man, third son of John, bishop of Chester, and husband of Katharine, daughter of Robert Lever of Great Lever), 195; John (bishop of Chester), 146, 195, 239, 250, 269; John (patron of Plemstall), 333n; Orlando (eldest son of the bishop of Chester, and Lord Keeper to Charles II), 195, 232, 334n

Bristol, 239

British church, 146, 310n, 316n, 322n

British Museum, 285, 293, 331n

Broadgate, 81, 146

Broadley, Matthew, 235

Brown, John, 279; *John Bunyan*, 279. *See also* Keynes family

Brown (of Westhoughton) family: John, 306n; William, 306n

Browne, Thomas, 191

Broxap, Ernest: *The Great Civil War in Lancashire*, 181–82, 195, 211

Brussels, 81

Bucer, Martin, 48, 104, 130, 176

Buckingham, George Villiers, duke of, 231, 316

Buenos Aires, 38

Bullinger, Henry, 49, 62, 122

Bungey, Cornelius, 78

Bunyan, John, 241, 279; *The Heavenly Foot-man*, 241; *Pilgrim's Progress*, 286

Burghley, William Cecil, Lord, 50, 52–53, 55, 59, 121–22, 131, 134, 164

Burnley, 314n

Burscough Priory, 301n

Bury, Lancashire, 330n

Bynneman, Henry, 57

Byzantium, 291, 333n. *See also* Constantinople

Caesar, Julius: *Gallic Wars*, 283

Calamy family: Ann (née Lever, of Darcy Lever), 325n; Edmund, Jr.,writes *The Nonconformists' Memorial*, 257

California, 38

Calvinism, 41, 55, 126, 139–40, 141, 149, 152, 162, 171, 174, 238, 247, 260, 266, 268, 275, 287

Calvin, John, 127, 165, 171, 329n

Cambridge, 94, 121, 241; Christ's College, 78, 80, 94, 160, 190, 313n; Corpus Christi College, 58; Emmanuel College, 39, 182; Jesus College, 257; King's College, 78, 104; Pembroke College, 52, 196, 305n, 306n; Peterhouse, 151; Queens' College, 52; St. John's College, 40, 47–48, 52, 55, 58, 92, 94, 121, 131, 138, 151, 240, 307n, 316n; Sidney Sussex College, 317n; Trinity College, 104, 186, 230, 233, 240, 303n; university, 37, 48, 81–82, 108, 126, 130, 150, 152, 182, 185, 247, 248. *See also* Pythagoras: "House" of

Canterbury, 98, 175, 316n

Canton, 279

Caribbean, 239

Carpenter, Edward, 288

Carr, Charles, 204

Carrington, John, 267, 269

Carter, Peter: headmaster of Bolton grammar school, 58; *Annotationes in Dialectica Ioan Setoni*, 299n

Cartwright family, 285

Cartwright, Thomas, 58–59, 131, 152

catechisms, 36, 56–57, 236

Catherine of Aragon (queen consort of Henry VIII), 95

Cecil. *See* Burghley; Salisbury

Ceres, 287

Chaderton, Laurence, 39

Chaldee, 130

Champney, Anthony: *Mr. Pilkinton his Parallela*, 316n

Chapman, Edmund, 234

Charles V (Holy Roman Emperor), 94, 95, 130–31

Charles I (king of England): and civil

war, 36, 85, 96, 154, 159, 246; financial policy, 195; as "martyr," 194, 199–200; portraits, 187; religious affairs, 128, 174–75, 227, 269, 276; trial and execution, 161, 183, 196, 206, 209, 226, 260, 319n

Charles II (king of England), 334n; and constitutional loyalists, 195–96, 204–5, 242; "ingratitude" of, 265; patron of Deane, 185, 271; religious affairs, 198, 226, 234, 245, 260; his restoration a cult at Tonge Fold, 216; and the "second civil war," 228

Chaucer, Geoffrey, 23, 177

Cheke, John, 80–81, 276; *Life*, by John Strype, 285

Cheshire, 31, 36, 79, 83, 183, 227

Chester, 25, 30–32, 78–79, 84, 86, 92, 96, 99, 105, 195; abbey of St. Werburgh (later cathedral), 23, 25, 30, 31–32, 68, 82, 96–97, 101–2, 129, 187, 195, 312n; city walls, 145; diocese, 300n; earldom of, 32, 83; Northgate dungeon, 86, 102, 154; siege of, 96, 195, 210

Chetham family, 191, 206; George, 192; Humphrey, Jr., 191, 257, 318n; Humphrey, Sr., 181, 184; Katharine ("consort" to George), 192

Chillingworth, William, 190

China, 279

Chishull, Edmund, 331n

Chorlton, John: "Life" of Henry Pendlebury, 318n

Churchill. *See* Marlborough, John Churchill, first duke of

Clayton, Leonard, 319n

Clegge, Lancelot, 184

Clement I (pope), 105

Cleopatra, 255, 281, 287, 292–93; portraits of, by Herbert Gilchrist, 293

Clough, A. H.: *Amours de Voyage*, 274

Coccium (Roman fort), 144

Cockerele, James, 200, 320n

Cockey Chapel, Ainsworth, 232, 257, 258

Coke, Edward, 166

Coldharbour, 135

Cole, Thomas, 208, 321n

Coleridge, Samuel Taylor, 235, 332n; "Frost at Midnight" (for son of, Hartley Coleridge), 283; "Kubla Khan," 279

Colet, John, 94

Coley: chapel, 249; curacy, 246; register, 338

Comenius, John Amos, 317n

commerce and industry (general), 91, 94, 107, 119, 132, 139, 146, 152–53, 181–82, 191, 207–8, 230, 232–33, 243, 246; banking, 45, 109, 289; bleaching, 317n; chemicals, 182, 188, 317n; coalmining, 38, 195; cotton, 38, 242, 255–56, 265, 278–79, 285; engineering, 182, 289; foundries, 38; fustian (wool and linen or cotton mixture), 263; glass, 140, 146; iron and steel, 37, 144–45; papermaking (including currency), 255, 320n; printing and publishing, 278–79; racketeers, 96, 117, 133, 152–53; textiles (general), 36, 42, 45, 62, 78, 87, 230–31, 322n; wool, 36, 256

Compton, Henry (bishop of London), 267

confession, auricular, 107, 109, 149, 170, 190

Congo, 165

Congregationalism, 189, 226. *See also* Independency

conscience, 27–29, 43–44, 49, 61, 85, 94, 103, 106–7, 109, 117, 129, 152, 169, 171, 192, 227, 237, 244, 252, 261, 265

Constantine the Great, 175, 226, 274, 316n

Constantinople, 273

conversion, 40, 232

Cotes, George, 95, 98, 100, 105, 119; bishop of Chester, 87, 90, 91, 93, 97, 102, 104, 154; master of Balliol College, Oxford, 93–94

Coton, Père, 169

Cotton, John, 322n

Covenanters, 184, 227, 260; religious practice of covenanting, 229, 233

Coventry, 50, 53, 60, 62, 78, 154, 297–98n, 332n; Bablake chantry, 50, 154; Bablake school, 51; grammar school of Henry VIII, 54; hospital of St. John, 51, 54; mystery plays, 50–51, 62, 78; Whitefriars, 51

Coventry and Lichfield, diocese of, 31, 50

Coverdale, Miles (bishop of Exeter): with

Lever at Aarau, 62; *Certain . . . Letters . . . of Martyrs,* 86, 108, 340; translation of the Psalms, 62
Cowper (sheriff of Chester), 103
Crabtree, Henry (curate of Todmorden), 269
Cranmer, Thomas (archbishop of Canterbury), 82, 107, 136, 151; homily on the "Salvation of Mankind," 151
Crashaw, Richard, 241
creeds, 28, 57, 97, 294 n
Crompton (of Darcy Lever) family, 91, 194
Crompton (of Bedford Grange, Leigh) family: William, Jr. (expelled minister of 1662), 173; William, Sr., 173–74, 177
Cromwell family: Mary, Lady Falconbridge, 196; Oliver, Lord Protector, 35, 185, 189, 196, 199, 204, 206–7, 227, 239, 289, 334 n; Richard, Lord Protector, 204, 225
Culloden (battle of), 252
Cuthbert, Saint, 132
Cyprian (bishop of Carthage), Saint, 46, 58, 232
Cyprus, 255

Dante, 255; *De Monarchia,* 292; *Divina Commedia,* 140, 256
Darcy Lever: and educational endowments, 164, 181; hall, 72; Hacken hall, 265; industrial microcosm, 38; Puritan heartland, 85–86, 88, 91, 289
Darlington grammar school, 121
Darwin, Charles, 247
David (king of Israel), 242
Deane, 88, 109, 120; Broadgate, 81, 146; Heaton chantry at, 295 n; Hulme Barn Farm, 109; moor, 109; parish, 15, 36–37, 81–82, 108, 145, 161–62, 185, 195, 232, 270, 285; parish church (St. Mary's), 36, 37, 56, 67, 184, 185, 324 n; parish school, 81, 106, 303 n; vicarage, 184–85; village, 202. *See also names of individual townships*
Declarations of Indulgence, 226, 234, 289
Dedham, Essex, 234–35; Presbyterian conference at, 234
Dee, John (warden of Manchester), 182
Delaware (river), 272
Demetrius (in Acts), 287

Derby, 78, 271
Derby, Charlotte Stanley (née de la Trémouille), countess of, 181, 183, 217, 226, 242
Derby, earldom of, 80, 83, 200
Derby, earls of: Edward Stanley (third earl), 82, 84–85, 88, 94, 96, 99–100, 112–13, 119; Edward Stanley of Bickerstaff(e) (eleventh earl), 206, 243, 265; Edward G. S. Stanley (fourteenth earl), 198–99, 279, 332 n; Edward Henry Stanley (fifteenth earl), 279; Henry Stanley (fourth earl), 304 n; James Stanley (tenth earl), 265; Thomas, Lord Stanley (first earl), 83, 199. *See also* Derby, James Stanley; Stanley family (general, seventh earl of)
Derby, James Stanley (1607–51), seventh earl of, 181–83, 184, 188, 203, 211–12, 226, 243, 265; burial, 242; execution, 198–201, 204, 215, 278, 320; as "martyr," 187, 194–200, 206; *Private Devotions,* 342; speech on the scaffold, 342
Derry (siege of), 252
Devereux family, 52. *See also* Essex, earls of
Diana of the Ephesians, 287
Dickens, Charles, 192; *Hard Times,* 284
Dido (queen of Carthage), 281
Dionysus, 139–41, 143, 274, 287, 309 n
Disraeli. *See* Beaconsfield, Benjamin Disraeli, earl of
Dobson, Joshua (minister at Cockey Moor), *Religious Gratitude . . . and Civil Liberty,* 310 n
Donne, John, 175, 197
Douglas (river), 145
Downham (Lancashire), 146
Drayton (Leicestershire), 239
Drogheda, 228; massacre, 227; obelisk, 281
Dublin: Trinity College, 257
Dudley family, 60, 95. *See also* Leicester, Robert Dudley, earl of; Northumberland, John Dudley, duke of; Warwick, Ambrose Dudley, earl of
Dudley, Lord Guildford (husband of Lady Jane Grey), 95
Dugdale, Richard, 219, 266, 267–69,

327–28 n; his mother, 269; his sister, 268

Dunster, Henry, of Bolholt, 39

Durham: castle, 131; cathedral, 121, 128, 131, 136–38, 154, 307 n; city, 132; college, 132; county, 121; diocese, 52, 131, 134, 237, 304–6 n; hospital (Sherburn), 52, 54, 305–6 n, 338

Eccles parish, 319 n

Edgeworth, 144; moor, 320 n

Edinburgh university, 161, 184, 235

Edward the Confessor (king of England), 28, 31

Edward, the "Black Prince" (prince of Wales), 51

Edward I (king of England), 32; Edward III, 267; Edward V, 204

Edward VI (king of England): ambiguities and opportunities of his minority, 42, 45–46, 91, 147, 161, 246; early death, 48; education, 77; religious affairs of reign, 40, 50, 82, 84, 100, 106

Egerton family: Elizabeth (née Ashaw), 242; Peter (Roundhead general), 242; Ralph, 328 n

Egypt, 108, 255, 281, 286–87

Eikon Basilike, 319 n

Eleazar, 248

Eleutherius (pope), 125

Eli, sons of, 248

Eliot, T. S., 285–86, 288; Four Quartets, 197, 280, 292–93; The Sacred Wood, 279; The Waste Land, 255, 280, 293

Elizabeth I (queen of England), 88, 103, 117; education, 81; enjoyments, 85, 136, 141; and Essex, 83, 146, 231, 331 n; as "Governor" of the Church, theory, and practice, 58–60, 77, 96, 105–6, 111, 120, 125–28, 131–32, 149, 163, 276; as icon of lamentation, 250, 338; and questions of "loyalty," 61, 121–22

Ely: bishopric, 120; cathedral, 120

Elyot, Thomas, 282

Emden, 36, 81, 120, 314 n

Emerson, R. W., 192

Engels, Friedrich, 181, 280

Ephesus, 287

Epictetus, 192

episcopacy, 50, 55, 58, 60, 105–6,

129–30, 131, 139, 195, 225, 226, 233, 312 n

Erasmus, Desiderius, 27, 94, 121, 126, 139, 142–43; De Libero Arbitrio, 153, 289; Praise of Folly, 93

Erastianism, 233, 240, 245

Essex, 235

Essex, earls of: Robert Devereux (second earl), 57, 83, 100, 146, 231, 331 n; Walter (first earl), 100, 298 n

Ethelbert (king of England), 322 n

Eton college, 78

Euripides, 143; Bacchae, 141, 327 n

Eve, 287

Exeter, John Holland, duke of, and earl of Huntingdon, 142. See also Wilde, Constance

Fagius. See Phagius, Paul

Falconbridge/Fauconberg, Lord, 329 n. See also Cromwell, Mary

Farnworth grammar school, Widnes, 148

Father, God the: concepts of, 28, 107, 126, 127, 150, 247, 276; as creator of destiny, 30, 126, 140–41, 276; as sanctioning transmitted authority, 24, 30, 103, 153, 162, 177, 259, 264–65, 270, 287–88. See also Providence, ideas of; Trinity, the Holy

Fell, Thomas (vice-chancellor of the duchy of Lancaster), 239

Fenner, Dudley (Puritan divine), 233

Fisher, John (bishop of Rochester), 92

Fletcher, Ralph 291

Fleury, Claude, 283

Flodden (battle of), 83–84, 312 n

Florence, 256

Fogg, Lawrence (1623–1718), of Darcy Lever, 289–93; dean of Chester, 280, 289; An Entrance into the Doctrine of Christianity, 289–90; A General View of the Christian Religion, 290, 293; rector of Hawarden, 289; Theologiae Speculativae Schema, 289–90

Fogg (of Darcy Lever) family, 91, 301 n; John, 332 n

Forster, E. M., 306 n; Passage to India (and connection with Whitman's poem of that title), 293

Fox, George, 238, 240; raised among descendants of George Marsh's friends, 239

Fox, Richard (bishop of Winchester), 93
Foxe, John, 118, 146, 149, 151; *Actes and Monuments*, 70, 86, 90, 105, 106, 108, 145, 340; edits James Pilkington's *Nehemiah*, 153; epicedium of, for Pilkington, 154
France, 36, 54, 160, 270; absolute monarchy, 169, 246
Frankfurt, 58, 62, 129, 163, 189
Franklin, Benjamin, 235
Frederick II (Holy Roman Emperor), 274
Fulke, William, 53, 297 n, 339
Furness, 88, 239; abbey, 301 n

Gardiner, Stephen (bishop of Winchester and Lord Chancellor), 80, 87, 88, 90, 95, 97–98, 101, 119
Gelasius of Cyzicus, 138; *Syntagma*, 308 n
Geneva, 36, 126, 129
George, Saint, 98
George III (king of England), 235
Gerard family: Anne (née Ratcliffe), 314 n; Gilbert (attorney-general), 164, 314 n
Germany, 94, 123, 240
Glencoe, Massacre of, 252
Glover, Robert, 78
Goodwin, John, 207
Goodwin, Richard: curate of Bolton, 182, 186; dissenting minister, 188; vicar, 182, 188
Gosnell, James (curate of Bolton): founds Gosnell lectureship, 164
Goudimel, Claude, 124
"Governor": as spiritual title, 31, 35, 40, 53, 62, 104, 125, 174, 198, 250, 295 n
Great Lever, 56, 91, 145–46, 195, 211, 250, 267, 269; hall, 195, *215*
Greek, 192, 256, 273–74, 280; and biblical humanism, 35, 93–94, 125–26, 130, 135, 142–43, 148, 150, 162, 264; and the irrational, 100, 191, 231; and literary sophistication, 80–81, 121, 135, 169–70, 252, 264, 287; particular meanings, 40, 138, 275, 290–92; and tragedy, 139–41. *See also names of individual authors*
Greenhalgh castle, 203
Gregory the Great (pope), 135, 175, 176, 317 n

Grey, Lady Jane, 42, 47–48, 94, 246, 296 n
Grindal, Edmund, 120; archbishop of Canterbury, 54, 59–60, 96, 148, 276; archbishop of York, 54, 122; bishop of London, 52, 53, 134; commissioner for the prayer book, 55; homily against "Gluttony and Drunkenness," 150
Grossteste, Robert (bishop of Lincoln), 176
Grundy, Tilsley, 320 n
Gualter, Rodolph, 135
Guernica (massacre, 1937), 183
Guise, Mary of, 37

Hackney, 284
Hadrian (Roman emperor), 287
Hales, John, 51
Halifax, 235, 251, 256, 257, 323 n; grammar school, 316 n
Halliwell, 186; *Township Book*, 341
Hammond, John, 193
Hampshire, 134–35
Hampton Court, 105, 281
Hanoverian dynasty, 270, 289
Hapsburg dynasty, 98, 288
Hardman, Richard (of Great Lever, d. 1623), 332 n. *See also* Pilkington (of Horwich) family
Hardy, Thomas: *Tess of the d'Urbervilles*, 279
Harley, John (bishop of Hereford), 77
Harrison, James (of the Society of Friends), 271–72, 323 n
Harpur, John (vicar of Bolton), 186–87
Hartley family: David, I, 235, 283; David, II, 235, 283–84; David, III, (1783), 235, 284
Harvard college, 39, 185
Haslam, Edward, 320 n
Hatton, Richard (vicar of Deane), 271
Haworth, 231
Hawthorne, Nathaniel, 82, 192, 330 n; *The Ancestral Footstep*, 82
Heapey: connections with Thomas Cole and the Bolton Whitmanites, 321 n
Heaton, 36; hall, 119, 120, 270; manor, 164, 314 n
Heaton (of Heaton) family, 36, 120, 164, 165, 301 n; George (Marian "sustainer"), 36, 40, 81, 120, 296 n; Joanna (née Bowes), 40, 119; Martin (bishop

of Ely), 40, 119–20; Ralph, 303n;
Richard (is father of Elenor), 36, 40,
295n; Richard of Westmeath, 314n;
Thomas (Marian "sustainer"), 36, 40,
81, 120, 296n
Hebrew, 100, 125, 130, 148, 192, 245,
248, 289
Henry II (king of England), 129; Henry
III, 32; Henry VI, 78, 104
Henry VII (king of England): dynastic
success of, 119, 163; and educational
investments, 80, 265; and neogoth-
icism, 83, 104, 146, 266; religious policy of, 28
Henry VIII (king of England), 95; as anarchist reactionary, 29, 30–32, 45, 117;
antichivalry of, at Flodden, 83; as "Defender of the Faith," 35, 129; founds
Trinity College, Cambridge, 104, 230,
240; "Head" of the Church, 97; sack
of religious foundations, 25, 31, 51,
276, 301n
Henry II (king of France), 36; Henry III,
304n; Henry IV, 168, 246
Henry (prince of Wales), 233
Herbert, George, 187, 227, 230–31, 234,
247; "The Church Porch," 249
Herrick, Robert, 182
Heton. See Heaton (of Heaton) family
Hewit, John (1614–58), 104, 161, 187,
194–200, 204, 206, 218, 234, 241, 289,
336–37; marries Lady Mary Bertie, sister to the earl of Lindsey, 196; portrait
of, at Lyme, 319n; preacher to Charles
I, 161, 195; royalist "martyr," 194,
196, 206, 276, 292; Prayers of Intercession, 104; Repentance and Conversion,
187, 196–97
Heyrick, Richard, 182, 184, 185, 285
Heywood, Nathaniel, Sr. (1633–77), 162,
225–44, 248, 269, 337; Christ Displayed, 241, 244, 264, 337; nephew of,
Benjamin, 228; son of, Nathaniel, Jr.,
228; son of, Richard, Jr., 228; vicar of
Ormskirk, 217, 242; wife of, Elizabeth
(née Parr), 239
Heywood, Oliver, Jr. (1630–1702), 162,
181, 186–87, 216, 225–52, 255–56,
263, 267, 269, 289, 337–38; journals,
226–27, 232, 233, 241, 251; son of,
Eliezer, 235, 248, 252; son of, John,

235; first wife of, Elizabeth (née Angier), 238, 245, 249, 251; second wife
of, Abigail (née Crompton), 244,
251–52. Works: Advice to an Only
Child, 235, 242, 251; Baptismal Bonds,
231, 235; Best Entail, 238; Closet
Prayer, 235; Family Altar, 235, 250;
Heart-Treasure, 230, 231–32, 234, 292;
Narrative of the Holy Life . . . of . . .
John Angier, 234, 245, 276; writings
(general), 233, 244, 247, 264
Heywood, Richard, Sr. (of Little Lever),
182, 186–87; 233; 240; 256; brother of,
John, 186; father of, Oliver, Sr., 232,
248; son of, John, 228; son of, Josiah,
228; son of, Nathaniel, Sr., 228 (see
also Heywood, Nathaniel, Sr.); son of,
Oliver, Jr., 228 (see also Heywood, Oli-
ver, Jr.); son of, Thomas, 228; wife of,
Alice (née Critchlaw), 232, 240, 271
Heywood, Thomas, England's Elizabeth,
250
Heywood (of Heywood) family, 231
Hill, Thomas (master of Trinity College,
Cambridge), 247, 322n
Hilton lectureship, 191
Hinton, William (vicar of St. Michael's
and archdeacon of Coventry),
297–98n
Hipperholme grammar school, 235
Hippocrates, 333n
Hitler, A., 239
Hobbes, Thomas: Leviathan, 199, 211,
266, 270
Hoghton family: Henry, 242; Katharine
(née Gerard), 314n; Mary (née Eger-
ton), 242; Richard, 314n
Holcombe chapel, 191
Holcroft, Thomas, 113
Holland, 246, 266, 326n
Holland family, 142, 309n. See also
Wilde, Constance
Hollingworth (a Presbyterian), 119
Holme, John (founder of Blackrod gram-
mar school), 306n
Holy Roman Empire, 95, 101
Homer, 169, 261
Hong Kong, 279
Hooker, Richard, 100, 190; Sermon on
Justification, 100–101, 110, 125

Hopkins, Gerard Manley (Jesuit curate at Bedford Leigh), 173, 177, 315–16n

Horace: *De Arte Poetica*, 127; *Epistles*, 94

Horne, Robert: bishop of Winchester, 127, 306n; dean of Durham, 128, 137

Horrocks, James (curate of Westhoughton, Deane), 232, 233, 236, 238, 247

Horwich, 285, 332n; chapelry, 185; manor, 255

Hotham, Charles (rector of Wigan), 204

Hull, Kingston upon, 233

Hulme Barn Farm, 109

Hulme, William (of Kearsley, Deane): endows Manchester grammar school, 181

Hulton, Nathaniel (factor to Richard Heywood, Sr.), 230

Hulton (of Hulton) family, 145, 194, 201; William (civil-war turncoat), 203; William (Peterloo magistrate), 291; William W. B. (dilettante), 331n

humanism. *See* Greek

hundreds (subdivisions) of Lancashire: Salford (southeast Lancashire), 36, 84, 91, 119, 173, 181, 201, 203, 235, 288; West Derby (southwest Lancashire), 36, 84, 173, 203, 260, 313

Hunt, Richard (Arminian dean of Durham), 308n

Huntingdon, 78

Hurst, Jeffrey, of Shakerley (brother-in-law of George Marsh), 106, 190, 310n

Hustler, William (M.P.), 283

Hyde family: Anne (duchess of York), 326n; Edward (first earl of Clarendon), 326n; Henry (second earl of Clarendon), 326n; Laurence (earl of Rochester), 260

Independency (or Congregationalism), 35, 189, 209, 226, 258

Innocent III (pope), 273, 276; "vicar of Christ," 273

Innocent IV (pope): sanctions torture, 274

Innocent VI (pope): wittily recognizes historical inconsistency, 316n

Ireland, 99–100, 165, 195, 227, 246, 267, 273, 281, 302n

Ireland, William (vicar of St. Michael's, Coventry), 297n

Isherwood family: Christopher (author of *Goodbye to Berlin*), 263, 316n; Mary (née Bradshaw), 263; Nathaniel (trader in fustian), 263; William, 320n

Isis, 220, 286–87

Italy, 95

James IV (king of Scotland), 83

James VI and I (king of Scotland and England): *Basilicon Doron*, 233, 255; imposes fines for refusing knighthoods, 85; religious affairs, 60, 120, 128, 149, 172, 257, 316n; theological interests, 120, 161, 173–74

James VII and II (king of Scotland and England), 268, 282; and Declarations of Indulgence, 226; as duke of York, 251–52, 271, 272; invades Ireland, 267; religious policies, 244, 245, 248, 257, 260; supplanted by Mary II and William III, 226, 258

James, Saint, 140

James, William: archdeacon of Coventry, 297n; Calvinist bishop of Durham, 139, 149

Jansenism, 264

Japan, 288

jazz, 249

Jerome, Saint, 291

Jerusalem, 146, 209, 239; Synod (1672), 294n

Jesuitism, 160, 164, 168, 176, 246, 260, 262, 264, 268, 302n

Jewel, John (bishop of Salisbury): *Apology of the Church of England*, 52; at Frankfurt, with Knox and Lever, 58, 189

Jezebel, 264

Joan of Kent (anabaptist), 106–7

John (king of England), 273

John, Saint (the evangelist), 240

John Chrysostom, Saint, 192, 204

John XXII (Avignon pope), 275

Johnson, J. (London publisher), 189

Johnson, John (Lostock baptist), 191, 275; founder of the "Johnsonians," 270, 318n; writings, 271, 290

Johnston, John, 278; *Visits to Walt Whitman in 1890–91 by two Lancashire Friends*, 293 (*see also* Wallace, J. W.); *Wastage of Child Life*, 332n

Jolly, Thomas, 267–68

Joseph of Arimethea, Saint, 310n

Judaism, 172, 239, 274, 292; necessity of imitating, in O. Heywood, 248; persecution of, in Germany, 274, persecution of, in Poland, 177, persecution of, in Yorkshire, 274

Julius II (pope), 93, 240

Juvenal, 283

Kafka, F.: *The Castle*, 98

Kaskaskin, Illinois, 333 n

Kearsley, 181

Kenilworth, 141

Kentucky Derby, 243

Kenyon (of Kenyon Peel Hall) family: Alice (née Rigby), 203; Roger, 203. *See also* Rigby (of Peel, Little Hulton) family

Keynes family: Florence Ada (née Brown), 279; Geoffrey, 279; John Maynard, 279

Khartoum, 288, 330 n

King's County. *See* Offaly

Kingsmill, Andrew (brother-in-law to James Pilkington), 127

Knowsley, 189, 190, 265

Knox, John, 51–52, 58, 95, 188, 189

Lancashire (south of the Ribble), 79; in Chester diocese, 31; in Coventry and Lichfield diocese, 31; educational experiments in, 80; and Ireland, 100, 227; a royal appanage, 83, 145, 270, 301 n; sectarian divisions in, 36, 201, 242. *See also* hundreds (subdivisions) of Lancashire

Lancaster, 78, 86–88, 96, 159, 244, 252; assizes, 192, 269, 270; castle, 82, 85, 86–88, 90, 92, 106; court of common pleas, 159; duchy, 159, 239; grammar school, 91; John O' Gaunt, second duke of, 83, 91, 92, 128, 204–5; priory, 90; royal house of, 78, 83, 88, 163

Langley family: Ralph (warden of Manchester), 92; Robert, 92; Thomas (bishop of Durham), 92, 137

Langton, Leicestershire, 77, 86, 88, 98, 109, 239

Lathom house, 78, 96, 104, 180–82, 183, 190, 244, 317 n; George Marsh at, 82–86, 110, 112–14; siege and sack of, 84, 188, 202, 203, 242

Latimer, Hugh (bishop of Worcester), 43, 46–47, 107, 139, 147; sermons, 45, 152

Latin, 80, 192, 283; borrowings from Greek, 40; confusion inherent in, 135; decadent rimed prose, 46; gossip, satire, and war in, 282; imperialist connotations of, 99, 281, 292; as jargon of scholasticism, 27, 175–76, 273; penumbral meanings of, 127, 290–91. *See also names of individual authors*

Laud, William (archbishop of Canterbury), 139, 175, 196, 198, 276

Leaf (London apprentice), 107

Lear (a king in Shakespeare), 44–45

Lee, Ann (Shaker "mother"), 272, 287

Leicester, 78

Leicester, Robert Dudley, earl of, 60, 146, 331 n

Leicestershire, 45, 77, 80, 86

Leigh grammar school, 316 n

Leix, 99

Lemprière, John: *Classical Dictionary*, 283; headmaster of Bolton grammar school, 324 n

Lenin, V. I., 98

Levellers, 184

Lever, Charles James, 332 n

Lever family/surname-solidarity group: Adam (a "papist"), 329 n; Christopher (author, *Defendors of the Catholique Faith*), 63, 338–39; John (minister at Cockey Moor), 329 n; John (vicar of Bolton), 271, 329 n; Margaret (née Isherwood), 329 n

Lever, John, Jr., 38, 121; Marian exile, 48, 62; founder-headmaster of Tonbridge grammar school, 58; rector of Washington, county Durham, 306 n

Lever, John, Sr.: cofounder of Bolton grammar school, 36, 38, 94, 296 n; daughters of, Helene and Jane, 305 n; son of, Gilbert, 305 n; sons of, John, Jr., Ralph, and Richard, 38; son of, Roger, 305 n; son of, Thomas, Sr., 38; wife of, Elenor (née Heaton), 36, 40, 81. See also Lever, John, Jr.; Lever, Ralph; Lever, Richard; Lever, Thomas, Sr.

Lever, Ralph (d. 1585), 38, 42, 48, 52–53, 57, 60, 121, 305–6 n, 339; archdeacon of Northumberland, with episcopal powers in the interregnum after Pilkington's death, 121, 305–6 n; Marian exile, 58; *vagus, 62.* Works: *Arte of Reason, rightly termed, Witcraft,* 57, 100, 298 n; "Assertions touching canon law," 111; *The Most Noble play,* 60, 297 n (*see also* Pythagoras)

Lever, Richard, of Little Lever, 38, 305 n, 306 n; granddaughter of, Heth Lever (daughter of Jenett and Thomas, Jr.), 305 n; great-grandson of, John Andrews (son of Heth and Nicholas), 182, 236, 305 n; son of, Thomas Lever, Jr., 305 n. *See also* Andrews family; Bolton (of Bolton) family; Lever (of Darcy Lever) family; Longworth (of Longworth) family

Lever, Thomas, Sr. (1521–77), 35–62, 77, 79, 81, 85, 87, 94–96, 106, 117, 120, 125, 129, 164, 182, 189, 236, 305 n; archdeacon of Coventry, 50–52, 59–60, 98; canon and prebend of Durham, 52–53, 121, 134; colonist at Aarau, 38–39, 62, 87–88, 96, 186, 299 n; master of St. John's College, Cambridge, 47–48, 98; master of Sherburn hospital, Durham, 52, 54, 121; letters, 42, 49, 121. Works: *Epistle to the Council,* 42, 47; preface, etc., to John Bradford's *Meditations,* 42, 53, 228, 306 n; *Sermons,* 42, 43–48, 61, 69, 85, 106, 140, 147, 161, 185, 188, 205, 241, 290; *Treatise of the Right Way,* 36, 56–57, 60–61, 88, 106, 112, 137, 282; writings (general), 40–41, 55, 58, 112, 117, 133, 148, 165, 274, 339–40

Lever (of Darcy Lever) family: Ashton (of the Leverian museum), trustee of Bolton grammar school, 331 n; Robert, Jr., refounder of Bolton grammar school, 66, 181, 221, 236, 325 n; Robert, Sr., 305 n. *See also* Andrews family; Darcy Lever

Lever (of Great Lever) family: Leverhulme, W. H. Lever, first baron Lever and first viscount, 133, 146, 181, 279, 288. *See also* Bridgeman family; Tillotson and Son

Lichfield, 50

Lincoln family: Abraham, 293; Mary (née Todd), 293

Lindsey, Montagu Bertie, second earl of, 196

Linus (pope), 105

litanies, 26, 104–5, 109, 124, 197–98

Little Hulton, 202–3

Little Lever, 36, 38; chapel, 186; hall, 38; manor, 37–38, 145, 165, 305–6 n

liturgies, 41, 52–53, 56, 90, 133–34, 138, 185, 236–37, 249, 275, 289

Liverpool, 96, 100, 270, 290

Livesey, James (1625–82), 191–93, 196, 204–5, 210; writings listed, 340

Livy, 283

Locke, John, 279; *Thoughts upon Education,* 283

Lodge, John (deputy-keeper of the muniments of Ireland), 331 n

Lollardism, 50, 80, 91, 234–35, 288

London: under Alfred the Great, 145; financial capital, 107–8, 145, 181, 279, 289; persecution in, 81, 86, 171; printing and publishing center, 35, 48, 189, 234, 255, 267, 289; and the Wyatt rebellion, 49. *See also* All Hallows; Merchant Taylor's School; Phoenix Tavern; Plumbers' Hall dissenters; St. Gregory's; St. Paul's

Londonderry. *See* Derry (siege of)

Longinus: *On the Sublime,* 292

Longworth, 52, 232, 271, manor, 145, 165

Longworth, Richard (1533–79), 340; canon and prebend of Durham, 53; dean of Chester, 54, 100, 236; master of St. John's College, Cambridge, 52–53, 58

Longworth (of Longworth) family: Adam (fellow of Corpus Christi College, Cambridge), 58; George (trustee of Bolton grammar school), 306 n; Jenett (Mrs. Thomas Lever, Jr.), 305 n; Peter (trustee of Blackrod grammar school), 306 n; Richard, 52–54 (*see also* Longworth, Richard); Roger (of the Society of Friends), 272; Thomas (nephew of Richard), 52, 298 n

Lostock, 36, 270; Baptist chapel, 191, 270; hall, 159, 164, 213, 270, 313 n; maypole, 286

Louis XIV (king of France), 265, 266, 268, 283

Louvain, 39, 246

Love, Christopher, 185
Lucan, 245, 286
Lucius (a British king), 125
Luke, Saint, 143, 290
Lutheranism, 41, 62, 95, 127, 171
Luther, Martin, 42, 191; *De Servo Arbi-trio*, 125, 153, 289; *Ninety-Five The-ses*, 93
Lydgate, John, 23

Magna Carta, 273, 277
Maintenon, Madame de, 265
Malta, 51, 298 n
Mancetter (near Coventry), 78
Manchester, 38–39, 78, 85–86, 92, 107–8, 144, 181, 184, 201, 239, 265; Chetham's hospital and library, 181, 184; college, 119, 182, 272; collegiate church, 92; grammar school, 78, 94, 181, 182; university, 181
Manicheism, 96
Marcellus II (pope), 124
Markievicz, Constance (née Gore-Booth), Countess, 288
Marlborough, John Churchill, first duke of, 265
Marsh family: George, 77–113 (*see also* Marsh, George); Giles (co-founder of Deane parish school), 303 n; Hum-phrey, 81; James (a Victorian descend-ant of George, at Broadgate), 146
Marsh Fold (Rumworth), 81–82
Marsh, George (1515?–55), 37, 57–58, 70, 77–113, 117, 124, 153, 164, 171, 189, 209, 225, 228, 230, 236, 238, 244, 252, 290, 293; children, mother, other relatives, 106, 108; curate of Langton, 77, 98, 239; descendants, at Wes-thoughton, 232; letters, 58, 79, 85, 88, 91, 108–10, 117, 133, 142, 144, 148, 162, 212, 241, 274, 284, 289, 340; mar-tyrdom, portrayed in Foxe, 70, 292; spurious letter, 145, 310 n, 340; wife of, 108
Marston Moor (battle of), 138, 184, 202, 210, 233
Martin of Tours, Saint, 96
Marx, K., 98; *Das Kapital*, 288
Mary I (queen of England): acclaimed queen, 48; builds Trinity College chapel, 103–4; denounced by the pope, 104, 129; at Hampton Court, 105;

Hapsburg alliance, 51, 77, 88, 94–95, 97, 110, 281; last illness and death, 105–6, 117, 119; persecution under, 77, 81, 171, 269; propaganda against, 36, 81, 87; reconciled to the pope, 84, 90; and the Wyatt rebellion, 49
Mary II (queen of England), 258, 266, 326 n; elegy to, 332 n; funeral music, 281; at Hampton Court, 281
Mary Magdalene, Saint, 142
Mary of Modena (queen consort to James VII and II), 258, 271
Mary, Queen of Scots, 37, 53–54, 119, 120, 134, 163
Mary, Saint, 102, 291
Mass, Roman Catholic, 26, 28, 37, 40, 56, 60, 77, 88, 90, 108, 110, 119, 120, 161, 165, 166–67, 177, 190–91, 261, 270
Massachusetts, 186
Mather, Increase: *Trials of the New En-gland Witches*, 267
Maulcbone, Humphrey, 204
Maximilian I (Holy Roman Emperor), 93, 97
Maximus (emperor of the west), 96, 97–98, 101
Mead, Richard, 284
Medici, Catherine de', 36, 151
Melanchthon, Philip, 79, 94, 108, 110, 300 n, 312 n; *Baccalaureate Theses*, 100–101; *Propositions on the Mass*, 108; *Wittenberg Concord*, 113
Menander, 169
Merchant Taylor's School, London, 196, 316 n
Mercia, kingdom of, 31–32
Mersey (river), 144, 145
Methodism, 189
Middleton parish, 56, 232. *See also* Ains-worth; Great Lever
Milan, 96
Mill, J. S., 235, 322 n; *Utilitarianism*, 97
Milton, John: *Paradise Lost*, 228
Missouri, 285
Model Army, 202, 228
monasteries, 23, 31, 32, 35, 43, 51, 77, 95–98, 109, 131, 145, 164, 187, 228, 263, 298 n, 301 n
Montreal, 38
More, Thomas, 191; idea of "utopia," 98

Morton, Thomas, 175; bishop of Chester, 176; writes *Catholike Appeale*, 175
Moon, 208
Morwen, John, 130
Moses, 136
Muncer (rebellion), 240
Murray, Mr., 338

name of God: as expression of totalitarianism, 201
Nantes, edict of, 168, 245–46
Napier, Robert: invades Abyssinia, 279
Naples, 163
Napoleon I (emperor of the French), 287
Nayler, James: prosecuted for blasphemy, 239, 261
Nehemiah, 135, 146, 231
Neile, Richard (Arminian bishop of Durham), 139, 149
Nero (Roman emperor, impresario, and poet), 105, 245, 283
Netherlands, 98. *See also* Holland
Neville family, 137–38. *See also* Westmorland, Charles Neville, sixth earl of
New England, 38–39, 62, 108, 189, 249, 266
"new learning." *See* Greek
Newman, J. H., 273; *Fifteen Sermons*, 97
New Testament (general), 94, 149, 176, 231, 252, 288; Acts, 130, 143, 229, 231, 255, 275, 287; 1 Corinthians, 44, 192, 290; Ephesians, 231; Galatians, 71, 135, 250, 308 n; John, 225, 261; 1 John, 169; Luke, 107, 139–41, 143; Mark, 61; Matthew, 107; 1 Timothy, 291; 2 Timothy, 290. *See also* Bible; Old Testament (general)
Newton, Adam, 338
Newton, Isaac, 230, 247
New York, 38, 272
Nicene Council, 138
Niger, 279
Norman Conquest, 31, 129, 144
Norres, or Norris, Alexander, 318 n
Norris, Edward, 306 n
Northampton, William Parr, marquis of. *See* Parr family
Northowram, 235; chapel, 235; register, 338; school, 235, 283
Northumberland, John Dudley, duke of, 47–48; 60; 95

Northumberland, Thomas Percy, seventh earl of, 121–22
Nottingham, 183
Nowell, Alexander (dean of St. Paul's): *Catechism*, 56–57, 61, 298–99 n

Oberammergau, 239
Ockham, William of, 27, 113, 136, 273–76, 282, 287, 308
Offaly, 99
Oldham, Hugh (bishop of Exeter), 93–94
Old Testament (general), 30, 108, 135, 149; Ezekiel, 192; Genesis, 169, 287, 288; 2 Kings, 264; Leviticus, 276; Nehemiah, 118, 135–36, 151; Psalms, 62, 88, 192, 205, 264, 273; 1 Samuel, 248; 2 Samuel, 242. *See also* Bible; New Testament (general)
Ormond, James Butler, earl of, 196, 227
Ormskirk, 226, 242, 257; Stanley tombs at, 242
Orrell (of Turton) family, 165, 191, 299 n; citation for recusancy, 181, 296 n; William (trustee of Bolton grammar school), 306 n
Osiris, 287
Overall, John (bishop of Norwich), 257; *Convocation Book*, 258, 264, 265
Over Hulton, 194
Overton, William (bishop of Coventry and Lichfield), 60
Oxenbridge, John (rector of Southam), 60
Oxford, 27, 93, 131; Balliol College, 93–94; Bodleian Library, 120; Brasenose College, 311 n, 316 n; Christ Church, 316 n; Corpus Christi College, 93; Durham College, 132; Gloucester College, 294 n; university, 182, 278, 291

Palestrina, G. P. da: *Missa Papae Marcelli*, 124
Pankhurst family (pioneers of women's suffrage), 288
papacy: and allegiance of all Christians, 29, 77, 90, 96, 104–5, 173, 273; and canon law, 53, 101; and the deposing power, 29, 93, 96, 166–67, 171, 173, 175, 190, 273; dogmatic statements of, 27, 55, 101, 135, 273; and the empire, 93–99, 125, 274; and philosophic realism, 44, 171–72, 274–75

Paris, Treaty of (1783), 235, 243
Park, or Parke, Robert (vicar of Bolton), 233, 322 n
Parker, Alexander (of the Society of Friends), 238
Parker, Matthew (archbishop of Canterbury), 131, 134, 298 n
Parker Society, 134, 296–97 n
Parliament (general), 35, 160, 166, 169, 181, 204, 211, 225, 266; and Anne, 263; "Barebone's," 207; under Charles I, 182; under Charles II, 228, 250, 261; and Civil War, 60, 173, 183, 186, 195, 210, 227; under the Commonwealth, 185, 240, 255; under Elizabeth, 49, 134; and the Hanoverian succession, 263; under Henry VII, 28; under Henry VIII, 31; under James I, 168; and James II, 258; and the Janeites, 94; under Mary I, 77, 90, 95; and the "Revolution" of 1688–89, 267, 277; "Rump," 198, 207; sovereignty of "Crown in Parliament," 278, 289, 333 n; under the Stuarts, 226
Parliamentary Reform Act (1832) 278, (1867) 199
Parma, Margaret, duchess of, 120
Parr family: Catherine (queen consort of Henry VIII), 36; Elizabeth (kin to Richard), 239; Richard (bishop of Sodor and Man, and kin to Catherine), 323 n; William (marquis of Northampton, and brother to Catherine), 36–37
Partington, Solomon: George Marsh, 309 n; Winter Hill Right of Way, 309 n
Paslew, John (last abbot of Whalley), 56
patchwork, form and meaning in, 252, 271
Patrick, Saint, 100
Patten family (merchants of Preston), 243
Paul, Saint, 44, 135, 142, 193; martyrdom of, 291–92; as Saul, 149
Paul III (pope), 130, 307 n; Paul IV, 302 n
Pearce, Zachary (bishop of St. David's), 292; translator of Longinus, 292
Pearson, John (bishop of Chester), 271
Peasants' Revolt, 103, 141–42
Pelagius, 274
Pemberton, Phineas (of the Society of Friends), 271–72; wife of, Phoebe, 271–72
Pendle. See witches
Pendlebury, Henry (1626–95), 187, 189–91, 196, 340–41; wife of, 190. Works: The Books Opened, 189; Invisible Realities, 189, 191; Plain Representation of Transubstantiation, 189
Penn, William, 272
Perkins, William (Calvinist divine), 126–27, 247
Persia, 146
Persius: Satires, 283
Peter the Great, Czar, 289
Peterloo (massacre of), 145, 198, 201–2
Peter Martyr (Pietro Martire Vermigli), 127
Peter, Saint, 99, 142, 149, 170, 260
Petrarch, 121
Phagius, Paul, 104, 130
Phoenix Tavern, 286
Philip II (king of Spain), 51, 77, 88, 94, 95, 97, 99–100, 104, 105, 134, 281
Piel Island, Furness, 88
Pilgrimage of Grace (1536), 35, 268
Pilkington, Gilbert: Tournament of Tottenham (1350), 309 n
Pilkington, James (1519–75/76), 37, 52–53, 79–80, 91, 117–54, 163, 190, 236, 263–64, 305 n, 341; bishop of Durham, 52, 80, 106, 118; commissioner for Cambridge, 130–31, 150, 152, 176; commissioner for the prayer book, 52, 55, 105, 133, 275; daughters of, Deborah, and Ruth, 308 n; founder of Durham city, 132; founder of grammar schools, 71, 81, 121, 133, 284; master of St. John's College, and regius professor of divinity, Cambridge, 52; sons of, Isaac, and Joshua, 146; ideas and writing style (general), 58, 105, 112, 117–18, 127, 130, 133–34, 140, 148, 171, 274. Works: Burnynge of Paules Church, 58, 125–26, 135–36, 138, 162, 284, 307 n; Haggai (includes homily against "Excess of Apparel," 150, 311 n), 105–6, 123, 138, 143, 149–50; Nehemiah, 112, 122, 135, 141, 144, 146–54, 162, 174, 177, 186, 284; Obadiah, 149. See also Pilkington, Richard, Sr.

Pilkington, John, 52, 305 n; archdeacon of Durham, 52, 317 n; associate of Ascham, 176; (acting) master of Pembroke College, Cambridge, 52; neoplatonist, 176; prebend of St. Paul's, 53. See also Pilkington, Richard, Sr.

Pilkington, Leonard, 305 n; excommunicated, 305 n; master of St John's College, and regius profesor of divinity, 52, 58; treasurer of Durham, 121. See also Pilkington, Richard, Sr.

Pilkington, Matthew: A Rational Concordance . . . of the Bible, 329 n

Pilkington, Richard, Sr., 304 n; daughters of, Janet, Katherine, and Margaret, 304–5 n; grandson of, Richard, Jr. (archdeacon of Carlisle), 174, 177, 314 n; son of, Charles, 305 n; son of, Francis, 305 n; son of, George, 121; 145, 304 n; sons of, James, John, Laurence, and Leonard, 305 n; wife of, Alicia (daughter of Lawrence Asshaw of Heath Charnock), 243, 304 n

Pilkington (of Horwich) family: James, 287–88; Mary, (née Hardman), 332 n; Richard, 332 n

Pilkington (of Pilkington) family, 128, 142, 200, 204–5, 299 n, 307 n; Robert (seneschal to Lord Halton), 309 n; Thomas (knight of the body to Richard III), 307 n

Pilkingtons, (glassmakers), 146, 317 n

Pius V (pope), 129, 163

Plato, 126, 176–77, 247, 317 n; Crito, 300 n, 303 n; Laws, 153, 312 n; Phaedo, 80–81, 124–25, 140, 228, 274; Phaedrus, 125; Symposium, 125

Plumbers' Hall dissenters (London), 53, 297 n

Pole, Reginald (archbishop of Canterbury and papal legate), 77, 90, 104, 148

Pope, Alexander, 284; "Epistle to a Lady," 239; Rape of the Lock, 284

Port Arthur: naval battle at (1904), 288

Pound, Ezra, 286

Pozzo, Andrea, 286

Prague, 131

prayer books, 40, 41, 52, 55, 86–87, 104, 133–34, 138, 197, 250, 286, 333 n

predestination, 42, 110, 126–27, 149–51, 162, 306 n

Presbyterianism, 49, 58, 127–28, 131, 138, 152, 154, 170, 171, 182, 184–93, 198, 205, 209, 226–52, 258, 271, 306 n, 312 n

Preston, 144, 184, 228, 235, 243; battle of (1648) 227, (1715) 270

Preston family: John, 315 n; Thomas (benedictine), 315 n. See also Anderton (of Lostock) family

priesthood, 41, 107, 166–67, 261, 288, 289, 312 n

Priscilla (in Acts), 143

Privy Council, 46, 49, 54, 97, 121, 129, 269

"prophesyings" (Puritan tradition of preaching conferences), 59–60, 77, 96, 239, in Robert Ainsworth, 287; in Oliver Heywood, 234, 251; in James Pilkington's Nehemiah, 152, 154, 299

Protectorship, the Cromwellian, 195–96, 198, 204, 206, 207, 225, 239, 264

Protogenes (Greek sculptor), 255

Providence, ideas of, 30–32, 44, 51, 103, 149, 151, 162–63, 225, 256, 258–59, 261, 263, 265, 266, 277

Prussia, 284

Prynne, William, 195–96

Pugin, A. W. N., and E. W.: their work at Scarisbrick, 243

Purcell, Henry, 281

Pym, John, 199

Pynson, Richard, 282

Pythagoras: game of, 48, 53, 60, 120; "House" of, 48

Quakers. See Society of Friends

Queen's County. See Leix

Racine, J.: Athalie, 264

Radcliffe, John, 328 n; Radcliffe Infirmary, 328 n

Rasbotham, Dorning: "History of Lancashire" manuscript, 331 n

Rayner, William: Apologia Protestantium . . . per Ioannem Brerleium, 177

recusancy, 168, 181, 185

Rhodes, 255

Ribble (river), former boundary between feudality of Scotland and English royal appanage, 144–45, 270

Richard I (king of England), 252; Richard II, 101, 103, 142, 205; Richard III, 83, 128, 300n

Ridley, Nicholas (bishop of London), 40, 107

Rigby, James (acting curate of Turton), 204

Rigby (of Arley) family: Alexander, 306n

Rigby (of Aspull) family: Alexander, 203; Joseph (d. 1671), 203–7, 211, 225, 341

Rigby (of Middleton, Goosnargh) family: Alexander, Jr. (Roundhead colonel), 202; Alexander, Sr., 203

Rigby (of Peel, Little Hulton) family: George, 202–3; spy headquarters at Peel Hall, 214. See also Kenyon (of Kenyon Peel Hall) family

Ripon, 138

Rivington, 128, 133, 138, 177, 288; chapelry and township, 144–46; grammar school, 71, 81, 121, 133, 134, 143, 177, 284; manor, 128, 145, 165; moors, 146, 293; Presbyterian chapel, 239, 285, 323n; Unitarian manse, 288

Rochdale, 257

Rogers, John, 90, 97, 111

Roman law, 169, 273

Rome, 99–100, 139, 160, 241, 283, 292; meaning "brute force," in Greek, 292; music school, 124; St. Peter's, 93; pope's Lutheran mercenaries, 95

Roosevelt family: Eleanor, 267; Franklin Delano, 267, 279

Roscow family: James, 203, 320n; Ralph, 320n

Rothwell family: James (vicar of Deane), 100, 106, 113; Richard (Puritan exorcist), 100

Rotterdam, 233

Roubiliac, L.-F., 284

Rupert, Prince, of the Rhine, 183, 198, 202, 208, 227–28

Russia, 288

sacrament, eucharistic, 43, 48, 96, 107, 111–13, 125, 189, 236–37, 263, 265; as analogy of monarchy as constitutional talisman, 199; bleeds, 176–77; and the commercial and legal system, 207–8; and the "commonweal," 37, 41–42, 44–47, 51, 60–62, 91, 112, 138–41, 182, 185, 187–88, 197, 206, 241; as

consecrating "place," 25, 37, 104; as dynamic, 40, 61–62, 290; as guardian of the mind from evil, 27–28, 103, 190; as personal, rather than merely bodily, presence of Christ, 41, 111–12 ; reception of, as an act of the intellectual will, 290; and the royal person, 25–26, 35, 46–47, 161, 170, 205, 263; as the "shadow" of Christ, 230; and sovereignty, 24, 35, 41, 49, 61–62, 117, 148, 160–61, 165–66, 183, 188, 190, 205; as vibrative, 187. See also Son, God the; Zwinglian memorialism

Sarcerius, Erasmus (author, Novum Methodium in Praecipiis Scripturae Divinae Locis), 302n

St. Gregory's, London, 196

St. Louis, 285

St. Omer, 263

St. Paul's, London: cathedral, 44, 56, 136; cross, 47,149, 307n; school, 94

Salamis (naval battle) (480 B.C.), 288

Salisbury, Robert Cecil, first earl of, 338

Salvian, 252, 325n

Sancroft, William (archbishop of Canterbury), 257, 264, 267

Sandys, Edward, 113; archbishop of York, 60, 305n; founder of Hawkshead grammar school, 141; vice-chancellor of Cambridge, 48

Saul (king of Israel), 242

Saunders, Lawrence (vicar of All Hallows, London), 77–78, 82, 86, 90, 91, 106–7, 111, 135

Saunderson, Ellis (vicar of Bolton), 164

Saxon monarchy: gender stereotyping, 250

Scarisbrick, Anne (of Scarisbrick), 243; ancestors and family, 243

Scarisbrick Chapel, 242, 243

Scot, Cuthbert, 104

Scot (jailer at Lathom), 104

Scotland, 83, 100, 120, 145, 154, 170, 185, 188, 227, 246, 251, 270

Sedbergh grammar school, 47

Seddon, Arthur, 320n

Seneca, 192

Seville, 313n

Shakerley, 106

Shakers: origins of, in Bolton, 272, 287

Shakespeare, William, 85; Antony and

Cleopatra, 255; *King Lear,* 44–45; *Othello,* 255; *Richard II,* 266; *Richard III,* 300–301n; *The Tempest,* 137

Sharp, John (archbishop of York), 289

Sherlock, William (master of the Temple), 326n

Shuttleworth, Richard (Roundhead colonel), 203–4, 211–12

Sidney, Philip, 146, 231

Simnel, Lambert, 88, 204–5, 266, 307n

Simonds, Hugh (vicar of St. Michael's, Coventry), 297n

Sixsmith, Charles, 288–89

Sloane, Hans, 331n

Smithills, 186; hall, 78, 81–82, 109, 144, 196, 270; Oldhams farm, 295n

Smyth, William (bishop of Lincoln), 311n

Society of Friends, 136, 207, 236–37, 240, 268, 270, 271–72, 307–8n, 323n

Socrates, 79, 80–81, 88, 109, 124–26, 142, 150–51, 228, 283, 300n

Some, Robert, *Treatise against Oppression,* 151–52

Son, God the: as an actor or esthetic projection, 225, 230, 239–40, 244; as the biblical Jesus, 190, 238, 267, 271, 291; as that which is bodily present, 24, 41, 61, 87, 101, 111–12, 276; as bridegroom of the soul and vivifier of shared creation, 25–26, 41, 62, 89, 111–12, 244; concepts of, 28, 103, 107, 126, 206, 228, 247, 271, 291; and sovereignty, 24, 26, 41, 47, 53, 59, 62, 160–61, 165, 206, 208–9, 238; as subversive, 44, 59, 60–61, 141. *See also* sacrament, eucharistic; Trinity, Holy

Sophocles, 121, 150; *Oedipus at Colonus,* 135; *Oedipus the King,* 122

Southam, 60

Southwell, 183

Spain, 51, 54, 96, 160, 168; claims Naples, 163; Spanish Armada, 99

Spenser, Edmund, 56, 146, 206; *Shepheardes Calender:* "Julye," 276

Spirit, God the Holy: concepts of, 97–98, 100, 247; as creating the inner life, 248, 271, 275; as inspiring pathos, 227, 230, 241; as a possession and talisman, 107, 111, 148, 229; as prompting discretion and restraint, 78, 109, 117,
124, 233; and questions of assurance, loyalty, and assent, 24, 27–28, 77, 85, 87, 89, 98–99, 100, 103, 109, 112, 117, 161–62, 225, 227. *See also* Trinity, Holy

Sports, *Declaration* of: for Lancashire (1617), 316n

Staffordshire, 25

Stanley family (general), 80, 83–85, 100, 119, 128, 189, 204, 212, 304; at Bosworth (Sir William), 83, 300–301n; "kings" of Man, 195; and Mary Queen of Scots (Edmond, Thomas), 304n; tombs, at Ormskirk, 242. *See also* Derby, earls of

Stanley (of Bickerstaff or Bickerstaffe) family: Edward (d. 1640), 206; Edward (d. 1776), eleventh earl of Derby, 206; Elizabeth (née Patten, wife of Thomas, Jr.), 243; Elizabeth (née Scarisbrick, born 1516), 243; Mary (née Egerton, wife of Thomas, Sr., and grandmother of Thomas, Jr.), 242; Thomas, Jr., 243; Thomas, Sr., 243, 265

Stonyhurst, 267

Strafford, Thomas Wentworth, earl of, 196, 198

Strype, John: *Annals of the Reformation,* 285; *Life of Sir John Cheke,* 285

Stuart, Charles Edward (also "Bonnie Prince Charlie," "The Young Pretender"), 144, 271

Stuart dynasty, 144, 199, 226, 248, 265, 270. *See also names of individual monarchs*

Stuart, James Francis Edward (also "James III," "The Old Pretender"), 145, 252, 258, 268, 270

Sturt, John, 286; engraving of the veiled Isis, 220

Sudan, 108, 279

Surey, 266. *See also* Dugdale, Richard

Sussex, Thomas Radcliffe, earl of, 121

Swift, Jonathan, 228; *Tale of a Tub,* 327n

Switzerland, 38, 42, 59, 88, 135

synods, 49, 288, 294n

Tacitus, Caius Cornelius, 99; *Annales,* 105

Taylor family: Abigail (née Ward, Mrs. Zachary, Sr.), 257; Anne (second Mrs. Zachary, Jr.), 327n; Barbara (née Stanley of Bickerstaff, first Mrs. Zachary, Jr.), 206, 327 n; Robert Eveleigh, 333 n; Zachary, Jr., 257; Zachary, Sr., 206, 257–58. *See also* Stanley (of Bickerstaff or Bickerstaffe) family

Taylor, John (bishop of Lincoln), 77

Taylor, Zachary, Jr. (1653–1705?), 245, 256, 257–71, 276, 327 n, 342; curate of Wigan, 206, 257, 264; king's preacher, 260; "the Lancashire Levite," 257; rector of Croston, 327 n; vicar of Ormskirk, 257. Works: *The Death of the Righteous,* 262; *The Decency of Christian Mourning,* 262; *A Dissuasive from Contention,* 260–62; *Obedience and Submission,* 258, 263, 264; *Surey Impostor,* 219, 267–70

Ten Commandments, 42, 77

Thales: on "place," 208

Theodosius I (emperor of the west), 130

Thomas Aquinas, Saint, 135, 274; *Summa Theologica,* 170

Thomas à Becket (archbishop of Canterbury), 129

Thomas à Kempis, 247; *Imitation of Christ,* 82, 111

Thornley, Roger: repairs the Tudor Bolton grammar school, 318 n

Throgmorton, John (recorder of Coventry), 51

Tillotson, John (archbishop of Canterbury), 189, 289

Tillotson and Son, 278; John, 278; Mary (née Lever of Great Lever, Mrs. W. F.), 279; William Frederick (son of John), 330 n

Tilsley, John (1614–84), 184, 202, 210, 285, 317 n; marries Margaret Chetham, 184, 317 n; verses to Joseph Rigby of Aspull, 204–6; vicar of Deane, 161, 184, 319 n

Tirinus, 192

tithes, 109, 176, 185, 207

Toleration Act (1689), 226

Tolstoy, Leo, 288

Tonbridge grammar school, 306 n

Tonge Fold: royalist commemoration at Dog and Kennel Inn, 216

Tonge with Haulgh: Mrs. Robinson, wife of the Commonwealth J. P., 320 n

Toxteth, Liverpool, 100, 227

transubstantiation, 26–30, 35, 42, 48, 57, 96, 101, 110, 113, 131, 136, 138, 165, 176, 190, 208, 241, 273, 274, 289, 294 n, 317 n

Trevelyan, G. M., *England under the Stuarts,* 183

Trieste, 332 n; Austrian naval port, at Fiume, 332 n

Trinity, Holy: concepts of, 24, 28, 103–4, 127, 247, 267, 271, 288, 290. *See also* Father, God the; Son, God the; Spirit, God the Holy

Tudor dynasty, 31, 36, 48, 51, 55, 77, 78, 80, 83, 85, 94, 106, 117, 131, 145, 212, 292. *See also* names of individual monarchs

Tunstall, Cuthbert (bishop of Durham), 132, 301 n

Turks, 171–72, 191, 287

Turton: chapel, 185, 189, 195; Presbyterian ordinations at (1650), 185, 189; tower, 181, 194–95, 214, 270; township, 165, 195

Tyre (siege of), 248

Ulster, 100

Ulverston, Furness, 239

Unitarianism, 189, 191, 271, 329 n

Ursula, Saint, 62

Van Dyck, Anton, 187

Vaux, Laurence (1519/20–85), 36, 56, 246, 263, 342–43; *Catechisme,* 36, 56–57; sub-prior of Louvain, 39, 246; warden of Manchester, 39, 119

Vawdry (deputy chamberlain of Chester), 103

Venn, Humphrey (vicar of Holy Trinity, Coventry), 298 n

Venus, 255, 256

Victoria (queen of England), 267, 281, 293

Virgil, 133, 136; *Aeneid,* 281

Virginia, 228; tobacco, 252

Voltaire, F. M. A. de, 271

Wagstaffe, Thomas: *An Answer . . . to . . . Obedience and Submission,* 259, 262

Wales, 83, 96, 99–100, 103, 145, 183, 227, 289; principality of, 83

Wallace, J. W., 293, 303–4 n. *See also* Johnston, John; Whitman, Walt: Whitmanites, of Bolton

Walmsley, 232; chapel, 271

Walters, Thomas (of the Society of Friends), 323 n

Warburton: Marsh's companion at Lancaster, 87; Ellen, mother of Robert Ainsworth, 301 n, 330 n; Thomas, married by Lever at Aarau, 87

Ward, Professor, 286

Wardley, James and Jane (early "Shakers"), 272

Ware, 60

Warrington, 183

Warwick, Ambrose Dudley, earl of, 60, 310 n

Warwickshire, 60, 154, 286

Washington, county Durham, 303–6 n

Waterfield (Shaker colony), New York, 272

Webb, Beatrice (Fabian socialist), 288

Wenslow, George (chancellor of Chester), 94

Werburgh, Saint, 25, 27–28, 30–32, 40, 68, 82, 100, 145, 187, 250, 292–93

Wesel, 62

Wesley, Charles, 331 n

West, James (president of the Royal Society), 286

Westchester, New York, 38

West Chester, Cheshire. *See* Chester

Westhoughton: chapelry, 185; curacy, 246

Westminster, 28, 56, 95

Westmorland, Charles Neville, sixth earl of, 121–22, 138

Wexford, 228

Whalley, 146, 195, 211, 266, 268; abbey, 56, 211–12, 267; grammar school, 268, 299 n

Wharton, Philip, Lord, 238

Whewell (Derby's headsman), 320 n

Whiggery, 195, 206, 243, 246, 248, 256, 259, 266, 267

Whitaker family: Thomas (schoolmaster at Burnley), 314 n; William (master of St. John's College, Cambridge), 55, 311 n, 313 n

Whitehall, 161, 183

Whitehead, Edward, 288–89

Whitfield, George (Calvinistic Methodist), 189

Whitgift, John (archbishop of Canterbury), 55, 120, 129, 149–52, 276, 311 n

Whitman, Walt, 188, 208, 288, 293; *Leaves of Grass,* 278; "A Passage to India," 293, 321 n; "Song of Myself," 231; Whitmanites, of Bolton, 239, 321 n, 332 n

Whittingham, William (Puritan dean of Durham), 132, 134, 136–37

Wigan, 145, 264, 325 n; grammar school, 299 n; rectory, 195, 204, 269. *See also* Aspull township

Wild, Fred (early memories of Bolton grammar school), 303 n

Wilde, Constance, Mrs. Oscar (née Holland), 309 n

Wilkins, John (bishop of Chester), 185, 189, 334 n

William I ("the Conqueror," king of England), 31

William III (king of England), 189, 226; fulfils Janeite dream, 246; hatred of France, 266; meets the requirements of the advocates of Lambert Simnel, 206; his providentially confirmed administrative "authority" dispossesses divinely sanctioned "rights," 258–59, 263; "settles" the Church, 189, 289

William the Silent (prince of Orange), 226

Willis, Thomas: *Pathologiae Cerebri . . . Specimen,* 267

Willoughby of Parham, Lords: Francis (fifth baron), governor of Barbados, 255; Hugh (fifteenth baron), buried at Horwich, 285–86; Hugh (twelfth baron), a pupil of Oliver Heywood, 239, 255, 323 n, 328 n; Thomas (eleventh baron), Roundhead major resident at Horwich, 255

Winchester, 52, 134, 145; diocese, 306 n; Fecknam (Marian abbot of), 296

Winstone (servant at Smithills hall), 82

witches, 267–69

Wither, George, 204

Wolsey, Thomas (cardinal): holds see of Durham *in commendam,* 132

Woolf, Virginia, 281, 293, 330 n

Worcester (battle of), 198, 228

Wordsworth family: Dorothy (at Halifax), 323n; William (at Hawkshead, receptive of Puritan influences), 141, 235, 252, 322n

Wren, Christopher, 281

Wrench (schoolmaster at Chester), 101

Wyatt, Thomas, 49

Wycliffe, John, 103, 113, 141, 247; befriended by John O' Gaunt, duke of Lancaster, 91; visiting "master" of Balliol, 93; preaches against transubstantiation, 27, 113, 131; temporal claims of the papacy, Wycliffian, 167

York, 121, 175, 182, 184, 210, 235, 274, 314n, 316; All Saints North Street, 318n; castle, 252; grammar school, 316n

Yorkshire, 202, 226, 231, 235, 247, 289

Young, Thomas (archbishop of York), 134

Zenobia (queen of Palmyra), 292

Zwinglian memorialism, 35, 41, 43–44, 47, 56, 57, 60, 110